PQ
442
.P56

Pondrom, Cyrena N.

The road from
Paris

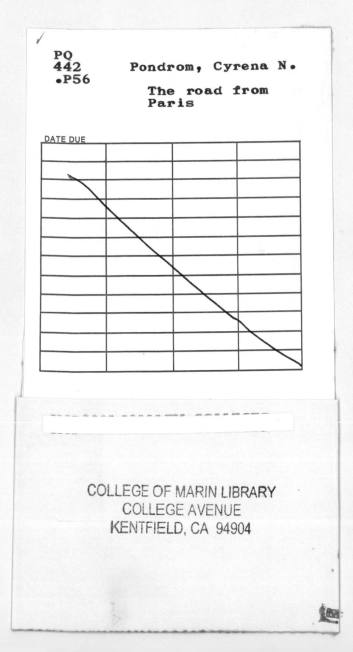

THE ROAD FROM PARIS

French Influence on English Poetry, 1900–1920

THE
ROAD FROM PARIS

French Influence on English Poetry
1900–1920

CYRENA N. PONDROM
Professor of English, University of Wisconsin

CAMBRIDGE
AT THE UNIVERSITY PRESS

Published by the Syndics of the Cambridge University Press
Bentley House, 200 Euston Road, London NW1 2DB
American Branch: 32 East 57th Street, New York, N.Y. 10022

© Cambridge University Press 1974

The Approach to Paris © 1974 Ezra Pound. By permission of
Dorothy Pound, Committee for Ezra Pound.

Library of Congress Catalogue Card Number: 72-80593

ISBN: 0 521 08681 7

Composed in Great Britain by
Alden & Mowbray Ltd
at the Alden Press, Oxford

Printed in the United States of America

TABLE OF CONTENTS

CONTENTS

ACKNOWLEDGEMENTS

The author and publisher would like to thank the following for permission to include copyright material:

The Ann Elmo Agency for the essay by Nicolas Beauduin, the two essays by Remy de Gourmont and the three essays by Richard Aldington.

Mrs Lindsay Auchterlonie for the essay by T. E. Hulme.

Editions Gallimard for the letter from Guillaume Apollinaire to F. S. Flint.

'The Approach to Paris' from Ezra Pound, SELECTED PROSE 1909–1965, edited by William Cookson. Copyright © 1974 by the Estate of Ezra Pound. Reprinted by permission of New Directions Publishing Corporation and Faber & Faber Ltd., London.

Fasquelle Editeurs for Florian-Parmentier's letter to F. S. Flint.

Ianthe Price for the four essays by F. S. Flint.

The New Statesman for the two excerpts by Aldous Huxley and the essay by André Lhote (all of which are reprinted from *The Athenaeum*).

For all remaining copyright material permission has been sought from appropriate sources.

PREFACE

I should like to thank the American Council of Learned Societies and the Graduate Research Committee of the University of Wisconsin for the fellowship and research support which enabled me to advance this project substantially during a leave year in 1968–9. I also am most grateful to the permanent staff of the Institute for Research in the Humanities in Madison, Wisconsin, for the hospitality and facilities extended to me during that year.

Mr Robert Yahnke, Mr John Hofer, Mr Michael Routh, and Mr Jerry Cousins substantially helped me by proof-reading, typing initial transcriptions of some of the documents, and tracing needed books and articles. I also wish to thank Mrs K. F. Schofer for advice on the proper reading of handwritten documents in French and for proof-reading some of the French material. Mrs Nancy Pellmann and Miss Diane Gest were of invaluable assistance in preparing the final typescript of the manuscript with patience and exactitude, and Mrs Susan Friedman deserves my sincerest gratitude for proof-reading the manuscript and, with Mr Routh, preparing the index.

Mrs Mary M. Hirth, Librarian of the Academic Center Library, The University of Texas, was generous in helping me obtain access to the Flint manuscripts held there, and Professor Stephen G. Nichols, Jr of Dartmouth College gave valuable suggestions during the original planning of the project. To two of my colleagues, Professor L. S. Dembo of the Department of English and Professor Germaine Brée of the Department of French, I wish to express my particular gratitude both for specific suggestions and for the discussion of pertinent topics; they know how deeply I am in their debt. Finally I should like to thank my husband for his understanding and support.

THE ROAD FROM PARIS

INTRODUCTION

I

T. S. Eliot, in 'A Commentary' in *The Criterion* in 1934, observed that: 'Younger generations can hardly realize the intellectual desert of England and America during the first decade and more of this century.' He continued:

The predominance of Paris was incontestable. Poetry, it is true, was somewhat in eclipse; but there was a most exciting variety of ideas. Anatole France and Remy de Gourmont still exhibited their learning . . .; Barrès was at the height of his influence . . . Péguy, more or less Bergsonian *and* Catholic *and* Socialist, had just become important, and the young were further distracted by Gide and Claudel. Vildrac, Romains, Duhamel, experimented with verse which seemed hopeful, though it was always, I think, disappointing; something was expected of Henri Franck, the early deceased author of *La Danse devant l'arche*.[1]

Nor did Eliot stop with homage to literary France. He recalled the importance of the sociologists Lévy-Bruhl and Durkheim, of Janet, the psychologist, of Loisy, of Faguet, and above all of Bergson, whose metaphysic 'was apt to be involved with discussion of Matisse and Picasso'. This account of the intellectual dominance of France in the years before World War I is matched, more succinctly, by Eliot's statement of the impact of those currents on English poetry. 'I look back to the dead year 1908', he wrote, 'and I observe with satisfaction that it is now taken for granted that the current of French poetry which sprang from Baudelaire is one which has, in these twenty-one years, affected all English poetry that matters'.[2]

The view of Eliot's fellow exile in London, Ezra Pound, was even more sweeping. In one of his earliest articles on contemporary French poetry, 'The Approach to Paris' in 1913, Pound declared: 'For the best part of a thousand years English poets have gone to school to the French, or one might as well say that there never were any English poets until they began to study the French. . . The history of English poetic glory is a history of successful steals from the French. . . The great periods of English have been the periods when the English showed the greatest powers of assimilation'.[3] Whether Pound's assertions are accurate for all of English literature or not, they are right for his own period, for he correctly defined the source of the poetic renaissance in early twentieth-

1 'A Commentary', *The Criterion*, XIII, 52 (April 1934) 451–2.
2 'Books of the Quarter: *Baudelaire and the Symbolists*', *The Criterion*, IX, 35 (January 1930) 359.
3 'The Approach to Paris, II', *The New Age*, XIII, 20 (11 September 1913) 577.

century England. In partial demonstration of his assessment, his own statement appeared in a series of articles which was one of his attempts to 'school' English poets in the achievements of the French poetic *avant garde*. The effort had already been launched by F. S. Flint, Ford Madox Ford, T. E. Hulme, John Middleton Murry, and even some lesser figures. Pound himself, in this article, was offering poems from Remy de Gourmont's *Le Livre des Litanies* as an illustration of accomplishments in verse-rhythm that English poets should seek to equal. In fact, the imagist poets for whom Pound then spoke had already 'stolen' the theory and technique of *vers libre* and adapted both as important elements of their own poetry. And in the two years immediately after this essay, Pound and his fellow vorticists Wyndham Lewis and Henri Gaudier-Brzeska assimilated the aesthetic views of cubists, futurists, and abstract expressionists and articulated the precepts of a British movement of abstract art.[1] The abstract poetics Pound shaped in this period still illuminates and often guides much American poetry today.

Of course, the origins of modern poetry in England are far too complex to be seen only in terms of a foreign influence. The attention of Richard Aldington and Hilda Doolittle (H.D.) to classical Greek lyric cannot be attributed originally to French inspiration; Pound had begun to study the troubadours before he became an exile in Europe; even the scientific formulation of wave patterns as a description of the motion of sound and matter made a contribution to new ideas of form; and 'influences', finally, can never *explain* individual accomplishment. But with these caveats in mind, one may summarize French presence in early twentieth-century British poetry thus: French influence was ubiquitous in the innovative movements of poetry in London between 1908 and 1920; French intellectual currents were far more extensive and important than those of any other foreign origin in this period; and the rhythm, metric, subject, and form in imagist, vorticist and immediately succeeding poetry all exhibit properties which were inspired or reinforced by French practices or by poetry or criticism in the French language. Neither Eliot nor Pound was excessive in his emphasis upon the paramount influence of France on the English poetic world between 1908 and 1920.

One can examine this influence as it appears in the development of individual writers or as it is manifest in the currents of London literary history. Studies of the influence of particular French poets on the work of Ezra Pound, T. S. Eliot, T. E. Hulme, Edith Sitwell, Hilda Doolittle, and John Gould Fletcher already exist, and they have the virtue of fully documenting specific examples of direct imitation and of showing the French influence on major portions of the careers of individual

[1] See William C. Wees, *Vorticism and the English Avant-garde* (Toronto, 1972).

poets.[1] The present volume provides many of the materials for a broader literary historical study of the impact of French literary culture on the development of poetry in England between 1900 and 1920 – a study, that is, of the way ideas, themes, and techniques common to important segments of the French literary community came to be important in London, where they had an independent and parallel development, reinforced in part by continuing developments in France.[2] Examining the period rather than individual writers enables one to assess the full range of French influence in England, to identify the ideas or techniques most important to the period as a whole, and to examine the course of transmission rather than the effects of influence alone. Observing the course of transmission lays the foundation for the revaluation of some literary reputations: both F. S. Flint and John Middleton Murry, neither highly regarded for his own creative work, made important and in the case of Flint extremely extensive contributions to the transmission of French influences, and thus played a significant role in shaping the course of English poetry.

Viewed from the perspective of literary history, French influence passed through several slightly overlapping but reasonably clear stages between the years 1900–20. The first stage is the period of the persistence of nineteenth-century symbolist influence of the type prevalent in the British 1890s.[3] This kind of 'French presence' is characteristic in much work from the years 1900–10, before the great modern poetic revolution got well underway. Essays on the French mostly harked back to the achievements of the symbolist period – as did F. S. Flint's reviews for *The New Age* on 11 July 1908 and 11 February 1909; or Francis Grierson's 'Paul Verlaine' and 'Stéphane Mallarmé', André Beaunier's 'La Littérature française contemporaine', and Catherine Verschoyle's 'On Beauty and Some Modern French Poets', which all appeared in the first months of 1910.[4] In poetry the characteristic note of this phase of

[1] A selected bibliography of these studies includes, for Pound, Eliot, H.D., and Fletcher, René Taupin, *L'Influence du symbolisme français sur la poésie américaine (de 1910 à 1920)* (Paris, 1929); and individually, John J. Espey, *Ezra Pound's 'Mauberley': A Study in Composition* (Berkeley and Los Angeles, 1955); Edward J. H. Greene, *T. S. Eliot et la France* (Paris, 1951); Alun R. Jones, *The Life and Opinions of T. E. Hulme* (London, 1960); Ihab H. Hassan, 'Edith Sitwell and the Symbolist Tradition', *Comparative Literature*, VII (Summer 1955) 240–51.

[2] Attention is given to the French contributions to imagism by Stanley K. Coffman, *Imagism: A Chapter for the History of Modern Poetry* (Norman, Okla., 1951) and by Wallace Martin, 'The Origins of Imagism', in *'The New Age' under Orage: Chapters in English Cultural History* (Manchester, 1967), pp. 145–81. I have a book-length study of French influence on English poetry, 1900–20, in progress.

[3] The fullest available study of the transmission of French influence into England in the latter part of the nineteenth century is Ruth Z. Temple's *The Critic's Alchemy: A Study of the Introduction of French Symbolism into England* (New Haven, c. 1953).

[4] Flint, 'Recent Verse', *The New Age*, n.s. III (11 July 1908) 212–13, and review of *For Christmas*

influence was struck by the imitations of Swinburne, Dowson, and Symons in Pound's early collections *A Lume Spento* (1908), *Personae* (1909), and *Exultations* (1909);[1] by the *symboliste* manner in many poems of Flint's *In the Net of the Stars* (1909); and by some passages in Yeats' *In the Seven Woods* (1904). One of the most important critics still was Arthur Symons, whose *The Symbolist Movement in Literature* of 1899 – perhaps the apogee of French influence in the 1890s – was republished in 1908; and the standard anthology of French poetry was the two-volume Adrien Van Bever and Paul Léautaud *Poètes d'aujourd'hui*, a thorough selection of French symbolist verse by poets active before 1900.

The second stage of French influence in the first two decades is that of the rapid spread of interest in symbolist *cénacle* and post-symbolist French poetry and theory. This stage corresponds to the beginnings of the modernist movement in English poetry in the years 1909–14. It is marked by the widespread adoption of *vers libre*, development of a poetic theory heavily indebted to Bergson's aesthetic views, attention to some aspects of the French stress on a renewed classicism, and use of realistic, industrial, and lower or middle class subjects and diction in poetry. All of these developments are clear in the beginning and growth of imagism, a movement itself modelled on the coteries which dominated the post-symbolist French poetic world in the years from 1900 to 1914. The important sources or models were no longer the symbolist masters (like Mallarmé, Verlaine, or Rimbaud) but the men active in the years following the formal establishment of the symbolist school, a development usually dated from Jean Moréas' use of the name *symbolisme* in *Le Figaro*, 18 September 1886. Among these *cénacle* figures, for example, Gustave Kahn was an important source for Hulme's advocacy of free verse in 'A Lecture on Modern Poetry' (1909), Émile Verhaeren a shaping influence on the *vers libre* of Flint's transitional volume *In the Net of the Stars* (1909), and Remy de Gourmont and Henri de Régnier the models Pound suggested to English language poets for, respectively, 'rhythm' and 'simplicity of syntactical construction'.[2] Hulme and Flint spread information about poets of the symbolist *cénacle* in the secession Poets' Club of 1909.[3] In addition, a larger British audience was introduced to these French writers by means of essays in journals like *The*

MDCCCCVIII, The New Age, n.s. IV (11 February 1909) 327–8; Grierson, 'Paul Verlaine', *The New Age*, n.s. VI (6 January 1910), and 'Stéphane Mallarmé', *The New Age*, n.s. VI (10 February 1910) 351–2; Beaunier, *The Nineteenth Century and After*, LXVII (January 1910) 48–64; Verschoyle, *The Thrush*, II, 1 (April 1910).

[1] Discussions of Pound's use of a British 1890s variety of *symbolisme* appear in N. Christoph de Nagy, *The Poetry of Ezra Pound: The Pre-Imagist Stage* (Bern, 1960); Thomas H. Jackson, *The Early Poetry of Ezra Pound* (Cambridge, Mass., 1968); and Hugh Witemeyer, *The Poetry of Ezra Pound: Forms and Renewal 1908–1920* (Berkeley and Los Angeles, 1969).

[2] Ezra Pound, 'Editorial Comment: Paris', *Poetry*, III, 1 (October 1913) 26–7.

[3] F. S. Flint, 'The History of Imagism', *The Egoist* (1 May 1915) 71.

New Age; both characteristic and significant are Flint's review of Verhaeren's volume of poetry *The Sovereign Rhythms* and Richard Buxton's 1911–12 series on de Régnier, Moréas, Francis Vielé-Griffin, Stuart Merrill, Francis Jammes, Paul Fort, and Albert Samain.[1]

At almost the same time, London poets began to know of the French generation that succeeded the *cénacle* – the post-symbolist poets who were ranged in competing coteries like *unanimisme, néo-Mallarmisme, néo-paganisme, paroxysme, fantaisisme,* and a cluster of others. The two earliest extensive sources of information about these poets in London were F. S. Flint's 'Contemporary French Poetry' in 1912 and Pound's series 'The Approach to Paris' in 1913, and they shared two significant features: both discussed the post-symbolists in the context of *cénacle* poets like Fort, de Régnier, Jammes, and Kahn, and both emphasized, among *les jeunes,* the *unanimistes* and their supporters, like Jules Romains, Charles Vildrac, Georges Duhamel, and André Spire. Other essays – like Tristan Derème's 1912–13 series for *Rhythm*[2] and Flint's regular 'French Chronicle' for *Poetry and Drama* in 1913–14 – treated more innovative French contemporaries, like Guillaume Apollinaire, Henri-Martin Barzun, André Salmon, and Paul Claudel. These essays made somewhat less of the symbolist heritage and thus prepared for English writers to look to their *current* French counterparts as the source for aesthetic innovation.

The third stage of French influence, in 1914, 1915, and 1916, is that of Anglo-American assimilation of contemporary developments in poetry and abstract aesthetics. It was a time of attention to the ideas of cubism, futurism, and abstract expressionism and a period of regular reporting on *les jeunes poètes* of France. The most dramatic aesthetic development in the London of these years was the formation of the vorticist movement as a correlative to the Continental schools of non-representational art. The process of assimilating Continental theories of aesthetics began in earnest late in 1913, although the roots of the process go back as far as 1910,[3] and the effects of these influences were manifest theoretically in T. E. Hulme's art criticism in early 1914 and in the vorticists' aesthetic statements of 1914 and 1915. The effect of these new theories on poetry became clear only after the period of assimilation of influence was largely over. Some poems of 1914–16 hint at new techniques (one thinks of Pound's 'Heather' or 'Dogmatic Statement on the

---

1 'The Sovereign Rhythms', *The New Age* (22 September 1910) 496–7. The Buxton essays appeared respectively, on 14 September, 28 September, 12 October, and 2 November 1911, and 11 January, 8 August, and 24 October 1912.

2 'Lettre de France, i–v', *Rhythm*, June, August, October, December 1912, and February 1913.

3 F. T. Marinetti gave his first London lecture on futurism in March 1910, and Roger Fry held the first Post-Impressionist Exhibition at the Grafton Gallery in the fall of the same year.

Game and Play of Chess'), but the full significance of abstract aesthetic theories for poetry began to emerge only with the publication of Pound's first three cantos in summer, 1917, 'Homage to Sextus Propertius' and 'Canto IV' in 1919, and 'Hugh Selwyn Mauberley' in 1920, and Eliot's 'The Waste Land' in 1922. In these years of most active interest in aesthetic theory France was important both as the point of origin of significant influences – like post-impressionist painting, cubism, and the poetry of Apollinaire and Max Jacob – and as broker for intellectual currency from throughout Europe. The Italian futurists, for example, spoke and often wrote in French, and their propaganda in London was very often published in French rather than in translation from Italian.[1] The Oriental influence so important to those years was also imported through French versions, as well as English ones.[2]

At the same time that Pound, Wyndham Lewis, Henri Gaudier-Brzeska, and T. E. Hulme led the way toward the formation of an aesthetic theory which integrated many Continental experiments in abstraction, Richard Aldington and Hilda Doolittle, as literary editors of *The Egoist*, consolidated the achievements of imagism and made *The Egoist* the means of continual, non-partisan commentary on current events in French poetry. Aldington was not really exaggerating when he wrote in 1915: '*The Egoist* has been hammering at people to read French poetry.'[3] Unlike the introductory essays by Buxton, Flint, Pound, and Derème in the preceding years, comments on French poets in *The Egoist* were predicated on the accurate assumption that a lively interest in literary France and at least some knowledge did exist among the *avant garde*. Thus, from 1914 through 1916 *The Egoist* offered selections of recent poetry in French,[4] translations of Remy de Gourmont's novel *The Horses of Diomedes* and Lautréamont's *The Songs of Maldoror*, regular reviews of new French books, more extensive essays

[1] The leader of literary futurism, F. T. Marinetti, wrote his poetry in French up until 1914. The first futurist manifesto in 1909 was published in French in *Le Figaro*, and later manifestoes very often appeared either originally or simultaneously in that language. When Marinetti travelled about London to lecture and converse, he spoke in French and relied on Aldington, Pound and others to translate for the benefit of the relatively small number of literati who could not understand. Gino Severini, the futurist painter with the largest number of English connections, lived in Paris and received English guests in Parisian *avant garde* company that included Apollinaire. For anecdotes about the futurists and English writers see Richard Aldington, *Life for Life's Sake* (New York, 1941), p. 108, and C. R. W. Nevinson, *Paint and Prejudice* (New York, 1938), p. 64.

[2] French sources for the early imagist interest in Japanese poetry are discussed in Earl Miner's *The Japanese Tradition in British and American Literature* (Princeton, 1966), pp. 97–107. Glenn Hughes in *Imagism and the Imagists* (New York, 1960) notes that John Gould Fletcher's interest in Chinese poetry (p. 138) and Amy Lowell's attention to Japanese verse (p. 204) both were first stimulated by French translations of the Oriental poems.

[3] 'New Poetry', *The Egoist*, II, 6 (1 June 1915) 89.

[4] These selections included (but are not limited to) poems by Paul Fort, 1 March 1915; P. J. Jouve, 1 July 1915; Guy-Charles Cros, 2 August 1915; and André Spire, 1 December 1915.

on such figures as Léon Deubel, Charles Péguy, Joris-Karl Huysmans, and Remy de Gourmont, and in each issue a lengthy French literary causerie entitled 'Passing Paris' by Muriel Ciolkowska. During the first two years of the war there were few competing *avant garde* journals; *The New Age*, however, also continued to open its columns to those interested in French poetry and the new aesthetics. Pound and Hulme published there frequently during this period, and extracts from Max Jacob's 'cubist' prose poems appeared in the issue for 6 May 1915.

The fourth stage of French influence began in the later years of the war and continued through and beyond 1920. It was marked by a more reserved attitude toward most contemporary French poets and by greater interest in the French nineteenth century. By this time a strong and independent modernist movement in English poetry existed, and a new generation of English poets – including Edith Sitwell, Aldous Huxley, and Herbert Read – were beginning to take their places in this new tradition. Since the appearance of the fourth stage of influence is characterized by a subtle change in attitude toward France on the part of London literati, a precise beginning date cannot be specified. The presence of this new attitude is clear, however, in the first cycle of *Wheels* in 1916, in *The Egoist* from June 1917, when T. S. Eliot became literary editor, and from the first number of *Art and Letters* in July 1917. The 'new generation' of English modernist poets was active in all three journals. Although the contemporary French no longer occupied the authoritative position in poetic experiment they had held before the war, by this time French and English literary worlds were so contiguous that anyone seriously interested in poetry was presumed to be acquainted with recent French literature. The French post-symbolist coteries, like the *unanimistes, fantaisistes, paroxystes* (*ad infinitum*) – largely disrupted by war – no longer offered technical inspiration to the English, and coterie spirit of the Bloomsbury kind did not lead to the formation of significant French-style poetic movements, like imagism or vorticism. Rather, individual English poets, like Edith Sitwell or Aldous Huxley, turned to selected French figures for inspiration – particularly to the proto-surrealist Lautréamont or to Baudelaire, Rimbaud, and Mallarmé. The one contemporary French poet really acclaimed in Britain was the man who most fully represented French symbolism in the twentieth century, Paul Valéry. Here too the new independence and strength of judgement of the English modern poetry movement was clear; Valéry's extremely important volume *La Jeune Parque* was first fully appreciated – in either country – by John Middleton Murry in the *Times Literary Supplement* for 23 August 1917.[1] This British independence meant an eclectic,

---

[1] The author of the anonymous *TLS* review is identified by Charles Du Bos in 'Letters from Paris, v: On the Symbolist Movement in French Poetry', *The Athenaeum* (30 July 1920) 159.

7

individual approach to contemporary French poetry and some resistance to imitation of recent Continental currents. Eliot, for example, drew on St.-John Perse, particularly on the *Anabase* (1924),[1] though the French poet was neither popular nor widely known in England in the 1920s. The English return to the French symbolists was paralleled (and perhaps to some extent prompted) by a new attention in Paris to the French late-nineteenth century, to Rimbaud, Lautréamont, and Jarry; and two significant French post-war movements in poetry, dadaism and surrealism, grew out of this concern. These movements were discussed in London by 1920, but chiefly by the one critic who had been really devoted to thorough reportage on current French poetry in the years before the war – F. S. Flint. He treated the new developments in three essays: 'Some Modern French Poets (A Commentary, with Specimens)' in *Chapbook*, October 1919; an abbreviated version of the same article for the *Times Literary Supplement* leader for 2 October 1919; and most important, 'The Younger French Poets: The Dada Movement' in *Chapbook*, November 1920. Flint himself had almost stopped writing poetry; his influence with *avant garde* poets had been through the defunct imagist movement and with the end of war he had resumed his work in literary circles as journalist and translator rather than as a member of *les jeunes*. Meanwhile, John Middleton Murry and Aldous Huxley were directing British attention to exciting developments in French prose – to the novels of Marcel Proust and André Gide. Perhaps consequently, Flint's early and significant essays on French dadaism went largely unheeded in the circles of poetry; critical journals were slow to follow his lead; and it was not again until the 1930s that a French movement, surrealism, belatedly became important to English poetry. For the interim decade or so it was fair to say, as T. S. Eliot did in the same essay in which he praised the France of pre-war years, that 'the intellectual primacy of Paris' was 'not what it was' in the vital, tumultuous years in which a modern English poetry was shaped.[2]

II

In terms of understanding both the importance of French influence and the complicated origins of modern English poetry, the most interesting stages of influence are the years of the discovery and widening knowledge of symbolist *cénacle* and post-symbolist poets and of the assimilation of abstract aesthetic theories – that is, 1909–16. It is with the disputed origins of imagism, which lie in the years 1908 or 1909, that one can best begin to examine the extension of French influence in twentieth-

[1] Edward J. H. Greene, *T. S. Eliot et la France* (Paris, 1951), pp. 135–6.
[2] Eliot, 'A Commentary', *op. cit.*, 53.

century England. Literary revival was brewing in England in 1908. Only William Butler Yeats, the writers of the Irish renaissance, and occasionally Thomas Hardy had continued to do really significant work in poetry during the years since the demise of *The Yellow Book* in April 1897. But in 1908 T. E. Hulme and other members of a first Poets' Club were meeting to discuss the techniques of poetry, and in December of that same year, Ford Madox Ford launched one of the important journals of the half-century: *The English Review*. At about the same time A. R. Orage became editor of *The New Age* and shaped that weekly into an important source of information on foreign literature and *avant garde* theories in philosophy and aesthetics. The Poets' Clubs, *The English Review*, and *The New Age* all served to spread the influence of the French.

One part of the story begins with the emergence of a young working-class man, Frank S. Flint, as a poetry reviewer with an unusual gift for language. A self-educated man, Flint studied French in a workingman's night school just after he entered the civil service at age nineteen,[1] approximately 1904. By 1906 he had begun literary work,[2] and in 1908 he became the regular poetry reviewer for *The New Age*. In his first essay there, 11 July 1908, he spoke of the tanka, the haikai (using, as Earl Miner points out, the French form of that term),[3] unrhymed verse, broken cadences, and Stéphane Mallarmé.[4] The first Poets' Club, which had been meeting throughout 1908, issued in January 1909, an anthology of its work: *For Christmas, MDCCCVII*, and in February 1909, Flint reviewed it for *The New Age*. Flint particularly liked Hulme's 'Autumn' – later to be regarded as a paradigm imagist poem – but he compared the Poets' Club to the discussions of poetry in French cafés, and concluded: 'Those discussions in obscure cafés regenerated, remade French poetry; but the Poets' Club – ! . . . the Poets' Club is death.'[5]

As subsequent descriptions of the period have often recorded, the review led to a meeting between Flint and Hulme, and the formation in March 1909, of a second or secession Poets' Club, attended by Flint, Hulme, Edward Storer, Florence Farr, Joseph Campbell, Francis Tancred, Ezra Pound (who began attending with the fourth meeting),[6]

---

1 'Obituary: Frank S. Flint, Imagist Poet', *The Times*, 29 February 1960, p. 14.
2 A typed manuscript of *The Agora: A Journal for All and None*, dated November 1906, is held in The Academic Center Library of The University of Texas. It consists of poems and articles by Flint and others.
3 Miner, *The Japanese Tradition in British and American Literature*, p. 101.
4 *The New Age*, n.s. III (11 July 1908) 212–13.
5 'Recent Verse', *The New Age*, n.s. IV (11 February 1909) 327.
6 The quotation and most of the foregoing information is from Flint's 'History of Imagism', *The Egoist*, II, 5 (1 May 1915). See also Wallace Martin, *op. cit.*; Pound, 'Preface' to 'The Complete Poetical Works of T. E. Hulme' in *Ripostes* (London, 1912); and Patricia Hutchins, *Ezra Pound's Kensington* (London, 1965).

and, as one of Hulme's organizing letters indicates, Ernest Radford and Ernest Rhys.[1] 'We were all much influenced by the French symbolists', Flint said of that group – and it was back toward those 1909 meetings that both Pound and Flint pointed[2] as sources of inspiration for the imagism that had its real development in 1912 and 1913. Three members of that group have laid claim to priority in transmitting French influence or have been pointed out by later critics as chiefly responsible for introducing London poets to crucial aspects of contemporary French poetry and criticism – T. E. Hulme, Ezra Pound, and F. S. Flint. Both unpublished letters and the files of *avant garde* journals or little magazines make clear that Flint holds priority. His first published references to French literature in *The New Age* reviews which began 11 July 1908, certainly preceded Pound's interest in the French. They did not precede Hulme's *interest* in French poets, but it is reasonably certain that the earliest Flint reviews preceded Hulme's first formal and public use of recent French poetic ideas in 'A Lecture on Modern Poetry', which was probably given early in 1909.[3] Flint's knowledge of the contemporary French scene was far more extensive than that of Hulme or Pound, though less the product of personal friendships. His publications on the subject are far larger than even those of Pound or Richard Aldington; and the judgements revealed by his choice of subjects, though not guided by a zeal to advocate a particular kind of poetic technique, were on the whole no less reliable than those of his more famous London contemporaries. For example (if one may look ahead chronologically), Flint was aware of the significance of Apollinaire, Paul Claudel, Charles Péguy, Jean Cocteau, and Paul Eluard before Pound was.[4] Flint did underestimate the significance of Valéry, and he exhibited a tolerance for minor poets like Lucien Rolmer, Charles Périn, and Drieu la Rochelle that led critics and competitors for the title of chief interpreter of French poetry to fault his critical judgement.[5] He was, moreover,

[1] Hulme to Flint, unpublished card postmarked 24 March 1909. The manuscript is in the Academic Center Library of The University of Texas.

[2] See footnote 6, page 9.

[3] The exact date of the lecture is unknown. I have presented several arguments for the probability of January 1909, in 'T. E. Hulme's "A Lecture on Modern Poetry" and the Birth of Imagism', *Papers on Language and Literature*, v, 4 (Fall 1969), pp. 465–70.

[4] The essays in which Flint first really discusses these figures are the 'French Chronicle' in *Poetry and Drama* for December 1913 and March 1914 (Apollinaire); March and December 1913 (Claudel); December 1914 (Péguy); and 'Some Modern French Poets (A Commentary, with Specimens)' in *Chapbook*, October 1919 (Apollinaire, Cocteau, Eluard).

[5] The *Chapbook* essay on 'Some Modern French Poets' omitted reference to Valéry, and Flint was severely criticized for this in the short notice and letters columns of *The Athenaeum* for 31 October and 7 November 1919. Richard Aldington defended him in a letter which appeared 7 November, and Flint himself explained in a letter to *The Athenaeum* on 14 November that he had omitted Valéry because he had been unable to secure a review copy of *La Jeune Parque*.

himself an unassuming man and a minor poet, able to exploit in his own work only a few of the many technical achievements he described in French literature. As an essayist he deliberately set himself the task of giving full and fair description of the French *avant garde* rather than that of being an evaluative critic sifting the better poets from the worse or telling English readers whom to prefer. The role he chose was properly suited to the times and to his readers. As T. S. Eliot has noted:

A critical introduction to contemporary poetry may take one of two forms, according to the degree of knowledge of the material that may be attributed to the audience addressed. If the poets to be discussed are almost unknown, the critic's chief service is to bring their work to the notice of readers who are likely to appreciate them; and his critical acumen will be most appropriately exhibited by copious and well-chosen quotation. His main task is to persuade his readers that his poets deserve their attention, and to send them eagerly to the poetry itself.[1]

Such a task – sending readers by well-chosen quotation to the poetry itself – was one Flint performed with zeal and skill. It would be a grave mistake in literary history to confuse Flint's standing as a poet or his lack of interest in critical evaluation with his crucial role as transmittor of information about French poetry to a London *avant garde* seeking just such a catalyst to expedite – or make possible – the development of a modern poetic tradition. It is in the latter role that Flint's primary importance lies.

At the time of Flint and Hulme's meeting in February 1909, following the review of *For Christmas, MDCCCCVIII*, both men had acquaintance with a few (and different) poets of the symbolist *cénacle*. One of Flint's most important sources at that time was the two-volume symbolist anthology, *Poètes d'aujourd'hui*, which he alluded to in the same essay in which he discussed the Poets' Club anthology. In some large measure as a result of Flint's influence, it seems, that anthology became a standard handbook for the imagist poets. (Flint included translations of two poems from it in collections of his own work; Pound recommended it as a French text in 1913; Richard Aldington modelled an attempt at a prose poem in *Images (1910–1915)* on a verse from Paul Fort that had appeared there; H.D. borrowed Flint's volumes in 1917 because she temporarily could not obtain Aldington's copy; and as René Taupin has observed, Amy Lowell used it as a basic source for her critical study *Six French Poets*.)[2] Flint demonstrated that his reading in

1 'Foreword', in *Contemporary French Poetry* by Joseph Chiari (New York, 1952), p. vii.
2 Flint, 'Cleopatra' after Albert Samain and 'Odelet' after Henri de Régnier in *Otherworld* (London, 1920); Pound, 'Paris', *Poetry*, III (October 1913) 29. Comparison of Aldington's 'Night Piece' with Fort's 'Des "Ballades de la Nuit"' will appear in my forthcoming critical–historical study of French influence on English poetry, 1900–20; letter, 30 August 1917, in 'Selected Letters from H. D. to F. S. Flint', ed. Cyrena N. Pondrom, *Contemporary*

French literature had exerted an influence on his poetry as well as on his criticism in his first volume of verse, *In the Net of the Stars*, which also appeared in 1909. There he attempted the irregular line length, rhyme in successive very long and very short lines to give a strong cadence, internal rhyme or assonance, and repetition of phrases characteristic of the *vers libre* of Emile Verhaeren.[1] Only a few poems in the volume showed these experiments with free verse, but they were enough to demonstrate that Flint was moving metrically (if not in the handling of the image) in the same direction as his friend, T. E. Hulme, at about the same time.

The direction that Hulme was going was clearly shown in the two poems which appeared in the Poets' Club anthology which Flint reviewed. The following passage, for example, is part of 'A City Sunset' from that collection:

> A frolic of crimson
> is the spreading glory of the sky
> heaven's wanton
> flaunting a trailed red robe
> along the fretted city roofs[2]

This passage, which could have been written no later than 1908, shows irregular line length and assonance which replaces end-rhyme (wanton / flaunting), and employs the single dominant, metaphoric image which characterizes the benchmark poems of imagism, like H.D.'s 'Oread'. Whereas Flint's inspiration appeared to come chiefly from Verhaeren, probably with assistance from Henri de Régnier, Hulme was probably relying particularly upon Gustave Kahn, whom he cited in his 'Lecture'.[3] He had spent seven months in Brussels in 1907 teaching English and learning French and German,[4] and at about the same time he had read André Beaunier's book on the symbolist *cénacle* poets, *La Poésie nouvelle*.[5] Perhaps partially under the impetus of Ford Madox Ford (*né* Hueffer), then at the helm of the new *English Review*, Hulme codified his reflections upon Kahn and other *cénacle* poets and explained his current experiments in free verse in 'A Lecture on Modern Poetry', probably

---

Literature, xi, 4 (Fall 1969) 584; René Taupin, *L'Influence du symbolisme français sur la poésie américaine (1910–1920)* (Paris, 1919), p. 168.

[1] Compare, for example, 'He meets Her in a Wood at Night' with 'November' from *Poètes d'aujourd'hui*.

[2] *Further Speculations: T. E. Hulme*, ed. Sam Hynes (Lincoln Nebraska, 1962), p. 215.

[3] Wallace Martin, '*The New Age*' under Orage, op. cit., p. 157, has shown that passages of Hulme's 'Lecture' are directly translated, without acknowledgement, from Gustave Kahn's 'Sur le vers libre', *Premiers Poèmes* (Paris, 1897).

[4] 'Introduction', *Speculations: T. E. Hulme*, ed. Herbert Read (New York, n.d.), p. ix.

[5] In a review in *The New Age*, n.s. ix (24 August 1911), p. 400, Hulme says he read the Beaunier book 'some five or six years ago' – that is, about 1906, or the year before Read indicates Hulme really learned French. The date thus, is merely approximate.

delivered, as I have noted, in January 1909, some six months after Flint's first review for *The New Age*. 'There were certain impressions I wanted to fix', he said. 'I read verse to find models, but I could not find any that seemed exactly suitable. . .until I came to read the French vers-libre. . .'[1] Such a comment seems as appropriate to the two Hulme poems in *For Christmas, MDCCCCVIII*, published before Hulme and Flint met, as to his later work; and one should conclude, I think, that Hulme had begun to assimilate his knowledge of symbolist *cénacle* poetry before he came to know Flint in January 1909.[2] In any case, Hulme went on in the 'Lecture' to explain that Kahn's technique 'consisted in a denial of a regular number of syllables as the basis of versification. The length of the line is long and short, oscillating with the images used by the poet; it follows the contours of his thought and is free rather than regular. . .'

Thus when Hulme and Flint became friends they brought together their knowledge of French poets and their slightly differing approaches to *vers libre,* and they shared this information in a poets' discussion group (attended by Pound) which thoroughly implanted the idea of experiment with cadenced or free verse in London poetic circles. Throughout the year, the two continued to exchange poems and comment on each other's efforts. On 7 September 1909, for example, Hulme dashed off a card to Flint bearing a 'draft poem' and one ironic comment:

> Maria Aboda whose bent form
>
> The sky in arched circle is.
>   ever mourning
> Seems ∧ ~~weeping~~ for a grief unknown
>   cry (~~say~~)
> Yet on a day, I heard her xxxxx [whisper ?]
> "Damn the roses and the singing poets,
>   try."
> Josephs all, not tall enough to xxxxxxxx [kiss me ?]
>
>   This truly inspiration, quite sudden.
>   T. E. HULME[3]

After this year of being a poet, however, Hulme began to devote himself more to philosophy and its applications to poetic theory. His greatest interest was philosopher Henri Bergson, whose aesthetic views were interpreted to provide a rationale for much post-symbolist art in both

---

1 *Further Speculations, op. cit.,* p. 68.
2 Alun Jones, I think, overstates the case when he says it was through Flint that Hulme 'was brought into contact with contemporary French poetry', since by 'contemporary' he seems to mean the *cénacle* poets. *The Life and Opinions of T. E. Hulme* (London, 1960), p. 32.
3 Unpublished postcard to Flint, postmarked 7 September 1909. The manuscript is in the Academic Center Library of The University of Texas.

France and England. Although this change of interest did not separate Hulme either from poetic theory or from France, it did deflect him from further poetic ambition of his own and it led him away from sustained study of contemporary French poets.

At this time others were taking note of Continental poetry and urging a break with traditional metric. As early as 1909 *The English Review* printed Emile Verhaeren's poem 'La Prière' (March 1909) and the editor called for technical experiment in phrases that have some similarity to sentences in Hulme's 'A Lecture on Modern Poetry'. 'The literature of today is a poor thing', Ford Madox Ford wrote, 'because we have no trained writers who, bursting the bonds of conventions which have trained them, have achieved an ease of phrase, a mastery of form'.[1] Soon thereafter, in the important preface to a collection of his poems, in 1913, Ford urged the English poet to write 'exactly as he speaks' and pointed to France and Germany for models of such poetic diction.[2]

In August 1910, *Tramp*, a journal edited by Douglas Goldring, one of Ford's associates on *The English Review*, carried on the demand for experiment by printing a letter from F. T. Marinetti and extracts from the first futurist manifesto, published in Paris in *Le Figaro* on 20 February 1909. This first extended British notice of futurism – apart from Marinetti's lecture earlier in 1910 – included the declaration of war on tradition: 'The essential elements of our poetry will be courage, audacity, and revolt...We will sing the multicoloured and polyphonic surf of revolutions in modern capitals; the nocturnal vibration of arsenals and docks beneath their glaring electric moons; greedy stations devouring smoking serpents, factories hanging from the clouds by the threads of their smoke...'[3] The same issue also contained news of the impressionist coterie in Paris, 'An Impressionist Symphony' by Edgcumbe Staley.

Symbolism was attracting attention at Oxford, and the young John Middleton Murry in Easter 1910, was struggling to read Mallarmé and Rimbaud in the original. His efforts largely foundered on a poor command of French, and the Christmas vacation of 1910–11 saw Murry, aged 21, in Paris, learning French from the Parisian *avant garde*. He met fauve artist J. D. Fergusson there, studied Bergson's *L'Evolution créatrice*, and laid plans for a magazine that would bring Parisian literary, artistic, and philosophical excitement to England.[4] The 'modernism' he

---

[1] Review by 'E.R.' in *The English Review*, 1 (January 1909) 374. The author has been identified by David Harvey in *Ford Madox Ford, 1873–1939: A Bibliography of Works and Criticism* (1962).
[2] *Critical Writings of Ford Madox Ford*, ed. Frank MacShane (Lincoln, Nebraska, 1964), p. 141.
[3] *The Tramp*, 6 (August 1910) 487–8.
[4] F. A. Lea, *The Life of John Middleton Murry* (London, 1959), pp. 18, 20.

intended his journal (which appeared in summer 1911, as *Rhythm*) to express meant 'Bergsonism in Philosophy – that is a really *Creative* Evolution with only in the end an Intuition to put the individual at its heart roots; an intuition which is the raising of Personality to the nth degree, a conscious concentration of vision'. He went on, in the same letter of April 1911, to Philip Landon to make the poetic significance of his new philosophical interest clear: 'Now Bergsonism stands for Post-Impressionism in its essential – and not in the sense of the Grafton Exhibition: it stands for a certain symbolism in poetry on the one hand; and a certain definite rejection of suggestion on the other. It stands equally for Debussy and Maehler [*sic*] in music, for Fantaisisme in Modern French literature...'[1]

Murry's interpretation of what Bergson should mean to English poetry was in some ways like Hulme's and both marked out the direction to be taken by imagism. Essential to all three views is a belief in art, in poetry, as the expression of a higher realism. Symbolism's appeal to an otherworldly realm of truth, accessible to the artist, was abandoned: hence the 'certain definite rejection of suggestion'. Truth was present, empirical; the artist's direct intuition of the object (mental or physical) and his presentation of it by image and analogy could be the occasion for an intuition of essential reality by the reader. Hence, in Murry's elliptical (and somewhat imprecise) phrasing, the retention of a 'certain symbolism in poetry'. The result was akin to the 'higher empiricism' Bergson attributed to his own philosophy. Acute perception and acute description of the object were imperative, for reality lay in the empirical world; yet it was the direct apprehension of the object that was important, and an art of psychological realism was at the same time an art of the poet's superior sensitivity and inner vision. The mystical aesthetic of spiritual vision characteristic of many symbolists had been reshaped in the post-symbolist world, under the impact of mechanistic and scientific philosophies. It had emerged as an aesthetic that laid claim to a higher realism by dint of affirming the essential truth that could be revealed by the present, empirical consciousness of the artist. Murry, in his essay on Bergson for the first issue of *Rhythm* in summer 1911, gave a fuller development to the position:

We attain to the truth not by that reason which must deny the fact of continuity and of creative evolution, but by pure intuition, *by the immediate vision of the artist in form.* But the pure intuition is no mystical surrender of reason and personality to a vague something, which, because it is nothing, is called God. It is the triumph of personality, the culmination and not the negation of the reason. The intuition is that point, as it were, at which the reason becomes most wholly itself, and by its own heightened working *conquers the crude opposition of subject and object*, from which at a lower level it

[1] The letter to Landon is quoted in full in Lea, *op. cit.*, pp. 24–5.

cannot become free. Here human personality by the consciousness of reason *drags reality into its knowledge*, into itself, the rational self asserting its ultimate triumph over an externality, which is, while merely external, meaningless.[1]

Anticipating the 'higher realism' of imagism, Murry in the same essay also anticipated the endorsement of abstract and essential forms which Hulme and Pound reached only in the winter of 1913–14 under the impact, respectively, of Worringer and Kandinsky. In the same essay of 1911 Murry, already acquainted with the *avant garde* art world of Paris, continued:

The artist attains to the pure form, refining and intensifying his vision till all that is unessential dissolves away ... He must return to the moment of pure perception to see the essential forms, the essential harmonies of line and colour, the essential music of the world.[2]

At about the same time that Murry was studying *L'Evolution créatrice* and working out its aesthetic implications, Hulme was journeying to Bologna to the Philosophical Congress in April 1911, where he extended his own acquaintance with Bergson. In the intervening two years, Hulme had played a very substantial role in popularizing Bergson in England. As Sam Hynes has pointed out, Hulme's first essay on Bergson was published in 1909, and by the end of 1912 he could claim at least eighteen published items on the subject.[3] Where that study, coupled with his own prior inclinations, had brought him by approximately 1911 is clear from two comments, published posthumously. His belief – like Murry's – that the poet seeks to render an empirical reality, and at the same time to convey an inner vision of that reality, is explicit in 'Notes on Language and Style': '...the poet is forced to use new analogies, and especially to construct a plaster model of a thing to express his emotion at the sight of the vision he sees, his wonder and ecstasy... Perhaps literary expression is from *Real to Real* with all the intermediate forms keeping their *real* value.'[4] And in 'Bergson's Theory of Art' Hulme identifies the French philosopher as the source of the view he shares of the poet as one who gives form to essential truths which are accessible, by intuition, in the empirical consciousness of the artist:

To use the metaphor which one is by now so familiar with – the stream of the inner life, and the definite crystallized shapes on the surface – the big artist, the creative

[1] 'Art and Philosophy', *Rhythm*, I, 1 (Summer 1911) 9–10. See pages 54–7. Italics mine.
[2] *Ibid.* 12.
[3] *Further Speculations, op. cit.*, pp. 221–2.
[4] *Further Speculations, op. cit.*, p. 78. Italics are Hulme's. The date of these notes is particularly unclear. Martin, *op. cit.*, p. 172, suggests a date of about 1907–11 for entries titled 'Notes on Language and Style'. From a comparison with Hulme's explicitly dated comments, I would conjecture that this entry was written about 1911.

artist, the innovator, leaves the level where things are crystallized out into these definite shapes, and, diving down into the inner flux, comes back with a new shape which he endeavours to fix. He cannot be said to have created it, but to have discovered it, because when he has definitely expressed it we recognize it as true.[1]

Such revisions of the symbolist approach in the light of Bergson's aesthetic comments had been a fundamental part of the post-symbolist movements of France of the first decade. One of the most thoroughgoing of these critical statements was Tancrède de Visan's *L'Attitude du lyrisme contemporain*, which Hulme gave enthusiastic review in *The New Age* in August 1911 (see pages 58–60). What is more, some of the formulations in that volume reappear in the rhetoric of imagism.

Hulme's dissemination of his version of Bergsonian poetics extended beyond his frequent appearance in journal columns and lecture halls. His living room was the scene of the weekly 'Frith Street gatherings', which Pound scoffed at as 'diluted with crap like Bergson',[2] and he was credited with the translation of Bergson's *What Is Metaphysics?* (tr. 1913) and Georges Sorel's *Reflections on Violence* (tr. 1916). Some of those translations were in progress as early as 1912. Hulme, however, does not deserve the whole or perhaps even the major credit for the work, beyond his role as literary entrepreneur. In one of his characteristically ill-typed letters in mid-1912, Hulme berated his old acquaintance F. S. Flint at length for protesting about his small reward for working with Hulme on translations:

If you felt that it wasnt [*sic*] worth while you should have said o so [*sic*] and I should have got some one else to do it who had offer [*sic*] The point is that it was not worth my while to give more * I could not afford it * If I had to give more *I should partly have done it myself* I will send you an extra giunea [*sic*] for the Bergson and the other money for the Sorel in a few days ...[3]

Whether Flint or Hulme deserves primary credit for making available to the British public Bergson's very important *What Is Metaphysics?* and Sorel's *Reflections on Violence*, both men clearly played a significant part. These facts stress Flint's role in conveying two highly influential French

1 *Speculations*, ed. Read, *op. cit.*, p. 149. Martin, *op. cit.*, p. 172, places this lecture in 1911; I think it very likely it is actually Hulme's 'Bergsonian' lecture on 'The New Philosophy of Art as Illustrated in Poetry', advertised by *The Poetry Review* 7 (July 1912) 295 for Clifford's Inn Hall, 15 July 1912.

2 Pound, 'This Hulme Business', *The Townsman*, II, 5 (January 1939) 15.

3 Unpublished two-page typed letter from Hulme to Flint, without date but accompanied by matching envelope postmarked 9 August 1912. Italics mine. The phrase between asterisks is an insertion. Other letters dealing with Flint's translation duties have attached envelopes postmarked 6 April and 16 August 1912, and 8, 21, and 26 August 1913. An apparently earlier, undated, letter suggests that the collaboration began with Flint simply correcting Hulme's French, though this quotation implies Hulme came to pay small sums for Flint to do the work himself. All these Hulme letters are in the Academic Center Library of The University of Texas.

currents which are usually associated with other, more prominent, names.

In addition to the widespread interest in Bergson, and particularly in Bergsonian aesthetics, 1911 brought more attention to current developments in French art and *fantaisiste* poetry and to the major figures of the symbolist *cénacle*, to the men who had accomplished the transformation of French metric and diction. For example, as well as Murry's article on Bergson and poetry, the first issue of *Rhythm* carried art by Picasso and an article on fauvism; the winter 1911 number printed two French poems by *fantaisiste* Tristan Derème, and the issue for spring 1912 carried both a poem by *fantaisiste* Jean Pellerin and a survey of French *avant garde* magazines by Murry.

During the same period of time, *The New Age* began publishing a series of essays by Richard Buxton on Henri de Régnier (14 September 1911), Jean Moréas (28 September 1911), Stuart Merrill (2 November 1911), and Francis Jammes (11 January 1912). Two other essays by Buxton, on Paul Fort on 8 August and on Albert Samain on 24 October appeared later in 1912. Buxton was not a member of the poetic *avant garde*, and his series of articles did not have as much acknowledged effect as Flint's work. He did, however, provide an extended and reliable description of six members of the *cénacle*, including three – de Régnier, Jammes, and Fort – who were to receive considerable attention from one or more members of the imagist group. He expressed a preference for 'subjective' poetry, but he accurately noted the tendency of several of his subjects to move from a period of influence by Verlaine and Mallarmé, to a period of more independent mastery of symbolist *vers libre*, and finally into a return to a more objective, classical, or Parnassian verse. And in describing the practice of the symbolists, he too used the diction of the Bergsonian reinterpretation of that aesthetic: 'The meaning was presented by means of a series of pictures which, in their rapid succession, were to print an image on the mind of the reader which was none of them and yet which was composed by all of them.'[1]

Throughout much of 1911, relatively little was heard from the poets who would form the earliest ranks of imagism. Up at least until that year Flint had maintained his connections with the poetic movement that was slowly gathering strength in England. He was quite possibly the means by which both Hulme and Storer became contributors to *The New Age*;[2] he frequently contributed a poetry column to that journal himself until late September 1910; and he continued to write poetry which appeared in *The English Review* and in Goldring's *The Tramp*. Then he was rather less active until he was brought into the group

[1] *The New Age*, n.s. IX (14 September 1911) 471.
[2] Martin, *op. cit.*, p. 166.

which was to form imagism, probably very late in 1911, and no later than the first days of 1912. Richard Aldington, then just 18, was in London for an abbreviated enrollment at the University of London and had begun early in 1911 to write *vers libre*. Aldington several times claimed to know nothing of the French at that date;[1] a university friend has recalled, however, that Richard was already corresponding with Remy de Gourmont and lending around a copy of *Le Latin mystique*.[2] Pound had returned to London after an extended trip to the United States, and H.D. arrived there in the fall. At about the turn of the year Aldington met Pound, H.D. and Flint,[3] and the discussions that led to imagism began. One of the important catalysts in this group was Flint's knowledge of current French poetry – which, with the possible exception of Aldington, the others knew little about. In a letter to his mother on 21 February 1912, Pound said Flint had introduced him to 'some very good contemporary French stuff: Remy de Gourmont, de Régnier, etc'.[4] And on the same day Pound thanked Flint for lending him some of the work of Albert Samain, and scheduled a meeting – to include H.D. as well – for later in the same week.[5] Within about two months, all of the group but Flint had gone to Paris for a few weeks, and Pound was actively involved with the *Mercure* crowd.[6] Meanwhile, Flint, who was preparing an article for the new *Poetry Review* on 'Contemporary French Poetry', was carrying on a staggeringly extensive correspondence in French with some members of the Parisian *avant garde*. And that too, had its significant effect: 'In the spring or early summer of 1912', Pound wrote, '"H.D.", Richard Aldington and myself decided that we were agreed upon...three principles...Upon points of taste and of pre-dilection we differed, but agreeing upon these three positions we thought we had as much right to a group name as a number of French "schools" proclaimed by Mr. Flint in the August number of Harold Munro's [*sic*] magazine for 1911 [*sic*].'[7] Pound was right about one date – the early spring 1912, starting point for imagist discussion – and wrong about another; Flint's essay appeared in August 1912, not in 1911. In addition, Pound was undoubtedly right about the importance of Flint's essay.

1 Letter from Aldington to Amy Lowell, 20 November 1917. The manuscript is in the Harvard University Library.
2 'Sir Alec Randall', in *Richard Aldington: An Intimate Portrait*, ed. Alister Kershaw and F.-J. Temple (Carbondale and Edwardsville Illinois, 1965), p. 115.
3 Aldington to Lowell, *op. cit.*; Charles Norman, *Ezra Pound* (New York, 1960), pp. 60, 68.
4 Letter from Ezra Pound to Isabel W. Pound, 21 February 1912. The manuscript is in the Yale University Library.
5 Letter from Ezra Pound to F. S. Flint, n.d., accompanied by matching envelope postmarked 21 February 1912. The manuscript is in the Academic Center Library of The University of Texas.
6 Postcard, 9 May 1912, 'Selected Letters from H. D. to F. S. Flint', *op. cit.*, p. 559.
7 Ezra Pound, 'A Stray Document', *Make It New* (London, 1934), p. 335.

Pound and Aldington did not have to wait for the appearance of the essay to hear all about Flint's new information on French poetry. Members of the group were in touch with Flint for frequent meetings throughout the spring,[1] while Flint composed the article and received books and letters from French poets. Pound's first actual reference to an 'imagiste' poem came in an 18 August 1912, letter to Harriet Monroe, immediately after Flint's article appeared. And in the same letter Pound instructed Miss Monroe, 'you must keep an eye on Paris'.[2] The coincidence between new information from Flint about current French work and the formation of the movement which was the starting point for modern poetry in English appears in very few ways coincidental.

Flint's responsibility for spreading information about the French in the formative days of imagism was recognized by René Taupin in his early study, *L'Influence du symbolisme français sur la poésie américaine* (1929). Taupin, however, stressed his judgement that Pound, Aldington, and H.D. had all written some poems unmistakably using the new techniques before Flint told them of contemporary French work,[3] and later critics have sometimes followed that lead in emphasizing the purely English elements of imagism.[4] Such emphasis depends upon a view that 'influence' is present almost exclusively when actual imitation of specific poems – especially technical imitation – can be shown, and it takes rather less account of conceptual and theoretical influence. New *ideas* about how poetry may be written, about form and order, may be transmitted by very limited examples or even by theoretical paraphrase and critical description, and the transmission of a key idea may very well be the occasion of the recreation of a parallel aesthetic in the recipient literary milieu. A view that influence is reliably shown only in the presence of specific verbal imitation also fails to deal with the reciprocal influence of literary currents which interact over several years to extend and reinforce each other. English poetry between 1908 and 1914 benefited both from the reception of key ideas and from the intensifying effect of contact with parallel aesthetic developments in France. Impressionist theory, the Bergsonian definition of the function of the image, ideas of asyntactical poetic form, and a concept of poetry

[1] See, in addition to footnote 6, page 19, letters from Pound to Flint dated 3, 6, and 21 February; 1 and 5 March; 2 April; and 31 July 1912. Several specifically comment on poetry, and one (5 March) alludes to Parisian poetic standards. All are in the Academic Center Library of The University of Texas.

[2] 18 August 1912, *The Letters of Ezra Pound*, ed. D. D. Paige (London, 1951), p. 44.

[3] Taupin, *op. cit.*, p. 90. 'Pendant l'automne de 1911, Mme Patmore, H.D., Pound, et Aldington se réunissaient pour prendre le thé. Bientôt Flint se joint à eux c'est par lui qu'ils apprennent à connaître la poésie française des symbolistes . . . Je crois nécessaire de répéter que jusqu'alors, ni Pound ni Aldington ni H.D. n'avaient cherche leur technique chez les Français, et pourtant tous les trois avaient déjà écrit des poèmes définitifs.'

[4] Hoffman, *op. cit.*, pp. 84–5; Glenn Hughes, *op. cit.*, p. 22.

as one of the non-representational arts played decisive roles in the formulation respectively of impressionist, imagist, and vorticist (and subsequent formally abstract) poetry in England. The development of *vers librist*, 'classical', and abstract movements in London received significant intensification from the analogous movements in France. Few of these developments, however, can be shown in the specific imitation of a French poem by an English writer. Even in the case of such more restricted influences, the imitation may recall its model only in the most general ways. In a column exhorting his fellow poets to turn to France for inspiration, Ezra Pound himself urged the 'creative' or 'original' use of French models:

> There are two ways of being influenced by a notable work of art: the work may be drawn into oneself, its mastery may beget a peculiar hunger for new sorts of mastery and perfection; or the sight of the work may beget simply a counterfeiting of its superficial qualities. This last influence is without value... The first influence means a new keenness of the ear, or a new flair for wording, or a deeper desire for common sense if the work is what is properly called classic.[1]

With such an explicit doctrine of the proper use of models expressed by the imagist leader, it is not surprising that in the work of the two best of the four imagist poets he treats in detail – Pound and H.D. – Taupin could find only a few examples of specific imitation. The absence of slavish imitation is no denial, however, of the significance of French poetic ideas and examples.

Further, Taupin's warning that major imagists had adopted a *vers librist* and imagistic technique before Flint introduced them extensively to French poetry – while useful to bear in mind – must be qualified in one additional way. There is no question that Flint explicitly directed the attention of Pound, H.D., and Aldington toward French contemporaries in the first days of 1912. But, as we have seen, Flint had begun to write of the French in 1908; Hulme had been energetically preaching Bergson for about two years, and throughout 1911 there was a steady and very significant increase in English attention to French poetry and theory. Thus Aldington's and Pound's poetic experiments in 1911 – and one must not forget Flint's and Hulme's earlier efforts – took place in a milieu in which contemporary French intellectual currents were already beginning to play an important role.

Those currents grew deeper in the first half of 1912. Harold Monro, who was born in Brussels and lived there during his first six or seven years, returned to London in autumn 1911, from a two-year Continental sojourn which included both Paris and Florence, and he set about organizing a new magazine for serious current poetry.[2] He announced

---

[1] 'The Approach to Paris, II', *op. cit.*, 577.
[2] Gsant, *Harold Monro and the Poetry Bookshop, op. cit.*, pp. 5, 21, 23.

in the first issue of *The Poetry Review*, January 1912, that a special issue would be devoted to French poetry, and it was this essay Flint was invited to contribute. In April 1912, following the influential London opening in March of the Exhibition of Works by the Italian Futurist Painters, *Tripod* published in its first issue F. T. Marinetti's 'Le Futurisme pictural'. Virtually every succeeding issue of *Tripod* contained another article on futurism, usually an essay written in French by a member of the futurist coterie (e.g. 'La Sculpture futuriste' by Umberto Boccioni in November 1912). *Tripod* was a Cambridge magazine; not to be outdone, *The Blue Book*, which first appeared in Oxford, in May 1912, contained 'The Past and Present of Futurism' by Michael Sadleir (*né* Sadler), another of the founders of *Rhythm*. Even a more popular journal, like *T.P.'s Weekly*, then enjoying a literary revival through the influence of Holbrook Jackson, commissioned John Middleton Murry to write an article on Émile Verhaeren, for which, in March 1912, Murry received his 'first literary earnings'.[1]

Despite increasingly frequent news from France, there had been in 1912 in England no systematic exposition of French experiment. The special issue of Monro's *Poetry Review* was designed to remedy that. As a result of the commission, Flint set out to learn as much as possible about French poetry by writing the poets themselves, requesting books, personal information, and as many comments about the poetic scene as they were prepared to volunteer. (See pages 64–83.) One whom Monro had first approached, Alexandre Mercereau, responded with voluminous generosity. In the course of many pages of handwritten comment on his poetic colleagues, Mercereau gave Flint a participant's knowledge of the French literary milieu. (A participant's knowledge, though more directly in touch with events, has the drawback of limited point of view; Flint came to feel that these early comments on French poetry were distorted by undue emphasis on minor figures.)[2] To these instructions Flint added numerous other briefer letters and a careful study of available books of poetry and treatises on poetic technique. In the course of this article Flint discussed and quoted from the work of Henri Ghéon, Jean Royère, André Spire, Henri-Martin Barzun, Alexandre Mercereau, Théo Varlet, Paul Castiaux, Georges and Cécile Périn, Jules Romains, René Arcos, Georges Duhamel, Charles Vildrac, Lucien Rolmer, Nicolas Beauduin, Valentine de Saint-Point, Berthe Reynold, Tancrède de Visan, Henri Hertz, and F. T. Marinetti. His discussion ranged over the *vers librists*, 'Néo-Mallarmisme', l'Abbaye de

[1] John Middleton Murry, *Between Two Worlds* (London, 1935), p. 191.
[2] Letter to the editor, *The Egoist*, 21 February 1917. The letter, which is very hostile to Pound, did not appear in the journal and may have remained unsent. The manuscript is held in the Academic Center Library, The University of Texas.

Créteil, 'Néo-paganisme', 'Unanimisme', the 'Whitmanistes', 'L'École de Grâce', 'Paroxysme', and 'Futurisme', and he provided an introductory section on antecedent symbolism in which he quoted Baudelaire, Gustave Kahn, Vielé-Griffin, Mallarmé, and Henri de Régnier. The article further served to call the attention of the readers of *The Poetry Review* to the major recent books on literary history or technique and to the important French little magazines or literary journals. Flint cited among his sources *L'Attitude du lyrisme contemporain* (1910), the volume by Tancrède de Visan Hulme had earlier reviewed; *Du Rhythme, en Français* by Robert de Souza; Duhamel and Vildrac's *Notes sur la technique poétique* (1911), a book which gave direction to imagist discussions of metric;[1] *La Littérature et l'époque* (1911) by Florian-Parmentier, an account of French poetry by 'schools'; Francis Vielé-Griffin's 'La Discipline Mallarméenne' in *La Phalange*, May 1907; and – significantly – Bergson's 'Introduction à la Metaphysique' from *Revue de métaphysique et de morale*, January 1903, which he and Hulme were shortly to translate.

Among the literary magazines Flint drew upon – and cited – were *Pan, Les Rubriques Nouvelles, La Flora, Beffroi, La Phalange, Vers et Prose, Poesia* (Marinetti's journal), *Nouvelle Revue Française, La Vie,* and *Les Bandeaux d'Or*. The mention of these magazines did serve to stimulate interest in them: the Flint correspondence preserves a letter passed on to Flint by Monro requesting the address of *Les Bandeaux d'Or*. Flint replied with the address and a recommendation of another journal. Moreover, the special issue created a stir in the London literary world. One extent of the response is suggested by the pleased comment Flint addressed to René Arcos, 18 November 1912: 'Mon article dans *The Poetry Review* a eu, à ce qu'on m'a dit, un grand succès'.[2] In fact, the article generated so much interest that it was profitable for Flint, in a subsequent letter asking for review copies from French publishers, to sign himself 'auteur de "Contemporary French Poetry"'.[3] Pound himself, ill-temperedly, summarized the importance of Flint's essay: 'that rotten *Poetry and Drama*, established itself solely by Flint's French number which everybody had to get; it was the first large article on contemporary stuff.'[4]

---

[1] See, for example, Pound's references to the volume in 'A Few Don'ts by an Imagiste', *Poetry*, 1, 6 (March 1913) 206. Reprinted in *Literary Essays*. The matter is discussed by one of my former students, Professor James Naremore, in 'The Imagists and the French "Generation of 1900"', *Contemporary Literature*, xi, 3 (Summer 1970).

[2] The manuscript is in the Academic Center Library, The University of Texas.

[3] Unpublished, stencilled letter, n.d., later than October 1919. The document is in the Academic Center Library, The University of Texas.

[4] Letter to Harriet Monroe, 28 March 1914, *The Letters of Ezra Pound, op. cit.*, p. 74. The reference should be, of course, to *The Poetry Review*.

Flint followed this success by volunteering to handle French reviewing for Monro's new periodical, *Poetry and Drama*. A delighted Monro made the appointment, and the result was the regular feature, 'The French Chronicle', which began with the first number of *Poetry and Drama*, March 1913, and lasted until the journal suspended publication during the war, in December 1914. This column offered regular attention to current trends in French poetry and criticism. Flint was careful to take account of developments in three different areas: he reported on the new books or recent honors of the most influential older figures; he kept up with first or second books by the young men he considered either representative or individually significant; and he provided a running chronicle of the rise and fall of literary coteries or schools of critical thought. To guarantee the accuracy of his comments as a reflection of *poèsie actuelle* he corresponded with literally dozens of French writers, including the poetry critics for the *Mercure* (Georges Duhamel) and the *Nouvelle Revue Française* (Henri Ghéon) and leaders of individual movements like Jules Romains, F. T. Marinetti, and Henri-Martin Barzun. In addition, Flint received and read most of the major French *avant garde* periodicals and ordered review copies of books which attracted his attention. The extent to which he was *au courant* can easily be shown by an example: when in March 1914 he discussed the *fantaisiste* movement Flint included representative poems by Tristan Klingsor and Apollinaire which did not appear in book form until, respectively, 1921 and 1925.

He clearly saw the current generations as developments from symbolist *cénacle* aesthetics, and he ranked Émile Verhaeren, Remy de Gourmont, Paul Fort, Francis Jammes, and Francis Vielé-Griffin as the leaders among the poets and critics of that generation. Among the countless younger figures he discussed, he devoted particular attention to expositions of the *unanimiste*, futurist, and *fantaisiste* groupings and to the critical controversy between adherents of classicism and romanticism.[1] Thus he commented upon Jules Romains, René Arcos, F. T. Marinetti, Guillaume Apollinaire, André Salmon, and Charles Maurras. Among figures not easily defined by these major groupings, he devoted attention to H.-M. Barzun, to Péguy, to Valery Larbaud, and to the poetic dramatists, including O. W. Milosz, a major figure then only slightly known.

Of all his French contemporaries, the single figure to whom he gave the highest praise – accurately, in terms of literary accomplishment in

---

[1] See, for example, the chronicles for, respectively, June and December 1913; September 1913; May and June 1914; and March and June 1913. A fuller discussion of the relation of Flint's comments on these movements to the development of English poetry appears in the introduction to the chronicles, on pages 201–3.

1913, and long before other British critics followed suit – was Paul Claudel. He singled out in his work the achievement the imagists, in slightly different fashion, also sought: 'The difficulty is the difficulty presented by genius', Flint wrote. 'Paul Claudel is undeniably a great poet in every sense. . . The development of his thought does not proceed by a logical dovetailing of phrases, but by the accumulation of images and rendered visions. . .'[1] Then he went on to cite from *Cinq grandes Odes* a statement of aesthetic principle portentous in an era coming to regard the work of art not as simple representation nor as transcendental vision but as the creation of significant form: 'For a poem is not just a heap of words, it is not merely / The things it signifies, but is itself a sign, an imaginary act, creating / The time necessary for its own resolution / Modelled upon man's action, examined in its springs and its weights.'[2]

Consistently throughout the chronicles Flint stressed technical achievements in cadenced or free verse and the communicative power of the image. He did not refuse to discuss adherents of the more traditional metrical styles, but he devoted so much more space and praise to the *vers librists* that his column must be cited as an important contribution to the milieu in which poetry was freed to experiment, not merely with new verse forms, but with abandonment of syntax and logical meanings themselves. He was, moreover, in touch with some of the most experimental of the French *avant garde* journals, including Apollinaire's *Les Soirées de Paris*, which Flint called 'a very modern review, futurist, cubist',[3] and to which he contributed an article on imagism in July–August 1914.

At about the same time that Flint published his first major essay on the French, in summer 1912, Tristan Derème began a series on the current Parisian poetic scene in *Rhythm*. Derème also discussed the romanticism–classicism controversy and laid heavy emphasis on the *fantaisistes*. His much briefer series, however, treated only a small fraction of the subjects taken up by Flint.[4]

It was not until the fall of 1913 that Ezra Pound began a serious round of propagandizing for the French, and the series of essays in which he did so, 'The Approach to Paris' (11 September–16 October 1913, *The New Age*), is an important landmark in the history of the development of modern poetry. The most interesting aspect of Pound's

[1] F. S. Flint, 'French Chronicle', *Poetry and Drama*, I, 4 (December 1913) 473. See page 227.
[2] Paul Claudel, 'The Muses', *Five Great Odes*, trans. by Edward Lucie-Smith (London, 1967), p. 16.
[3] Flint, 'French Chronicle', *Poetry and Drama*, II, 2 (June 1914) 220.
[4] The series rates in importance only behind the contributions of Flint and Pound as an early source of information pertinent to imagism, however. For a full discussion see 'Introduction', 'Lettre de France', p. 146–51.

'approach' to Paris was neither his long overpraise of Francis Jammes nor his predictable tribute to Henri de Régnier; it was, rather, his extended attention to the parts of the work of Jules Romains which stressed new conceptions of the order or structure of reality. The *unanimistes*, for whom Romains was undisputed leader, had already enjoyed considerable attention in London. Charles Vildrac had spoken chiefly on the *unanimiste* poets at the second Post-Impressionist Exhibition at the Grafton Gallery in the fall of 1912.[1] When Jethro Bithell in the spring of 1912 had published an anthology of recent French poetry in translation he had limited his comments on the current generation to Romains and his fellows.[2] And F. S. Flint, though he stressed the *unanimistes* were but one group among many, had presented extensive information on several of those associated with the group, both in his 1912 essay and in his subsequent columns. Pound's contribution was his recognition that Romains was proposing or popularizing new definitions of being in which the poet played a major role as the intelligence which gave voice to a vision of order not part of the traditional ways of viewing experience. Pound chose to translate the long concluding section to *Puissances de Paris*, in which Romains asserts: 'Already our ideas on *the being* (l'être) are correcting themselves...one ceases to believe that *limit* is indispensable to beings...A being has a centre, or centres in harmony; a being is not compelled to have limits. Many exist in one place...a second being begins without the first having ceased...All intercrosses, coincides, cohabits...'[3] It was such conceptions of multiple perspectives and of the continuous, interpenetrating nature of matter (or, in this case, of *groups*) that lay behind such steps toward artistic abstraction as analytical cubism and futurism. Romains explicitly saw the poet as giving voice to these new orders or previously unperceived structures of reality – that is, as Pound interpreted it, the poet becomes a ' "crater" or "vortex" and "the crowd must think his words" '.[4] Pound on this date was still some four and one half months away from his first articulation of his own abstract aesthetics,[5] and one might well regard Romains as one step on Pound's route to a new poetic.

Pound was also about to enter a period in which he wrote a significant amount of satiric, scatological, and bitterly defamatory poetry – such as 'Salutation the Third', 'Monumentum Aere, Etc.', and 'Fratres Minores' which appeared in *Blast*, 1 (June 1914). (The candidness of

[1] F. S. Flint, 'French Chronicle', *Poetry and Drama*, 1, 1 (March 1913) 76.
[2] Jethro Bithell, *Contemporary French Poetry* (London, 1912).
[3] Pound, 'The Approach to Paris, III', *The New Age*, n.s. XIII, 21 (18 September 1913) 607. See page 179.
[4] Pound, 'The Approach to Paris, IV', *The New Age*, n.s. XIII, 22 (25 September 1913) 631.
[5] One may reasonably date the published development of Pound's abstract aesthetics from 'The New Sculpture', *The Egoist* (16 February 1914).

'Fratres Minores' for that era was such that the issue was suppressed until three lines of the poem could be blacked out with heavy ink.) In the light of such a direction in Pound's own immediately subsequent poetry, it is interesting to note the high praise he accords not only to Tristan Corbière, but even more unstintingly, to Laurent Tailhade. Tailhade's technique he equates with 'the presentative method' and identifies as 'the scourge of fools'. One may well see some of the interests antecedent to Pound's 'Hell Cantos' when he goes on to quote with approval Tailhade's scorn of the 'mufle' ('mugs') in lines like

> Trop de merluche et des lentilles copieuses
>
> .   .   .   .
>
> Enjolivent de certains rots édifiants
> La constipation des personnes pieuses.[1]

In the case of both Romains and Tailhade, Pound's essays are of interest paramountly for what they show of the influences on important stages of his own development. There are other respects, however, in which the essay series is important for its contribution to the general acceptance of attitudes or models which became significant to a number of poets. Pound's comments on the new rhythms achieved by Remy de Gourmont were among the first to direct full attention of English-speaking poets toward a figure who became a touchstone for the period. Perhaps even more fundamental, Pound urged the deliberate assimilation by English poets of the new aesthetic and technical achievements of the French, and he provided the rationale that the greatest periods of creativity in English poetry have consistently been such eras of assimilation of French influence. Whether in part at Pound's behest or not, the next five years did prove to be an era of the assimilation of foreign influence.

Pound contributed greatly to this assimilation by adapting Continental theories or experiments – more than other imagists – for use in his own poetry and poetics. His contribution through critical essays on the French, in pre-war years, is somewhat less than that of Aldington and significantly less than that of Flint. 'The Approach to Paris' in fall 1913, was Pound's first major essay on the French.[2] He summarized those conclusions for *Poetry* in a brief essay entitled 'Paris', in October 1913, and included passing allusions to French poets or theories in much of the literary journalism which he produced subsequently.[3] He

---

[1] Pound, 'The Approach to Paris, v', *The New Age*, n.s. XIII, 23 (2 October 1913) 662.

[2] He had earlier reviewed P.-J. Jouve's *Présences* for *Poetry* in February 1913, and Jules Romains' *Odes et prières* for the same journal in August 1913. These brief reviews, plus one of Paul Castiaux's *Lumières du monde* for *The New Freewoman*, 1 December 1913, join 'The Approach to Paris' and 'Paris' to comprise Pound's total output on modern French subjects through the end of 1914. See Donald Gallup, *A Bibliography of Ezra Pound* (London, 1963).

[3] For example, Pound alludes to Francis Jammes in 'Ford Madox Hueffer', *The New*

did not, however, return to major critical commentary on the French until the death of Remy de Gourmont in September 1915, an event which occasioned two significant essays from Pound, one in *Fortnightly Review* in December 1915, and another in *Poetry*, January 1916.[1] It was not again until near the end of the war that Pound produced extensive comments on French poetry. Then, in three years he contributed four major essays and several minor ones to American publications: 'Irony, Laforgue, and Some Satire', *Poetry*, November 1917; 'The Hard and Soft in French Poetry', *Poetry*, February 1918; 'A Study in French Poets', *The Little Review*, February 1918; and 'Remy de Gourmont: A Distinction', *The Little Review* (Special Issue on de Gourmont), February–March 1919.[2] In 1920–1 he translated poems by de Gourmont for *The Dial*, and in 1926 he issued his translation of de Gourmont's *The Natural Philosophy of Love*, with its postscript dated 21 June 1921. Thus Pound's largest critical contribution to the transmission of French influence belongs to the period after World War I rather than to the pre-war years in which French work was playing its catalytic role, and in that later period he directed more of his efforts toward the American literary world than toward the British. Nonetheless, on the strength of his personal influence, his series on 'The Approach to Paris', and his adaptations of Continental aesthetic theories, Pound's name may be justly associated with major contributions to pre-war French influence in England.

As the poetic revival gained strength in England and America, knowledge of current French work became a status symbol, and rivalry developed among those who claimed priority in introducing it to others. By 1914, Aldington, Murry, Hulme, Pound and Flint all had written substantially on current French poets or philosophers and even John Gould Fletcher, who contributed relatively little to the British periodical press, subsequently claimed personally to have introduced Pound, and hence London, to symbolist and post-symbolist French poetry. Of all of these, only Aldington fully and consistently acknowledged that Flint was the earliest, farthest-ranging, and most systematic commentator of the six.

The rivalry grew particularly sharp between Flint and Pound, and

---

Freewoman, 13 (15 December 1913) 251; he contrasts English and Continental aesthetic theories in 'Vortex: Pound', *Blast*, 1 (June 1914) 153–4; and he devotes a paragraph to young French poets in 'Status Rerum – the Second', *Poetry*, VIII, 1 (April 1916) 41.

[1] The two essays, entitled 'Remy de Gourmont I and II', are collected in *Pavannes and Divisions* (New York, 1918), pp. 112–28. They do not appear in *Literary Essays*.

[2] All but 'A Study in French Poets' are collected in *Literary Essays*. *Instigations* (1920) and *Make It New* (1934) reprint 'A Study in French Poets' together with shorter essays on 'Unanimisme' (April 1918), Jean de Bosschère (October 1918), and Albert Mockel (October 1918) under the general title 'French Poets'. See Gallup, *A Bibliography of Ezra Pound, op. cit.*

resentments over this issue contributed significantly to the schism which separated Pound from the imagists after summer 1914. Pound was always the most prominent figure among the imagists, and whether by accident or intent, he assumed or was given credit for transmission of French influence beyond that which may accurately be attributed to him. Part of the others' irritation originated in Pound's customary air of authority. When he agreed to be Harriet Monroe's foreign editor for *Poetry*, for example, he sweepingly volunteered: 'If I can be of any use in keeping you or the magazine in touch with whatever is most dynamic in artistic thought, either here or in Paris – as much of it comes to me, and I *do* see nearly everyone that matters – I shall be glad to do so.' The offer, at that date, could only have been grandiose; it was August 1912,[1] just after Flint's 'Contemporary French Poetry' essay had appeared. A year later, when he knew the Parisian poetic world much better, Pound himself conceded that his previous knowledge had been somewhat sketchy. He wrote in a *Poetry* essay summarizing the conclusions of his 'The Approach to Paris' series: 'I spent about four years [presumably 1909–13] puddling about on the edges of modern French poetry without getting anywhere near it.'[2] This modesty was not usually equalled, however, by his deference to those who knew the subject better than he. There was, for example, a hint of condescension in his comment at the end of 'The Approach to Paris': 'There are a host of younger writers who doubtless will receive fitting recognition at the hands of Mr. Flint.' Another, clearer, view of the dissension appears in Aldington's candid advice to Flint: 'It doesn't seem to me quite tactful to borrow Ezra's Corbière as he would certainly declare afterwards that he "introduced Corbière to you".'[3] These conflicts broke clearly into the open in the spring of 1915 in two different sets of events.

With the 'French Chronicle' abandoned at the end of 1914 because of the demise of *Poetry and Drama*, Harriet Monroe and Flint discussed the possibility of Flint's contributing frequent essays on the French to *Poetry*. Flint wrote on 10 May 1915: 'I should be quite happy to send you articles on French poets from time to time, but I do understand you consider Pound has definitely abandoned that field? I have established relationships with French publishers, and should I obtain books from

---

[1] 'To Harriet Monroe', [18] August 1912, *The Letters of Ezra Pound, op. cit.*, p. 44. At the time Pound's contacts appear to have been chiefly with the *unanimistes*. Even in 'The Approach to Paris', for example, he showed little deep appreciation of the work of Apollinaire and Claudel, who were more experimental and at least as influential.

[2] Pound, 'Paris', *Poetry*, III, 1 (October 1913) 29–30.

[3] Aldington to Flint, undated note. I would conjecture a date in 1914–15, since it was during this time that the imagists were most annoyed with Pound on this issue. The manuscript is in the Academic Center Library of The University of Texas.

them on the plea that I was going to write about them in "Poetry", it would be annoying if E.P. suddenly got ahead of my course and took the wind out of my sails! Perhaps you can suggest a means of preventing any such clash. The best way would perhaps be for you to tell him that you have asked me to write about French poets.'[1] In fact, a few Flint pieces did appear in *Poetry*, but because of personal difficulties he was never able to carry out his plan to become a regular contributor.[2]

At about the same time Aldington and H.D. planned an imagist special issue of *The Egoist*, one of the important enterprises undertaken by the movement since Pound's separation from it in summer 1914. In what is apparently a draft for his essay 'The History of Imagism', Flint wrote: 'Well, Mr. Pound came [to the Poets' Club of 1909] and listened to all we had to say on the theory and practice of verse...But he... added nothing of any value to the discussion. Most of the members of the group were pretty widely acquainted with French theory, and Mr. Pound had simply nothing to teach them; but he took very much.'[3] At another place in the same fragment, Flint put Pound's 'first illumination' on the subject of French poetry 'in the spring of 1912', and continued:

In August of the same year,...finally, he was led to discover the 'Approach to Paris' – which I had made for him. Alas! In his eagerness to be the first guide along that delectable road – which I had made – he cut such strange capers and said such strange things that the prudent have been suspicious ever since. The bottle-green guide who touts for credulous Americans outside the Louvre will take you, if you are fool enough, to some odd picture in an out-of-the-way corner and announce with much triumph and mystery that he is the only guide who shows you *that*. Mr. Pound's method was the same.[4]

In this case, as in several others, Flint thought better of his acerbity before he prepared the final copy, and his published 'history' does not include so direct an attack. It did, however, insist that Pound knew virtually nothing of modern French poetry in 1909. Even this, more muted, published version (see page 302) occasioned an acrimonious exchange of letters between Flint and Pound.[5] It is worth noting that

[1] Flint to Harriet Monroe, 10 May 1915. The manuscript is in the Academic Center Library of The University of Texas.

[2] For example, on 18 January 1916, Flint wrote Miss Monroe to apologize for not having been able to provide an article on Stuart Merrill he had promised.

[3] The manuscript is in the Academic Center Library of The University of Texas. It has been reproduced in Christopher Middleton's 'Documents on Imagism from the Papers of F. S. Flint', *The Review*, 15 (April 1965) 39–40. I have omitted stricken words without ellipsis, although they are included in parenthesis in the Middleton text.

[4] *Ibid.*, 39. The first sentence of this quotation was lined out, and for clarity I have slightly regularized its internal punctuation. In the remaining sentences I have, as before, omitted without ellipses the stricken words included by Middleton. Other marks show Flint's later determination to cancel the entire passage.

[5] Middleton, *op. cit.*, prints the two Flint letters and paraphrases Pound's.

while Pound in the exchange challenged Flint's history on five different points, he did not take issue with the assertions that most club members knew the symbolists and that he himself was ignorant of modern French poetry in 1909.

Nor was Flint the only one to believe he deserved credit for making possible Pound's 'Approach to Paris' series. John Gould Fletcher visited Pound in early summer 1913, to exhibit his new volume of *vers libre*, *Irradiations*. The two met again about a week later, and Pound launched into a detailed critique. In response, Fletcher says,

> I was able, by quotation and example to show him that my favourite French symbolists were using my own devices of internal rhyme, vowel assonance, and the like; and my remarks to that effect seemed to impress him with the thought that there might be something in the symbolists after all, *whom he had never actually read*. Accordingly, on his next visit to my flat, he borrowed an armful of my French books and departed. When I next saw him he was already enthusiastic over de Gourmont, Corbière, and the early Francis Jammes.[1]

When Pound emphasized those authors in 'The Approach to Paris', the success of the series roused Fletcher to some bitterness: 'I must confess I felt somewhat aggrieved at his taking credit, thus blithely, for introducing these poets to the English public, when I had not only discovered them in the first instance myself, but had discussed them with him minutely. I felt that he had simply exploited the knowledge I had gained before him to serve his own ends.'[2] The result of this feeling was a short breach between Fletcher and Pound, during which Pound returned to Fletcher all the French books. From an historical perspective it is clear that Fletcher was but one of several who offered Pound information about French poetry. Certainly he was not the first, since Pound himself spoke of being introduced to Remy de Gourmont by Flint in February 1912.[3] The account of jealousy and conflict is particularly interesting, however, because it suggests again how highly poets of the day rated the catalytic effect of French influence in the development of modern English poetry.

If Fletcher clearly did not first introduce Pound to the symbolists, it is less clear how he came to real knowledge of them himself. Spurred by Arthur Symons' work, he first read Baudelaire and the symbolists in translation during his junior year at Harvard, but it was not until his visit to Paris in late fall of 1912 that he 'began to study the French language seriously, bought a host of books dealing with the symbolist movement', and paid increasing attention to 'the art of Cézanne, Gauguin, Van Gogh, and other post-impressionist painters...'[4]

---

[1] John Gould Fletcher, *Life Is My Song* (New York, 1937), p. 73. Italics mine.
[2] *Ibid.*, p. 74.   [3] See footnote 4, page 19.
[4] Fletcher, *Life Is My Song, op. cit.*, p. 48.

Fletcher remained on the outskirts of literary affairs until a Parisian meeting with Pound in May 1913. Nonetheless, he was in London during the appearance of Flint's early reviews for *The New Age* and he met A. R. Orage, the journal's editor. He was also in London for several months right after the publication of Flint's 'Contemporary French Poetry' and frequented the premises of Harold Monro's *The Poetry Review*.[1] Fletcher himself does not credit anyone with prompting his genuine exploration of French poetry in late 1912 and 1913; he noted simply that Flint, whom he met late in 1913, then 'was, like myself, fully aware of all the literary currents in Paris'.[2] His independent study of the symbolists and their successors did, however, begin during the upsurge of interest in French poetry occasioned by Flint's essay in *The Poetry Review*.

Richard Aldington, in contrast, generously acknowledged his equals and predecessors in the field. In an essay in 1914 he identified Flint and Fletcher as the best informed: 'I believe I am right in saying that practically the only men in England who have sufficiently omniverous habits to read *all* the modern French poetry published are Mr. F. S. Flint and Mr. John Gould Fletcher.'[3] In his autobiography he acknowledged Amy Lowell's command of the topics: '...she knew French better than any of us except Flint. He introduced her to a whole new generation of French writers, the foundation of her book on that subject.'[4] And to Flint himself he was unfailingly appreciative. He wrote 12 September 1913: 'By the aid of Eugène Figuière's Anthologie and your article I am hectically endeavoring to get at least a superficial idea of French poetry ...'[5] In December of the same year he commented: 'My de Régnier article is "out" in the Outlook and "Living French Poets" is billed about the town! I feel guilty of stealing your thunder, and as if I ought to pay you a perpetual commission on everything I get for writing on French poetry.'[6]

Thus it is clear that by the end of 1913 Aldington, under the tutelage of Flint and Pound,[7] had become sufficiently well acquainted with recent French work to become a source of information on it himself. In the next two and a half years, from the time he assumed the literary

---

[1] Fletcher, *Life Is My Song*, pp. 40, 42, 48, 50, 59.

[2] *Ibid.*, p. 77.

[3] Aldington, 'Some Recent French Poems', *The Egoist*, I, 12 (15 June 1914) 221.

[4] Aldington, *Life for Life's Sake, op. cit.*, p. 137.

[5] Aldington to Flint, n.d., envelope postmarked 12 September 1913. The anthology to which he refers is almost certainly Florian-Parmentier's *Anthologie critique*, published in 1912 by Figuière. The letter manuscript is in the Academic Center Library, The University of Texas.

[6] Aldington to Flint, n.d., envelope postmarked 31 December 1913. The manuscript is in the the Academic Center Library, The University of Texas.

[7] Aldington acknowledged his debt to Pound in his autobiography, *Life for Life's Sake, op. cit.*,

editorship of *The Egoist* until his conscription in mid-1916, he wrote frequently on the post-symbolist and *cénacle* French poets and translated their essays. Much of his work appeared in *The Egoist*, from which six of Aldington's essays or translations have been included in this volume,[1] but he also contributed to *Poetry*, to *The Little Review*, and to better-established, less *avant garde* journals in England. His range of topics included frequent casual, journalistic reviews of recent books, both prose and poetry, careful treatment of neglected figures (e.g. Charles Péguy, *The Egoist*, 15 October 1914), regular support for the writings of Remy de Gourmont, and revival of recently past work which, in his judgement, deserved more attention. Thus he discussed J.-K. Huysmans in 'Decadence and Dynamism', *The Egoist*, 1 April 1915, and opened the pages of that journal to five installments of translations of *The Chants of Maldoror* by Lautréamont (1 October–16 November 1914; 1 January 1915). His interests were more eclectic than Pound's, less dedicated to definitive scope than Flint's. With the exception of the casual reviews, which were a routine part of his editorial responsibilities on *The Egoist*, Aldington selected his topics and French poems for reprinting in *The Egoist* with concern either for current critical debate (e.g. de Gourmont, Beauduin) or for publicizing writers whose work, in his eyes, merited wider Anglo-American attention (e.g. Lautréamont, Péguy).

His literary production during his military service was very small. When he returned to London in the spring of 1919, however, he obtained the position of French critic for the *Times Literary Supplement*. He elected to concentrate on French prose and asked his old friend Flint to take over the job of reviewing French poetry.[2] His translations and writing on French literature in the next years were extensive, and he particularly translated a great deal from de Gourmont. He was not primarily concerned with poetry, however, and, indeed, much of his writing dealt with the tradition of French literature rather than with the modern period.

One further major literary current of these years confirms the great importance of French influence on English poetry through the middle of World War I. Along with the British adoption of Continental theories of abstract form in the visual arts went an adaptation of these

p. 111: 'He gave me Villon, he gave me Verlaine, he gave me the Symbolistes ... We came to differ over a lot of things but ... I can't go back on the Ezra of 1912–14.'

1 For fuller discussion of Aldington's contributions to the transmission of French influence, see the introductions to each of those essays: 'Remy de Gourmont's *Le Latin Mystique*', 'Some Recent French Poems', 'Laurent Tailhade', 'Tradition and Other Things' by de Gourmont, 'Lautréamont' by de Gourmont, and 'The New Poetry of France' by Beauduin.

2 Aldington to Flint, n.d., envelope postmarked 9 June 1919. The manuscript is in the Academic Center Library, The University of Texas.

theories to poetry, fiction, and criticism. Beginning late in 1913 and continuing especially rapidly in 1914 and 1915, Ezra Pound, Wyndham Lewis, and T. E. Hulme, as well as others, incorporated French and German theories of abstract or geometrical art into new aesthetic statements of their own, which had significance for literature as well as the visual arts. They chiefly drew upon cubism, futurism, fauvism, expressionism, Worringer, Kandinsky, and, of course, Bergson.[1] They found in their midst a protegé, model, and fellow artistic revolutionary in French sculptor Henri Gaudier-Brezska, who became an enthusiastic vorticist.

All the central figures in this aesthetic development, including Pound and Lewis, had extensive personal contacts with Paris – but no such limited, individualistic view is adequate to describe the cultural interchange which took place at this time. The restatement and extension in England of Continental ideas of non-representational art is far too complicated, widespread a phenomenon to be traced to a few transmitters or cultural sources. After 1912, probably half the essays which treated post-symbolist French literature made direct or indirect allusion to the experiments in abstract aesthetics, and to these literary sources must be added the exhibitions of modern art and the prodigious energies of Roger Fry, Clive Bell, and those others whose concerns were almost exclusively in the visual arts. (Of particular significance for their impact on literary men, for example, are the Exhibition of the Works of the Futurist Painters at the Sackville Gallery in March 1912; Roger Fry's Second Post-Impressionist and Cubist Exhibition at the Grafton Gallery in November 1912; the Gino Severini one-man show in April 1913; the activities of the Omega Workshop in summer and fall 1913; F. T. Marinetti's London speeches about futurism in November 1913 and late spring 1914, together with a futurist exhibition at the Doré Gallery in April 1914; exhibitions by Kandinsky under the auspices of the Allied Artists Association from 1909 through 1913; and the publication of Apollinaire's *Les Peintres cubistes* in spring 1913, Clive Bell's *Art* in late fall 1913, and Michael Sadleir's translation of Kandinsky's *Concerning the Spiritual in Art* early in 1914.)

In the presence of these explorations of non-representational art, Pound, for example, moved from his earliest imagist stress on 'direct treatment of the "thing" whether subjective or objective',[2] to an assertion that he was not concerned about whether an artist is 'representa-

---

[1] For an excellent discussion of the contributions of cubism and futurism to the vorticist movement in the visual arts see William Charles Lipke, 'A History and Analysis of Vorticism', unpublished dissertation (Wisconsin, 1966), Chapters I–III.

[2] 'A Retrospect', *Literary Essays of Ezra Pound, op. cit.*, p. 3. The phrase was used in *Poetry*, I, 6 (March 1913) in an essay signed by Flint but inspired by Pound.

tive or non-representative'. Rather, he said, it was essential that the artist '*depend*...on the creative, not upon the mimetic or representational part in his work. It is the same in writing poems...'[1] He went on in the same essay to indicate that the poet is as much concerned with universal forms as the analytic geometer and that the work of art, like a geometric equation, can 'cause form to come into being'.[2] Some six months later, Pound continued his stress on the priority of form over content in this fashion: 'A painting is an arrangement of colour patches on a canvas, or on some other substance. It is a good or bad painting according as these colour-patches are well or ill arranged. After that it can be whatever it likes.'[3] Between the first, imagist, statement in early 1913 and Pound's later ones in 1914 and 1915, Apollinaire had noted: 'Real resemblance no longer has any importance, since everything is sacrificed by the artist to truth, to the necessities of a higher nature whose existence he assumes, but does not lay bare. The subject has little or no importance any more.'[4] And Kandinsky had written: 'Painting stands...at the first stage of the road by which it will, according to its own possibilities, grow in the abstract sense and arrive finally at painterly *composition*. For this ideal of composition, painting has...at its disposal...color...[and] form. Form can stand alone, as a representation of an object ("real" or not), or as an abstract limit to a space or surface.'[5] There can be no doubt about Pound's debt to such cubist and expressionist sources in shaping his own poetics. In regard to precisely these comments of Kandinsky's, he advocated: 'The image is the poet's pigment; with that in mind you can go ahead and apply Kandinsky, you can transpose his chapter on the language of form and colour and apply it to the writing of verse.'[6] He also readily acknowledged a like debt to cubist theory and practice, calling 'Picasso, Kandinski, father and mother, classicism and romanticism of the [vorticist] movement.'[7] Pound shows, in addition, at least equally significant *rapport* with the theories of the futurists, whom he attacked in battles of artistic ideologies as being merely 'accelerated impressionists', mimetic rather than creative in their fundamental artistic endeavor. F. T. Marinetti, in an essay translated for the September 1913, futurist special issue of *Poetry and Drama*, called not only for 'words at liberty' from syntax, but also for a

1 Ezra Pound, 'Vorticism', *Fortnightly Review*, xcvi (September 1914) 464.
2 *Ibid.*, 469.
3 Ezra Pound, 'Affirmations, II: Vorticism', *The New Age*, xvi (14 January 1915) 277.
4 Guillaume Apollinaire, *The Cubist Painters*, trans. by Lionel Abel (New York, 1962; 1st pub. spring 1913), p. 12.
5 Wassily Kandinsky, *Concerning the Spiritual in Art*, trans. by Michael Sadleir with revisions by F. Golffing, M. Harrison, and F. Ostertag (New York, 1966), p. 46. First publication, in German, was in 1912; Sadleir's unrevised translation into English appeared in 1914.
6 Pound, 'Vorticism', *Fortnightly Review*, *op. cit.*, 465.
7 Ezra Pound, 'Vortex: Pound', *Blast*, 1 (June 1914) 154.

'new orthography' in which words were 'deformed' in the interests of the fullest lyric expression. 'It matters little', he continued, 'if the actual word so deformed becomes equivocal. It will marry itself to the onomatopoeic chord or summary of sounds. It will permit us, shortly, to attain the...sonorous yet abstract expression of an emotion or pure thought.'[1] Such a demand was even more unreservedly open to literary 'abstraction' than Pound's suggestion, a year later, that poetry must find a way to go 'beyond the existing categories of language', and his assertion that 'the image', in such poetry, 'is the word beyond formulated language'.[2] Of all the modernists before dadaism, the futurists were the most insistent in declaring that the non-representational course of futurist art could and should be matched by analogous innovations in poetry. Pound rejected much from their doctrine, but he echoed and developed key suggestions about multiple meanings unconfined by normal syntax and superimposed and interacting formal patterns of language. Even when such specific theoretical influences and antecedents are less readily observable, it is clear that expressionists, cubists, and futurists with whom Pound was extensively acquainted were calling in 1913 and sometimes even earlier for developments in art and poetic theory somewhat like those Pound articulated in 1914 and after.

In following these currents Pound of course was participating in a cultural evolution that was not exclusively French. Kandinsky was Russian by birth and part of the art world of Munich in the pre-war years; Picasso was Spanish, though resident in Paris; Marinetti was Italian, though his literary work was in French, and even Apollinaire was not French by birth. Yet, as the French connections of these men suggest, Paris was one focal point for all the important movements of modern abstraction except expressionism, and even Kandinsky, until 1914, was exhibited in London in a context chiefly of British or French cubism rather than of the expressionists of Munich's *Blaue Reiter* artists. Certainly it was chiefly through the brokerage of Paris that the currency of modern art became common coin for Pound, and most others, in London.

Such French sources of information and innovation are as clear in the case of Wyndham Lewis as with Pound. Lewis had lived abroad studying art, chiefly in Paris, from 1902 until 1909. As early as 1909 his figure studies exhibited the characteristics of the primitive cubism of Picasso's *Demoiselles d'Avignon*.[3] As an English cubist movement began to appear by 1911, Lewis was clearly the most innovative or *au courant*

---

[1] F. T. Marinetti, 'Wireless Imagination and Words at Liberty', trans. by Arundel del Re, *Poetry and Drama*, I, 3 (September 1913) 326.

[2] Pound, 'Vorticism', *Fortnightly Review, op. cit.*, 466.

[3] Lipke, *op. cit.*, I, pp. 42–3.

of the British painters, and he held this title as he marked the beginning of the non-representational vorticist period in England by completing between 1 December 1913, and late January 1914 a dining-room decoration scheme using non-representational forms.[1] *Tarr*, the novel which he was writing at the same time, reflected in its style his attempt to achieve analogous formal effects in language.[2] Of that effort he later commented: 'In *Tarr* (1914–1915) I was an extremist. In editing *Blast* I regarded the contributions of Ezra as compromisingly passéiste, and wished I could find two or three literary extremists. In writing *Tarr* I wanted at the same time for it to be a novel, and to do a piece of writing worthy of the hand of the abstractist innovator (which was an impossible combination). Anyhow it was my object to eliminate anything less essential than a noun or verb. Prepositions, pronouns, articles – the small fry – as far as might be, I would abolish.'[3] Lewis thought better of this enterprise later, and the revised edition of *Tarr* in 1928 provided many of the elements of conventional style absent from the first versions. By that time, however, Pound had gone beyond Lewis's early attempts by developing the ideas of abstract poetic form implicit in the early cantos, 'Mauberley', and the edited text of *The Waste Land*.

Within his immediate circle, Pound had been urged in this direction as much by T. E. Hulme as by Wyndham Lewis. The immediate impetus to Hulme's adopting the cause of abstract art apparently was a long and seminal stay in Germany. He wrote Flint from Berlin in February 1913, that he was 'bursting with theories' and intended to return to Germany in October;[4] he acknowledged the influence of German art critic Wilhelm Worringer in a preface note to the second essay on modern art in his 1914 series for *The New Age*.[5] He used Worringer's theories of vital and non-vital or geometrical art, however, primarily to analyze the achievements of the French cubist movement and (in his view) its international followers, and in fact he went so far as to suggest Kandinsky's expressionist explorations with pure abstraction were 'dilettante' and 'a more or less amusing by-product...[of]

---

1 Lipke, *op. cit.*, I, pp. 89–90; II, p. 244. The work was done under commission from Lady Drogheda.
2 Although Lewis assigns the novel to 1914–15, a letter tentatively dated to 1914 indicates that he had just finished the book at that time and had been working on it for about a year. Lewis to Augustus John, *The Letters of Wyndham Lewis*, ed. W. K. Rose (Norfolk, Conn., 1963), p. 65.
3 Lewis to Hugh Kenner, 23 November 1953, *Ibid.*, pp. 552–3.
4 Hulme to Flint, n.d., envelope marked received in London 22 February 1913. The manuscript is in the Academic Center Library, The University of Texas.
5 T. E. Hulme, 'Modern Art, II: A Preface Note and Neo-realism', *The New Age*, XIV (12 February 1914); reprinted in *Further Speculations, op. cit.*, p. 120. Hulme made the same acknowledgement in his lecture to the Quest Society, 14 January 1914, on 'Modern Art and Its Philosophy'. See *Speculations: T. E. Hulme*, ed. Herbert Read (New York, n.d.), p. 80.

the main movement...which, arising out of cubism, is destined to create a new geometric and monumental art...'[1] He also explicitly interpreted this abstract tendency as the herald of a new way of viewing experience, a shift which in its full realization would affect literature as profoundly as art.[2] How extensive and enduring that shift was one cannot yet be certain. It is clear, however, that of all the myriad influences from Paris which bubbled among the poets of London in pre-war and early war years, these new theories of art wrought the most significant changes in the major poetry of these and immediately succeeding decades.

III

By the beginning of 1917 the literary currents which had directed British poetry since 1908 – and especially since 1912 – had lost momentum, and the coteries had been disrupted by war. *Poetry and Drama* and *Blast* were unable to continue publication; Aldington was conscripted and H.D. struggled often almost alone to maintain the literary columns of *The Egoist* and to keep the imagist anthology going. Hulme and Lewis both entered military service, Hulme to be killed, and Pound, shorn of a tumultuous literary milieu, had turned to the study of Oriental poetry and drama. In this partial hiatus a new generation launched its literary efforts. Edith Sitwell and her entourage began *Wheels* in December 1916. T. S. Eliot became literary editor of *The Egoist* in June 1917, and Frank Rutter and Herbert Read, soon to be joined by members of the Sitwell coterie, issued the first number of *Art and Letters* in July of the same year. Herbert Read identified the shift in generations in a diary entry on the day in 1918 when he first met Ezra Pound:

The Sitwells are rather too comfortable and perhaps there is a lot of pose in their revolt. But they are my generation whereas Lewis's is the generation before and it is with the Sitwells that I must throw in my lot...Ezra says we younger men must prepare for a ten-year period of spade work and...then we shall be entitled to act on our own.[3]

The apprentice period lasted much less than ten years. When former members of the literary vanguard like Aldington and Flint returned to poetry or criticism after the war, they encountered a world in which the patterns of associations and some of the literary issues, as well as their own attitudes, had changed.

There were a few writers who provided continuity. John Middleton

[1] T. E. Hulme, 'Modern Art, III: The London Group', *The New Age*, XVI (26 March 1914). Reprinted in *Further Speculations, op. cit.*, p. 130.
[2] Hulme, 'Modern Art and Its Philosophy', *op. cit.*, p. 91.
[3] Herbert Read, '28.x.18', 'A War Diary 1915–19', in *The Contrary Experience* (London, 1963), p. 141.

Murry began in December 1913, to submit articles on French poetry to the *Times Literary Supplement*. Assigned in mid-1916 to duty as a war translator in London,[1] he continued to publish there and in other major journals until he launched *The Athenaeum* on its scintillating two-year finale in April 1919. His usually acute critical judgement and his preference for the ideal, philosophical, and symbolist achievement showed itself both in his high praise for Claudel in the *Quarterly Review* in 1917[2] and in his persistent criticism of French poets for failing to achieve an intensity suitable to the trauma of war. Still more significant was his evaluation of Valéry's *La Jeune Parque*. (See pages 303–9.) This review for *TLS* on 23 August 1917, praised Valéry as 'the authentic and the sole disciple of Mallarmé himself'. It was not only the first full recognition in either country of Valéry's importance: the essay also signals renewed English concern with French achievements in idealistic or transcendental symbolism, an interest already shared by Edith Sitwell and soon to attract T. S. Eliot. This symbolist interest is a shift in emphasis from Pound's imagist attention to French attempts to reconcile the ideal and the real in the empirical world.[3]

A shift in what the British sought from France was even clearer in the cycles of *Wheels*. The first volume, in addition to poems by the Sitwells, contained Helen Rootham's translations of three prose poems by Rimbaud, and these poems in many respects were the keynote of new directions. Inspiration from Rimbaud is clear in Edith Sitwell's early poetry, and the result is generically different from the impressionist and imagist poems of pre-war years. In Cycle Two of *Wheels* (1917) in 'Lagoons' Miss Sitwell wrote:

> The Night, a blue wave flashed from tropic seas,
> Fills with a hollow sound that gourd the Sun –
> Drifted along its waters: ripples run
> Across the cities stilled with ecstasies.[4]

---

[1] F. A. Lea, *The Life of John Middleton Murry, op. cit.*, pp. 35, 54–5.

[2] John Middleton Murry, 'The Works of Paul Claudel', *Quarterly Review*, CCXXVII, 450 (January 1917), 78–94.

[3] By idealistic or transcendental symbolism I mean a poetry in which the meanings of individual images depend upon the relationships established within the poem and in which the poem's symbolic reference is to a non-empirical, absolute realm. Such a realm may have the mystical or religious significance found, for example, in the work of Rimbaud or Villiers de l'Isle Adam. (And the religious poetry of T. S. Eliot has some image patterns which function in this way.) The reference may also be to an absolute aesthetic realm, created by the poem and deriving its absolute significance from no empirical or ideal foundation beyond the poem itself; Mallarmé in his later poetry strove to create such a realm. Poets with an 'objectivist' aesthetic (like the imagists), in contrast, seek the ideal absolute in the empirical perception; their predecessors are Bergson, Husserl, and the Remy de Gourmont of *Le Probleme du style*.

[4] Edith Sitwell, 'From the Balcony: Lagoons', *Wheels* (Oxford, 1917), p. 76.

These first four lines of a poem which reveals the perception of visionary unity in a landscape illuminated at evening effect a metaphoric unity of 'waves' of darkness, light, sea, and sound. 'Night' is a 'blue wave' from 'seas', but it is 'flashed' like light, and it 'fills...that gourd the Sun' *with* 'sound' (and not simply *with the accompaniment of* sound). The 'waters' of these lines seem the dark waters of Night, in which (lines 5–6) 'syrens' float. But underlying similitudes are again suggested in lines 7–10, in which water is associated with the light of Day (either waning at sunset or reflected as moonlight):

> the heavens sift
> Upon them [syrens] watery atoms from the Day,
> Till domes and towers like fiery suns are drowned
> In the subtle ripples of a sense like sound –

These same lines continue a pattern of dissociation and reassembly in which objects are detached from their normal physical characteristics and perceived in terms of other senses. The heavens 'sift' 'watery Atoms' as if they were dust; these atoms drown 'domes and towers' in 'ripples' of

> a *sense like sound*
> Striking the burning cities like a lyre,
> And every wanderer seems a shaft of fire.[1]

These concluding lines achieve a final visionary metamorphosis: the waves of night, juxtaposed to 'watery atoms from the Day', have engendered a vision not of water or darkness but of a pillar of fire. Such a poem is neither an impressionistic rendering of an inner mood in terms of an external or imagined landscape (like Yeats' 'The Lake Isle of Innisfree') nor the accurate presentation of an aesthetic moment, in which the 'meaning' for both reader and poet is synonymous with the sensations elicited by the empirical image (like H.D.'s 'Oread').[2] It is the creation of a synthesis by the fusing or yoking of disparate and even antagonistic images and assertions; its tools are sensory images, but its source is the vision (and not simply the perception) of the poet. The poem in this case concerns the experience of light at sunset or evening, but one cannot specify beyond argument whether the light is sunset or moonlight. The poem's process and goal may best be suggested by Edith Sitwell's comments on Rimbaud's use of hallucination:

[1] Edith Sitwell, 'From the Balcony: Lagoons', p. 76. Emphasis my own.
[2] For a discussion of nature of the imagist poem see chapters one and two in L. S. Dembo's *Conceptions of Reality in Modern American Poetry* (Berkeley and Los Angeles, 1966), especially pp. 10–15. I am indebted to the author, my colleague at the University of Wisconsin, beyond the reaches of that book for innumerable conversations on the nature of modern poetry.

This hallucination consists, to my mind, not so much in transforming actualities into other actualities, as in making all things one, in abolishing time and place, in making all times as one, all places as one. He has found a formula in which to express, with the utmost acuity of all the senses, each scene that he puts before us.[1]

The technique of disordering sensory experience and dipping far into the recesses of hallucination or subconscious anticipates the surrealists, but Miss Sitwell clearly indicates how she believes Rimbaud's work (and her own) should be distinguished from these French correlatives:

The aesthetics of the Seer has something in it of a voluntary, active quality; it modifies, triturates, torments the real in order to transmute it, and tear its secret from it; in surrealism emphasis is laid on the passivity of the spirit, it is an uncontrolled interrogation of the unconscious.[2]

Her observations do much to explain what separated the English poetry which anticipated or borrowed surrealist techniques from the surrealist movement proper: most British poets – both during the years just after World War I when the influences of Rimbaud, Baudelaire, and to some extent of Lautréamont and Cocteau were important and in the 1930s and 1940s, after Breton and French surrealism had made a significant impact – never relinquished their belief in the poet's active control of his material. Hence for the most part they never accepted the aesthetics of chance which led French surrealists to experiment with a poetry which juxtaposed images without reference either to an *a priori* poetic conception or to a substratum of archetypal meaning. But the influence of Rimbaud, and hence the creation of a poetry with many rapports with surrealism, was pervasive at the end of World War I and in the first part of the 1920s. 'His influence', Miss Sitwell said, 'has been. . . nothing short of extra-ordinary. Indeed, it might be said that Rimbaud is, to modern English verse and American prose poems, what Edgar Allen Poe was to Baudelaire and Mallarmé.'[3] Several of her own poems – 'The Drunkard' from *The Mother and Other Poems* (1915) and 'Trams' from *Twentieth Century Harlequinade* (1916), for example – she regarded as too derivative from Rimbaud to be included in her *Collected Poems.*[4]

Her debt to the French nineteenth century does not cease with Rimbaud. She regarded Baudelaire as the better technician of the two[5] and a significant number of her early poems show his influence to the extent of unmistakable imitation. R. L. Megroz, for example, has called 'Vacuum' (*Wheels*, 1918; reprinted as 'Nocturne, I' in *The Wooden*

---

[1] Edith Sitwell, 'Arthur Rimbaud, An Essay' in *Prose Poems from 'Les Illuminations'*, trans. by Helen Rootham (London, 1932), pp. 44–5. The first of these translations to be published appeared in *Wheels*, 1916.

[2] *Ibid.*, p. 42.   [3] *Ibid.*, p. 39.

[4] *Ibid.* Miss Sitwell also lists 'Merrygoround' as too derivative from Rimbaud to merit inclusion in *Collected Poems*, and she names 'Pleasure Gardens' in *Troy Park* (which does appear in the collected volume) as another example of his influence.   [5] *Ibid.*, p. 38.

Pegasus, 1920) 'one of the most Baudelairean of English poems', and he has detected the same influence in the other three nocturnes and in many of the poems of *The Mother and Other Poems* and *Troy Park* (1925)[1] (although one must note that the dialogue and rhymes of the second nocturne, 'Et l'on entend à peine leurs paroles', are surely reminiscent of Laforgue rather than of Baudelaire). Other poems, like 'Clown's Houses' (*The Wooden Pegasus*) and 'Clown's Luck' (*Troy Park*),[2] recall both Laforgue's irony and his themes.

Beyond specific imitations, the most important way in which Miss Sitwell's poetry continues the tradition of the symbolist masters is by the use of symbols which draw their primary meanings from the self-defining context of the poem.[3] In the case of 'Lagoons', for example, the poem's meaning depends upon the metamorphic relationship among natural phenomena not even usually related by antithesis – night, water, sound, and light. These relationships culminate in a unitary 'shaft of fire' which depends for its meaning upon its position in the pattern of metamorphoses, established solely within the poem itself. Such dependence for meaning upon the poetic context (which may extend to whole sequences of poems) is characteristic to differing degrees of Mallarmé's 'Le Tombeau de Charles Baudelaire', Rimbaud's 'Le Bateau ivre', Baudelaire's 'La Beauté' – and of Edith Sitwell's *Façade* (1922).

It is worth noting that *Façade* also represents a creation of abstract, verbally contentless, formal patterns which clearly show the author's position in the twentieth-century development of an abstract poetic. These 'abstract' qualities of *Façade* also direct attention to similarities in the currents which bear upon the poetry of the latter part of the second decade. The development of an abstract poetic was spurred in the years before World War I by changes in aesthetics in the visual arts between 1907 and 1914. The Sitwells were among the chief proponents of that art in the immediate post-war years. Gertrude Stein, in part drawing upon her experience with cubism, had developed an abstract prose of her own during approximately the same pre-war years. Edith Sitwell was probably the most active person in trying to popularize Miss Stein's work in England immediately after the war.[4] Both facts link the Sitwells to post-symbolist developments. Yet, the disassociation of sensory experiences from their normal sources and the reassembly of

---

[1] R. L. Megroz, *The Three Sitwells: A Biographical and Critical Study* (London, 1927), pp. 136–7, 140. 143,

[2] *Ibid.*, 149.

[3] Calling such images 'extrinsic symbols', Ihab Hassan gives an extremely useful account of the general ways in which Miss Sitwell employs symbolist techniques. See 'Edith Sitwell and the Symbolist Tradition', *Comparative Literature*, VII (Summer 1965) 240–51.

[4] Osbert Sitwell, *Laughter in the Next Room* (Boston, 1948), p. 273.

the images derived from them in a pattern which reflects the author's vision – a technique in which Miss Sitwell particularly emphasized her debt to Rimbaud – may produce a poem which represents no material reality and which is all but impossible to distinguish from a poem designed from the outset chiefly to create abstract formal patterns. Furthermore, later poets and critics have suggested that Mallarmé created abstract verbal patterns in *Un Coup de dés* about a decade before the development of an abstract art.[1] It seems clear, thus, that in the years 1915–20 British poets' interest in the French symbolist period led them to models which reinforced the growth of an abstract poetic form earlier prompted by the revolution in the visual arts between 1907 and 1914. Both currents converged and their individual impacts henceforward often cannot be clearly distinguished, despite the fact that the nineteenth- and twentieth-century influences generally rest on different aesthetic foundations.

Some of Miss Sitwell's experiments with French techniques were also explored by her brothers, Osbert and Sacheverell (who, in addition to writing poetry, joined in August 1919, to organize the 'first large exhibition of modern French pictures held in London since 1914'[2]). Another of the contributors to *Wheels*, however, was more important in Anglo-French relationships than the Sitwell brothers, both for his own attention to French models and for his discussions of current French work in the *avant garde* journals of the day: Aldous Huxley. Although Huxley's stature now rests on his novels, he first earned a literary reputation as a poet, and in addition to his contributions to each of the six cycles of *Wheels* he issued between 1916 and 1920 four collections of poetry: *The Burning Wheel*, *Jonah*, *The Defeat of Youth*, and *Leda*. These collections present a panoply of experimentation with French models.

Like Edith Sitwell, he was particularly attracted to the symbolist period, and as she has noted,[3] the prose poems which first appeared in *Wheels* (1918) show the influence of Rimbaud's *Illuminations*. 'Gothic', for instance –

The apples on the trees are swaying in the wind, rocking to the clamour of bells. The leaves are of bright green copper, and rattle together with a scaly sound. At the roots of the tree sit four gargoyles playing a little serious game with dice. The hunch-backed ape has won from the manticore that crooked French crown with a hole in it which the manticore got from the friar with the strawberry nose...[4]

has sympathies of tone as well as technique with a poem like 'Après le Déluge':

1 'An Interview with Kenneth Rexroth', conducted by Cyrena N. Pondrom, *Contemporary Literature*, x, 3 (Summer 1969) 327.
2 Osbert Sitwell, *Laughter in the Next Room*, *op. cit.*, p. 31.
3 'Arthur Rimbaud, An Essay', *op. cit.*, p. 39.
4 Aldous Huxley, 'Gothic', *Leda* (London, 1920), p. 43.

As soon as the idea of the Deluge had subsided, A hare stopped in the clover and swaying flower-bells, and said a prayer to the rainbow, through the spider's web...[1]

There are equally strong echoes, however, even among Huxley's prose poems, of the ironic postures of Laforgue: 'One of the candles flickered, snickered. Was it a draught or was it laughter? / Flickering, snickering – candles, you betrayed mè. I had to laugh too.'[2]

His use of French models, particularly of Laforgue and Baudelaire, begin in his first collection *The Burning Wheel*. Titles alone suggest Huxley's reading when he assembled the collection: 'Villiers de L'Isle-Adams' [*sic*], 'Quotidian Vision', and 'Variations on a Theme of Laforgue' (a reshaping of some parts of 'Complainte du Roi du Thulé'). Other poems of that date which bear the marks of Laforgue include 'The Garden', 'The Ideal Found Wanting', and the sonnet 'Were I to die, you'd break your heart, you say', which recalls the French ironist's use of dramatic monologue. The Laforguian viewpoint as it appears in the volume is succinctly represented by 'Philosophy':

> "God needs no christening,"
> Pantheist mutters.
>
> .   .   .   .
>
> "Flesh, key-hole listening,
> Hears what God utters"...
> Yes, but God stutters.[3]

In addition, the first two poems in the volume, 'The Burning Wheel' and 'Doors of the Temple', both echo a Baudelairean fascination with the antitheses of radiance and darkness, passion and peace, 'God's radiant throne' and 'the fires of wrath and agony'.[4]

Within a year Huxley, like Eliot, had attempted to write in French himself. *Jonah*, December 1917, contains four French lyrics, including 'Zoo Céleste', and 'Hommage à Jules Laforgue'; and 'The Oxford Volunteers' in that collection goes beyond irony to recall the satiric poetry of Laurent Tailhade. Huxley's next 'hommage' was translation, and the succeeding volume, *The Defeat of Youth and Other Poems* contains his English rendering of Mallarmé's 'L'Après-midi d'un faune' and Rimbaud's 'Les Chercheuses de poux'. The volume also reflects the continued presence of Laforgue in Huxley's own verse; there is, for example, the 'Complaint of a Poet Manqué'. Huxley's interest in the

---

[1] Arthur Rimbaud, *Illuminations*, trans. by Louise Varèse (New York, 1957), p. 3. 'Aussitôt que l'idée du Déluge se fut rassise, / Un lièvre s'arrêta dans les sainfoins et les clochettes mouvantes, et dit sa prière à l'arc-en-ciel, à travers la toile de l'arraignée.'
[2] Huxley, 'Evening Party', *Leda, op. cit.*, p. 44.
[3] Huxley, *The Burning Wheel* (Oxford, 1916), p. 21.
[4] Huxley, 'Doors of the Temple', *The Burning Wheel, op. cit.*, p. 9.

French was enduring. He translated Remy de Gourmont's novel *A Virgin Heart* in 1921 and included a translation of Baudelaire's 'Femmes Damnées' in *The Cicadas and Other Poems* in 1931. In addition, as critics have sometimes noted, the sonnets of *The Cicadas* seem indebted, both in imagery and conception, to Baudelaire's poetry,[1] and Spandrell of *Point Counter Point* is based on Baudelaire as a man.[2]

Wheels appeared annually, and Edith Sitwell, Aldous Huxley, and other *Wheels* contributors whose poetry demonstrated their vital interest in the symbolists also published frequently in small collections and other *avant garde* journals like *Art and Letters, The Egoist, Coterie,* and *Oxford Poetry*. That in itself would have been enough to mark a new stage in the development of modern English poetry. These interests found an active critical voice as well, however, when John Middleton Murry agreed to revive the moribund *Athenaeum* in April 1919. Here too Aldous Huxley played a role, for Murry named him assistant editor (after J. W. N. Sullivan held the job only briefly). Huxley commented frequently on English and French poetry and French fiction. He paid alert attention (and qualified praise) to the poets associated with dadaism and *fantaisisme* – Eluard, Tzara, Soupault, Breton, Aragon, Picabia, Cendrars, and Salmon;[3] of the war poets he praised Romains and Duhamel highly for *Europe* and *Vie des Martyrs*;[4] he noted the classical tendency,[5] compared Verhaeren unfavorably to Rimbaud,[6] and gave very modest approval or no attention at all to most other poets of the pre-war years. The attention given to symbolist poets, however, far exceeded the coverage of current French experiment. For example, Murry obtained Valéry's 'The Spiritual Crisis' and 'The Intellectual Crisis' for the issues of 11 April and 2 May 1919. He engaged Charles Du Bos to contribute frequent essays and letters from Paris, including two essays 'On the Symbolist Movement in French Poetry', one on Proust, and two on 'Poe and the French Mind'.[7] He published J. W. N. Sullivan's long discussion of Valéry's *Introduction à la méthode de Léonard de Vinci* (27 August 1920) and he contributed himself two important essays on Baudelaire (22 October and 29 October 1920). In addition, *The Athenaeum* offered hospitality to T. S. Eliot recalling his first encounters

1 Alexander Henderson, *Aldous Huxley* (New York, 1936), p. 230. Henderson also sees Corbière as a poetic influence, and does not name Laforgue, although Laforgue's is the most insistent presence, in my judgement, in the early poetry.

2 John Atkins, *Aldous Huxley: A Literary Study*, rev. ed. (London, 1967), p. 82.

3 See Aldous Huxley, 'Marginalia' (signed Autolycus), *The Athenaeum*, 23 April and 10 September 1920; and 'Young French Verse', pp. 315–17 in this volume.

4 Huxley, 'A Guide-Book to Literature', *The Athenaeum*, 9 April 1920.

5 See 'Art and The Tradition', pp. 309–11 in this volume.

6 Huxley, 'Verhaeren', *The Athenaeum*, 19 November 1920.

7 The essays on the symbolist movement appeared 23 July and 30 July 1920; the one on Proust, 9 April 1920; the two on Poe, 7 January and 14 January 1921.

with symbolism and suggesting the importance of Remy de Gourmont in 'The Perfect Critic' (9 July and 23 July 1920); published regular discussions of modern French art by critics and painters like Clive Bell, Roger Fry, and André Lhote; and intelligently reviewed literally hundreds of French books in literature and the arts.

On *The Egoist* T. S. Eliot continued Muriel Ciolkowska's column 'Passing Paris'. However, the experimental energies of *The Egoist* were directed at this time more toward discussion of *Noh* drama and trying to effect the publication of *Ulysses* than toward French poetry. Thus the budding surrealist tendencies in Paris escaped the acute attention they might have received from *The Egoist* of earlier days. Eliot's own collection, *Prufrock and Other Observations*, which The Egoist press issued, in 1917, contained his widely known Laforguian imitations and thus helped to confirm the revival of interest in the French nineteenth century. The poems of this collection, however, had been chiefly written in pre-war years and shared aesthetic foundations with imagism, and Eliot's subsequent directions were not yet clear even in his later collection, *Ara Vos Prec* (1920).

Another member of the new generation, Herbert Read, also shared an early allegiance to imagist aesthetics and in many ways recapitulated the enthusiasms of pre-war poets. In a diary entry for 31 July 1916, he identified 'the essence of XXth century' in Bergson, Croce, the 'Anti-Humanists,...Sorel and his theories,...the Post-Impressionists and Futurists (on whom I am tremendously keen),...Henry James and the Imagist Poets'.[1] He read Donne, Browning, and the imagists at about the same time, he said, and thereafter, 'The modification of Browning's influence came from France – from Rimbaud and Laforgue, and from the early verse of Duhamel, Jules Romains, Jean de Bosschère, André Spire and Apollinaire...From this experience, which lasted from the year 1913 to 1917, I quickly evolved what I would have called my philosophy of composition'.[2] Read's heritage, thus, is exactly that which Flint, Pound, and Aldington provided during the most active stage of English assimilation of French post-symbolist influence. In the years just after the war one of Read's most important activities was his editorial activity with *Art and Letters*, which began in July 1917, while Read was still in the service, with Frank Rutter listed as its only editor. *Art and Letters* effected a temporary and probably uneasy alliance of the pre-war and post-war *avant garde*. The journal emphasized the art considered innovative in pre-war years, offering drawings by Gaudier-Brzeska, J. D. Fergusson, S. J. Peploe, Edward Wadsworth, Picasso, and Wyndham Lewis. It published imagists, like Aldington, and the poets of

[1] Read, *The Contrary Experience, op. cit.*, p. 73.
[2] *Ibid.*, pp. 172, 174.

Wheels. In 'Definitions toward a Modern Theory of Poetry', Read called for a poetry which expressed 'the mind's' vision: by means of 'significant form, which significant form is achieved by unity, vitality, exactness, concentration and decoration'[1] – a statement which brought into one sentence ideas apparently drawn from Clive Bell, imagist doctrine, and Rimbaud. And there were also articles on French poets important before the war. Read contributed 'An Approach to Jules Romains' in winter 1918–19, an essay which reflects the almost universal attraction the *unanimistes* held for English poets (indeed, critics as disparate as Pound, Flint, Aldington, Murry, Huxley, and Read all expressed their admiration for Romains and Duhamel). One other significant essay dealt with a Belgian poet of the same generation: Ezra Pound's 'Durability and De Bosschère's Presentation' in summer 1919. Osbert Sitwell bought an interest in the journal in the second volume, and under the joint editing of Rutter and Sitwell *Art and Letters* published still more of the work of the *Wheels* circle, as well as important poetry and criticism by T. S. Eliot. There still, however, was relatively little attention to more recent French poetry. In summary, the contents of the magazine do much to suggest a profile of the poetic *avant garde* in post-war years: they were sophisticated about modern art; well-read in French symbolism to the point of outright imitation; aware and respectful of the major French poets of the years before the war; absorbed in their own very significant poetic and critical endeavors; and, perhaps with some self-satisfaction, only mildly interested in poetic experiment currently in progress across the channel.

F. S. Flint, however, again provided – in *Chapbook* and *TLS* – extended, *au courant* accounts of the fads, movements, and genuine achievement of the whole French literary scene. Flint's thirty-nine page survey of the five years of war poetry, 'Some Modern French Poets (A Commentary with Specimens)' in 1919, treated eighteen figures, among them the heralds of new directions, Apollinaire, Cocteau, and Eluard; figures of pre-war eminence, Romains, Arcos, Spire, Jouve, and Claudel; and elder statesmen, Ghéon, Verhaeren, de Régnier, and Fort. The most interesting observations in that essay were Flint's speculations about the direction modern French poetry was about to take: 'After the comparatively slight blood-letting and the defeat of 1870–1, came the strange dreaming, the breaking-away from traditions, the exoticism, the revolt of the *décadence* and of Symbolism. After the exhaustion and victory of 1914–18, what?'[2] As partial answer he

[1] Read, 'Definitions toward a Modern Theory of Poetry', *Art and Letters*, I, 3 (January 1918) 78.
[2] F. S. Flint, 'Some Modern French Poets (A Commentary, with Specimens)', *Chapbook*, I, 4 (October 1919) 1.

quoted 'La Jolie Rousse' from Apollinaire's *Calligrammes*, two poems from Cocteau's *Le Cap de Bonne Espérance*, a dada poem from the journal *Sic*, and a lyric from Paul Eluard's *Le Devoir et l'Inquiétude*. Of the latter poems he astutely observed that they 'seem to have been conceived in a state of mind bordering on hallucination',[1] and he linked this development to the war itself.

The rest of the 1919 survey was devoted to the more conventional poetry of war, but Flint followed up his interest in the outer reaches of the *avant garde* by another monograph for Monro's *Chapbook* in the following year: 'The Younger French Poets – The Dada Movement'. This essay offered England a thorough introduction to both 'theory' and practice of dadaism. For example, Flint quoted from his literal translation of Tristan Tzara's original manifesto:

Every product of disgust capable of becoming a negation of the family is *dada*; protest with fists of all one's being in destructive action: dada; ...abolition of logic, dance of the impotent of creation (or to create): *dada*; ...trajectory of a word flung like a sonorous disc cry; ...to spit out like a luminous cascade one's harsh or amorous thought, or to caress it – with the lively satisfaction that it is just the same...Liberty: DADA DADA DADA, howling or irritated colours, interweaving of contraries and of all the contradictions, of grotesques, of inconsequences: LIFE.[2]

He corrected Huxley's labelling of Tzara's poetry as onomatopoeic with the observation that the onomatopoeic implies 'an attempt to convey something' whereas 'M. Tzara does not wish to convey'.[3] Then he went on to discuss theoretical analyses of the movement by André Breton and Jacques Rivière and to provide individual discussions of the poetry of Tzara, Picabia, Eluard, Breton, Soupault, Aragon, and Morand, accompanied by translations of poems, texts of the originals, and drawings by Picabia and Hans Arp.

Flint's comments, particularly those on Breton and dada's 'stratégie littéraire' directly raised the radical challenges modern literature has posed for established ideas of order, logic, and systems of values. Breton, he summarized, 'calls for...justice to be done to the arbitrary as a factor in the creation of a work or an idea'. He continued:

The obscurity of our words is constant...To read a book in order to know denotes a certain simplicity. The little even the best books teach us should turn us away from them. It is the thesis and not its expression that disappoints us...The poets who have recognised this fly hopeless from the intelligible. They know they have nothing to lose thereby.[4]

[1] F. S. Flint, 'Some Modern French Poets', 13.
[2] F. S. Flint, 'The Younger French Poets – The Dada Movement', *Chapbook*, 17 (November 1920) 5.
[3] *Ibid.*, 4.
[4] *Ibid.*, 13.

Theses such as these have shaped the course of much Continental literature from 1920 to the present. They have left their mark on some American poets of stature, and in time they made a confined impression on the course of English letters. In its own way, Flint's last major survey of French poetry in 1920 was as important a view of new directions as his first, in 1912. But in London, to return to the words of T. S. Eliot, 'the predominance of Paris' was no longer 'incontestable'. Drawing upon the French theory and practice of the last half-century that they had now assimilated as part of a vital and innovative modern poetic tradition of their own, British poets devoted themselves more to the creation of major achievements in their own poetry than to a search for further inspiration abroad.

A NOTE ON BIBLIOGRAPHICAL REFERENCES FOR QUOTATIONS

In many essays presented in this volume the author's citation of bibliographical material for quoted poems was scanty or lacking altogether. Wherever possible, for each quotation a French text has been traced, full bibliographical information supplied, and appropriate notation made of any departure from French publication. Some of the sources were ephemeral literary magazines and limited or private editions, however, and in some cases National Union Catalogue circularization produced no record of current holdings of the needed texts in England, France or the United States. When for this reason the French text could not be consulted, any available bibliographical information has been supplied and the footnote has been marked with the symbol ‡.

FLINT, THE HAIKU, AND THE SYMBOLISTS

This essay is the first of the regular reviews of English poetry which F. S. Flint contributed to *The New Age* from 1908 through 1910. It appeared as 'Recent Verse' in the issue for 11 July 1908, and it is of particular interest because it documents that at this early date Flint, who was to be a member of the imagist circle, was already acquainted with the Japanese haiku form and with the French or Belgian symbolist poets Stéphane Mallarmé, Maurice Maeterlinck, Charles Baudelaire, and Paul Verlaine. He had by this time appreciated some of the technical significance of Japanese and symbolist poetry, for he indicated the 'sword songs' should have been translated 'unrhymed' and suggested that 'more subtle rhythms and broken cadences' would have been preferable to Victor Neuburg's 'lofty rhymes'. The essay also shows that Flint held the view – common to British 'symbolists' of the 1890s – that the poet's most important task was to convey by symbols intimations of his own soul or of his visions of the spiritual world. Although under the impact of imagism he adopted for a few years the rhetoric and technique of precision, Flint never really abandoned his emphasis that the poem conveys an *impression* of the world and expresses the highly personal vision of the poet. In this lengthy excerpt of the review Flint evaluated: *Sword and Blossom Song* by T. Hasegawa;[1] *The Web of Life* by Wilfrid W. Gibson; *The Bridge of Fire* by James Flecker; and *A Green Garland* by Victor B. Neuburg. Comments on *Hero Lays* by Alice Milligan and *Songs of the Uplands* by Alice Laws have been omitted.

RECENT VERSE*

F. S. FLINT

As I turned over the pages of these Japanese Sword and Blossom Songs my fingers trembled with delight. Surely nothing more tenderly beautiful has been produced of late years than this delicate conspiracy of Japanese artist with Japanese poet! The Blossom Songs, taken from the famous Kokinshiu Anthology of A.D. 906, and the Sword Songs of later date, are completed and explained by the exquisite illustrations on each page. It is a pity, however, that the translators did not choose some other measure than the heavy English rhymed quatrain. It is probable that nearly all the spontaneity of the Japanese tanka has thus been lost. The Japanese, we are told, are quick to take an artistic hint; in fact, even the most lowly are all poets (or should we say, *were* poets?); and "to them in poetry as in painting, the half-said thing is dearest" – the suggestion not the complete picture (one thinks of Stéphane Mallarmé). A word will awaken in them, therefore, a whole warp and weft

---

[1] This ephemeral anthology is no longer held in United States libraries or in the British Museum.

* *The New Age*, n.s. III (11 July 1908) 212–13.

of associations. Take this haikai, typical of a common form of Japanese poetry:

> Alone in a room
> Deserted –
> A peony.

Or

> A fallen petal
> Flies back to its branch:
> Ah! a butterfly!

I could have wished that the poems in this book had been translated into little dropping rhythms, unrhymed; but the translators thought it due to the English Cerberus that they should be "done into English verse." The Sword Songs are akin in spirit to the similar songs in the Bard of the Dombavitsa.

To the poet who can catch and render, like these Japanese, the brief fragments of his soul's music, the future lies open. He must have the spiritual insight of the Maeterlinck of the Trésor des Humbles, and he must write, I think, like these Japanese, in snatches of song. The day of the lengthy poem is over – at least, for this troubled age; and Mr. Wilfrid Wilson Gibson is a dead man, for whom the preoccupations that have long agitated France and artistic Europe, even, in a small degree, England, do not exist. He has no new thing to tell us and his "Web of Life" is rather a shroud. There was a time when Mr. Gibson could write with a pang little songs of lovelorn queens and forlorn harpers, or sketch three dusty urchins at pitch and toss on the road, or a stonebreaker at his toil. He has given us, too, six little homespun plays with the tang of the earth in them. But since then he has grown ambitious. Perhaps his ambition is due to the bad influence of the Samurai Press, which set out with a banner and a trumpet blast, modest enough, proclaiming its intention to imagine its best and to strive for that best. Surely an artist can tie himself to no fixed principle, but can only *be*. The intellect is the father of principles and the prig, but the emotions and the imagination – and a poet should have nothing else – will always remain noble.

You may open Mr. Gibson's book anywhere, and find the same level of excellent, nay, brilliant writing, even when he tells you, in forty lines, that Beauty never dies, or that Song is imperishable, in twenty-four. He knows the rules well – when to alliterate, how to manage onomatopoeic effects and pauses, PFV, vocal harmony, and so on; but he leaves you cold; and one has the image, which Carlyle hated, of a man sitting down deliberately to write poetry – to imagine his best! He can paint in vivid colours:

> ...from his broad shoulders sprang
> His bronzed throat like a pillar; and his eyes

Burned bright beneath his turban, whose green folds
Were shot with scarlet, as, with little dark
Red poppies, the green wheat of Syrian plains.[1]

From Keats he has learned how to mass ornament, and he has steeped his learning in Swinburne; yet he is without Keats's haunting undertones, and without Swinburne's passion of utterance; so that, though pleasant to read, he lures us on to weariness and satiety. Mr. Wilson [*sic*] sees the world with eyes blinded by words. The one haunting passage to be found in his book, in the introduction to "Ferhad and Shirine," smacks of Mr. Yeats's "Shadowy Waters":

What shadows from the shadows of old days
Does the white magic of the moon recall
To tread once more the glistering desert-sands,
Clad in the light of their old ecstasy
That wakens in thine eyes an answering flame?[2]

. . . .

I confess I do not understand Mr. Flecker. He has been to Oxford, to London, and to Paris. He has dabbled a little in Sin, and translated Baudelaire's "Litany to Satan"; he has penetrated the secret of Mary Magdalen, been inspired by Francis Thompson, and walked along the Oxford Canal; and his translation and thoughts on these occasions seem to me the best part of his book. But his "Bridge of Fire" poem bewilders me. He has forsaken the creed of the Galileans, and is "the slave of fear and death." Those who would know more must buy his book.

After the first page or so of "A Green Garland," Verlaine's lines come into one's mind:

De la musique avant toute chose
Et pour cela préfère l'impair.

Mr. Neuberg's gods are Youth, Truth, Progress, Love, and "Mighty Reason"; but he says that all the gods are dead.

Prends l'éloquence et tords-lui le cou.

And we have here the diverting spectacle of a disciple of Nietzsche eloquently celebrating a Freethought Congress, glorifying Truth and Progress, and burning with indignation of the suggestion that a memorial tablet to Herbert Spencer,

[1] Wilfrid Wilson Gibson, 'Ferhad and Shirine', *The Web of Life* (Samurai Press: Cranleigh, Surrey, January 1908), p. 57.
[2] *Ibid.*, p. 52.

The vast colossus of the later days
And silver statue in the realm of thought![1]

should be placed in Westminster Abbey, the fane of the hated and pallid-spirited Galileans. It is not to be inferred from this that "A Green Garland" is without merit, despite the fact that a quotation from the "Daily Chronicle" at the head of a page might deter one from reading any more in that book. Mr. Neuburg has more intellect than imagination, and the beauty of young summer, the heat of the sun, and the scent of blossoms stir him to sing rapturously, sometimes obscurely, of the Dawn and the Day, when life will not be sicklied o'er with the pale cast of other worldliness. For the new humanity he builds the lofty rhyme; but it is to be feared, alas! that the new humanity will prefer more subtle rhythms and broken cadences, the song that will come and go like the wind on the leaf or the bourdon of a blond bee hovering over a bank of swaying mignonette.

[1] Victor B. Neuburg, 'An Agnostic View', *A Green Garland* (Probsthain & Co.: London 1908), p. 41.

BERGSON AND THE *AVANT GARDE*

John Middleton Murry's essay on the connection between Bergson and *avant garde* attitudes in art came just as the British were beginning to direct considerable attention to the French philosopher. His essay, however, was one of the most acute early attempts to explain the implications of Bergsonian philosophy for aesthetic theory, for even Hulme's writings on Bergson had so far stressed the philosophy more than its implications for art.[1] Murry showed how the theory of intuition led to simultaneous and compatible views that the artist is creative rather than simply imitative, and that art is nonetheless the 'only expression of reality' and a means to apprehending a higher realism.[2] This aspect of his discussion may well have been the most important in 1911, for such ideas underlie the imagist movement, which was soon to begin. In addition, Murry's attempt (perhaps not philosophically persuasive) to link Bergson to the Platonic tradition led him to emphasize some key ideas about form two years before they became fashionable among the literary *avant garde* in London. The 'pure perception' of the artist enables him to see 'essential forms', Murry interpreted, and 'the form and not the flesh is art'. These forms derive their essential quality – and their empirical validity – from the fact that they represent 'the rhythms at the heart of things'. The extent to which Murry in these assertions was both ahead of most of the *avant garde* and concerned with an issue fundamental to modernism *per se* is clear from comparing them to a text Pound relied upon during the development of his abstract aesthetics in 1914. Ernest Fenollosa in *The Chinese Written Character as a Medium for Poetry* wrote: 'The whole delicate substance of speech is built upon substrata of metaphor...But the primitive metaphors do not spring from arbitrary *subjective* processes. They are possible only because they follow objective lines of relation in nature herself. Relations are more real and more important than the things which they relate.'[3] A similar correlation between Murry's suggestions about the significance a Bergsonian aesthetic gives to form and the views of Worringer and Kandinsky, both popularized in London in 1914, could also be made. The importance of the article is extended by the fact that *Rhythm*, in which it appeared, was the most innovative little magazine published in 1911.

ART AND PHILOSOPHY*

John Middleton Murry

Art is consciously eternal. The creation of art is the expression of the continuous and undying in the world. It is the golden thread that runs through a varied texture, showing firm, brilliant, and unbroken when the fabric has fallen away. Art sweeps onward, and by its forward march

---

[1] By 1911, Samuel Hynes has pointed out, about 200 items on Bergson had appeared in England. (See *Further Speculations* (Lincoln, Nebraska, 1962), p. xiii.) Typical of Hulme's emphasis at this time on the philosophy rather than on its literary implications is 'Bax on Bergson', *The New Age*, IX (3 August 1911) 328–31. His lectures on Bergson and art came, so far as they can be positively dated, in 1913.

[2] For further comments on Murry's contribution in this essay to the post-symbolist tendency to accommodate the conflicting demands of idealistic symbolism and realism see the General Introduction, pages 15–17.

[3] Ernest Fenollosa, *The Chinese Written Character as a Medium for Poetry*, with a Foreword and *Notes by Ezra Pound* (London, 1936), p. 26.

* *Rhythm*, I, 1 (Summer 1911) 9–12.

alone has its being. It is imperishable because through all the ages it is life; because the artist's vision is a moment's lifting of the veil, a chord caught and remembered from the vast world music, less or more, yet always another bond between us and the great divinity immanent in the world.

The philosophy of Bergson has of late come to a tardy recognition in England. In France it is a living artistic force. It is the open avowal of the supremacy of the intuition, of the spiritual vision of the artist in form, in words and meaning. He has shown that the concepts of the reason, while the reason remains untrue to itself, fail before the fact of Life. The philosophies which would explain the universe are by their own nature debarred from touching its one great reality. They are but barren jugglings with worthless counters. As water through the meshes of a sieve, Life slips through their iron terminologies. We attain to the truth not by that reason which must deny the fact of continuity and of creative evolution, but by pure intuition, by the immediate vision of the artist in form. But the pure intuition is no mystical surrender of reason and personality to a vague something, which, because it is nothing, is called God. It is the triumph of personality, the culmination and not the negation of the reason. The intuition is that point, as it were, at which the reason becomes most wholly itself, and by its own heightened working conquers the crude opposition of subject and object, from which at a lower level it cannot become free. Here human personality by the consciousness of reason drags reality into its knowledge, into itself, the rational self asserting its ultimate triumph over an externality, which is, while merely external, meaningless. Just as prose becomes poetry when the passage of thought runs most swiftly, yet most consciously within its own power; so when the workings of the reason become most concentrated and intense it reaches that utter consciousness of its own all-embracing power, which the blind call mysticism; but which is the very essential rationality of reason. This is the truth which Plato declared so many years ago. Interpreted into the crude hallucinations of Neo-Platonism, it is the most blind and feeble of all doctrines. Taken in its real truth and meaning, it is the final word in aesthetic – a truth which Bergson, as I interpret him, is declaring once more to-day.

The eternality of art is openly proclaimed. It is eternal because it lives; and to be art at all it must live. It must go onward and forward. It lives for the present, striving to force fresh paths for its progress across the waste of dull dead matter which it vivifies. It is an evolution because it proceeds only by bringing something to birth. The past is judged by the present, not the present by the past; for in the present alone the past has its being.

Art is beyond creeds, for it is the creed itself. It comes to birth in irreligion and is nurtured in amorality. Religion and morality alike mean for the western world that this life fades away into the colourless intensity of the world to come. For them Life has neither meaning nor continuity, for its value begins with death. Only a creed which is of and for this world can give us art; for then it is art. Art is against religion or religion itself. It can hold no middle course. It seeks an expression that is new not merely because before it for generations there was nothing, but new because it holds within itself all the past. The artist must take up the quest where his fathers left it. He must identify himself with the continuity that has worked in the generations before him. His individuality consists in consciously thrusting from the vantage ground that he inherits; for consciousness of effort is individuality. He cannot palter with great problems under the cloak of a morbid humanitarianism. Art is movement, ferocity, tearing at what lies before. It takes nothing for granted; and thrusts mercilessly, pitilessly. It has been nearer the East than the West because their religion was their life, and their life a continuity. The future lies in a West that is conscious of the East.

The present is the all-in-all of art. Derive its very elements, the matter of its being, from the past if you will; it remains the creation of a new thing, and by these unending creations alone Life proceeds and Art exists. The search for individuality of expression may become bizarre; yet the search is of the essence of art, for art is self-conscious and works in travail and tears. To say that art is revolutionary is to say that it is art. In truth, no art breaks with the past. It forces a path into the future. The flesh and the bones of the new creation may come from the past, but the form is new; and the form and not the flesh is art. The attempt to compel the present to submission to the past is but the puny fiat that Life shall cease and the universe perish.

In the present alone does the past exist. The reality of Time is but the reality of Life; and those "high revelations of eternal truth" which wrapped the soul of Saint Teresa, of a living God who died daily, are now no longer the discredited phantasms of a fevered brain, but the clear and conscious vision of the artist, the true seer. To reject a chronology which esteems the past because it is the past, to concentrate every power on striking to the heart-roots of the present, to rise above the mere reactions of a dull mechanical routine and to be in acting free – such are the canons of the new Philosophy, and these are the principles made patent in all true art. False aestheticism and spurious criticism in art, rigid system and universal dogmatism in philosophy rest alike on a conception of Time which is false to philosophy and cripples art.

Art is the true and only expression of reality. It clothes itself in many forms. The intense gaze of the Assyrian and Egyptian saw through and round the object. The Japanese saw no shadow. The vision of the Renaissance was an absorbing delight in an object for a material and tangible thing, something to reckon with and conquer day by day. We are become sophisticated, and can no longer, like those children of the Gods, make matter into spirit by an abiding joy in its materiality. To the age of naive wonder we can never return, to the child-like joy in a woman's body, in a boy's face, in the ripples of the sea for their own reality's sake, unless it may be, Art and Life travel in a great cycle. For us, the artistic intuition must draw away from the practical. Art turns to regard the things of daily life with the eyes of the heightened reason; and in the moment of intuition once more to behold and make actual, though for a moment, the great continuity.

The artist attains to the pure form, refining and intensifying his vision till all that is unessential dissolves away – memories and that false knowledge which would bind him down to a mere existence, untrue because it is unlived. He must return to the moment of pure perception to see the essential forms, the essential harmonies of line and colour, the essential music of the world. Modernism is not the capricious outburst of intellectual dipsomania. It penetrates beneath the outward surface of the world, and disengages the rhythms that lie at the heart of things, rhythms strange to the eye, unaccustomed to the ear, primitive harmonies of the world that is and lives.

True art and true philosophy go side by side in a progress that breaks through convention and tradition for its own life's sake. The old familiar words of Plato become pregnant with a new and a truer meaning. Philosophy is the greatest art because art is the greatest philosophy. It is the recognition of the rational supremacy of art. A fantastic and reactionary aestheticism is art's greatest enemy. The artist looks to the past only to create in the present. In the end it may be that every note of the eternal music blends in one harmony; but a criticism and an aestheticism fixed in the past would create a symphony of a single chord, which has lost its living charm, unappreciated, almost unheard. Until the day when the last note is sounded the Life of the world and the Life of art hang upon seeking new chords to create new harmonies.

BERGSON AND THE THEORY OF MODERN FRENCH POETRY

T. E. Hulme's enthusiastic recommendation of Tancrède de Visan's *L'Attitude du lyrisme contemporain* is indicative of the importance in England of the adaptation of symbolist aesthetics to a Bergsonian philosophic view. His warm reception of the book was matched by Flint's response to it,[1] and a comparison of Pound's descriptions of the function of the image with those of de Visan's suggests that Pound too – directly or indirectly – drew upon such Bergsonian reinterpretations of symbolism in his own poetics. Although he praises the book highly, Hulme in his review does not touch upon the critical ideas in the volume which bear most directly on imagist theory. De Visan was concerned to define the symbolist – and Bergsonian – achievement as the perception and communication of a higher, but empirical, realism. He too inveighed against discursive analysis, the use of counter phrases, the putting of signs in the place of realities. 'Au contraire', he wrote, 'nos poètes prétendus symbolistes n'analysent pas, ils prennent une vision concrète ou *centrale* des choses, leur esthétique consiste à "posséder une réalité *absolument*, au lieu de la reconnaître *relativement*...."'[2] He concluded his analysis of the aesthetic of contemporary poetry with a description of a poem as the exteriorizing of a lyric intuition by means of accumulating images, a view that is fundamental to the imagist poetic: 'Le symbolisme ou attitude poétique contemporaine se sert d'images successives ou accumulées pour extérioriser une intuition lyrique.'[3] Thus, although he set out to offer an explanation of symbolism, de Visan in fact represented the tendency to accommodate the conflicting demands of positivism and idealistic symbolism, an effort which dominated the early days of the post-symbolist era. His book is an important expression of an aesthetic view readily assimilated by British poets already seeking relatively similar ends.

REVIEW OF DE VISAN'S
*L'ATTITUDE DU LYRISME CONTEMPORAIN**

T. E. HULME

This is an extremely good and an extremely interesting book. I recommend those who either know nothing of modern French poetry or who, knowing something, want their knowledge systematised, to buy it at once. (True inwardness of movement.)

I confess that its goodness was a surprise to me. When I first picked it up I saw that it was a collection of essays on all the poets that one has known about for some time. The names on the cover – Verhaeren, De Régnier, Mockel, Paul Fort, Maeterlinck, and Vielé-Griffin seem just the same as those in Beaunier's book, "La Poésie Nouvelle," that I read some five or six years ago. There were no new names. I found this

[1] F. S. Flint, 'Contemporary French Poetry', *The Poetry Review*, 1, 8 (August 1912) 355–6. See pages 86–7. It is clear that Flint's early aesthetic views significantly rely on de Visan's formulations.

[2] Tancrède de Visan, *L'Attitude du lyrisme contemporain* (Paris, 1911), p. 455. Emphasis appears in the original.

[3] *Ibid.*, pp. 459–60. The entire sentence is in italics in the original.

* *The New Age*, n.s. IX (24 August 1911) 400–1.

to be an illustration of one of my favourite theories – that French verse, after a short period of great interest, the most vital that had occurred for centuries, had now arrived at comparative stagnation, and had been succeeded by a period during which French philosophy, also for the first time for centuries was to. dominate Europe.

However, when I commenced to read the book I found it vastly different to what I had expected. It is not a mere collection of disconnected, though intelligent, essays on the fashionable moderns that we all of us know, the kind of thing which any literary man who is in the know can turn out at his leisure, but is really a definitely-thought-out attempt to exhibit all these poets as particular manifestations of the same general current of ideas.

It starts out from this thesis. That there is in each generation what Taine called a "température morale," which is to be found at the same epoch in all the different orders of mental activity, and which constitutes "l'état général de l'esprit de moeurs environnantes." To any tendency of poetry at a given time there is a corresponding tendency of philosophy. The psychology of one of Corneille's heroes corresponds to the pure Cartesian doctrine. To the Positivism of Comte and Littre [*sic*] corresponds in literature the spread of naturalism and the "Parnasse." The criticism of Taine, the poetry of Leconte de Lisle, the novels of Flaubert, the painting of Courbet, all live in one common atmosphere. The question then arises, what similar parallelism holds good of modern French literature and philosophy – Monsieur De Visan's book is a reasoned attempt to prove that the spirit which finds expression in the Symboliste movement in poetry is the same as that represented by Bergson in philosophy.

They are both reactions against the definite and the clear, not for any preference for the vague as such, not for any mere preference for sentiment, but because both feel, one by a kind of instinctive, unconscious process and the other as the result of reasoning, that the clear conceptions of the intellect are a definite distortion of reality. Bergson represents a reaction against the atomic and rational psychology of Taine and Spencer, against the idea that states of mind can be arrived at by the summation of more elementary states. He asserts the mental states form a continuous and unanalysable state of flux which cannot from its nature be ever represented clearly by the intellect, but must be seized by a process of intuition. The Symbolist reaction against the Parnasse is exactly the same reaction in a different region of thought. For what was the Parnassian attitude? It was an endeavour always to keep to accurate description. It was an endeavour to create poetry of "clear" ideas. They employed always clear and precise descriptions of external things and strove by combinations of such "atoms of the beautiful" to manufacture a living beauty. To the Symbolists this seems an impossible feat. For life is a continuous and unanalysable curve which cannot be seized clearly, but can only be felt as a kind of intuition. It can only be got at by a kind of central vision as opposed to analytic description, this central vision expressing itself by means of symbols. M. Visan would then define Symbolism as an attempt by means of successive and accumulated images to express and exteriorise such a central lyric intuition. This is the central idea of the book, and the working of it out in the detailed study of the poets of the movement is extremely well done. It is very interesting to see how a complex thought like that of Bergson should be unconsciously anticipated and find a tentative expression in a purely literary movement.

One amusing expression should be noted. He gives an interesting description of the eager little sets of students who used to attend Bergson's lectures at the Collège de France, and contrasts it with the present-day, when it is impossible to find a seat and the hall is overpowered by the feathers and "blasphemous scents" of women.

CORRESPONDENCE WITH *LES JEUNES*: THIRTEEN LETTERS ON FRENCH POETRY IN 1912

When Harold Monro returned from the Continent in fall 1911, and began preparing the first numbers of *The Poetry Review*, he laid plans for a special issue on French poetry. He wrote Eugène Figuière, the head of a Paris publishing firm, for assistance on the project, and he asked F. S. Flint to write the essay. Monro's request for help led to an extensive correspondence, exchanged chiefly between F. S. Flint and Alexandre Mercereau, but including René Arcos, Guillaume Apollinaire, Florian-Parmentier (all published here) and at least twenty-nine other French poets and critics before the special issue appeared. The immediate result of this correspondence was the monograph 'Contemporary French Poetry', which precipitated in August 1912, a major wave of British interest in French verse. A secondary effect of this project was to establish Flint as a special authority on French poetry who wrote frequently on the subject and carried on a voluminous correspondence with French poets throughout the second decade.

The letters themselves are of intrinsic value as a record of the responses of French poets to Flint's queries about themselves, their work, and their literary friends. They also show how much an *avant garde* British poet knew about the French when the correspondence began, what he regarded as the central literary issues, and how particular French poets and movements came to be widely known in England when others of similar interest did not. The letters published here include those which form the basis for Flint's essay. By far the largest amount of information was provided by Alexandre Mercereau.

Figuière referred Monro's introductory letter to Mercereau, who was the secretary of the literary section of the Salon d'Automne and director of *Vers et Prose*. Mercereau responded at the end of March or early in April and promised to have poets send the books or poems that Monro would need. He also suggested the names of two groups of poets who should be included: 'les aînes' – Émile Verhaeren, Francis Vielé-Griffin, Paul Fort, Gustave Kahn, René Ghil, and St Pol Roux; and 'les jeunes' – Tancrède de Visan, Jean Royère, Guillaume Apollinaire, André Salmon, Nicolas Beauduin, Jean Thogorma, Louis Mandin, Georges Périn, Henri-Martin Barzun, Henri Hertz and F. T. Marinetti. He called Monro's attention to the *avant garde* journals *Vers et Prose*, *La Phalange*, and *Les Rubriques Nouvelles*, and recommended de Visan's *L'Attitude du lyrisme contemporain*, his own *La Littérature et les idées nouvelles* and a forthcoming anthology, *L'Anthologie des poètes nouveaux*, for further reference.

By this time Flint had agreed to do the essay, and he acknowledged Mercereau's letter on 17 April 1912. Flint had already studied the two critical books which Mercereau had mentioned. He indicated he knew the poets of 'les aînes' and was most interested in the younger men, about whom he said he as yet knew little. He returned a list of poets that merged his own list with that sent by Mercereau, omitting the older men, but almost doubling the number of 'les jeunes', adding 'André Martin', André Spire, François Porché, Jules Romains, Charles Vildrac, René Arcos, Lucien Rolmer, Georges Duhamel, Henri Franck, Henri Ghéon, and Georges Chennevière. These additions interestingly suggest how much Flint already knew about current French poetry. 'André Martin' did not exist and was added to the list because Flint read 'H. Martin Barzun' (a name he presumably did not recognize) as two persons rather than one. Henri Franck had recently died, and beneath the weight of Mercereau's protest about Chennevière and silence on Porché, Flint later omitted those two from his study. But his additions also show that he already knew the poets he associated with *unanimisme* (Romains, Vildrac, Arcos, Duhamel and Chennevière) and the poets and theorists loosely in the symbolist and *vers librist* traditions. The *Notes sur la technique poétique* of Duhamel and Vildrac, for example, appeared in 1910 and provided important support and information for English advocates of free verse. Henri Ghéon, whose essays appeared in *La Nouvelle Revue Française*, was also a staunch defender of free verse.[1] Thus, although he did not have a full view, Flint started with some appreciation of two of the four or five most significant tendencies of the period. He added a third, more fashionable than significant, by asking for the names of the more important women poets.

Moreover, in this first letter Flint clearly established his purpose in writing the essay – he wished to give a clear and fair documentation of the French poetic scene. He asked that Mercereau send him all he deemed necessary for the essay to have 'at least a documentary, if not a critical, value'. This purpose did not shift, although Flint later felt that his account had been somewhat distorted by the information he received: 'In 1912, when writing about French poets and poetry, I too unwittingly fell into bad company, and was indoctrinated, and made much the same kind of blunders', he said in a letter attacking Jean de Bosschere's articles on Pound in *The Egoist*.[2] By 'blunders' Flint meant that his correspondence led him to give more attention to Mercereau and several of his friends than a truly faithful portrait of French poetic activity would have done. Pound's later criticism of Flint for his 'tolerance for all the faults and imbecilities of French poets',[3] when he never intended his article to be selection of what would survive in current French poetry or publicity for French trends most useful to English writers, caused Flint considerable annoyance. 'Let me say, however', he wrote in a manuscript draft left among his papers, 'that the notes on contemporary French poets which appeared in the August, 1912, number of *our Poetry Review* [*sic*] (and which have had a disastrous effect on Mr. Pound's own later development) were drawn up with no eye to discrimination; but simply with a view to giving general conspectus of what was being said and done in France, without regard to comparative or absolute merit...Mr. Pound knows very well that I have no illusions about the value of any of the poets whose work I presented.'[4] To some extent, Flint's importance lies precisely in this intent to record French poetic endeavor rather than his own taste. His personal preferences lay with Émile Verhaeren[5] and sometimes with minor figures like Georges Périn or Jean de Bosschère. In the course of his many articles in the second decade, however, he discussed with full acknowledgement of their stature virtually all of the French poets of real achievement, and thus he provided fundamental information to poets more gifted than himself.

[1] For example, Ghéon's speech at the 1909 'Séances littéraires' – 'La Mouvement dans la poésie française' – used André Spire and Vildrac as illustrations of the 'vitality' of free verse. See Cornell, *The Post-Symbolist Period, op. cit.,* p. 103.

[2] The letter is addressed to the editor of *The Egoist* and is dated 21 February 1917. It may not have been sent; at any rate it did not appear in *The Egoist*. The manuscript is in the Academic Center Library of the University of Texas.

[3] Pound to René Taupin, May 1928, *The Letters of Ezra Pound, op. cit.,* p. 292. Translation my own.

[4] The manuscript bears neither address nor date. The somewhat formal tone of the prose suggests it is rebuttal to attack, and it was possibly intended for a letters-to-the-editor column. The manuscript is in the Academic Center Library, the University of Texas.

[5] See 'Contemporary French Poetry', p. 87 in this volume.

Whatever defects Mercereau's assistance may have had, he was invaluable to Flint not only as a source of information but for eliciting very widespread co-operation from other French poets. When he next responded to Flint at the end of April he suggested seven additional, non-lyric, poets, named three women writers, and helped Flint understand differences in generations and reputations. What is more, he indicated that he had already asked every poet on the list to send poems and other information directly to Flint. He also began in this letter urging Flint's attention to dramatic poetry – to which Flint did give notable attention – and cautioning him not to overestimate the poets of *unanimisme* because of their skill at propaganda. Flint did not accept Mercereau's views of the *unanimistes*, but he showed far better understanding of their relative importance in French poetry than did, for example, Pound. Flint replied to this letter from Mercereau on 29 April.

By this time Mercereau's intercession with friends and Flint's direct inquiries to other poets had begun to bear fruit. That same morning Flint had received from Florian-Parmentier a long and informative letter (see pages 69–70) commenting on the enclosed copy of his *La Littérature et l'époque* and other topics concerning recent developments in poetry. Although the correspondence from Florian-Parmentier before the appearance of the article is confined to this major letter and some cards, he is one of the most important sources of Flint's essay and indirectly affected related developments in English poetry. His critical survey, *La Littérature et l'époque* (Paris, 1912), analyzes poetic developments exclusively from the standpoint of opposing schools. Even the introductory pages which deal with the symbolist roots of contemporary work and stress the metaphysically creative role of the poet approach the subject from the standpoint of such subdivisions as 'symbolisme', 'vers-librisme', and 'poésie scientifique'. This method Flint carried over into his own article; the effect was to make subdivision into minor schools both widely known and modish. And it was this, as Pound noted, which gave the initial impetus to the formation of imagism as a *cénacle* with its own credo and propaganda machinery.[1] Soon after, the air was for a short and hectic time swirling with -*isms*. Ford Madox Hueffer had already been talking about impressionism; now cubism, futurism, vorticism and imagism also became, in some circles, words to conjure with.

By the same date Flint had also received letters, books, or both from de Visan, Royère, Salmon, Beauduin, Thogorma, both Périns, and Castiaux. He had written Gaston Gallimard explaining his need for books and information as sources for the projected article, and he soon received from Jacques Nayral, *directeur littéraire* at Figuière, a letter containing information about his work. By the end of May Flint had received books or poems and information from Georges Duhamel, Henri Ghéon, André Spire, Théo Varlet, René Arcos, Guillaume Apollinaire, and Louis Mandin. Since Gallimard was director of the publishing house of *La Nouvelle Revue Française*, Ghéon one of the review's poetry critics, Duhamel (since March 1912) poetry critic for *Mercure de France*,[2] and Mercereau connected with *Vers et Prose*, Flint was in touch with many poets and with five of the major firms or journals publishing significant *avant garde* poetry and poetic theory.

He exploited these connections to inform British readers of the most recent collections or studies by each of the figures he treated, substantially before the uncertain channels of reviewing and commerce could have made the titles available in London. And he sometimes obtained, notably from René Arcos (see pages 75–7), genuinely intimate glimpses of important literary associations in France. The remaining correspondence, in June, shows Flint making final decisions about what to include in the

---

[1] Pound, 'A Retrospect', *Literary Essays*, p. 3.
[2] Cornell, *The Post-Symbolist Period, op. cit.*, pp. 108, 110, 119.

essay. Only two younger figures with really significant stature in 1912 escaped Flint's attention: Péguy and Claudel (whom he mentioned in passing), and it is noteworthy that he here was embarrassed by Mercereau. Not once in the endless list of names he sent to England did Mercereau ever mention these two major figures. Two poets, whose stature later grew, Flint elected to exclude as less important – André Salmon and Apollinaire, despite Apollinaire's correspondence. He corrected all four oversights in his columns on French poetry in the next two years. The Apollinaire omission in 1912, however, reveals how far the chief English spokesman for French experiment had come in understanding the literary innovations of Paris, and how far he had to go. The controversies on free verse Flint expounded with diligence and insight. Futurism he received with tolerance and some approbation. Confronted with the poetry of Apollinaire, he confessed to Mercereau, he did not know what to say. With these exceptions, Flint provided London with a panoramic account of French poetry which gave poets a vision of new possibilities in modern verse.

EDITORIAL NOTE

The previously unpublished letters on pages 65–83 are transcribed from manuscripts in the Flint Collection of the Academic Center Library of The University of Texas, with the permission of the manuscript committee. The Flint letters are published by permission from Mrs Ianthe Price; the letter from Apollinaire by permission from Gallimard; and the letter from Florian-Parmentier by permission from Fasquelle. The following editing procedures have been used.

1. In letter headings, unless the names of sender and receiver actually appear on the manuscript, brackets have been placed around the name supplied. The presence of brackets does not mean the identity of the sender or receiver is doubtful.

2. Omitted diacritical markings have been silently supplied. In most of the letters the authors rarely omit the proper mark. In some letters from Flint, the manuscript is a carbon copy of a letter written on an English typewriter. In these cases Flint wrote in only a few diacritical marks, and I have supplied the others. Since this procedure requires some decisions about intended meaning, I have identified in a note letters in which wholesale provision of marks was necessary.

3. Any other insertions in the manuscript appear in square brackets. The insertions include:

[?] The preceding word is partially illegible.
[sic] The form in the preceding words is that of the letter-writer.
[punctuation] The bracketed punctuation has been supplied for clarity.
[date of letter] The date has been supplied by the editor.

4. Uncertainties about date, sender, or recipient and clarification of unusually elliptical comments in the letters are discussed in notes.

5. The form of capitalization and punctuation in titles is that of the writer of the letter. No attempt has been made to impose consistency on such usage; as a result some titles are both quoted and italicized. For typographical convenience the quoted form "xxxx" has been used throughout, although some titles in manuscript are given "xxxxx,,.

6. The kind of manuscript is indicated after the heading. The following code is used, with appropriate combinations:

A – autograph	Ms – manuscript
T – typed	L – letter
S – signed	cc – carbon copy

Correspondence with Les Jeunes

Société du Salon d'Automne
[Between 22 March and 16 April 1912]

Monsieur et cher confrère,

Dès réception de votre honorée du 21-3-12, mon éditeur, M. Eugène Figuière m'a prié de me mettre en rapport avec vous, au sujet de votre si intéressant projet de groupement de la poésie française moderne. Ma situation dans la littérature active – vous la verrez énoncer par Jean Metzinger dans la brochure que mon éd. vous fait parvenir par ce courrier – me met à même de pouvoir vous donner les meilleurs renseignements et les plus impartiaux dans le sens qui vous intéresse.

Je suis moi-même Directeur d'une revue que vous connaissez certainement parce qu'elle est la meilleure revue française: "Vers et Prose" qui ne publie que les meilleures pages des écrivains les plus nobles. Elle porte en exergue "Défense et illustration et de la haute littérature et du lyrisme en prose et en poésie." C'est en effet toujours pour le haut lyrisme que j'ai lutté, ainsi que Paul Fort, le fondateur de "Vers et Prose" qui a bien voulu m'appeler à ses côtés comme directeur.

Je m'offre donc de vous faire parvenir les poèmes dont vous avez besoin.

Comptez-vous mettre les aînés également: Verhaeren, Viclé-Griffin, Paul Fort, Gustave Kahn, René Ghil, Sᵗ. Pol Roux, ou seulement les jeunes. Parmi ces derniers il est indispensable pour être vraiment représentatif de la poésie jeune dans ce qu'elle a de supérieur, de faire figurer M.M: Tancrède de Visan (qui, entre autre a publié au *Mercure de France* un volume de 500 pages sur *l'attitude du lyrisme contemporain*) Jean Royère (Directeur de "la Phalange") Guillaume Apollinaire, André Salmon, Nicolas Beauduin (Dir. des Rubriques Nouvelles) Jean Thogorma, Louis Mandin[,] Georges Périn, H. Martin-Barzun, Henri Hertz – et peut-être Marinetti qui, en dépit de la mauvaise réputation que lui a donné son Futurisme, est un des poètes les plus lyriques qu'il soit.

Un numéro de revue qui comprendra tous ces noms exprimera vraiment la quintessence de la poésie moderne lyrique. Vous les trouverez groupés avec une quinzaine d'autres poètes dans "*l'Anthologie des Poètes Nouveaux*" qui paraîtra dans un mois ou deux, et qu'a préfacée M. Gustave Lanson, professeur à la Sorbonne et le seul officiel d'esprit très avancé.

Je suis, Monsieur et cher confrère, à votre entière disposition pour toute démarche qu'il vous plaira en France[.]

Veuillez croire à mes remerciements au nom des poètes français, et à ma vive considération[.]

Alex Mercereau

[Left margin, page 4]
Vous recevrez par ce courrier mon volume *"La littérature et les Idées nouvelles"* (que M. Stephen Swift & Co. Ltd, 10 John Street, Adelphi, London a pris à sa firme pour l'Angleterre) et les Thurbulums [*sic*] affaissés, poèmes lyriques de moi, volume épuisé que je vous serais reconnaissant de me rendre.

[Left margin, page 3]
M. Stephen Swift, et M. Arthur Ransome (Manor Farm Hacht; Tisbury, Wiltshire, critique que vous connaissez certainement) pourront vous donner sur moi des renseignements, si vous ne me connaissiez pas.

[FLINT TO MERCEREAU] (TccL)

le 17 avril, 1912

Cher Monsieur,

Le directeur de la *Poetry Review*, M. Harold Monro, m'a chargé de lui bâcler l'étude sur la poésie française moderne, à laquelle, comme il vous l'a annoncé, il va consacrer son numéro d'août.[1] Et il m'a remis la lettre que vous lui avez écrite.

Je connais un peu déjà votre situation dans la littérature active, que me confirment les livres que vous avez fait parvenir jusqu'à nous, surtout votre si turbulemment intéressante "Littérature et les Idées Nouvelles," et les renseignements que vous pourrez me donner, et que vous nous offrez de si bonne grâce, me seront précieux. En effet, ce sont les aînés chez vous que je connais le mieux. Les jeunes, je ne les connais qu'imparfaitement et qu'épars dans les revues, telles le *Mercure* et *Vers et Prose*. Mais j'avais déjà dressé une liste de ceux-ci. Ma liste à moi cependant comprend des noms que vous omettez dans la vôtre, tandis que la vôtre contient des noms que je n'ai cru inclure. Voici donc les deux listes mises au point:

Tancrède de Visan	(j'ai passé de belles heures de soleil et d'exaltation sur son "Attitude du Lyrisme Contemporain,["] mais je connais peu ses poésies)
Jean Royère	
Guillaume Apollinaire	
André Salmon	(c'est plutôt un aîné, n'est-ce pas?)
Nicolas Beauduin ⎱	
Jean Thogorma ⎰	Des tonnerres?
Louis Mandin	
Georges Périn	
A. Martin	

---

[1] Diacritical marks are omitted on this carbon manuscript and have been supplied by the editor.

Barzun
Henri Herz [*sic*]
√Marinetti
Alex. Mercereau
√André Spire
√François Porché
√Jules Romains
√Ch. Vildrac
√René Arcos
√Lucien Rolmer   M. de F.[1]
√Georges Duhamel
√Henri Franck   (dead to Gaston Gallimard)[1]
√Henri Ghéon
√G. Chennevière
   et autres

et puis, il y a toute une...théorie de jeunes femmes poètes, un million au moins! Pourriez-vous m'en indiquer les deux, ou trois, ou quatre qui comptent?

Vous voyez, la liste est assez longue, et encore est-ce complete [*sic*]?

Je me prévaudrai donc de votre aimable offre de nous envoyer tout ce que, en fait de livres de poésies, de renseignements, etc., vous jugerez utile pour que notre étude ait une valeur au moins de documentation, sinon de critique. Cela doit faire, ce me semble, un bel article d'avant-garde.

Quant aux aînés, je crois que c'est l'intention de M. Monro d'en faire un court article, mais ce sont surtout les jeunes qui importent, nous trouvons.

Veuillez accepter, Monsieur, dès l'instant nos remerciements pour tout ce que vour [*sic*] ferez pour nous, et croire à mon estime bien sympathique.

[F. S. Flint]

MERCEREAU TO [FLINT] (ALS)
Société du Salon d'Automne
[Between 18 April and 28 April 1912]

Mon cher confrère,

Je suis rentré à peine du Luxembourg et d'Allemagne où j'ai passé quelques jours, et, trouvant votre lettre, j'ai commencé mon action.

Parmi les noms que vous me citez, quatre avaient été omis par moi, parce que la première lettre de M. Monro les contenait. D'après M. Harold Monro, il s'agissait de la jeune poésie *lyrique*, or la liste ainsi comprise contient quelques poètes moins que lyriques, et si ceux-là y sont, il

---

[1] These notations and all checkmarks are added to the carbon in ink. M. de F. refers to *Mercure de France*, the major literary journal which did much to spread Rolmer's reputation in the years just before this letter. Henri Franck died in 1912, and the addition by his name is almost certainly made following response to a letter Flint wrote about him to Gallimard on this same date.

est d'autres noms bien plus importants parmi les jeunes et qui doivent alors figurer: M. M. Castiaux, Théo Varlet, Roger Allard, Léon Deubel, Divoire, Sylvain Bonmariage, G. Ch. Cros (il y en aurait encore beaucoup) sont de ceux qui appartiennent avec le plus de droit à la jeune littérature active. Vous recevrez de leurs poèmes et des renseignements par eux-mêmes, je les ai tous avertis.

Parmi les poètesses: Mme Cécile Périn, Valentine de Saint-Point, Berthe Reynold sont des meilleures, les autres bonnes poétesses appartenant déjà aux générations passées.

André Salmon (30 ans) n'est pas un aîné. Son premier recueil date de 1905. Les aînés là-dedans seraient plutôt Jean Royère, André Spire, Henri Ghéon, qui ont de 40 à 45 ans, mais ils ont commencé à publier très tard.

Henri Franck est mort.

Vous aurez une liste, non pas complète, mais bonne et éclectique. Si l'on y met Chenevière [sic], nouveau venu et encore très peu important, d'autres noms évidemment de beaucoup plus représentatifs devraient y figurer: J. A. Nau, Guy Lavaud, G. Gaudion, Pierre Fons, Clary, Cottinet[,] Florian-Parmentier, Roger Frène, O. Hourcade[,] J. Nayral, Fritz Vanderpijl[,] Ed. Malfère, R. Canudo, Roger Dévigne entre autres, car les bons poètes ne manquent pas. Mais on ne s'arrêterait pas. Il serait pourtant juste de les citer dans votre article.

Dans quelques jours vous aurez à peu près tous les documents. Je vais demander à M. Florian-Parmentier de vous faire parvenir, en même temps que son livre d'une haute conception philosophique *"Par les Routes humaines"* une brochure qu'il vient de publier *"La littérature et l'époque"*[.] Elle donne impartialement le résumé de toutes les écoles qui se divisent les jeunes, quoique, à la vérité une seule tendance est [sic] nouvelle – c'est-à-dire se dessine comme devant être plus forte qu'aux autre époques parce qu'elle a existé de tout temps comme le romantisme, le symbolisme, le naturalisme. Mais atteindra avec fotre génération au sommet – cette tendance c'est le dramatisme. Le dramatisme seul peut enclore toutes les doctrines des jeunes, depuis celles qui sont la queue des doctrines aînées (comme l'unanimisme emprunté par Romains, comme poésie à Whitman et Verhaeren, comme prose à Paul Adam et Rosny aîné, comme théorie à Durkheim, Le Bon, Tarde qui l'ont exploitée depuis vingt ans) jusqu'aux [all following words appear in the margin] nouvelles. J'ai oublié de changer mon pseudonyme de jeunesse Eshmer-Valdor pour mon vrai nom Alexandre Mercereau sur mon livre de poèmes, mais vous le ferez je pense pour moi.

Salutations les plus distinguées[.]

Alex Mercereau

FLORIAN-PARMENTIER TO [FLINT] (ALS)

Paris, le 29 Avril 1912

Monsieur et cher confrère,

Je vous ai adressé hier mon dernier livre de vers et un petit livre que je viens de publier sur *La Littérature et l'Epoque*. J'ai appris, en effet, que vous préparez un important travail sur la nouvelle Poésie Française. Mon ouvrage pourra vous être utile, car il résume tout le mouvement poétique depuis 25 ans. Vous y trouverez un exposé complet et absolument impartial de toutes les écoles. Mais si ce petit livre ne vous suffisait pas, vous pourriez vous addresser à moi en toute confiance: je me tiens à votre disposition pour tous reseignements.

En ce moment, il y a en France un mouvement considérable, qui est une sorte de renaissance idéaliste. La dernière tentative matérialiste a été l'*unanimisme*; mais elle a complètement avorté. Toute la jeunesse s'en détache, parce que les tendances réelles ne sont pas là. Néanmoins, il est juste de dire que M. Jules Romains, un jeune poète qui s'était mis à la tête de ce mouvement, publia en 1908 un volume d'une réelle valeur et qui faisait espérer beaucoup de lui: *La Vie Unanime*. Malheureuscment ce poète, nommé professeur de philosophie, s'est confiné depuis à une philosophie matérialiste qui a découragé tous ses partisans. Actuellement, les jeunes poètes sont tous imprégnés de sciences *occultes*, et il y a, en France, une agglomération poétique qui est comme le moyen-âge de la pensée contemporaine. Tous les poètes sont métaphysiciens, et ils ont les plus hautes ambitions ésotériques. M. Alexandre Mercereau, est un grand esprit, autour duquel se groupent de plus jeunes, et dont les aspirations philosophiques, mystiques, scientifiques et émotionnelles sont tout à fait dans la tradition nationale. Ceci nous rapproche d'ailleurs de l'Angleterre, car, de plus en plus, les écrivains français renient les races latines pour se sentir davantage en affinités avec les races du Nord. Le génie gallique et celtique inspire tous nos jeunes poètes de talent: les Tancrède de Visan, les Théo Varlet, les Louis Mandin, les Guillaume Apollinaire, les Pierre Rodet, les Martin-Barzun [*sic*], André Salmon, les Fernand Divoire, les Raymond Christoflour, les Léon Deubel, les Pierre Fons, les Henry-Marx, les J. J. Van Dooren, etc.

Parmi les poètes un peu plus âgés, très admirés, et qui suivent cette même direction, dans laquelle ils seront suivis à leur tour de plus en plus, il convient de rappeler les noms de Paul Fort, Philéas Lebesque, Saint-Georges de Bouhélier, Michel Abadie, René Ghil, Francis Jammes, Gustave Kahn, Louis Le Cardonnel [*sic*], Sébastien-Charles Leconte, Camille Mauclair, Victor-Emile Michelet, Han Ryner, Albert Saint-Paul, sans parler des maîtres définitifs comme Emile Verhaeren,

Léon Dierx, Maurice Maeterlinck, Henri de Régnier, André Gide, etc[.] dont la réputation est universelle.

Comme vous les verrez par mon petit livre, j'ai toujours coopéré avec activité et avec conviction au mouvement actuel, et je puis dire même que je l'ai accéléré, que j'y ai orienté nombre de jeunes poètes, en fondant l'*Impulsionnisme*. Vous trouverez pages 47 à 54 un bref exposé de la doctrine, et de la technique qui s'en dégage. J'ai eu le plaisir et l'honneur d'être écouté de la jeunesse et même, en 1905–1906, j'aurais pu déterminer un mouvement considérable si je n'avais été entravé par des refers de fortune des plus cruels. – En tout cas, il est à noter que les idées émises à cette époque trouvent leur complet épanouissement dans la jeunesse d'aujourd'hui.

Encore une fois, si vous avez besoin de renseignements, d'adresses de poètes, etc. vous pouvez compter sur mon entier dévouement. Je joins à la présente lettre, une notice, extraite d'un catalogue de M. Gastein, (éditeur qui habite la même maison que moi); cette notice vous reseignera sur moi au point de vue bibliographique.

Croyez, Monsieur [et] & cher confrère, à tous mes meilleurs sentiments.

Florian-Parmentier

Florian-Parmentier
17, rue Fontaine, 17
Paris, 9ème

[FLINT TO MERCEREAU] (TccL)

Cher Monsieur,   le 29 avril, 1912

J'ai bien reçu votre dernière lettre.[1] Vous avez raison: les bons poètes français ne manquent pas. Cela m'effraient, [*sic*] tant ils sont nombreux. Il s'agit bien de la jeune poésie *lyrique*, mais il n'y a que celle-là? Quoiqu'il en soit, mon travail ne sera pas tant une oeuvre de critique qu'une exposition des différentes tendances. Je connais les noms de la plupart des poètes que vous me citez pour avoir lu de leurs oeuvres dans *Vers & Prose* ou le *Mercure*; mais ce n'est pas assez de connaître un nom et une partie d'une oeuvre: il faut les situer dans leur époque par rapport les uns aux autres; et c'est pour tirer au clair les divers groupements que me sera si utile la brochure de M. Florian-Parmentier, La Littérature et l'Epoque, dont vous me parlez, et qui m'est parvenue ce matin.

Je vous remercie bien chaleureusement, cher Monsieur, de tout ce que vous avez fait dans ce sens pour moi.

Voici donc, je crois, la liste des poètes à qui vous avez demandé de m'envoyer de leurs oeuvres et des renseignments [*sic*] sur eux-mêmes:

[1] Diacritical marks are omitted on this carbon manuscript and have been supplied by the editor.

T. de Visan	
J. Royère	(j'ai Soeur de Narcisse Nue – un peu...abscons!)
G. Apollinaire	
A. Salmon	(a promis d'envoyer de ses poèmes, etc)
N. Beauduin	(a envoyé son oeuvre complète, *etc.*)
J. Thogorma	(a envoyé Crépuscule du Monde: mérite une verte semonce pour sa préface)
G. Périn	(a envoyé Le Chemin, l'Air qui Glisse...j'aime beaucoup ça)
L. Mandin	
Barzun	
H. Herz [*sic*]	
Castiaux	(a envoyé La Joie Vagabonde)
Théo Varlet	
R. Allard	
L. Deubel	
F. Divoire	
S. Bonmariage[1]	(un Belge. Je sais que M. Monro songe à un numéro Belge)
G. Ch. Cros	
Mmes Cécile Périn	(a envoyé Variations du Coeur Pensif. Quelle délicieuse antiphonie!)
Valentine de Saint-Point	
Berthe Reynold	

Si j'ajoute à cette liste le groupe de l'Effort (sans oublier Marinetti et vous-même) et que je glisse quelque part une mention des autres noms contenus dans votre lettre, on aura, je pense, une idée assez complète du lyrisme contemporain en France. Et Tristan Leclère (Klingsor) ne mérite-t-il pas une mention...honorable?

Encore une fois, cher Monsieur, je vous remercie et vous prie de croire à ma haute estime.

[F. S. Flint]
(66, Pyrland Road, London, N.)

[P.S.] Pour ce qui est de M. Salmon, c'était une bévue de ma part. J'écrivais Salmon et pensais Mockel, bien que mes souvenirs des deux soient, naturellement, très distincts les uns des autres.

MERCEREAU TO [FLINT] (ALS)

[Between 29 April and 7 May 1912]

Mon cher confrère,

"La littérature et l'époque" vous sera en effet je suis sûr, vu *sa complète impartialité*, fort utile. Il ne faut commencer cette brochure qu'à la p. 14[;] le reste étant d'une interprétation un peu particulière. Les jeunes écoles commencent à la p. 45 avec l'*impulsionnisme*[.]

Le somptuarisme (p. 40) a été fondé par Pol Lowengard [*sic*] et H.

---

[1] The name is crossed out by hand on the manuscript.

Fleichmann [*sic*] (deux jeunes) mais ne donna aucune oeuvre. Les poèmes n'étaient que des pastiches d'aînés notoires et les deux adeptes ont fini par le plus bas feuilletonnisme journalistique.

Pour avoir collaborré [*sic*] aux "*Ecrits pour l'art*" et à "*La Phalange*" Deubel, Mandin, G. Lavaud, Varlet, Castiaux, V. de Sr Point, moi-même n'avons pas moins toujours été des indépendants – admirateurs des aînés que prônaient ces revues, mais nullement suiveurs de leur trace.

Le néo-romantisme ne fournit que des poètes de vingtième ordre et qui ne comptent pour personne. *L'abbaye* (p. 55) fut fondée par M.M. H. Martin Barzun, René Arcos, Charles Vildrac et Alexandre Mercereau (plus des peintres, musiciens etc) eux seuls y habitèrent et y firent un travail manuel, menant là la vie communiste. Nous groupâmes autour de nous des indépendants comme Varlet, Castiaux, Périn, Romains quoique leur vision fût nettement distincte de la nôtre.

Jules Romains (p. 57) prit sa théorie dans Durkheim, Le Bon et Tarde sans y ajouter un mot, et son procédé dans Verhaeren, Whitmann [*sic*], Paul Adam, Rosny aîné, il se rattache aussi au naturalisme, à l'humanisme et au naturisme très fortement. René Arcos doit toute sa philosophie à Bergson mais son "style"[,] sa "manière" en ont fait quelque chose de personnel que n'a jamais pu avoir Romains. Arcos et Vildrac sont les plus personnels, les plus intéressants *du groups unanimiste*, groupe que sa mauvaise camaraderie, sa prétention injustifiée, son désir de passer sur tous les confrères aux dépens de toute sa génération ont fait mettre au ban de tous les jeunes, même ceux qui ont le plus soutenu ses poètes, pas supérieurs[,] il s'en faut à Martin-Barzun, Apollinaire, Salmon, Hertz, Deubel, Visan, etc, mais très débrouillards.

J'insiste sur cela, parce que ce bannissement total – que seuls exceptent "*L'effort*" et "*Les Bandeux d'or*" leurs revues – leur a conféré une place presque à part dans la jeune poésie et paraît les mettre en avant. L'anthologie française que vient de publier en anglais M. Jethro Bithell le démontre. A la stupéfaction de tout le monde en France "*Contemporary french poetry*" ne comprend comme jeunes que le groupe unanimiste. Cela démontre une documentation plus que légère et qui va provoquer ici des attaques indignées. Contrairement à ce que loyalement font ici les autres jeunes, lorsque c'est aux unanimistes qu'on demande des renseignements ils se mettent tout seuls en avant. "*Les Propos critiques*" de Georges Duhamel, les articles de leurs amis ne parlant que d'eux, voilà qui donne aux étrangers une fausse idée du mouvement actuel. Je vous mets en garde contre cela pour ne pas que vous tombiez dans l'erreur de M. J. Bithell[.]

Pour le "Visionnarisme" (p. 57) il donna un écrivain de talent et que j'avais oublié dans mon énumération: c'est M. Roger Dévigne (Georges Hector Mai). Je lui écris de vous envoyer des renseignements utiles.

Dans le "Primitivisme" (p. 60) M. Georges Gaudion est[,] par certains poèmes[,] de tout premier ordre. Je lui écris.

M. Max Jacob (p. 64) est un fort agréable fantaisiste, très doué mais qui n'a encore rien publié qu'un ou deux contes.

Les Renaissances (p. 65) n'ont donné qu'un poète de talent[,] Thogorma.

Le "subjectivisme" (61) le "sincérisme", (62) le "bonisme" (66) n'ont donné que des prosateurs.

Je vous ai parlé de tous ces poètes d'une façon *absolument impartiale* et désintéressée, je suis en contradiction formelle d'oeuvres et de formules avec plusieurs d'entre eux – (Thogorma entre autres)[.] Mais je tiens à ce que vos lecteurs ait [*sic*] une idée de la génération de 1900† aussi parfaite que les lecteurs de l'anthologie de Van Bever et Léautaud en ont une de la génération de 1884.‡ Je tiens à cela beaucoup plus qu'à tâcher de me mettre en avant et d'y mettre mes amis, pour qu'ils en fassent autant à mon égard. Vous aurez de cette façon quelque chose de complet et qui n'obéisse ni à la prétention, la vanité des uns, ni aux querelles particulières qui hélas! morcellent notre génération.

Veuillez agréer,

Mon cher confrère, l'assurance de mes sentiments les meilleurs

Alex Mercereau

(Tournez S.V.P)[1]

† génération "dramatiste"
‡ génération symbolistes [*sic*]

P S. J'oubliais de vous parler de Tristan Klingsor. C'est un fantaisiste du plus aimable, du plus délicieux talent et que je serais heureux de voir figurer dans votre numéro, mais il faudrait le mettre un peu en avant de nous avec Royère, Spire, Ghéon qui sont, comme je vous l'ai dit nos demi-aînés. Paul Fort aura, j'espère, parmi les aînés la grande place qu'il mérite avec Verhaeren, Vielé-Griffin, René Ghil, Gustave Kahn, F. Jammes etc.

Dois-je écrire aussi à Klingsor?

FLINT TO MERCEREAU (TccLS)

66, Pyrland Road,

Highbury, London, N.

le 7 mai, 1912.

Cher Monsieur,

Mes vifs remerciements pour votre dernière lettre. Si mon mérite littéraire était à la hauteur de votre dévouement pour les lettres

[1] The postscript appeared on the following page.

françaises, je ne craindrais pas de faire un tort à la poésie française en
parlant d'elle. Toutefois, je ferai de mon mieux. Entretemps, [*sic*] je
vous prie d'accepter un petit livre de moi – c'est mon dernier exem-
plaire – que je vous expédie par ce même courrier. Vous y verrez que,
moi aussi, j'au [*sic*] subi l'influence et le charme du vers libre et de
l'assonance. Au fait, ces deux éléments musicaux ont trouvé peu de
fauteurs ici. La poésie anglaise ne brille pas en ce moment; nous
sommes le faubourg du monde, – aucun signe de vie, aucune curiosité
technique ou psychologique, à part quelques jeunes, dispersés et tous
influencés par l'art continental; et, en dépit de ce club de fumistes, The
Poets' Club, ou de cette société pour jeunes demoiselles, *pfaffen*, et
vieilles bourgeoises, The Poetry Recital Society – tous les deux la
négation même de la poésie et actifs comme la peste – nous sommes ici
en plein croupissement. C'est pourquoi je lis la poésie française, qui vit,
elle.

Voici donc où nous en sommes avec notre fameuse liste:

Les Demi-Aînés.

Royère ⎫ Spire ⎬ J'ai assez de leurs livres pour pouvoir en parler. Ghéon ⎭	
Klingsor	Auriez-vous l'amabilité...?

L'Abbaye.

H. Martin Barzun	M'a envoyé L'Hymne des Forces; je lui écris pour avoir des renseignements quant à ses livres précédents.
Varlet	M'a envoyé ses Poèmes Choisis etc. Proteste qu'il n'est pas unanimiste!
Castiaux	M'a envoyé La Joie Vagabonde etc. Proteste qu'il n'est pas unanimiste!
Mercereau	—
Périn	M'a envoyé un livre, etc.
Arcos ⎫ Vildrac ⎬ Romains ⎬ Duhamel ⎭	Groupe unanimiste. M'ont tous envoyé des livres, excepté Romains.

Paroxystes.

Beauduin	Je tiens l'oeuvre presque complète. Il n'aime pas non plus les unani-mistes!
Thogorma	J'ai le Crépuscule du Monde et deux opuscules, dont Lettres sur la Poésie, d'où: il méprise les unanimistes (!), les verslibristes et autres: mais tirez sa matière au clair, il est bien vers-libriste lui-même, d'une sorte.

Sans Classement,

T. de Visan	J'ai ses Paysages Introspectifs, etc.
A. Salmon	A promis d'envoyer des ses poèmes: A oublié peut-être.
H. Herz [*sic*]	A envoyé deux livres etc.

G. Apollinaire L. Mandin R. Allard L. Deubel F. Divoire C. C. Cros Mmes de Saint-Point Berthe Reynold Cécile Périn	N'ont donné signe de vie.
	A envoyé un livre, etc.

Futuriste.

Marinetti   Va envoyer ses livres.

J'aurai avec ces noms-là plus qu'il ne me faut pour remplir le cadre de mon article. Grand dieu, cher Monsieur, vous me créditez d'une ambition en parlant de l'Anthologie de van Bever et Léautaud! Quant au travail de Mr. J. Bithell, vous avez raison; mais il faut lui rendre cette grâce – il a omis Rostand et gens de la même taille. Vous ne soupçonnez peut-être pas combien est méritoire pour un anglais le fait d'avoir introduit au public anglais à un prix ridicule (neuf pence) les meilleurs poètes français parmi les aînés: y avoir inclus quatre des jeunes, même à l'exclusion d'autres aussi bons ou meilleurs, est prodigieux, et fait preuve d'une intelligence anglaise supérieure. Qu'auriez-vous dit si le livre ne contenait que des traductions d'Auguste Angellier[1] ou du sublime auteur (v. propos de l'Empereur d'Allemagne) de l'Hymne au Soleil? C'était à craindre!

Je voudrais comprendre exactement le sens de votre mot "dramatisme."

Je suis très touché, cher Monsieur, par la noblesse de votre désintéressement, et vous prie de croire à une estime qui n'est pas seulement la terminaison d'une lettre.

F. S. Flint

Alex Mercereau

ARCOS TO [FLINT] (ALS)

Paris 29 Mai 1912.

Cher Monsieur,

Excusez-moi, je vous prie, d'avoir tant tardé à tenir ma promesse. D'importants travaux m'ont entièrement accaparé ces derniers jours. Je profite d'un instant de loisir pour vous écrire ces quelques lignes[.] Je ne pourrai, hélas, vous donner qu'une faible idée de ce que fut notre Abbaye; Une journée de conversation n'épuiserait pas le sujet!

---

[1] Minor French poet (1848–1911), some of whose work was published in England. Bithell mentions him only to dismiss him in his 'Introduction' to *Contemporary French Poetry* (London, 1912), pp. lxiii–lxiv.

L'entreprise qui dura 14 mois remonte déjà à 5 années! Nous étions alors bien jeunes, ayant tous, à peu près, une trentaine d'années aujourd'hui.

La loi de la "vie en société" pesait durement sur nous. Nous étions pleins d'aspirations que nous ne savions comment réaliser quand nous eûmes l'idée d'assembler nos ressources, de quitter la ville et de vivre en commun de notre travail, en artistes. Je crois que notre tentative n'eût pas laissé indifférent Ruskin dont les idées nous sont familières et bien sympathiques.

Par un jour pluvieux d'Octobre, Vildrac et moi, découvrîmes la retraite idéale qui devait abriter mieux qu'un rêve – c'était une vaste propriété abandonnée située à Créteil à 17 kilomètres de Paris. Je ne peux vous dire quelle émotion nous eûmes en parcourant pour la première fois les allées de l'immense parc mouillé et frissonnant. Les herbes folles avaient tout envahi, les buis dépassaient la hauteur d'un homme. Toutes les espèces d'arbres voisinaient dans ce parc féerique et si heureusement "mal peigné." Le verger, à l'abandon, était dans un état lamentable! Il put cependant nous nourrir de ses fruits tout un été. Je n'ai rien dit encore de la maison inhabitée depuis des années et dont aucune fenêtre et porte ne fermait! Des branches d'arbres entraient dans une pièce par les vitres brisées, et l'humidité avait soulevé le parquet en plusieurs endroits.

Nous louâmes cette maison, à un prix fort exagéré. Le propriétaire ayant eu vent de notre qualité augmenta son loyer. La maison nous plaisait et nous acceptâmes ses volontés. Elles devaient plus tard nous écraser.

En possession de la maison, notre premier souci fut de la rendre habitable. Tour à tour: peintres en bâtiment, menuisiers, serruriers, jardiniers, nous nous donnâmes de tout coeur à cette besogne. Au bout d'un mois, la propriété était méconnaissable. Je taillai moi-même les arbres fruitiers, grimpé dans les branches, cependant que Vildrac, debout au pied, me lisait à haute voix le manuel du parfait jardinier. Un ami nous ayant avancé quelques fonds, nous pûmes installer une petite imprimerie chez nous. Nous comptions vivre en faisant de l'édition d'art. Le métier d'imprimeur n'eut bientôt plus de secrets pour nous. Tous les matins nous travaillions à l'imprimerie. Chacun avait la libre disposition de l'après-midi pour travailler à son oeuvre personnelle.

Le dimanche était consacré aux amis.

Nous donnions de temps en temps des réceptions dans notre parc. On faisait de la musique, on lisait des poèmes. Les peintres réunissaient leurs toiles dans notre plus grande salle où on pouvait les visiter.

Une des photographies que je vous adresse (une carte postale) fut prise un de ces dimanches. Une autre représente "la Marne" rivière passant devant notre parc et où nous nous baignions presque chaque jour l'été.

Notre oeuvre eut un retentissement considérable. Tous les journaux de France et de Navarre nous consacrèrent des articles. Malheureusement, nous ne pûmes jamais surmonter les difficultés matérielles. Nous n'avions pas assez de travaux et nous fûmes aussi les victimes de gens indélicats qui abusèrent de nous.

Apres un hiver terrible (sans feu et sans beaucoup de nourriture, il nous fallut quitter la maison!) [*sic*] Je sortis le dernier, avec mes déménageurs, par un affreux jour d'hiver.

L'exemple ne sera pas perdu. Nous avons montré que notre idée était réalisable. Que d'autres, plus fortunés et mieux organisés[,] la mènent à bien!

Je voudrais vous raconter mille anecdotes sur notre vie à "l'Abbaye". Je ne veux pas non plus abuser de votre complaisance à m'écouter.

Cette aventure n'est plus déjà qu'un souvenir, mais quel souvenir! Nous la raconterons quelque jour tout au long dans un livre et on sera émerveillé –

Il y avait là, comme poètes: Vildrac, Duhamel, moi-même, Jules Romains qui faisit de fréquentes apparitions – Mercereau –

Les peintres étaient: Esleiyes, Doucet, Mahn. Nous ne fûmes jamais plus d'une dizaine (femmes et enfants en plus) à habiter l'Abbaye. Mais le dimanche, nous étions quelquefois 3 cents!

Les photographies vous donneront une idée de ce qu'était notre "couvent[.]" Je vous serais obligé de me les retourner quand vous les aurez bien examinées.

Nous vous remercions vivement, Cher Monsieur, d'avoir eu l'idée de parler de "l'Abbaye" à vos lecteurs anglais et nous vous en sommes bien reconnaissants.

Trouvez ici le gage de notre amitié, de la mienne particulièrement.

René Arcos

25bis *rue de l'Armorique XVè*

[P.S.] Vous pouvez garder comme petit souvenir la carte postale *rouge* représentant une entrée de l'Abbaye.

APOLLINAIRE TO [FLINT] (ALS)

[late May 1912]

Paris, 1 [?] rue La Fontaine –

Monsieur,

Monsieur Alex. Mercereau m'a engagé à vous envoyer quelques poèmes que v/trouverez ici. J'ai publié un ouvrage poétique mêlé de

vers et de prose: *L'Enchanteur pourrissant* (in 4° publié à 105 [?] exemplaires[,] Paris, Kahnweiler, 1909) avec bois gravés d'André Derain;
La poésie symboliste (Paris, l'Edition 1909, in-18 à 3 fr. 50) en collaboration avec P. N. Roinard et V. E. Michelet; *L'Hérésiarque et Cie* (in-18 à
3, 50, Paris[,] Stock 1910) dont on a beaucoup parlé et qui obtint le
plus grand nombre des voix au premier tour du vote pour le prix
Goncourt en 1910; *Le théâtre italien* (in 18 illustré, Paris, Michaud, 1910)
Le Bestiaire ou Cortège d'Orphée, poèmes (in 4° tiré à 120 exemplaires,
Paris Deplanche 1911) avec des bois gravés par Raoul Dufy. J'ai fondé
diverses revues, *Le Festin d'Esope* (1903–1904) *La revue immoraliste* (1905)
Les Soirées de Paris (1912) qui paraît toujours. Je suis un des fondateurs
de *Vers et Prose*[.] J'ai collaboré au [*sic*] journaux: *le Matin, Le Gil Blas,
Le Petit Bleu* etc. Je collabore à beaucoup de jeunes revues comme *La
Phalange, Les Marges* etc. à des journaux comme *Paris-Journal* etc. et
j'ai des rubriques régulières au *Mercure de France*, (la Vie anecdotique) à
l'Intransigeant (critique d'Art). Comme critique d'Art j'ai été longtemps
le seul à défendre les écoles avancées de peinture et de scupture [*sic*]
(Fauves, cubistes etc.)

La littérature actuelle prend une tendance qui me séduit infiniment
parce qu'elle est la mienne: c'est la tendance du *Dramatisme* qui
succède au *Romantisme*. Ceux que je préfère parmi les jeunes sont Théo
Varlet, A. Mercereau, H. M. Barzun, H. Hertz, F. Fleuret, Max Jacob,
T. de Visan, Deubel, Royère, etc. etc.

Veuillez agréer, Monsieur, mes compliments très empressés.

Guillaume Apollinaire

MERCEREAU TO [FLINT] (ALS)

Rec'd Sat. 1 June 1912[1]

Mon cher confrère,

Excusez-moi de vous avoir tenu si longtemps dans le silence mais un
travail fou a retardé toute ma correspondance.

J'ai bien reçu votre volume et vous remercie vivement de me l'avoir
envoyé. Je trouverai l'occasion d'en faire parler dans "La Revue
Indépendante" – revue hebdomadaire dont je m'occupe, et d'en faire
dire le bien que j'en pense. M. Martin-Barzun vous l'a déjà dit.

Avez-vous reçu tous les volumes et les renseignements, s'il vous en
manque, ne craignez pas de me le faire savoir et d'user de moi. Beaucoup sont très négligents, il faut les relancer souvent. Je vous ai fait
adresser par M. Gastein-Serge [?] "L'anthologie critique"[;] vous y
trouverez des renseigments [*sic*] et poèmes utiles: Apollinaire, Deubel,

[1] Note in Flint's hand.

Divoire, Florian Parmentier, Pierre Fons (qui mérite une mention quoique plutôt prosateur, comme je l'ai dit dans mon volume) Louis Mandin, A. Mercereau, Jacques Nayral, Jean Royère, T. de Visan plus les aînés : Bouhélier, Dierx, Paul Fort, René Ghil, F. Jammes, Gustave Kahn, Maeterlinck, Verhaeren, qui sont les meilleurs.

Abadie, L. Le Cardonnel, Seb. Charles Leconte, C. Mauclair, V. Emile Michelet, Han Ryner (surtout prosateur, n'a presque pas fait de vers) Ed. Schuré (prosateur) sont à citer seulement dans les aînés, quant aux autres c'est tout à fait inutile[;] plusieurs ne comptent pas du tout et sont franchement très mauvais, les autres sont juste quelconques.

Avez-vous reçu Spire, Ghéon, Klingsor, Salmon (qui avait déjà fait un 1er envoi depuis 10 jours quand vous m'avez écrit ne pas l'avoir. il m'en a promis un second) Mandin, Apollinaire, Allard, Divoire, G. Ch. Cros, Mme St Point et B. Reynold, – Marinetti ?

Faites-le moi savoir s.v.p. Pour ceux qui sont dans l'anthologie-critique, prenez-les là. Les portraits de Divoire, de Deubel, de moi, sont de notre extrême jeunesse[.] Nous avons changé depuis !

Il y a p. 37, après la préface[,] quelques notes supplémentaires. Pour ma part il n'y a à ajouter de nouveau que dans l'*iconographie* : "Excelsior" (1912)

Un petit mot de vous me fera plaisir cher confrère.

Croyez à mes sentiments trés devoués

Alex Mercereau

88 Bd Port Royal

[FLINT] TO MERCEREAU[1]

66, Pyrland Road, London, N
le 4 juin, 1912.

Cher Monsieur Mercereau,

Non, je n`ai pas reçu tous les livres ; même s'ils m'arrivaient tous, d'un coup, j'en serais au désespoir ! Je suis presque au bout de mon article, et au bout de mes forces. Le jour, j'ai des fonctions ; le soir, je m'acharne, m'évertue, m'ahanne [*sic*] à la poésie française ! C'est une journée, quoi ! Mais, plaisanteries à part, des poètes mentionnés dans ma dernière lettre voici ceux qui ne m'ont rien envoyé :

Klingsor
Salmon (Je ne sais m'expliquer la non-arrivée de l'envoi promis et dont vous parlez)
Allard
G. C. Cros
Deubel

---

[1] This manuscript is not a carbon copy but a handwritten draft. It is unsigned and may be incomplete.

Apollinaire m'a envoyé quelques poèmes.[1] Je ne saurais trop quoi en dire. Divoire m'envoie *L'Amoureux*. Idem. Avec *l'Anthologie critique* dont vous me parlez et qui n'arrive pas, il me sera peut-être possible d'ex-cogiter quelque chose. Tous les autres m'ont envoyé assez de documents pour en parler en connaissance de cause. J'ai reçu une lettre de Henry Marx, réclamant, de par ses mérites, une place. J'ai répondu poliment, ai reçu une brochure, et...passe outre. R. Devigne m'a envoyé des poèmes qui m'intéressent, mais je ne saurai, je crois, en parler. Voilà!

Fini mon article, j'en aurai pour 36 à 40 pages contenant chacune autant qu'une page de *Vers et Prose*, environ. J'ai obtenu de M. Monro qu'il consente à cet arrangement, et qu'il y consacre véritablement toute la revue.

Je ne gagne rien à ce travail, puisque la Poetry Review n'a que des ressources qui lui permettent de s'imprimer, en dépit d'un nombre de lecteurs relativement grand; et j'ai pensé qu'il me serait possible plus tard de publier mon travail – plus réfléchi, et élargi – en livre. Il y aura alors de la place pour d'autres poètes. Je connais un des associés de la maison Stephen Swift, qui est en relations d'affaires avec Figuière. Je l'approcherai. Mais croyez-vous qu'une recommandation de Figuière serait utile dans cette conjoncture, et voudriez-vous avoir l'amabilité de me la procurer, cette recommandation, – si toutefois mon travail méritait la forme livresque?

[F. S. Flint]

MERCEREAU TO [FLINT] (ALS)

Received 9/6/12[2]

Mon cher confrère,

Vous avez dû cette fois-ci recevoir l'anthologie critique de Florian-Parmentier – il vous l'a envoyé [*sic*]. Vous y trouverez des renseigne-ments sur: Apollinaire, Deubel, Divoire, Parmentier, Mandin, Mercereau, Nayral, Royère, Visan et de leurs poèmes. Plus ceux sur les grands aînés: Léon Dierx (parnassien, nommé Prince des Poètes à la mort de Stéphane Mallarmé et pour remplacer celui-ci.) Paul Fort,

[1] See Apollinaire to [Flint], [late May 1912].
[2] The manuscript bears a jotted notation in Flint's hand indicating date of receipt. The phrase has previously been read 'Received 9/11/12', but internal evidence shows the date should be read 9/6/12, an interpretation the handscript does not preclude. Specifically, in Flint's usual practice '9/11/12' would be 9 November 1912, but the first paragraph indicates that the information in this letter is intended for an essay which will appear before October. Even if '9/11/12' were read as 11 September 1912, it is highly unlikely that the letter's contents could be incorporated in an essay in time for publication before October. More important, the last paragraph of the letter is clearly a reply to an inquiry Flint had made in a letter sent 4 June 1912 (see preceding letter), as are other statements throughout. Consequently the reading 'Received 9 June 1912' seems highly reliable.

Ghil, Jammes, Kahn, Maeterlinck[,] Verhaeren (Il manque Griffin) *les seuls du volume de Parmentier qui soient essentiels*. Pour Deubel, servez-vous des poèmes qui sont dans ce livre. Pour Allard, signalez-le seulement en vous servant des quelques mots que j'ai mis sur lui p. 298 de *"La Littérature et les Idées Nouvelles."* Pour Cros, citez seulement son nom, on peut l'omettre dans une étude faite avant le prochain livre qui paraîtra seulement en Octobre au "Mercure de France" et *bien supérieur à ses autres livres*. Pour Dévigne, mettez au moins quelques lignes sur lui d'après "La littérature et l'Epoque" de Parmentier.

Pour Apollinaire, servez-vous de ce que j'en ai dit p. 286–287 de mon volume quoique ça s'adresse surtout au prosateur. Le poète est curieux, fantaisiste, raffiné, très souple, expert en notations subtiles, aiguës, rares.

Pour Devoire, mon volume (p. 80 à 90) donne le prosateur, celui de Parmentier (anthologie-critique) dit suffisamment sur le poète. (que pour ma part j'aime moins que le prosateur, l'intelligence le dominant trop dans ses vers cirieux mais froids)

Ma "Littérature et les Idées Nouvelles" parlent [*sic*] aussi de : Marinetti, Fort[,] Verhaeren, Arcos, Griffin, Spire, Nayral, Périn et Mme, Varlet, Castiaux. Puisez dedans tout ce que vous voudrez, et ne craignez pas de me demander des renseignements supplémentaires si besoin.

Je puis, si vous le désirez vous prêter mes livres de Klingsor. Demandez-les-moi si vous voulez.

Vous me disiez dans une précédente lettre que vous mettriez Romains, Arcos, Vildrac, Duhamel comme unanimistes. Je dois vous dire que depuis quelque temps ils protestent tous qu'ils ne sont pas "unanimistes," mot dont Jules Romains se sert pour désigner l'"interpsychologie" de Tarde, et qu'il s'est arrangé à faire passer pour le nom d'une école qu'il prétendait fonder et dont ses amis étaient prétendus représenter les élèves. Mais les pseudos-élèves se révoltent et protestent chaque fois qu'ils le peuvent, car ils doivent aux mêmes sources que Romains et non à Romains, leur tendance, c'est-à-dire à Whitman, Verhaeren, Paul Adam. Henri Ghéon, leur porte-parole, vient de faire dans le dernier numéro de la *Nouvelle Revue Française*, que refait M. Monro, un article à ce sujet et les appelle les "Whitmanistes[.]" Je crois qu'il vaudrait mieux laisser à Romains le titre d' "unanimiste" et nommer les autres simplement poète [*sic*] du groupe de l'abbaye, avec Martin et moi, car il y en a au moins un qui n'est pas Whitmaniste, c'est René Arcos qui suit pas à pas la philosophie de Bergson. D'ailleurs toutes ces tendances diverses ne peuvent valoir que par leur degré de lyrisme, de dramatisme, d'art, leur étiquette n'a pas d'importance.

81

C'est moi-même qui ai fait connaître à mon éditeur M. Figuière M. Granville, l'associé de M. Stephan [*sic*] Swift, c'est vous dire que je me ferai un plaisir de vous appuyer moi-même auprès de lui, et même de faire signer en votre faveur une pétition des jeunes poètes français, reconnaissants pour votre noble et désintéressé labeur.

Mille amitiés,
Alex Mercereau

[Left margin, page 4.]
Prière de me renvoyer ces deux coupures. Duhamel avait déjà envoyé une lettre de protestation un mois avant Arcos contre l'unanimisme comme doctrine neuve.

(Left margin, page 3.]
Les portraits de moi, de Divoire, de Deubel que vous verrez dans l'anthologie de Parmentier datent d'il y a 10 ans environ. Ils ne nous ressemblent plus. En voici un plus nouveau paru dans l'*Excelsior*.

[FLINT TO MERCEREAU] (AL draft)

66 Pyrland Road,
Highbury, London N
le 11-VI-1912

Cher confrère,

Il me faut perdre, moi aussi, ma quatorzième[1] page; mais il me sera au moins permis de me rappeler les noms qui s'y trouvaient et de les citer. Je crains que je n'aie déjà excédé l'espace qui m'est réservée [*sic*] et qu'il ne m'aille falloir raccourcir. Par conséquent, il ne me sera possible de faire plus que de mentionner, comme e'tant de ma 14ème page, les noms, avec quelques mots d'appréciation, de Klingsor, Salmon, Apollinaire, Deubel, Divoire, Mandin[,] Allard, etc. Mon travail comportera alors dans sa forme d'à présent:

1° une petite [*sic*] ~~notice~~ historique[2] de la poésie française au 19me siècle du point de vue technique particulièrement, pour introduire

2° une notice avec citations de chacun des poètes suivants:

Ghéon ⎫
Royère ⎬ Les Demi-Aînés
Spire ⎭

---

[1] The allusion is to a banquet given in honor of Paul Fort in February 1912, when the honoree, intending to respond with praise for the younger men present, mislaid his fourteenth page and was unable to commend everyone. Flint refers to the incident again in the essay 'Contemporary French Poetry'.

[2] This manuscript is a handwritten draft rather than a carbon; it contains an unusually large number of uncorrected errors and illegible and stricken words. Here, for example, Flint exchanged a feminine noun for a masculine one without altering the modifiers.

Note sur l'Abbaye

Abbaye
- Mercereau
- Théo Varlet
- P. Castiaux
- H. M. Barzun
- G. Périn
- J. Romains ⎤ Groupe dit unanimiste, mais dont Romains seul est
- R. Arcos ⎟ unanimiste. Groupe toutefois par des affinités et des
- G. Duhamel ⎬ amitiés, donc classé ensemble. Je ne donne pas de la tête
- Ch. Vildrac ⎦ dans l'étiqueté J'ai remarqué qu'il n'y avait qu'un unani-
  miste.

Lucien Rolmer et l'Ecole de Grâce (c'est une tendance)

N. Beauduin ⎫
Thogorma ⎬ Paroxystes

Florian-Parmentier et l'Impulsionnisme

Cécile Périn ⎫
V de S-Point [*sic*] ⎬ Trois Muses
B. Reynold ⎭

T de Visan

H. Hertz

F. T. Marinetti

Soit 22 poètes. Je sais bien qu'il peut y avoirs [*sic*] dans cette liste des poètes qui ne valent peut-être pas d'autres poètes, non-inclus; mais je n'en peux mais; j'ai fait de mon mieux, et pour l'article il ne me reste plus de temps pour ré-établir [*sic*] les hiérarchies! Voilà, j'exulte, je secoue les langes du labeur: demain ce sera l'affaissement devant des pages qui m'écoeurent!

Quant à l'Abbaye, j'ai eu des détails de M. Arcos, qui m'a envoyé aussi des photographies. Je vous envoie la page que j'en ai faite. Voudriez-vous la contrôler?

Si l'éditeur se présente et le temps se trouve, il me sera possible d'élargir à mon gré, et alors. . . la fête de ces messieurs de la quatorzième. C'est pure chance, vous comprendrez, leur absence. Malheureusement j'ai lâché un sarcasme dans le New Age au sujet de M. Granville, qui m'a agacé en me citant de travers dans les annonces d'un de ses livres, et puisque M. G. a été, lui aussi, collaborateur à ce journal, il en gardera mémoire et peut-être m'en voudra. Il est défendu aux poètes et aux soi-disants [*sic*] poètes de se faire éditeur!

Je suis content que mon livre[1] vous plait. [*sic*] Il y a des pièces dans la première partie, *Preoccupations*, que je ne rimeprimerai [*sic*] pas; mais enfin le livre est une confession et c'est moi là: c'est une autobiographie inintentionnelle. [*sic*] [The draft continues in shorthand notes for a few lines.]

[F. S. Flint]

[1] Flint's first book of poetry, *In the Net of the Stars* (1909).

THE FIRST MAJOR SURVEY OF THE FRENCH
*AVANT GARDE**

When F. S. Flint published 'Contemporary French Poetry' in August 1912, he placed before the literary world of London an entirely new poetic generation. Occasional essays on the French symbolists had continued to appear in intellectual journals since the 1890s, and since Flint himself had begun to write for *The New Age* in 1908 these articles had been increasingly frequent. Almost all of them had one thing in common – they spoke of the poets of the symbolist *cénacle* (like de Régnier, Kahn, Moréas, Jammes) as if they were the current generation in Paris. Nothing of significance had yet been written on the post-symbolist poets, the *unanimistes*, *futuristes*, *Whitmanistes*, *paroxystes* and others who would become the acquaintances of the London *avant garde*. Flint specified the change in generation as soon as he began; 'Symbolism', he said, '. . . is itself in process of evolution into other, different forms'. Besides introducing London to important new poets, the most significant contribution of his essay was his discussion of where that evolution of symbolism had led on two central French critical issues – the definition of symbolist aesthetics and the debate on *vers libre*. Both discussions contributed directly to the development of English poetics.

Flint adopted the Bergsonian language of the French post-symbolists when he asked, 'What was symbolism?' 'Ultimately', he said, 'it was an attempt to. . .set vibrating the infinity within us, by the exquisite juxtaposition of images'. Important in this definition is the allusion to images and the placing of 'infinity' within the psyche, rather than in a transcendental sphere. In the months ahead, even the word 'infinity' would be avoided by some of the English poets stressing the accurate rendering of the 'thing itself'. But the location of the infinite within the poet was the major step toward a new, psychological empiricism.

What is more, Flint, under the tutelage of Tancrède de Visan, whom he was paraphrasing, was using the idea of *infinity* in a way distinctly reminiscent of Bergson's 'true empiricism'.[1] Flint continued: 'The symbolist poet attempts to give you an intuition of the reality itself and of the forces, vague to us, behind it, by a series of images which the imagination seizes and brings together in its effort to insert itself into and express that reality, and to evoke at the same time the infinity of which it is the culmination point in the present.' Behind this statement is Bergson's 'Introduction to Metaphysics'. Any reality, Bergson said, can be seen in two ways. By an act of imagination, one may enter into an object and view it from within, intuitively. Such a view is an absolute and 'indivisible apprehension'.[2] One may also view the same object from without, analytically, and from such a stance one never ceases to enumerate the possible views of the object. 'Now', said Bergson, 'what lends itself at the same time to an *indivisible apprehension* and to an *inexhaustible enumeration* is, by definition, an *infinite*'.[3] Both de Visan and Flint seem to suggest that the poet, by means of his 'series of images', presents the object in such a fashion that one may apprehend it at once intuitively and analytically, and that one is thus put in touch with absolute and infinite reality.

Relying on Bergson's own suggestion that juxtaposed images offer the best way to lead a reader to an *intuition*, de Visan and Flint (and, after them, Pound) accorded the poet a privileged place in helping men to know reality. The poet, they implied, like the Bergsonian metaphysician, employs the only method which 'allows one to pass

---

* For other extended comments on 'Contemporary French Poetry', see the General Introduction (pages 1–49), the introduction to 'Correspondence with *Les Jeunes*' (pages 61–4) and the letters themselves (pages 65–83).

[1] Henri Bergson, 'Introduction to Metaphysics', in *The Creative Mind*, trans. by Mabelle L. Andison (New York, 1946), p. 175.　　[2] *Ibid.*, p. 161.　　[3] *Ibid.* Emphasis mine.

beyond idealism as well as realism'.[1] When Flint used de Visan's Bergsonian re-definition of symbolist poetics he helped to bring London into the post-symbolist search for an aesthetic that would reconcile the conflicting claims of transcendental symbolism and the positivism of a Comte or Taine.

Flint also introduced English readers to intricacies of the seething French debate over *vers libre*. Gustave Kahn's 'Préface sur le vers libre' in *Premiers Poèmes* in 1897 had been but the first of hundreds of monographs and statements of position. Some of the most important recent viewpoints appeared in Marinetti's *Enquête internationale sur le vers libre* (1909), Duhamel and Vildrac's *Notes sur la technique poétique* (1910), de Souza's *Du Rhythme, en français* (1912), and Henri Ghéon's essays, including those in *Nos Directions* (1911), and Flint referred to each of these volumes in his discussion. Ghéon urged the use of the 'analytical strophe' rather than 'vers libre', and asserted that in such a poem 'each expressive unit of the thought, each logical unit of the dis-course, will create a rhythmic unit in the strophe...which is the total, harmonious expression of a thought...' Vildrac and Duhamel interpreted that 'free verse' was not totally free, but based on the use of a 'rhythmic constant' of a fixed number of syllables that appeared in some position in every line, accompanied by a variable number of additional syllables. Despite the difficulty of applying French metrical discussions to English verse, these conflicting theories implicitly emphasized three conclusions: the abandoning of traditional forms was not just a symbolist experiment but the enterprise of most of the younger French poets; the use of 'free verse' was not a flight from the difficult, or the prerogative of the rare poet with a particularly gifted ear, but a respectable subject for experiment and theorizing; and the practice of 'vers libre' was not the abandoning of pattern but the creation of an original and perhaps very complicated metrical form suitable to each poem. It may well have been these observations that led the imagists to urge composition 'in the sequence of the muscial phrase' with the belief that they 'had as much right to a group name...as a number of French "schools" proclaimed by Mr. Flint...'

Flint's interest in the poets who sought an analogy with the musical phrase in the poetic line was insistent throughout the essay. He also discovered and praised in the French many of the other characteristics that came to be associated with imagism: the effort to strip poetry of rhetoric, the subordination of rhyme to the cadence of the verse, the more frequent use of assonance, the creation of images to convey emotion. One important element of imagist doctrine was not foreshadowed in his essay, how-ever, as it often is not reflected in his poetry: compression. Flint was not attentive to French attempts to eliminate from a poem all but the minimum necessary words.

The eclecticism of the essay lent it a significance beyond the confines of imagism. Flint noted the use of an ironic mask by Henri Hertz, and linked the practice to Laforgue and Corbière. He discussed the work of a 'vagabond poet', Théo Varlet, whose 'Tramp's Notebook' and poems of 'discord between the sun and smoke-laden fog' have their parallels in the *Autobiography of a Super-Tramp* of W. H. Davies and the poems of countless Georgians. Both in description of the work of poets like Barzun, Marinetti, Romains, Spire, and Vildrac, and in the extended citation of poems them-selves, Flint underscored the expansion of poetic subject-matter to include the urban, the industrial, and the painful. And he emphasized again and again the importance of French use of poetic drama, a genre that attracted a number of minor figures in London in the second decade, but (with the exception of Yeats, whose inspiration clearly lay elsewhere) no one of the stature of Claudel. Finally, but significantly, Flint provided not only the titles of books but, in effect, a substantial anthology as well. The readers of 'Contemporary French Poetry' who wanted to know more about

[1] *Ibid.*, p. 184.

85

Romains' use of images, Hertz's irony, or Vildrac's use of dramatic narrative could begin with a more thorough study of the quoted poems themselves. The essay, thus, did more than simply inform; it laid the foundation for the individual knowledge a generation of English poets acquired of the poetry of France.

CONTEMPORARY FRENCH POETRY*

F. S. FLINT

It seems to me that the nineteenth century in France – with the revolution and Napoleon I, his vicissitudes, the alternations of Napoleonic dynasty and Republic, the Franco-Prussian war, – kept the French mind in a constant state of excitation, wherein it was impossible for the spirit to vegetate and moulder; and that the literary activity of France during that period, the poetic production – for only in so far as literature is poetry, creation, is it estimable – was, therefore, greater and more diverse than at any other period of France's history. School followed school: Romanticism, Parnassianism, Naturalism, each in turn denied its forerunners and was denied; and the latest comer of all, Symbolism, which denied all, is itself in process of evolution into other, different forms.

What was symbolism? First of all, a contempt for the wordy flamboyance of the romanticists; secondly, a reaction against the impassive descriptiveness of the parnassians; thirdly, a disgust of the "slice of life" of the naturalists. Ultimately, it was an attempt to evoke the subconscious element of life, to set vibrating the infinity within us, by the exquisite juxtaposition of images. Its philosophy, in fact, as M. Tancrède de Visan has shown in that profound book, *L'Attitude du Lyrisme Contemporain*, was the philosophy of intuitiveness: it has been formulated by Bergson.[1]

The forerunner was Baudelaire:

> La Nature est un temple où de vivants piliers
> Laissent parfois sortir de confuses paroles;
> L'homme y passe à travers des forêts de symboles
> Qui l'observent à travers [*sic*] des regards familiers.
>
> Comme de longs échos qui de loin se confondent
> Dans une ténébreuse et profonde unité,
> Vaste comme la nuit et comme la clarté
> Les parfums, les couleurs et les sons se répondent.[2]

---

* *The Poetry Review*, I, 8 (August 1912) 355–414.

[1] See, notably, the *Introduction à la Métaphysique*, in the *Revue de métaphysique et de morale*, jan. 1903. [Flint's note.]

[2] Charles Baudelaire, 'Correspondances', *Les Fleurs du mal*, *Oeuvres complètes*, IV (Paris, 1930; 1st pub. 1857), p. 17. The line should read: 'Qui l'observent avec des regards familiers'.

Its first prophet was Stéphane Mallarmé, whose influence on his generation is not to be calculated. "Mallarmé dreamed the superhuman dream of putting the reader in direct contact with the infinite, by the choice of words which could give the sensation thereof, and in such a way that the poem would convey simultaneously the divination of musical, plastic, philosophical and emotional analogies."[1] The youth of his generation sat at Mallarmé's feet on Tuesdays in his apartments of the rue de Rome, and listened while he "evolved seductive and lofty doctrines of poetry and on art, on the prose poem and on the chronique, on music and on the theatre."[2] In the measure that a man may do so, Mallarmé formed the mind of all that was best in the youth of his generation. "There is not one among writers posterior to Mallarmé and worthy of consideration who does not owe to the poet of *Hèrodiade* and of *L'Après-midi d'un Faune*, but above all to the wonderful talker of those Tuesdays of the rue de Rome something of his thought and its expression."[3] Albert Mockel called him "*le type absolu du poète*," and he was so to Edouard Dujardin, Félix Fénéon, René Ghil, Gustave Kahn, Jules Laforgue, Charles Morice, Henri de Régnier, Laurent Tailhade, Francis Vielé-Griffin, Charles Vignier, Paul Claudel, André Fontainas, André Gide, A. Ferdinand Herold, Pierre Louys, Camille Mauclair, Stuart Merrill, Adolphe Retté, Marcel Schwob, Paul Valéry...[4] I am naming the subtlest prose-writers and the best poets of an age which, as Remy de Gourmont has said, has never been equalled in the number of its poets and in the quality of its poetry. And, this generation which produced Laforgue, Kahn, de Régnier, Vielé-Griffin, Verhaeren, Maeterlinck, Paul Fort, Claudel, Francis Jammes – men who retested the capabilities of a language and who widened the boundaries of consciousness, men who were the instruments through which a new spirit found a voice – was called decadent. It chose the designation *symbolist* as an alternative. As M. de Visan has pointed out, the word was both well and badly chosen.[5] A symbol is a sign used in place of a reality, as in algebra; but the symbolist poet attempts to give you an intuition of the reality itself and of the forces, vague to us, behind it, by a series of images which the imagination seizes and brings together in its effort to insert[6] itself into and express that reality, and to evoke at the

---

[1] Flint translates from Florian-Parmentier, *La Littérature et l'époque* (Paris, 1911), pp. 19–20. The same source also includes the stanzas quoted from Baudelaire.

[2] Flint paraphrases a comment by Bernard Lazare in *Figures contemporaines* (1895) which was quoted in *Poètes d'aujourd'hui*, 1, ed. A. Van Bever and Paul Léautaud (Paris, 1910), p. 345.

[3] Vielé-Griffin, *La Discipline Mallarméenne*, in *La Phalange*, mai 1907. [Flint's note.]

[4] Both the quotation from Mockel and the list of names – down to Claudel – are to be found in the critical and historical notes on Mallarmé in *Poètes d'aujourd'hui*, *op. cit.*, p. 345.

[5] This and the succeeding three sentences are translation and condensation of Tancrède de Visan, *L'Attitude du lyrisme contemporain*, *op. cit.*, pp. 454–5.

[6] Bergson's word. [Flint's note.]

same time the infinity of which it is the culminating point in the present. To convey these images, the symbol is necessary, and is a means of expression only. The word *symbolism* is badly chosen, therefore, if used to indicate an aesthetic; and well-chosen, if used to describe the mechanics of its expression.

But the symbolist poets did more than astonish a "Siècle d'âpreté juive et d'ennuis protestants" with beauty; they created a new manner, the *vers libre*.

In 1885, the year of birth, we may say, of the symbolist movement, French poetry had become stagnant. The art of Leconte de Lisle, de Vigny, Banville, Heredia and the other parnassians had stultified the regular alexandrine. M. Gustave Kahn, in a lecture on the *vers libre* delivered recently at the Maison des Etudiants, said that everywhere there were poets who were making the same verse; a worthy man, Emmanuel des Essarts, had enumerated them. Having cited those of Paris in a long article, he drew up a list of the Provincials in a still longer article. They were to be found in all the towns, and *Le Dictionnaire des Communes de France* could have been revised by adding, after the name of the town and its industrial product, the name of its poet, as thus

Pithiviers,	pâté d'alouette:	poète, Jules Béor
Nivers,	faïenceries:	poète, Achille Millien
Morcens,	buffet, célèbre:	poète, Evariste Carrance.[1]

Verlaine, influenced by Rimbaud, gave the *coup de grâce* to the old alexandrine, which had already been very much dislocated by the romanticists; but M. Gustave Kahn is commonly supposed to have invented the French *vers libre*. At the banquet given in the latter's honour in 1896, Mallarmé terminated his speech with these words: "To construct a verse as far removed from the constant mould as from prose, irreducible to either, viable, – what an extraordinary honour in the history of a language and of Poetry." To Jules Laforgue, also, and even to a poetess of Montmartre, Marie Krysinska, the merit of its invention has been attributed.[2] But however that may be, M. Kahn was undoubtedly the first theorist of the new technique. It has been said, too, that the introduction of *vers libre* was due to the influence of Whitman and of German poetry. I agree with M. Florian-Parmentier[3] that in a question of purely French technique, the names of foreign poets cannot be invoked. The French poets were impelled by an interior necessity to rid

---

[1] Flint translates from Gustave Kahn, 'Le Vers libre', *Vers et Prose*, xxviii (January–March 1912) 41.

[2] Cf. *Poètes d'aujourd'hui*, i, *op. cit.*, pp. 203–4.

[3] Flint refers the reader again to *La Littérature et l'époque*, *op. cit. Vide* pp. 14–16 ff.

their art of the grossness of the sleep that had fallen upon it – to bring it nearer to pure music.[1] The classic verse without *enjambements* had become unendurably monotonous; the verse of the romanticists, with its *enjambements*, its *rejets*, and its *chevilles*, retained only the semblance of regularity; the parnassian verse was a thing in itself, worked up, and then fitted to another verse, similarly fabricated. But the symbolists sought in their verse a variety, which the classic verse, a logic, which the romantic verse, a living flow of speech, rhythm, which the parnassian verse, did not possess. Their element was the strophe, of no conventional form, composed of verses that were free from exterior law. But this *vers libre* was misnamed. It is by no means free; it must follow rigorously the interior law of the poet's emotion and the idea which has given it birth. "Is it not easier," remarks M. Robert de Souza, one of the most ardent and even scientific theorists of the *vers libre*, "for mediocrities to fill a fixed form than to create at the same time idea and form? With the *vers libre* there is no drawing with tracing paper, no model to imitate; the poet must be personal and an initiator; he must have the thought which generates his form. This necessity seems elementary; yet it is not always apparent in poems with fixed forms, pompous displays of 'sonorous inanities.' "[2] The *vers libre* is the most difficult form of all. Indeed, only when a poet's inspiration is upon him at its strongest, only when he is really under the influence of the strange bursting exaltation which goes with all creation, is he capable of *vers libre*. Then, perhaps, he will produce such emotional music as this "*Thrène, In Memoriam Stéphane Mallarmé*," of Vielé-Griffin:

> Si l'on te disait: Maître!
> Le jour se lève;
> Voici une aube encore, la même, pâle;
> Maître, j'ai ouvert la fenêtre,
> L'aurore s'en vient encor du seuil oriental,
> Un jour va naître!
> – Je croirais t'entendre dire: Je rêve.
>
> Si l'on te disait: Maître, nous sommes là,
> Vivante et forts,
> Comme ce soir d'hier, devant ta porte;

---

[1] Cf. Florian-Parmentier, *La Littérature et l'époque, op. cit.*, p. 20.

[2] Flint refers this quotation to Robert de Souza, *La Poésie populaire et le lyrisme sentimental* (Paris, 1899), as if he were translating directly. No close correlative of these sentences appears in the volume he names, however. Flint goes on to annotate at this point: 'M. de Souza has established (see *Du Rythme, en français*) that the rhythm of French verse depends on accent and quantity. The results obtained with the apparatus invented by the Abbé Rousselot, which is in use at the Phonetics Laboratory of the Collège de France, and which registers the duration of spoken syllables, admit of no contradiction. These results also prove that the traditionalists, with their mute *e*, haven't a foot, or have only *lamed* feet to stand upon'! For the source of Flint's note see *Du Rythme, en français* (Paris, 1912), pp. 14–19.

Nous sommes venus en riant, nous sommes là,
Guettant le sourire et l'étreinte forte,
– On nous répondrait: Le Maître est mort.

Des fleurs de ma terrasse,
Des fleurs, comme au feuillet d'un livre,
Des fleurs, pourquoi?
Voici un peu de nous, la chanson basse
Qui tourne et tombe,
– Comme ces feuilles-ci tombent et tournoient –
Voici la honte et la colère de vivre
Et de parler des mots – contre ta tombe.[1]

The function of *vers libre* was to strip poetry of rhetoric...

Another innovation brought about by the symbolists was the restoration into modern French poetry of the assonance. The parnassians had made rhyme the be-all and end-all of poetry. Banville wrote in his *Petit Traité de Poésie Française*: "Rhyme is the only harmony in verse; it is the whole of the verse...The imagination of the rhyme is before all the quality which constitutes the poet...Only the word which is the rhyme is heard in a verse...So long as the poet expresses truly his thought he rhymes well; the moment his thought is confused, his rhyme is also confused, becomes feeble, dragging, and vulgar; and the reason is easily understood, since for him thought and rhyme are one."[2]

Oh [*sic*] qui dira les torts de la rime!
Quel enfant sourd ou quel nègre fou
Nous a forgé ce bijou d'un sou
Qui sonne creux et faux sous la lime![3]

Inevitable!

What Banville wrote of rhyme is perfectly true of rhymed verse; but it is not true of poetry, since it is to be presumed that Homer, Virgil and Shakespeare wrote poetry. But the parnassians did not consider this: They went to extraordinary trouble to find the *rime riche* with its *consonne d'appui* – pored over historical works and atlases, dived into scientific books and...catalogues, until poetry became a kind of punster's game, which reached its nadir of abjectness when Alphone [*sic*] Allais wrote:

Par le bois du Djinn, où s'entasse de l'effroi,
Parle, bois du gin ou cent tasses de lait froid.

[1] Francis Vielé-Griffin, 'In Memoriam Stéphane Mallarmé', *Plus loin* (Paris, 1906). The poem appears in *Poètes d'aujourd'hui*, II, *op. cit.*, p. 358, and is cited by de Souza, *Du Rythme, en français*, pp. 62–3.
[2] Théodore Banville, *Petit Traité de poésie français* in *Oeuvres* (Paris, 1891), pp. 52, 53, 65.
[3] Paul Verlaine, 'Art poétique', *Jadis et Naguère*, in *Oeuvres complètes*, I (Paris, 1959), p. 513.

The force of Nature could no further go; and the exhausted Parnassus sank into an idiocy of echolalia. Reacting against this servility to rhyme, the symbolists established the principle, which is sound aesthetically, that rhyme should be subordinated to the general music of the verse, and that where the music demanded it, rhyme should give place to assonance. The effect to be produced, and no rigid rule, was the sole arbitrament. On the appearance of Charles Guérin's *Le Sang du Crépuscule* [*sic*], Mallarmé wrote to the author in that curious prose of his:

Habitude du mètre en [*sic*] les complexité et fluidité, aussi, en la pensée, rien que de sûr parmi votre invention; même[,] une des toutes premières fois, l'assonance y suffisant à marquer le vers, comme coloration, apparaît dans son feu plus nu presque plus précieuse que la rime.[1]

Almost more precious than rhyme...no, as precious, in its place. Listen:

> Si j'ai parlé
> De mon amour, c'est à l'eau lente
> Qui m'écoute quand je me penche
> Sur elle; si j'ai parlé
> De mon amour, c'est au vent
> Qui rit et chuchote entre les branches;
> Si j'ai parlé de mon amour, c'est à l'oiseau
> Qui passe et chante
> Avec le vent;
> Si j'ai parlé
> C'est à l'echo.
>
> Si j'ai aimé de grand amour,
> Triste ou joyeux,
> Ce sont tes yeux;
> Si j'ai aimé de grand amour,
> Ce fut ta bouche grave et douce,
> Ce fut ta bouche;
> Si j'ai aimé de grand amour,
> Ce furent ta chair tiède et tes mains fraîches,
> Et c'est ton ombre que je cherche.[2]

With many of the younger generation, rhyme has fallen into complete disrepute. Rhyme, they say, is, in theatrical language, a "super," useful perhaps:

[1] Stéphane Mallarmé, 'Preface au *Sang des crépuscules*', *Oeuvres complètes*, ed. Henri Monder and G. Jean-Aubry (Paris, 1945), p. 858. The misprinted word is *ou*.

[2] Henri de Régnier, 'Odelette', IV', *Les Jeux rustiques et divins* (Paris, 1911), pp. 228–9. The poem appears in *Poètes d'aujourd'hui*, II, p. 133, and in the only two differences in spelling or punctuation in the two texts, Flint follows the reading found in the anthology.

To mark sometimes the end of a few verses of a dull rhythm.
To clash and roll when you must have cymbals and the drums,
To beat the step of a little dance, which makes do with it.
To give a heightened touch of preciousness to a poetic miniature.
To gild the edges of a madrigal.
To put on red heels in a "fête galante."
To polish the harness of bombast, if need be.
To fringe a curtain with tassels.
To give airs of refinement to imitations.
To make amusing little jokes.[1]

But assonance is rhyme with a mute, having, moreover, an unexpected-ness, nuances, and subtleties to which rhyme cannot attain; and the choice of an assonance is more difficult than the choice of a rhyme (which is very true, since to choose an assonance one must have a trained ear; to choose a rhyme one needs memory only); and even if a rhyme should offer itself – the old habit! – then tuck it away carefully in the body of the verse! Yet, they continue, the use of assonance as a rule would be as dangerous as the constant use of rhyme.

This, then, was the heritage left by the symbolist generation to the poets of to-day...Liberated from the tyranny of the ancient metrical system, they had bequeathed to them, not a form but a free spirit, capable of finding expression in an infinite variety of forms. The music of their language had been so enriched that it was like the revelation of the chromatic scale to a nation that had only known the diatonic; and the rhyme, which was dominant in the old scale (if I may dare use the phrase) had been subordinated to the general harmony of the new, lapsing into discreet assonances or disappearing altogether, if need be. And, with all, the conception of their art had been enlarged until it was as wide and deep as life itself: the poet was the instrument – which is an emotion wherein dailiness is solvent...

THE GENERATION OF 1900

In his speech at the banquet given last February in his honour, M. Paul Fort – the wonderful singer of *Les Ballades Françaises*, of which too little is known in England – tried to say an amiable word about every one of the younger generation that seethed around him. Alas! he mislaid the fourteenth page of his *palmarès*, and many names with many adjectives were lost. Anyone who writes about modern French poetry must lose his fourteenth page. I know that mine contains the names of the deliciously fantastic poets, Tristan Klingsor and André Salmon, of Roger Dévigne,

---

[1] Flint here translates from Georges Duhamel and Charles Vildrac, *Notes sur la technique poétique* (Paris, 1925; 1st pub. 1911), p. 43.

the apostle of "Visionnarisme," who has lived and suffered with the people, of Jacques Nayral, Fernand Divoire, the singer of the sufferings of poor children and of the "Urbs," of Henri Franck (who is dead), of Guillaume Apollinaire, a curious, fantastic, keen, supple poet, expert in subtle and piercing notations,[1] of Roger Allard, a cultivated, musical poet, who manipulates rhythm and phrase with a sure touch, of Léon Deubel, about whom M. Fernand Gregh wrote that his verses were "*sensitifs, frissonants, fluides, comme fleuris à la cime d'une lueur argentée,*" of Louis Mandin, an Ariel appealing to the Ariel in other men, of Guy Charles Cros, Fritz Vanderpijl, Jean Antoine Nau, Emile Cottinet...
– their names flow unceasingly to my pen; only the space at my disposal is limited...

In the following pages will be found grouped together some of the most representative poets of the present generation. There is hardly a common trait among them, even in the so-called "unanimist" school, unless it be that each is determined to sing only to the dictation of the daemon within him; so that the work of one is distinct from the work of any other. The confluence of the streams of romantic, parnassian and symbolist verse which carried them into the twentieth century seems to be bearing them on to that province of their art where poets speak the language of inspiration and intuition to assembled men: poetic drama.

I have to thank MM. Mercereau (especially), Florian-Parmentier and René Arcos for the very real assistance they have so willingly given me; and all the poets I have cited for the pleasure I have found in their work.

THREE DEMI-AÎNÉS: HENRI GHÉON AND THE "VERS LIBRE"

In reply to the inquiry regarding the *vers libre* which M. F. T. Marinetti, futurist and editor of *Poesia*, addressed to poets of all nations, M. Ghéon said that *vers libre*, both as verse and as free, had died on the day when the united effort of its apostles had set on foot the *analytical strophe*. Now was the period of construction...of rationalism. Besides, the only liberty in Art is the choice of a discipline. And the word verse, meaningless now in the academic sense – *versus*, will, if used at all, designate the rhythmic units, which, though each is given a line to itself, only count by their grouping, proportions and reciprocal relations in the strophe-organism uniting them:[2]

> Saine ivresse quotidienne,
> si connue

---

[1] Compare this statement with the one in the letter Flint received from Alexandre Mercereau on 9 June 1912 (pages 80–2).
[2] Henri Ghéon, 'Lettre sur le vers libre', *Nos Directions* (Paris, 1911), p. 223. Flint gives partial citation of this source for his translation.

que le coeur ne s'en défie point,
jour après jour,
je l'aurais bue
comme sans amour
– et mon coeur est plein:
plus d'autre soif,
plus d'autre faim
quand le vent pass![1]

There it is: each expressive unit of the thought, each logical unit of the discourse, will create a rhythmic unit in the strophe (as in the one above) which is the total, harmonious expression of a thought, i.e., an idea, a sentiment, or an image. That is M. Ghéon's rule, rational and no longer empirical. By it he claims to enter into the line of tradition. These logical rhythmic units have been received from every poet worthy of the name who has sung in the French language. According to the spirit of their age, Racine grouped together units of the same value, Hugo diversified them; and as, in the course of time, thought became more subtle, less calm, less evident, so the groups of units became richer, more numerous, and more varied, until, throwing off the external envelope of the alexandrine, they have attempted to exist by themselves. Moreover, existing by themselves, they can take full advantage of the musical resources of rhyme and assonance, placing these, undeterred by the reasonless exigency of the twelfth syllable, so that they bring out the rhythm of the strophe, and their values are never cribbed and crabbed.[2]

It will be seen that M. Ghéon is perfectly conscious of his Art. In *Du Rythme, en Français*, M. R. de Souza says that, with M. Francis Vielé-Griffin and M. Albert Mockel, *il est un de nos meilleurs et rares conscients*; but that his expression, *analytical strophe*, is as bad as that of *vers libre*, and in no way can it be opposed to the *verse*; for many ideas, sentiments and emotions do not lend themselves easily to this passionate shortening of our breathing – since small rhythmic elements set apart by themselves demand stoppages and renewed respirations; besides, there is a natural physiological tendency to pronounce in one breath successive groups of rhythmic feet, and the rhythmic content in this average length of a breathing can only be called a *verse*.[3]

[1] Henri Ghéon, 'Foi en la France', *Nouvelle Revue française*, IV (1 July 1910) 37. Flint cites the poem not from *NRF*, but from Robert de Souza's *Du Rythme, en français*, in which exactly these lines are quoted as an example of 'le rythme strophique'. Flint's quotation follows de Souza in two readings which differ from the *NRF* appearance. See de Souza, *op. cit.*, pp. 35, 38.

[2] The foregoing paragraph is a paraphrase of Ghéon, 'Lettre sur le vers libre', *op. cit.*, p. 225.

[3] As Flint indicates, he here is translating from Robert de Souza, *Du Rythme, en français*, *op. cit.*, p. 23.

In print, M. Ghéon's poems sometimes look like this:

C'est Alger
où tout germe
où tout fleure
où tout fleurit
mûrit:
voici
toutes les graines,
tous les fruits,
d'ici
d'ailleurs...
semez!
cueillez![1]

See how the typographical arrangement lends a superficial cleverness to the malicious critic who said that M. Ghéon was the only poet who wrote with a pin! And yet, if you discount a slight staccato effect, which is either involuntarily felt by the reader or forced on the poet by his form, you will find that these short lines, read correctly, have a very cunning rhythm. Not all M. Ghéon's books are printed in this way. *Chansons d'Aube*, the earliest, has the normal appearance of *vers libre*. *Le Pain, tragédie populaire*, is printed as prose, with dashes between each rhythmic unit.

Le Pain, which was only recently played – much altered – and printed, was written ten years ago, but it is nevertheless a manifestation of the renascence of poetical drama which has been preparing for some time past in France, and which seems to be on the point of complete fruition, – a drama neither romantic nor realistic, but classic, the classicism which unites Euripides, Sophocles, Goethe, Racine and Shakespeare: equilibrium in the groupings of beings and in their psychological construction, such as traits, sentiments, gestures, by which a personage appears really to exist, – precision and concordant generalities, capable of creating a "life" and "men" by the side of life and humanity.[2] *Le Pain* is the story of a town in famine after a war and of a visionary master-baker, Pierre Franc, who gives rather than sells and, in giving, rouses the suspicion of proletarian agitators. There is a hidden store of flour (his wife's father's) in the town, which Pierre discovers too late to stop rioting and bloodshed. He speaks plaintively:

– Coule le sang! – la flamme s'éteigne – dans les yeux clairs et joyeux! – Celui qui la gardait du vent – souffle son haleine sur elle!

(*Silence*)

[1] Henri Ghéon, *Algérie* (Brussels, 1906), p. 6. [Flint's note.]
[2] The idea that a new poetic drama which is neither romantic nor realistic, but classical, is developing in France. Flint refers to Ghéon, 'Notes sur le drame poétique', *Nos Directions, op. cit.*, p. 37.

– Caille le sang! – la vie se fane – sur sa tige de chair virile! – celui qui la devait soigner – comme une plante bien aimée, – la laisse ronger par le mal, – à la racine!

(*Silence*)

– Sèche le sang! – l'âme se retire[,] – des corps sains, jeunes et puissants! – Celui qui devait les nourir – les abandonne.

(*S'animant*)

– Et celui-là, rien ne l'excuse, – à la portée de sa bonté, – il avait tout, – la plus riche des nourritures. – Il ne lui fallait qu'un peu se pencher... – c'était beaucoup... – il n'a pas su le faire!

(*Silence*)

– Il a connu la détresse publique; – pas à pas, il en a suivi le progrès; – le remède était là, – oh dites! – qu'a-t-il fait – pour la prodiguer à ses frères malades? – D'heure en heure, de jour en jour, il recula, – jusqu'au jour irrémédiable!

(*Silence*)

– Devant le peuple, au matin du crime, – il allait parler... – Un de ses mots eût décidé – du destin de toute une ville! – Son pouls battait une horrible fièvre... – le mot touchaitses lèvres: – il l'a tu.

(*Silence*)

– Coule, caille, – sèche le sang! – des corps puissants – la chaleur s'en aille; – je l'ai voulu...

(*Il retombe abattu*)[1]

The selfishness of his wife and the suspicions and hatreds of the people bring Pierre Franc to his death, – at the hands of those whom he has nourished. A noble play.

But here is a dramatic verse which is not arbitrary, which can be made as living as a poet's genius can order it,[2] and one which, in its presentment, as M. Ghéon has found, leaves the actors in no doubt of the author's intentions.

M. Ghéon is the author of: Poems, *Chansons d'Aube, La Solitude de l'Eté, Algérie*; Plays, *Le Pain, L'Eau de Vie*: Novels, *Le Consolateur, La Vieille Dame des Rues*. He contributes a monthly article on poetry to the *Nouvelle Revue Français*.

JEAN ROYÈRE & "LE NÉO-MALLARMISME"

M. Jean Royère is the editor of an important and valiant review, *La Phalange,* and has grouped around him as his collaborators many of the most reputed of the symbolists, as MM. André Gide, Gustave Kahn, Stuart Merrill, Henri de Régnier, P. N. Roinard, Robert de Souza,

---

[1] Henri Ghéon, *Le Pain, tragédie populaire* (Paris, 1912), pp. 81–3. The ellipses appear in the original.

[2] It must be understood that there is a point beyond which, in the disposition of its rhythmic units, a regular verse form cannot go, and still retain its form. [Flint's note.]

Laurent Tailhade and Vielé-Griffin,[1] besides younger poets, as MM. Léon Deubel, Guy Lavaud, Louis Mandin, Tristan Klingsor, John Antoine Nau, Jules Romains, Charles Vildrac, André Spire, Georges Périn. M. Royère has submitted to the "Mallarmean discipline." To the accusation of obscurity which has been brought against him he answers that his poetry is as obscure as the lily, escaping all syllogism, but not intuition; it does not express because it evokes: *elle a la pudeur de l'infini...La poésie que j'aime,* he says, *est une quiétude intense.*

Not understanding him – I avow it frankly – I will quote from an article by John Antoine Nau, for whom M. Royère is a great poet. He says that Jean Royère is a poet endowed in an admirable fashion, a most original artist, who has understood that the Mallarmean shadow is more divinely nuanced, more poignant, with its subtle diversity of reflections, than the eternal though beautiful savageness of the sun in its fullness, forever blue and gold, red and gold, blond and gold; and out of M. Royère's verses he proceeds to build the magic palace of his art, which, situated on a large plateau overlooking abysses and furious and calm forests, is furnished with all discreet and beautiful things.[2]

But what is "Néo-Mallarmisme"? It is this: everything having been said, in poetry, on a superficial domain, a profound poetry is henceforth indispensable; inspiration is more complex: the poet must recreate his soul, empty his mind of reminiscences, and let his poetry become a creation, whose source is necessarily his interior being – a *discovery*, *concrete* and *sensuous*. The poem will be an harmonious flow of nuances, abhorrent of any philosophy or abstraction, obscure for minds working under their sway; and as at each moment the weft of its thought will be threaded by the shuttle of sensation and feeling it will be a tissue of analogies, divinations and intuitions. It is, therefore, a music, and demands a musical rhythm, a *vers libre.*[3]

Thrène

Ce bandeau de ciel las aux tempes de la ville
M'apaise – gris léger, gris de l'âme. – Je vois

---

[1] The foregoing is virtually a translation from Florian-Parmentier, *La Littérature et l'époque, op. cit.*, p. 44.

[2] John Antoine Nau, 'La Demeure de poète Jean Royère', *Vers et Prose*, XIII (March–May 1908) 87.

[3] The foregoing paragraph is made up almost exclusively of phrases translated from Florian-Parmentier and arranged in very slightly different order. Cf. *La Littérature et l'époque, op. cit.*, p. 45. The comparison is instructive as a guide to Flint's handling of literary debt. He indicates a reference, on this occasion, to the correct page; it is unclear without comparison, however, that the one text is almost a translation of the other. When Flint straightforwardly translates without rearrangement, he usually gives a reference to the book and precedes his translation with the phrase 'the author says'. When he paraphrases, even with minor changes, his citation of sources is frequently unclear and many times is omitted, although a general expression of debt may appear somewhere in the essay.

Des regards qu'atténue un mirage, et des voix
Naissent presque du nimbe épars comme ingénues;
Qu'est-ce qui tinte ainsi sous le dôme des nues,
Ephémère!...Recule au faste oriental
De l'enfance la joie éclatante! Serviles
Cieux splendides et nus où flambait le brutal
Soleil: matins de gloire et pourpres vespérales,
J'ai sur vos parvis d'or secoué mes sandales!
O fronts spirituels de l'aube, ondes d'un soir
Cerclé d'ombre au Jardin des Ombres, seuls asiles,
Je ne goûterai pas un autre nonchaloir
Que vos reflets peuplés d'extases puériles,
Vos arrière-regards! Les voûtes du dortoir
Offrent un rêve éteint à la lune qui hante
Le parc silencieux où se fête une absente...
Ci-gît tant de passé!

                      Certes l'écueil où brise,
Avec la nef, le flot des heures se précise
Déjà pour toi, pour toi, mélancolique! et tel
Que se dressait aux jours d'imposture l'autel
Funéraire. Au tournant d'une de tes allées,
Parle, si tu le veux, aux chères Immolées
Dont tu tissais jadis le voile hyménéal –
Et songe que tu dois une hostie à Baal.[1]

M. Royère is the author of *Exile Doré* (1898), *Eurythmies* (1904), and *Soeur de Narcisse Nue* (1907). The poem I quote is from the last book, his best.

ANDRÉ SPIRE

I approach the work of M. André Spire with some emotion, for I know – his books tell you – that here is a man whose heart has been wrung by the spectacle of life, which he has seen with the curiously keen and unsophisticated vision of a child with a man's intelligence. There are suffering, stupidity, callousness, sordidness and purse-pride on every side of you, he cries, *et vous riez!* The irony of it is not lost on him; he is of the same spiritual and terrestrial race as Heine. He wanders through the cities watching men and women at work; he is not afraid to write of a servant dusting and the gritty loathsomeness to her of the dust. He sees a peasant woman, and challenges us:

Vois cette femme, ces mains gercées, ce cou ridé,
Ces cheveux jaunes, cette peau rouge et ce gros ventre
Et[,] chante, si tu l'oses encore, chante
Le Travail, le Soleil et la Maternité.[2]

---

[1] Jean Royère, 'Thrène', *Soeur de Narcisse nue* (Paris, 1907), pp. 65–7.
[2] André Spire, 'Paysanne', *Et Vous Riez* in *Versets* (Paris, 1908), p. 39.

But in spite of all his exhortations to the people, *le peuple* –

> Il n'a pas relevé la tête.
> Il a gémi:
> "A quoi bon ces grands cris sur mes épaules lasses."[1]

And he concludes:

> Non, je ne chanterai pas pour toi, Peuple.
> Grand peuple dépouillé, grand peuple malheureux,
> Nous n'irons plus troubler ta torpeur résignée.
> Sans remords de nous être arrachés de toi-même,
> Nous irons loin de toi mener nos fortes vies.
> Mais, n'oubliant jamais d'où nous sommes sortis,
> Nous irons nous grouper, parfois, sur ton passage,
> Et, tristement pleurer sur ton destin tragique,
> O fleuve infortuné de germes avortés.[2]

M. Spire, who has studied in the laboratories of the Abbé Rousselot,[3] though he went there only to confirm his own intuitions, writes in a free rhythmic form, rarely rhyming; but what need?

> J'ai cueilli cette branche de saule fleurie,
> Près du fleuve ivre encore des orages de mars.
> Longtemps je l'ai portée à travers la campagne;
> Et ses chatons de soie me chatouillaient les tempes,
> Comme les frisons fous de tes tempes dorées;
> Et ses chatons poudrés, me caressant la bouche,
> Remplissaient l'air sucré d'un parfum chaud, pareil
> A l'odeur de ton corps lorsque tu sors du bain.[4]

M. Spire's book *Versets* (1908) is in two parts, *Et Vous Riez*, from which I have quoted, and *Poèmes Juifs*, dedicated to all those who lived, fought and died for the raising of the Jewish dignity; as an epigraph to these sad, noble, and yet exalted, and yet exalting, poems, he writes, "You ask me why I love these parias, the only proletariat in whom I can still hope" –

> – O mes frères, ô mes égaux, ô mes amis.
> Peuple sans droits, peuple sans terre;
> Nation, à qui les coups de toutes les nations
> Tinrent lieu de patrie,
> Nulle retraite ne peut me défendre de vous.[5]

A sincerity which will not allow itself to be led into cheap deceits animates all his poetry. I will quote one poem in full:

---

[1] 'Au Peuple', *Ibid.*, p. 22.
[2] *Ibid.*, pp. 22–3.
[3] Cf. note 2, p. 89.
[4] 'J'ai cueilli cette branche de saule fleurie...', *Ibid.*, p. 51.
[5] 'Rêves juifs', *Poèmes juifs* in *Versets*, *op. cit.*, p. 180.

Nudités

> Les cheveaux sont une nudite.
>
> *Talmud.*

Tu m'as dit: Je veux être ta camarade;
Je veux entrer chez toi sans avoir peur de te troubler[;]
Nous passerons de longues soirées, en causeries;
Nous penserons ensemble à nos frères qu'on tue;
Nous irons, à travers le cruel univers,
Découvrir un pays où reposer leur tête.
Mais, je ne veux pas voir tes prunelles briller,
Ni les veines brûlantes de ton front se distendre,
Car je suis ton égale et non pas une proie.
Regarde! Mes habits sont chastes, presque pauvres,
Et[,] tu ne vois pas même la base de mon cou.

Moi je t'ai répondu: Femme, tu es nue.
Les cheveux de ton cou sont frais comme une coupe;
Ton chignon qui s'écroule palpite comme un sein;
Tes bandeaux sont lascifs comme un troupeau de chèvres...
Fais couper tes cheveux.

Femme, tu es nue.
Sur notre livre ouvert se posent tes mains nues;
Tes mains, la fin subtile de ton corps,
Tes mains sans bagues, qui vont toucher les miennes tout à l'heure...
Femme, mutile tes mains.
Femme, tu es nue.
Ta voix chantante de ta poitrine monte;
Ta voix, ton souffle, la chaleur elle-même de ta chair,
Qui sur mon corps s'étale, puis pénètre en ma chair.
Femme, arrache ta voix.[1]

Since he published *Versets*, spring has lured M. Spire *Vers les Routes Absurdes*, and he has walked along them with the same clairvoyant irony, tenderness and passionate humanity.

L'ABBAYE

The story of l'Abbaye, the story of a few young men, who, *exaltés de ferveur artistiques et avides de remplir [librement] leurs jours selon leurs voeux, résolurent de bâtir leur Thélème, d'y rassembler leurs vies et d'y subsister,*[2] is one of the most moving stories that has come out of France. The poets among these young men (all of about twenty-five years of age) were Henri-Martin Barzun, René Arcos, Charles Vildrac and Alexandre Mercereau.[3] There were also painters, among whom, Albert Gleizes,

[1] 'Nudités', *Ibid.*, pp. 195–6.
[2] Charles Vildrac, 'Avertissement', *Images et Mirages* (Paris, 1908), p. 11.
[3] René Arcos, in a letter to Flint on 12 August 1912, protested the account of the formation of the Abbey, especially the list of poets Flint indicated were associated with the founding. Flint defended himself in a letter of 20 August: 'Vous dites que j'ai négligé les détails que

sculptors, engravers and musicians. The law of society weighed heavily upon them all. They were full of aspirations which they could not realize, and so they determined to gather together their resources and to live in common as artists. On a rainy day in October, MM. Vildrac and Arcos discovered the ideal retreat which was to shelter their dream. It was a vast abandoned property situated at Créteil, about fourteen miles from Paris. With an emotion that cannot be described, they ran over for the first time the paths of the immense wet and quivering park. The wild grasses had invaded everything; the bushes had grown taller than men. Every kind of tree grew in this faery park that was so happily "ill-combed." The neglected orchard was in a lamentable state. Not a door nor a window of the house, which had been empty for years, would shut. Branches entered the rooms by the broken panes, and the damp had ruined the floorings. But the house pleased them and their comrades, and they took it, at an exaggerated rental, for the owner had got wind of their quality.

In possession of the house, their first care was to make it habitable, and they became in turn house-painters, carpenters, locksmiths, gardeners, giving their whole heart to the task. One of them, for instance, would be in the branches of a fruit-tree, pruning it, while a companion below read to him the manual of the perfect gardener! At the end of a month the property was unrecognizable.

A friend having advanced the funds, they installed a small printing press in the house. They hoped to be able to live by publishing artistically printed books. Each morning they worked in the printing room; in the afternoon they were free for their own personal work. Sunday was consecrated to friends; and from time to time they gave open-air recitals of their poems, while in their "salon" would be an exhibition of their paintings and etchings. There were never more than ten men at l'Abbaye (there were also women and children); but on Sundays three hundred people would foregather there.

But, alas! in spite of the widespread interest they awakened, the publishing business did not pay its way; the heavy rental crushed them;

vous avez bien voulu me donner sur l'Abbaye. Mais, mon cher Monsieur, voyez donc à la page 369. De "The law of society weighed heavily upon them all" jusqu'à "*Je rêve l'Abbaye*," c'est-à-dire, le gros, le fond, de cette partie de mon article, c'est une traduction et une adaptation de votre lettre. Je n'ai fait que la généraliser un peu, et qu'arranger un peu différement, selon un ordre dicté par mes lectures par-ci par-là, les noms que vous m'avez donnés, en y ajoutant quelques uns.' The defense offers accurate insight into Flint's methods of composing the essay, for a comparison with Arcos's letter of 29 May 1912 (published on pages 75–7) shows that Flint's account of the Abbey is indeed largely a close paraphrase, even translation, of the information Arcos sent. Because of the influence of Mercereau, Flint did, however, assign Alexandre Mercereau and Henri-Martin Barzun an inaccurately large role in the founding of the Abbey. The unpublished Arcos–Flint exchange is in the Academic Center Library, The University of Texas.

indelicate people abused them; and after fourteen months of heroic effort, after a terrible winter passed without fire and without sufficient food, they were obliged to give in, and leave the house which had harboured so much hope.

Je rêve l'Abbaye – ah, sans abbé! –
Je rêve l'Abbaye hospitalière
A tous épris d'art plus ou moins crottés
Et déshérités...

En telle Hellade très-fleurie,
Et pas pourvue d'académies,
Bien loin, je rêve l'Abbaye
Gaie et recueillie,
Où vivre libres, en thélémites passionnés!
Où vivre quelques-uns et quelques-unes,
Artistes, artisans, buveurs de lune...

Nous nous aimerions mieux que des frères;
Elles s'aimeraient mieux que des soeurs,
Et nous seraient douces comme des fleurs;
Tout n'est-il pas possible en rêve...

Je rêve l'Abbaye...[1]

It was something more and something less than a dream to these artists, and it will be a dream to them for the rest of their lives...Other poets, more independent financially, who gathered round the Abbaye group and formed part of it, were MM. Georges Duhamel, Jules Romains, Théo Varlet, Paul Castiaux, and Georges and Cécile Périn. All are now accredited poets...

HENRI-MARTIN BARZUN

M. Henri-Martin Barzun, following his elder, M. Remy de Gourmont, that keen, genial mind, maintains that the poet has no longer the right to be ignorant of any of the manifestations and the results of human curiosity and probing.[2] The bearing of an idea, of a fact, may be incalculable; and an art that excludes these from its purview must become inferior. A poet, above all, is forbidden to be ignorant, for does he not, by the knowledge of every evidence, nourish the truth of his intuitions, and become the pioneer of future accomplishment? The only impure element in art will be that which has not been assimilated by the consciousness and thereafter transfigured by vision.

[1] Charles Vildrac, 'Je rêve l'Abbaye...', Images et Mirages, op. cit., pp. 33–4.
[2] In this statement and most of the succeeding two paragraphs Flint condenses major points in H.-M. Barzun's L'Ere du drame (Paris, 1912), especially from pp. 16–53 passim. Flint's fourth paragraph is drawn chiefly from pp. 77–9 of the same volume. From the succinctness of the summary it is clear that Flint was thoroughly familiar with the book.

M. Barzun sees that the psychology of humankind has to go through four main stages of development. First the individual – in the early ages, a man conceived himself as an entity; then the collective – men became conscious of themselves as groups and nations; then the human – electricity having made humanity global, the whole world quivers with every catastrophe, every tragedy of magnitude; and lastly, the universal – the prescience of sidereal life, the scientific knowledge of the cosmos, the philosophic search for the divine: human life being but a feeble offshoot of universal life. From the universal, by a natural return on himself, man is led once again to the conception of the individual, but an individual enriched by many more points of contact with a life conceived cosmically.

Poetry, too, must pass through these stages, and is now, M. Barzun thinks, in the era of drama, which will reach its apogee in the present generation. The philosophers, Durkheim, Le Bon, Tarde, having lit, the poets, Verhaeren, Paul Adam and Rosny,[1] having led, the way, a poet is now capable of revealing his multiple vision of the individual, in its vital relationships, instincts, pleasures, love; of the collectivity, in its elementary, aggregative relationships – appetites, interests, sentiments, religions; of the human, in its evident physical and biological solidarity (races, peoples, languages, countries) – in its conflicts, disasters, discoveries, destiny; and of the universal, in its cosmogonic revelations, its identity, mystery, divinity. And in the vast synthesis that M. Barzun has in mind, simple lyricism becomes absorbed by a manifold, superior lyricism: voices, presences, entities, crowds, speak, and the *poem* becomes *drama*. With this conception, all the forms of poetry may be impregnated, renewed, magnified: novel, poem, epic, play, legend, mystery – every form...The poet becomes the interpreter of the universal consciousness, the inspired bard, the supreme judge of the age; and his song changes from the monodic to the polyphonic, wherein life is dramatized psychologically by its multiple voices, the form being a long rhythmic melody, whose cadence, purely musical, is determined internally by the poetic emotion.

In this sense, M. Barzun has composed his own work, *La Terrestre Tragédie*, of which, so far, four parts have appeared. The first volume, *Poème de l'Adolescence* (lyrical) has only, he says, a chronological value (1903–1904). The second, *Poème de l'Homme et Chant de l'Idée* (1904–1906), conceived under the influence of his elders, is *interpsychological* – Tarde's word for the collective psychology – and shows a striving after dramatization. The third, *La Montagne*, a poetical drama of love and the earth, develops a purely psychological action (deliberately anti-

---

[1] I know that Paul Adam and Rosny are novelists; but in *my* language they are called poets, preferably. [Flint's note.]

103

theatrical), wherein entity-personages move about in a legendary atmosphere. Its dramatization is amplified by a collective hymn, evolving in the course of five episodes. The fourth is *l'Hymne des Forces* (1912), a dramatic song, wherein are heard the multiple voices of the world: heroes, prophets, athletes of the ideal, mages, geniuses, poets, visionaries, pioneers, apostles, God; it aspires to intuitive expression, to the identification of the human with the universal. It ends with a long hymn, *Apothéose des Forces*. The verses I quote are from the *Chant d'Agonistès* in the section *Antagonisme* of *l'Hymne des Forces*. *Antagonisme* is the word M. Barzun uses to typify the sentiment of struggle, resistance and contradiction which has always existed in opposition to the collective, human, universal will.

Agonistès

I

Contre mes craintes, sans répit,
Contre le mal qui m'envahit,
Contre mes goûts, mes habitudes,
Mes désirs et mes volontés,
Contre toutes mes servitudes,

Une voix me crie de lutter
Pour m'affranchir du joug des hommes,
Pour m'affranchir de mes propres entraves,
Pour exister et dominer
En victorieux parmi les hommes.

Contre mes joies et mes tendresses,
Contre les forces qui m'oppressent,
Pacifiques ou meurtrières,
Contre l'esprit et la matière
Ne pas me dresser pour lutter,

Ne pas être *l'Antagoniste*!

C'est renier ma destinée.

II

Regardant près de moi, sans cesse,
Je vivifie mon âme par l'example:

La chêne au sein de la forêt,
Dérobe aux arbres qui l'entourent
L'air et la lumière du jour.

Dans les abîmes de la mer
Règne la force des espèces
Successives maîtresses de la vie,
De la puissance à la faiblesse,
Du monstre aux infusoires infinis.
En l'espace, les lointains astres
Immobiles aux yeux aveugles,

> Bondissent fous dans l'Insondable,
> Livrés au joyeux rythme universel,
>
> Tournoyant, avançant parallèles,
> S'attirant, s'expulsant et jamais se heurtant
> Sur leur orbites de mystère,
>
> Adversaires dans l'univers fraternel;
>
> S'absorbant vers en centre parfois,
> Pour renaître bientôt en un géant soleil
> Fulgurant, formidable:
>
> Mais déjà la vie impatiente
> S'éveille au flanc du nouvel astre,
>
> Créant dans son rayonnement
> L'inconnu destin planétaire.

IV

> Hardiment, je m'avance et passe
> A travers les individus:
> Indifférents, dispersés sur l'espace,
> Groupés, délibérant compacts.
>
> Je ne demande à leur présence
> Qu'une lueur pour mon esprit,
> Qu'un palier nouveau pour mon âme,
>
> En m'accroissant à leur contact
> Selon l'image de la vie
> Qui a traversé tous les âges,
>
> Fluide en la chaîne des espèces
> Triomphant de tous les combats,
> Pour venir éclater en moi,
> Divine foudre.[1]

M. Henri-Martin Barzun was the principal founder of l'Abbaye,[2] and the first poet of his generation to voice the hymn of the collectivity.

ALEXANDRE MERCEREAU

M. Alexandre Mercereau is an interesting and attractive personality. He began his literary career in 1901, contributing poems and critical articles to the *Oeuvre d'Art Internationale*. In 1904, he founded a review, *La Vie*. In 1906, he was in Russia, editing a fabulous review, *La Toison d'Or*; he was also on the staff of the Muscovite review, *The Balance*. He was one of the founders, in 1907, of L'Abbaye. In 1909, he organized

---

[1] Henri-Martin Barzun, 'Agonistès', *L'Hymne des forces* (Paris, 1912).‡

[2] This statement is simply incorrect. Arcos and Vildrac were the principal founders of the Abbey. Flint's statement, as he explained to Arcos in his letter of 20 August 1912 (see footnote 3, page 101) was founded on a similar assertion by Alexandre Mercereau. See *La Littérature et les idées nouvelles* (Paris, 1912), p. 300.

and became director of the literary section of the Salon d'Automne. He is, with Paul Fort, co-editor of the best French review, *Vers et Prose*; he contributes largely to other reviews; and he is the secretary of La Société Internationale de Recherches Psychiques and of L'Oeuvre du Jardin de Jenny (a society whose object apparently is to provide work-girls with window flower-gardens). During these years, M. Mercereau published *Les Thuribulums affaissés*, poèmes (1905); *Gens de là et d'ailleurs*, contes psychologiques (1907); *Les Contes des Ténèbres* (1910); *La Littérature et les Idées Nouvelles*, a survey of the French literary movement of the last few years, especially of the year 1911; *La Conque Miraculeuse*, légendes de la Mer; and *Paroles devant la Vie*, a book of lyrical and moral disserta-tions (1912). M. Mercereau is a very active critic, with a formidable erudition, and a most disinterested[1] propagandist in the field of art, ever ready to publish the merit of other artists, expending his energies prodigally wherever art or life may be served. He is the kernel of a group of young French poets who are impregnated with the occult sciences, and who have metaphysical, mystical and esoteric aspirations. M. Mercereau is a very remarkable man.

The lyricism of *Les Thuribulums affaissés* has been well characterized by M. Jean Metzinger.[2] He says that M. Mercereau wished to see whether it was possible to adjust to new conceptions the old poetical material of symbolism. A troubled and charming art resulted, barbarous and precious; reason espouses fantasy; metaphysical anguishes are mingled with human clamourings. Swans float towards heroines who gather stars on the crepuscular water. The moon abets grammatical phantasmagorias. Barrel-organs bray in the walkyrian nights. Chimney-pots vibrate with chivalric echoes; wind and death howl under the doors. Sometimes a flash lights up solemn and spiritual vistas, and a grief, whose depth is measured by the duration of the thinking world, engulfs the faery islets. Here is one short poem.

Les Heures Tombent des Horloges

La rafale ébranle des cloches
dont le son s'essaime en mon coeur.
Les heures tombent des horloges
avec des sanglots de douleur.

Un orgue vieux de Barbarie
a le las du deuil en la voix;
il est si loin des rêveries
monotones des autrefois...

---

[1] As the angry response of René Arcos to distortions concerning the Abbey showed (see footnote 3, page 100), Mercereau was neither so disinterested nor so unbiased as Flint supposed at the time of the writing of this essay.

[2] The source of the succeeding sentences Flint attributes to Jean Metzinger, *Alexandre Mercereau, essai critique* (Paris, 1912).

Ces crissements des girouettes!
Oh! complaintes sans variété!...
On dirait passer la brouette
de l'identique éternité!

Dans les ruelles solitaires
mon triste corps est tant secoué
que je sens s'égrener à terre
ma pauvre âme déracinée.[1]

But M. Mercereau has abandoned verse. His lyricism seems to demand the larger measures of prose. *Paroles devant la Vie* are poetry, if by poetry one is to understand words creating by their reverberations the illusion of an intenser life. These *Paroles* might even be printed as blank verse, were it not that their effect as prose is somehow nobler.

[Flint quotes an extended prose passage of 'Paroles devant la femme enceinte' from *Paroles devant la vie,* and suggests that Mercereau's lyricism shows itself even in his short stories. He concludes:]

M. Mercereau is a thinker who is an artist, and an erudite, who, as a poet, has carried lyricism in prose to the summit of his intelligence.

THÉO VARLET, PAUL CASTIAUX, *LES BANDEAUX D'OR* AND "NÉO-PAGANISME"

One of the most interesting and the most devoted to pure letters of the innumerable *revues des jeunes* is *Les Bandeaux d'Or*, which was founded in 1906 by Théo Varlet, Paul Castiaux, P.-J. Jouve and E. Charpentier. MM. Varlet and Castiaux are both apostles of an intellectualized sentiment, which has been called *néo-paganisme*, and which is, in expression, a desire to live life fully, and, in expending its riches largely, to find once more the profound joys of the animal spirits.[2]

M. Varlet, although an active writer – he was *directeur* of *l'Essor* in 1898–9, was also one of the founders of the *Beffroi*; has contributed to some thirty reviews; and publishes his "Tramp's Notebook" regularly in *Les Bandeaux d'Or* – is an aristocrat of letters, and, disdainful of public opinion, he has had most of his books – those containing his best work – printed for private circulation only. He is a vagabond poet, loving to wander over Europe, watching its life with an intelligence that has been nourished on the classics and modern biology, and sharpened by the philosophies of Spinoza, Goethe and Nietzsche; but always the horror of the industrial north, with its factories and smoke, sends him back to

---

[1] Alexandre Mercereau, 'Les Heures tombent des horloges', *Les Thuribulums affaisés* (Paris 1905).‡
[2] P.-J. Jouve, *Les Bandeaux d'Or*, November, 1911. [Flint's note.]

the blue skies and seas of the Mediterranean shore, where he has elected his home.

If his poetry can be said to have a dominant theme, it is this discord between the sun and smoke-laden fog, between the amenities of the south and the brutalities of the north. If his poetry can be said to have a predominant pitch, it is the high pitch of an uncompromising individualism. M. Varlet is in many respects an isolated poet; but he is a rare poet also, loving words, and ideas, and rhythms, and music. He is one of those challenging spirits, like Nietzsche, who seem to have been thrust among men and cities to be their incarnate criticism, and at the same time creators of beauty – a beauty that is pungent with contempt for ugliness.

Brise Marine

Azur sur la verdure infinie des prairies,
Azur tout plein le ciel, azur, soleil et vent,
C'est le printemps sur les polders de Flandre.

Le vierge vent marin, venu des dunes blanches,
Jusques au fond de l'horizon
S'écoule infiniment sur les prairies du Zwyn,
Sans nul – ô joie de mes poumons profonds –
Sans le moindre, des lieues à la ronde,
Tuyau d'usine.

Polychromie, là-bas, parmi, les prairies vertes:
Rouges, noires et blanches,
Le vieux troupeau chrétien des vaches ruminantes
Broute l'herbe – l'herbe émaillée de pâquerettes.

Et moi, debout sur les talus des digues,
– Reniant votre étable empouacrée, ô villes,
Et mes frères humains, et leurs rêves séniles –
Je tette
– Non, vaches, non! tout n'est pas dit, tout n'est pas bu! –
Je tette à pleins naseaux
Le vent.

O Flandre en matin neuf, azur, soleil et vent,
Poison nouveau;
Drogue syprême,
Salut!
Que l'oubliée ivresse du vierge oxygène,
Vent marin, vent du Nord, vent toxique,
Regonfle la vigueur des désirs ataviques.

Assez brouté, troupeau, ton destin nonchalant,
Assez cassé, couard, tout héroïque élan,
En route!
La mer est là, toute
La mer:

Viens-y rêver, bon mythologue, aux âges
Où bifurquèrent
Vers notre humanité les frères mammifères.

Debout, fils ruminant de chrétiens et de lâches,
La mer païenne, la mer libre,
La mer charrie encore, peut-être, en quelque fond,
Le rire à pleine chair des antiques tritons;

Et peut-être, joie baptismale, y jaillirai-je
Natif
Nu jusqu'au coeur, dans le soleil et le vent vierge!

Bah! – Les vaches aussi, jusqu'à la fin des temps
Brouteront, vaches, les pâquerettes du printemps!

Car rêver de renaître heroïque et brutal,
C'est facile
Loin des villes!
Mais que vaudra, tantôt,
Contre les asphyxies en bêtise fatale
Du troupeau?

Azur! Soleil de juin! – Et, tandis que ruminent,
Blanches, rouges, et noires, les vaches de Zwyn,
Le coeur gros de spéculations philosophiques,
Je m'assieds sur la digue et bourre une autre pipe.

Or, lente, et délaissant le fraternel bétail
Que stupéfie la joie des médiocres mangeailles,
Une vache aberrante est venue devant moi
Aux ronces de l'enclos gratter ses fanons gras.

Dis, bonne vache pas-comme-les-autres,
Ton mufle à reniflé l'air d'un destin plus beau,
Et dans tes yeux pensifs de belle zélandaise
Passe la nostalgie d'héroïques genèses.

– Ah! n'être pas de ceux qui dans leur sort se vautrent
Et s'en aller hors du troupeau
Tout le long de la mer aux prairies infinies,
Vers le miraculeux gazon des Utopies! –

Survache! toi aussi, n'est-ce pas? – ô survache
Ma soeur, viens, faut que moi, surhomme, je t'embrasse![1]

M. Varlet is the author of *Heures de Rêve* (1898), *Notes et Poèmes* (1905), *Le Dernier Satyre* (1905), *Notations* (1906), *Poèmes Choisis* (1906–10): the last three are *hors commerce*.

M. Paul Castiaux, who was also one of the founders of the *Beffroi*, has been director of *Les Bandeaux d'Or* since 1908.

M. Castiaux is a musician (he is a critic of music), using words as his

[1] Théo Varlet, 'Brise marine'.‡

medium. Much of his poetry is a pure paraphrase of musical motives, as M. Théo Varlet has shown in the *Beffroi*. Fragments of Debussy:

> Caresse – à peine – aux moiteurs tièdes de vertige
> Calme – plus calme encore – apaise la langueur
> Immatérielle ainsi qu'une grande fleur pâle... [1]

of Wagner:

> Et d'un geste suprême domptant leurs chevaux,
> Debout sur les arçons, porteuses des héros,
> Emplissant d'un seul cri d'airain l'immensité,
> Les Walkyries saluent le Walhalla qui s'ouvre! [2]

abound in his work. But the appeal of music – that intoxication wherein the material vibration has so large a part – is not alone; it is accompanied by the illumination of vivid imagery:

> Au ras des dunes,
> Classiquement importune
> A ce soir parfumé d'essences recueillies,
> La pleine lune
> Caresse d'inutile ivoire le ciel vert. [3]

With an ear so cunningly attuned to music, and an eye so keenly sensitive to colour atmosphere – an interpenetration that harmonizes elsewhere than in space – and M. Castiaux has rarely need of rhyme. His verse has an interior music. Repeat this *Lied au Crépuscule*:

> Parmi la solitude tiède le soir chante:
> Le soir, tout frémissant comme un sanglot d'amour,
> Se dorlote aux terrasses bleues du crépuscule.
> Et des langueurs de lied caressent de l'extase.
>
> Sur le marbre poli de la terrasse blanche,
> Le crépuscule, tout vibrant d'agonie lente,
> Se parfume indiciblement de violettes.
>
> Il fait très doux, et sur le ciel en reposoir
> Des nuages d'or blond, fluides chevelures,
> En longues soies à la dérive s'infléchissent.
>
> Le cristal inouï d'archets crépusculaires
> Fond une pluie – caresse infinie – de pétales
> Sur la mer sommeillant aux préludes de l'ombre.
>
> C'est le premier beau soir d'été. Nous contemplons
> Radieux, débordants des philtres éternels
> Qui coulent clairs sur nos désirs comme des sources,
> La nuit glissant ainsi qu'un long troupeau de fleurs[.]

[1] Paul Castiaux.‡   [2] Paul Castiaux.‡
[3] Castiaux, 'Crépuscule de septembre' *La Joie Vagabonde* (Paris, 1909), p. 20.

Oh! les fleurs de la nuit se pressent sur nos lèvres
En larges thyrses ruisselantes d'étoiles bleues.
Par delà l'horizon ineffable, la lune[,]
Comme un baiser d'opale, monte vers notre étreinte.

Écoute: la nuit change ainsi qu'une féerie
Des rhapsodes [*sic*] d'amour aux harpes de l'Extase!
Écoute: sous les doigts d'invisibles caresses,
La nuit, la pure nuit[,] berce des encensoirs.

Des gouttes de parfum [*sic*] pleurent sur nous dans l'ombre:
Regarde mon regard. Donne-moi tes mains nues,
Que je les presse sur mes yeux comme deux fleurs![1]

[Flint includes one further representative of Castiaux's poetry – 'Souviens-toi de ce soir des hautains atavismes' – and then concludes:]

Multiply M. Castiaux's exquisite sense of music by his power over pictorial words and by his voluptuousness, and you have a three-dimensional conception of a poet: in intoxication, illumination, and ardour. He is the author of *Au long des Terrasses* (1905), and *La Joie Vagabonde* (1909).

GEORGES PÉRIN

He has been likened to van Lerberghe, the clear magician of the *Chanson d'Eve* and *Entrevisions*, and like his wife, Cécile Périn, he has something of Verlaine which is not Verlaine. His verse? –

Voici un clair baiser d'adolescent...
Voici une goutte d'eau sous la branche...

Voici ma vie – oh! j'en suis fier – qui tremble.[2]

His verse is limpid water seen through a crystal vase, wherein the words, like rose petals – pink, crimson, cream and yellow – fall; but he is anxious, a little, and timid; his breath troubles the surface of the water; and the perfect harmony of the colours glows through the crystal refracted into a slow flight of assonances. Or it is the music of an April morning, when the birds pipe inconsequently, when each little musical motive seems inconsequent and unrelated to any other; yet back of all is a spirit binding all. Or the luminous candour of narcissi, the golden transparencies of daffodils in sunlight. It is impossible to avoid these comparisons in speaking of his poetry; one has to think of imponderable, beautiful, diaphanous things, or of the music of a sylvan flute.

[1] 'Lied au crépuscule', *Ibid.*, pp. 79–81. The two misprinted words should read *rhapsodies* and *parfums*.
[2] Georges Périn.‡

De tes doigts, émus et bourdonnants,
De ta pluie – oh! de ta douce pluie! –
Va, délie aventureusement
Les parfums, cher Avril tout tremblant!

Avril!...Guirlandes aux abandons
Légers, buissoniers, au mouvement
Qui se fie et dessine l'attente,
Guirlandes si mollement pliantes!...

Saura-t-on quels oiseaux familiers
De mon jardin aux belles présences
En auront plus de goût à chanter?

Quel mystère qui, là, se balance,
Voudra – dis-moi? – se donner raison?

Va, délie aventureusement
Les parfums, cher Avril tout tremblant!

Ta tiédeur sera dans quelle gorge?
Celle-ci dont le thème est ainsi?
Ou cette autre?...Il n'importe...Ou cette autre?[1]

[Flint follows this by four stanzas of 'Tu jeux cessent...'; he then continues:]

And yet he is not easy to read; he is not for those who run; he is subtle, evokes rather than states. "He is all persuasion; which permits him not to affect power. His *métrique* is so supple that he has been able, within the limits of a prosody almost regular, to give himself many of the airs of the *vers libre*. His vocabulary is that which a classic poet would choose; yet it is impossible to say for what mysterious reasons of atmosphere the words have at the same time, mystery and transparency; they shake out a fine sparkling dust which binds them, like the fresh air between the grasses of a plain."[2]

M. Périn is the author of *Les Emois blottis*, poèmes (1902), *L'Expiation*, roman (1905), *La Lisière Blonde*, poèmes (1906), *Le Chemin l'Air qui Glisse*, poèmes (1910), and *Les Rameurs*, roman (1911).

"UNANIMISME"

It was *La Vie Unanime*, a poem published in 1908 by L'Abbaye, which brought M. Jules Romains, its author, into prominence, and gave rise to the catchword, *école unanimiste*. Roughly, it may be said of the principal members of the group which, by reason of friendships and intellectual affinities, has been dubbed *unanimiste*, and which is not *unanimiste* (M. Henri Ghéon has quite recently found the name "whitmanistes" for

[1] Périn.‡
[2] Flint here translates, as he notes, from Georges Duhamel, *Propos Critiques* (Paris, 1912), p. 140.

them), – it may be said that M. Romains considers life in relation to the god crowd; M. Arcos, in relation to the birth of the god in man; M. Vildrac, in relation to the human being, its common humanity;[1] and M. Duhamel, in relation to himself. The only *unanimiste* is M. Romains. The group has been influenced by the works of Durkheim, Le Bon, Tarde, – "unanimisme" is Tarde's "interpsychologie" – Verhaeren, Whitman, Richard Dehmel, Paul Adam, the elder Rosny, and the *Instrumentiste* poet, René Ghil.[2] But a poet only goes to his elders to affirm what he finds in himself...An anthology, containing poems by other poets than those represented here, and published by *L'Effort* (à "La Mérigote," Poitiers) is the most important collective manifestation of the group. The presence in it of translations from Whitman and the evident inspiration of Whitman explain the term "Whitmanistes."

JULES ROMAINS

The first prophet of a religion that may in time be the religion of the world – Jules Romains, *Unanimisme*. It has been said that he found the principles and elements of his religion in the good doctors of philosophy; but did not Jesus Christ, he too, study the wise men as well as confound them? So it is to be supposed that M. Jules Romains did not suddenly, like another Minerva, spring fully armed from the brain of his god; but that he was conceived and nourished slowly in its bowels, until he had fortified with appropriate juices the creative impulse within him. However, having discovered that:

> Les vérités de maintenant
> Naissent où il y a beaucoup d'hommes,
> Et s'exhalent des multitudes,[3]

M. Jules Romains has established this hierarchy: the god-couple, wherein each member becomes something different, and fuses into one being; the god-group, a changeable god, liable to fierce hatreds that may overthrow kings, or as peaceful and powerful as the diurnal dinner party; the god-family, the god-street, the god-village, almost static gods; and greatest god and chiefest god of all, the god-town, an omnipotent god, drawing and controlling all men. The datum is easily understood: given men, a power greater than each is born from their necessary association, and that power may, without any undue materialism, be

---

1 Flint's analysis here appears to owe much to Duhamel. The chapter titles in *Propos Critiques*, *op. cit.*, include 'Jules Romains et les dieux', 'Charles Vildrac et les hommes', and 'René Arcos et *Ce qui naît*'.

2 These comments paraphrase information given Flint by Alexandre Mercereau. Cf. Mercereau's letter to Flint, sent between 29 April and 7 May 1912 (pages 71–3).

3 Jules Romains, 'Poème du métropolitain, XI', *Deux Poèmes* (Paris, 1910), p. 53.

called a god; and humanity may, indeed, come to conceive itself, as
M. Romains conceives it, and become god-like – in the old sense of the
word – in its attributes.[1] We have had in England a poet, John Davidson, whose later work was inspired by a similar idea; but he was
egotistic and cried:

> It may be that the Universe attains
> Self-knowledge only once, and when I cease
> To see and hear, imagine, think, and feel,
> The end may come...[2]

and there are other big differences. But around that conception of a
humanity which is unanimistic, and which may one day become conscious thereof, M. Romain [sic] has constructed, with a patient, un-
deviating labour, his whole work. He has willingly put on the yoke and
burden of a philosophy and its consequences which he seems determined
to drag on to the end, depositing, at different stages of his road, the
sensations he has accumulated thitherto. For in spite of all his philosophical baggage, it is still with his sensations that he makes the reson-
ance of his books. They are, verse – L'Ame des Hommes (1904); La Vie
Unanime (1908); Premier Livre de Prières (1909); Un Être en Marche (1910);
Deux Poèmes (1910); L'Armée dans la Ville, an heroic play (1911); prose –
Le Bourg Régénéré (1906); Manuel de Déification (1910); Puissances de
Paris (1911); Mort de Quelqu'un, a novel (1911). It will be seen that
Unanimisme is a religion that has already a manual and a book of prayers.
The manual contains precepts like these:

Si quelqu'un meurt de ceux que vous aimez, ne dites pas: "Je le retrouverai un jour;
il est impossible que tout finisse ainsi et que nous soyons séparés à jamais." Mais
travaillez à ce qu'il survive.

Prends conscience de ton corps avec soin et gravité. Mais ne lui témoigne pas une
satisfaction trop épaisse. Ne lui laisse pas trop deviner qu'il t'est précieuse. Entre lui
et toi, conserve les distances.[3]

The book of prayers is composed of invocations to the gods formed
of men, from the couple to the town; it contains some of its author's best
work, rich in imagery and passion.

M. Romains is a great creator of images. He is the epic poet of modern
life, aspiring always to the highest generalities.[4] What other poet would

---

[1] The foregoing two sentences present a summary closely similar to that provided by Duhamel
in Propos Critiques, op. cit., pp. 41–2.
[2] John Davidson, 'The Gods in Perdition', The Testament of John Davidson (London, 1908)
in Poems, selected by R. M. Wenley (New York, 1924), p. 135.
[3] Jules Romains, Manuel de déification (Paris, 1910), pp. 33, 44.
[4] Cf. Duhamel, Propos Critiques, op. cit., p. 51. The stress Flint places on the use of imagery
in Romains' poetry corresponds to a similar and earlier emphasis in Duhamel. Imagism
is clearly one expression of a concern with the poetic image prevalent in France as well as
England.

dare to make an epic poem, as he has done in *Un Être en Marche* – a poem that grips and convinces, developing a world that is our world, but strangely new – of a school girls' outing? Or would celebrate with fervour the underground railway (*Deux Poèmes*)? M. Romains seems to know nothing of the past. Imagine a man who wanders through a large town, brooding over the ever-changing spectacle that unrolls before him, alternately exalted and depressed, but always rendering his vision and his sensations by words that reproduce exactly what he has seen, except that it has become intensified and serried in passing through his emotions and his imagination, so that it is illuminated by a many-coloured fire of analogy; for M. Romains, being a visionary, does not see the same tree that a fool sees:

> Un passé monte autour de chaque âme
> Comme tournoie et monte une fumée autour
> Du berger à genoux qui fait un feu d'automne...
>
> ...son clocher d'ardoise est plus haut que les toits;
> C'est un pieu biseauté qui perce le village
> Et le cloue au vallon pour qu'il ne glisse pas...
>
> Je nais de la maison comme d'un ventre noir...
>
> Le long du trottoir froid les passants se calfeutrent
> Dans un terrier d'habits dont ils ferment les trous...
>
> Pourquoi s'est-il mis à frémir tellement,
> En longeant la rue, un homme qui est moi?
> J'ai crispé mon coeur; j'ai détendu les mains;
> J'ai senti que j'étais rouge, puis pâle
> Comme s'il venait de passer un péril.
> Je ne marche plus sur le bord du trottoir;
> Je trouve à chaque roue un moyeu cruel
> Qui s'avance comme on renifle une proie.
> Je frôle les murs aussitôt que je peux.
> Mais quelque chose d'agile s'est sauvé
> Tel un lièvre roux qui part entre les jambes.
> J'ai presque eu peur et je reste plus pauvre.
> N'est-ce pas cela dont frissonnent les gens
> Qui s'écartent et qui regardent le sol,
> En face de la boutique aux volets jaunes?
> Et je crois bien que si le cheval a bronché
> Tandis que son poitrail devenait rocheux
> Et que ses crins allaient lui battre l'échine,
> C'est qu'il voyait aussi courir quelque chose.[1]

M. Romains writes in a very dense form of regular verse, rarely using rhyme and assonance, but replacing these by "rapports de sonorités," which is his own original contribution to modern verse

[1] Jules Romains.‡

technique. It is in this regular verse, with groups of lines of varying syllabic values, the value of the line for each group being determined by the emotional moment, that he has composed his drama, *L'Armée dans la Ville*, a play which is in conformity with its author's intentions:

Jouable, destiné à la scène, non au livre; simple de structure; dépouillé d'artifices extérieurs; moderne quant au sujet, mais doué de la plus haut généralité; une action remassée en une crise; un conflit aussi essentiel et aussi élevé que possible, où s'engagent les forces les plus internes de l'univers; un drame religieux par les profondeurs de l'âme qu'il révélera, et par l'emotion qu'il provoquera chez le spectateur.[1]

M. Romain's ambition is to resuscitate in France great dramatic art, which has been dead since the failure of *Les Burgaves*. It is the common ambition of all young French poets of to-day.

RENÉ ARCOS

It has been said that the pre-Bergson symbolist poets, writing under the influence of their age, and reacting against superficial parnassianism, imagined themselves into the centre of life, the interior of consciousness; it was their attitude with regard to life and to their art;[2] but it was an attitude taken up intuitively and not consciously directed. Later, Bergson formulated the whole philosophical outlook of the period: and poets now are writing, not wholly in obedience to the spirit of a time, but partly according to the suggestion of a philosophy. I do not think it is unfair to say that M. Arcos is one of these. The idea of *real duration* was surely behind these verses:

> Le temps enfle sans cesse et tout s'avance en lui
> selon le pas à pas de la conquête lente
> qui fait un bruit de pulsations.
>
> Voici l'espace empli des battements d'un coeur
> qui palpite et qui saigne à grosses gouttes d'astres,
> et, sous les nappes _ ruisselantes _ d'un sang d'or,
> comme ivres d'un sang noir, voici dans l'ici-bas,
> les hommes acculés _ par l'infini _ contre la terre.
> . . . .
> Le temps enfle sans cesse et tout s'avance en lui,
> plein la surface du présent.
> Et nous allons, oh! seulement si nous allions
> de notre pas, à nous, et selon notre gré,
> mais on nous pousse et nous savons

[1] Jules Romains, 'Préface', *L'Armée dans la ville* (Paris, 1911), p. x. The sentence following this quotation is a paraphrase of the same source, p. viii.

[2] Flint here refers to his earlier citation of Tancrède de Visan, *L'Attitude du lyrisme contemporain op. cit.*, pp. 454–5.

quelles escales et quel port nous toucherons.
– J'entends les temps faucher ma vie derrière moi.
Chaque seconde est un de mes épis qui tombe.[1]

Or the idea of *flux, continuity*, behind these:

Quelque chose, partout, ne cesse pas de naître.

Cette naissance en moi et de toute seconde,
simultanée aux coups du coeur,
qui emprunte un [*sic*] corps et donne à l'esprit
ce battement d'ailes...[2]

But M. Arcos exhorts and adds – for he is a poet – let this birth be the
birth of a god:

Il faudrait d'abord n'être pas trop l'homme,
n'être pas trop où meurt le corps,
pour être plus où naît le dieu.[3]

The god of M. Arcos, however, is not the god, or one of gods, of M.
Romains, it is rather inspiration. This is the scheme of one of his poems:

Beneath our lamps at night a god grows...In the silence of his room a man sits
motionless. He is the centre of innumerable memories. Suddenly he moves. Space
has put something in his presence, something has passed in his eyes with a flash, some
taste has come to his lips. He smiles, breathes more quickly. Something more than
himself has been born. He walks up and down his room, expending the superfluity
which has grown in him; he has attained his paroxysm; and now knows the giddiness
of his own dimensions. He breathes quickly; his step quickens, and reaching the
window, he throws it wide open. The nocturnal silence...the infusion of the stars...
and the whole fresh night greedily drinks him up.[4]

The god arrives after meditation has purified the vessel – after it has
fused in one glowing sensation all the scrap-metal of experience that we
have gathered in our walks abroad. He may come even after lassitude,
disillusion and the exhaustion of all suffering:

Nous avions épuisé sans fruit tout le pâtir
et rien n'avait parlé, divinement, comme un indice.

Nous avions affrété, en vain, tous les espoirs
et disloqué, à l'usage, tous les systèmes.

Nous étions las, si las! d'avoir vu tant de soirs,
comme les fossoyeurs éternels du destin,

[1] René Arcos, 'Le temps enfle sans cesse et tout s'avance en lui...', *Ce qui naît* (Paris, 1911)
pp. 35, 37.
[2] 'Quelque chose, partout, ne cesse pas de naître...', *Ibid.*, p. 33. The misprinted word
should be *au*.
[3] 'Le plus mauvais moi, le plus triste moi...', *Ibid.*, p. 43.
[4] Flint here offers a prose condensation of 'Réduit de quantité', *Ibid.*, pp. 99–103.

enfouir tant de matins où chantaient nos vigueurs;
dans nos fronts bas il y avait tant de défaites
et dans notre fierté tant d'agenouillements
que, déjà, nous avions, comme on abdique et à jamais,
dans le silence indifférent des hauts espaces,
repris le vieux chemin des pentes
et sonné, sous les yeux des astres étrangers,
peuplant notre agonie d'impassibles grandeurs,
sonné, loin et longtemps, triste à susciter Dieu,
la retraite de tous ceux qui allaient à la conquête,
sonné, loin et longemps [*sic*], le déclin des puissances.

Il y a dans l'air un goût de conquête;
une conquête _ qui ne veut _ d'aucun sommeil.
Elle n'accorde pas de repos, même aux morts,
et son galop nous a repris et emportés,
brisant encore les amarres _ de notre fierté.

Nous nous sommes raidis dans notre volonté,
ne voulant pas, ne voulant plus le jeu de dupe.
Le dur galop nous a soulevés malgré nous,
bousculés, submergés, roulés dans ses remous,
bâillonnés de vitesse,
et nous sommes partis
sans pouvoir un cri,
rigides et crispés,
la tête avec colère
rejetée en arrière,
et, dans notre désir têtu de l'inertie,
refrénant des deux poings la monture emportée!
Et l'on nous vit passer roides dans le galop
comme des morts restés debout sur les chevaux,
rebondissant à triples allure
dans une charge de bataille.
Mais la grande clameur du lyrique délire
a traversé nos corps comme une onde électrique
et, tout à coup jaillis, droits sur les étriers,
dardant, de tous nos yeux, une force en avant,
le coeur battant, cheveux au vent, en fuite d'ailes[,]
nous avons, frissonant d'émotion jusqu'aux moelles
et la face inondée de larmes frénétiques,
augmenté d'un grand cri la clameur héroïque.[1]

M. Arcos, then, appeals to the divinity in men,

Les hommes acculés _ par l'infini _ contre la terre.[2]

And the divinization he wishes is not to be obtained by any trick:

Des évangiles et des tables,
des livres, tant de livres!

[1] 'Nous avions épuisé sans fruit tout le pâtir...', *Ibid.*, pp. 95–8. The misprint should read *longtemps*.

[2] 'Le temps enfle sans cesse et tout s'avance en lui...'. *Ibid.*, p. 35.

Mais tes mains tombées,
mais ton chef branlant,
d'incrédulité;
mais l'impuissance du mensonge
malgré l'esprit industrieux
mais l'artifice à toute base...
Et pas de dieu non plus au prix d'un strategème.[1]

No, only when the spirit of heaviness has been driven away; only when you can say there is no man, no men; one speech sways all the worlds; one triumph swells its curve; there are no faces, nothing which declines, only currents and arteries of an obscure power bursting from the earth, feeding some birth immensely – only then can you cry:

Il est dans l'espace un goût de conquête
et l'air que je respire en est chargé.

La terre se dilate, à travers l'homme, dans l'espace.
Des hommes ont souffert d'une tension divine.

.   .   .   .

Chaque homme fait dieu, un péu, avec sa vie.[2]

M. René Arcos is a noble poet, constantly perfecting his thought and his rhythm. He is the author of *L'Ame essentielle* (1902), *Sur la Tragédie des Espaces* (1906), and *Ce Qui Naît* (1910).

GEORGES DUHAMEL

Besides the *Notes sur la Technique Poétique* (1910), written in collaboration with M. Charles Vildrac, from which I have already quoted, M. G. Duhamel is the author of four books of poems, *Des Légendes, des Batailles* (1907), *L'Homme en Tête* (1909), *Selon Ma Loi* (1910), *Compagnons* (1912); a play, *La Lumière* (1911, produced at the Odéon); and a book of critical essays, *Propos Critiques* (1912), wherein he has established his predilections. M. Duhamel has followed Pierre Quillard, the poet, who died recently, as critic of verse for the *Mercure de France*.

The *Notes sur la Technique Poétique* of MM. Duhamel and Vildrac explain the rhythmic principles on which they have constructed their poems. A *poétique*, they say, is based on metrical and phonetic relationships. The cadence of a strophe or poetical paragraph is due to the repetition in each verse of a fixed numerical quantity or *rhythmic constant*, which beats the time of the continuous melody.[3] The traditional alexan-

---

[1] 'L'humiliation avec amour...', *Ibid.*, p. 72.
[2] 'Il est dans l'espace un goût de conquête...', *Ibid.*, pp. 129, 130.
[3] Georges Duhamel and Charles Vildrac, *Notes sur la technique poétique* (Paris, 1925; 1st pub. 1910), pp. 13–14.

drine had a rhythmic constant of six syllables, and a line was composed of two of these. But the modern verse is composed of a constant of any number of syllables, plus an element numerically variable, which gives it an individuality closely adapted to the sense. The rhythmic constant has no fixed place in the verse; it may begin it, support it in the centre, or terminate it. A strophe may be governed by one or two rhythmic constants, and although the constant has been given a numerical value, this may be modified by the quantity of the syllables, the only law here and always being the instinct of the poet.[1] An example:[2]

> *S'il leur faut demain* | franchir une porte
> *Où l'on ne peur pas* | être deux de front,
> *Où il faut que l'un* | passe après l'autre,
> *Devant cette porte* | ils s'arrêteront
> AYANT UN PLI MAUVAIS | sur le front,
> AYANT UN OEIL MAUVAIS | pour s'épier.
> Ch. Vildrac, Les deux Buveurs.

The first four of these lines have a constant of five, which suddenly changes to a constant of six in the last two, as with change of tempo in music. . .

The poetry of M. Duhamel has perceptibly been influenced by Whitman's work:

> Recevez-moi, mes compagnons, accueillez-moi!. . .
> . . .Acceptez l'homme qui se présente
> Avec cette figure anxieuse et troublée.[3]

Besides, read his titles, *Selon Ma Loi*, *Compagnons*. But it is a Whitman with a scrutinizing and critical eye, out of which peers the unquiet soul of the twentieth century, that is re-weighing, re-measuring, re-adjusting all its standards, all its values. He has hardly any of that lyricism which is the outward song of passion: his verse seems to meditate inwards; thence outwards, perhaps, to catch at some everyday emotional motive, such as the passing in the street for years of the same person, which is brought in and pondered over. M. Duhamel ponders life. I say it in no disrespect to him, but I am reminded of a spider in its web, a poetical spider, brooding at the centre of a web of sensations. M. Duhamel seems ever on the watch for the significant human gesture which will be the starting-point of a meditation or an exhortation. He is keenly aware that small things, suddenly noticed, will turn the whole course of a man's feelings. You catch a glimpse of a friend's ear; you see for the first time that the lobe is crinkled, and you hate him! –

[1] George Duhamel and Charles Vildrac, *Notes sur la technique poétique*, p. 15.
[2] *Ibid.*, p. 18.
[3] Georges Duhamel, 'Ode à quelques hommes', *Compagnons* (Paris, 1918), pp. 12–13.

Mère! je suis plein de rancune.
Tu n'as pas bien fait ton devoir;
Le coeur que tu m'as donné n'est pas simple,
Peut-être aussi n'est-il pas bon,
Mais je vois trop [tout] ce qu'il faudrait ne pas voir.[1]

He analyses silences, marvellously sometimes, as in *L'Attente dans la Nuit* of *Selon Ma Loi*. He sees humanity as a system of forces surrounded and acted on by innumerable other forces:

Le Gardian [*sic*] Vigilant

Cet homme qui se tient debout,
La main sur le bouton docile de la porte,
Cet homme, je le reconnais,
Son coeur seul secoue l'antichambre noire.

Demeurer ou partir...
Des motifs de forces égales
Appuient de l'épaule et du poing
Sur les deux faces de la porte,
Et le bouton ne saurait pas tourner tout seul.

Partir ou demeurer...
Mille raisons d'être dehors
Fleurissent au delà des marches.
Aucune n'est assez soudaine
Pour séduire à la fois tous les muscles du corps
Et dominer dans la minute suffisante.

Demeurer!
Mille raisons de rester là
Sont à leur place, sur les meubles:
Aucune n'est assez tenace
Pour s'enrouler autour des membres
Et durer, seulement une heure.

Et rien ne vient de secourable,
Nul ne marche dans l'escalier,
Pas de courant d'air pousse la porte,
Pas le moindre bruit qui puisse intriguer,
Nul souvenir à satisfaire,
Rien qu'un choeur de menus motifs, sans coryphée.

Rien ne surgit de décisif.
L'intérieur se tait odieusement;
Les livres sont connus, dans la bibliothèque...
La cordialité des fauteuils
A quelque chose de servile et qui répugne.
La chaleur de cette maison
N'est ni trop pauvre ni trop forte,
Et quant au labeur...il est fait
Mais éternellement à faire.

[1] Georges Duhamel, 'Chez eux', *Selon ma loi, poèmes 1909–1910* (Paris, 1910), pp. 58–9.

L'homme, immobile auprès de la porte impassible,
Ecoute détonner [*sic*] son coeur, entre les murs,
Et ne siat trop pourquoi l'étreinte qui l'écrase
N'arrête pas aussi ce coeur trop vigilant.[1]

L'Homme en Tête is a book apart from the others. It is the legend of any of humanity's guides: infancy and adolescence of germination and heroic deed apart; then, the crowd having discovered a leader in him, they start in quest of the terrestrial paradise, troubling on their way the contentment of the fat, smug yahoos. But when the last ravine at the last summit has been passed, and the promised land seems to lie before them, the crowd rush by their leader and pour into death over a precipice. The leader returns with despair in his soul; and not until he has driven from him his two companions, his Evil-Genius and his Most-Intimate-Thought, can he sing:

Je vais dans un beau pays de santé
Où doit mourir un grand coeur
Pour avoir pâmé d'une caresse venimeuse.

Je vais dans un beau pays de beauté,
Où je veux, bien blanc et bien nu, rentrer,
Léger de savoir, léger de sagesse.

Les plus belles raisons y sont sans raison,
Les plus belles raisons n'y seront que des chansons.

Je vais dans un beau pays de joie,
Pour y aimer, par delà notre vie, la vie...
Et pour chérir cette irréalité des choses
Qui est le corps du songe, et la seule réalité.[2]

This is the bare outline – hardly that – of a poem rich in parable and psychological interest. The episode, *l'Epreuve*, is particularly fine.

CHARLES VILDRAC

A poet who loves men and loves life. Wherever he finds them, he finds himself; and wherever he finds himself, life thereby becomes exalted:

Il y avait moi, parmi tout cela,
Un peu celui-ci, un peu celui-là,
Il y avait moi,
Le rêve tendu désespérément vers des archipels
Et vers telle vie:
Une vie dans le vent, toutes voiles dehors,

---

[1] 'Le Gardien vigilant', *Compagnons, op. cit.*, pp. 41–3. The misprinted word in the body of the poem is *détoner*.

[2] Georges Duhamel, 'Epologue', *L'Homme en tête* (Paris, 1909), p. 187.

> Chair, esprit et le coeur et les yeux – extase ou larmes –
> Ou oui, furieusement, toutes voiles dehors:
> Une vie sans rien de commun avec la mort...[1]

Nothing is too mean for his transfiguring touch: a piece of waste ground, for instance, covered with the rubbish, the rubble, and the clinker of industrialism:

> Mais on y trouvait, quand même, en cherchant,
> Une bonne place d'herbe grasse,
> On trouvait quand même, en écoutant,
> Un bruit de feuillage
> Et d'oiseaux qui pourchassent... [sic]
> Mais si l'on avait assez d'amour,
> On pouvait quand même demander au vent
> Et des parfums et des musiques
> .   .   .   .
> On pouvait quand même emporter de là
> Un souvenir de la terre opulente,
> Un souvenir touffu et riche comme un bouquet,
> Durable autant que les chants de l'enfance
> Et pénétrant comme l'écho.[2]

Again, two men sit down to talk and laugh together under the pretext of drinking:

> Ils sont vraiment heureux d'être ensemble[;]
> Et cependant!...[3]

And yet to-morrow, if they met at a door wherein two could not enter abreast, they would frown and look obliquely and suspiciously at each other, and one of a thousand reasons which could set them fighting would have arisen. But at this moment:

> Il y a au fond de leur vieux coeur
> Un besoin secret d'embrassade et de liesse,
> Et pour cet instant de détente que laisse
> La mégère vie à leur pauvre vieux coeur,
> Les voilà qui se rient avec leurs yeux,
> Les voilà qui se tapent sur les épaules,
> Les voilà sans méfiance l'un pour l'autre,
> Les voilà qui veulent s'offrir à boire
> En se racontant de bonnes histoires.[4]

[1] Charles Vildrac, 'Il y en avait', *Livre d'amour, suivi des premiers vers* (Paris, 1959), p. 13. The extract Flint uses differs in punctuation from the text of the 1959 edition.

[2] 'Paysage', *Ibid.*, p. 48. There are minor differences in punctuation between the quoted text and the 1959 edition; the 1959 reading in the fifth line of the extract is *se pourchassant*, rather than *qui pourchassent*.

[3] 'Les deux Buveurs', *Ibid.*, p. 33.

[4] *Ibid.*, p. 34.

The method seems easy; the motives everywhere at hand: the poet walks along the street and rejoices that there are pretty girls; he passes the "carrefour des Chétives Maisons,"

> Elles sont trois, ces maisons,
> Blotties au même coin[,] toutes les trois,
> Il y en a deux qu'on n'habite plus,[1]

and the other is an inn where only the most miserable stop; he sees a poor woman walk along the country road, pushing a perambulator with a child in it; or a man suddenly remembers that he has a long outstanding promise to visit two humble friends, and he goes, although the rain pours down; or a sailor has been left to drown after shipwreck: all lowly subjects, it will be seen; but probe them and human tragedy will be found; consider the tragedy with love and imagination, and life will be exalted. And it is because M. Vildrac's inner consciousness is aware that he has brought love and imagination to bear on human wretchedness, meanness and pain that he has called his last book *Livre d'Amour* (1910). It is love that makes the inn at the "carrefour des Chétives Maisons" a place of hope; that makes the drowning sailor burst into song in his last agony:

> Ce fut la plus belle chanson
> De douleur, d'amour et de tristesse,
> Ce fut la plus poignante chanson d'amour [*sic*]
> Qu'un homme jamais eût chantée,[2]

and the poem is an exaltation. It is love, the humanity that makes the whole world kin, which is *La Seule Chanson*; listen to it:

> Ce soir, au vide lourd de son tombereau,
> Un charretier regagne son repos;
>
> A cent lieues de là, un grand seigneur
> Dans son grand parc erre tout seul;
>
> Et je sais un boutiquier de la ville
> Blotti au fond de sa boutique triste.
>
> En ce moment, ils profitent tous trois
> De ce qu'il [*sic*] sont seuls et que c'est le soir
> Pour laisser se tordre et se distendre leur bouche,
> Pour laisser rouler des larmes sur leur joue [*sic*],
> En pensant chacun à leur enfant qui est mort.
>
> A cause des lumières qu'il rencontre
> Et des autres voitures et des passants,

[1] 'Une Auberge', *Ibid.*, p. 35.

[2] 'L'Adieu', *Ibid.*, p. 89. The phrase 'chanson d'amour' is replaced in the 1959 edition by 'chanson d'homme'.

Le charretier se cache sous son feutre
Et dans le brouhaha...

Le grand seigneur, évitant les pelouses
Où ce qui reste de lumière
Se rassemble, s'effare et le dévisage,
Cherche les allées les plus noires...

Et le boutiquier[,] encore un peu recule
L'instant d'éclairer sa vitrine et ses yeux.
Or, s'ils étaient ici ce soir, ces trois hommes
Qui ne portent pas les mêmes habits,
Qui ne mangent pas le même manger,
Qui ne parlent pas de la même façon,
Qui ne savent pas les mêmes maisons
Ni les mêmes femmes,

S'ils étaient ici tous les trois, ce soir,
Assis sur un banc derrière toi[,] dans l'ombre,
Et que tu leur chantes
Cette chanson, tu sais, de l'homme aux pas menus
Qui va, les pieds dans l'eau et les épaules nues,
Qui va dans la nuit âpre et criarde,
Mais qui est bien heureux de couver des yeux
Et de bercer en le portant
Son petit enfant
Qui dort vien au chaud [*sic*]
Roulé dans son gros paletot,

Si tu chantais cela pour ces trois hommes,
O toi qui sais [la] langue
Qui retrouve et atteint dans leur nudité
Les hommes et les femmes avec qui tu es
Sur la terre,

Si tu chantais cela sans tourner la tête
– A cause des yeux et [de] la pudeur –
Tu n'entendrais peut-être
Que le bruit étranglé d'un seul sanglot.[1]

The last poem in *Livre d'Amour* tells of a symbolic conqueror (none other, surely, than M. Vildrac himself) who, without army or arms, goes afoot through a country, spreading, by his mere presence, his goodness of heart, until first one, and then many, and then the whole of the people become conquerors likewise.

There is an entire absence of rhetoric in M. Vildrac's poetry, which is simple and told with the vivid detail of naked vision. He is also the author of *Poèmes* (1905), *Images et Mirages* (1908), and of a drama, *L'Apothéose*.

[1] 'La seule Chanson', *Ibid.*, pp. 52–4. The readings in the 1959 edition differ in the following ways: stanza 4 – *qu'ils* and *joues*; stanzas 5 and 6 – no ellipses; stanza 9, last two lines – 'Qui dort bien au chaud / Roulé dans son gros paletot'; stanza 10 – *la* inserted as shown; stanza 11 – *de* inserted as shown.

LUCIEN ROLMER AND "L'ÉCOLE DE GRÂCE"

Under the aegis of Botticelli's Spring Maiden, who advances to you clad in flowers and diaphanous robes, as you pick up the review, *La Flora*, while the golden apples shine among the leaves overhead, M. Lucien Rolmer, who is its editor, has founded the School of Grace, which is to combat the evil influence of *unanimisme* and other schools of ugliness. In doing so, he is not so stupid, he says, as to suppose that he is creating an original formula. He wishes to convey in one word the delight of art and the human mind, the essential interior genius of a work of art, past and future glory, soul and form, love and harmony, the fine natural movement of thought, and his religion of the ancient illumination. *Fiat Lux*! As for the original formulae, all the roses are original. *Nascuntur*! The rest is cultivation, care, and, alas! chance. So with the poet.

Besides being the author of a number of novels, M. Rolmer is the singer of *L'Inconstance*, a lyrical poem, *Thamyris*, a lyrical poem, *Les Chants Perdus* (1907) and *Le Second Volume des Chants Perdus* (1911). In these last songs, M. Rolmer has not sought to paint the twentieth century, nor to convey any description or picture of our time (when he wishes to do that, he writes a novel); but he mourns sometimes its anxiety and he suffers with the human heart.

> Je n'ai jamais eu d'autre but
> Que d'aimer l'amour et la vie
> A la folie!
> Je n'ai jamais eu d'autre but,
> O Belzébuth![1]

Ardent, satirical at times, lyrical, the poetry of M. Rolmer has that grace whose absence he deplores in much of the work of his contemporaries. Ironical, tender, amorous, his verse has that Latin order which MM. Florian-Parmentier and the *verslibristes* repudiate, the first because he argues that the French are a northern race, Celts,[2] the second because they aver that the modern soul has profounder preoccupations. If I add that M. Rolmer is a devotee of English poetry, and that he has declared that he would sooner gain the suffrage of one young English poet, loving his language and its traditions, than the sympathy of ten young German poets (which is very amiable of him), perhaps the poem I quote may be read more curiously:

[Flint then cites 'L'Ode à la comète'.][3]

---

[1] Lucien Rolmer, *Le Seconde volume des chants perdus* (Paris, 1911).‡
[2] Cf. Florian-Parmentier, *La Littérature et l'époque, op. cit.*, pp. 15–16.
[3] In devoting significant space to Lucient Rolmer's 'L'Ecole de la Grâce' Flint permitted his desire for punctilious completeness to overcome his critical judgement and his sensitivity

The First Major Survey of the French Avant Garde

NICOLAS BEAUDUIN AND "LE PAROXYSME"

M. Albert Mockel, the penetrating and erudite critic, the delicious and fantastic poet and prosewriter, once defined the art of Emile Verhaeren, who is perhaps the world's greatest living poet. He showed that in Verhaeren's poems the plastic manner of classic art and the mystic manner of the Middle Ages were combined suddenly and violently, and he called the resultant flash "paroxysme." And there the word remained until it was flung at and adopted by M. Nicolas Beauduin and his school, the "paroxystes." For them, poetry is a lyric and inspired state; it is a faith, a religion, giving to life the value of an absolute – a passionate desire to exteriorize the manifestations of the inner ego, to transmute them into acts, and render them by means of adequate and eminently expressive rhythms.[1] Paroxysm, or "the objectivation of the radiant states of a poet's soul," lyric exaltation, faith, fervour, power and enthusiasm are the wings on which they would raise themselves to the sublime. Such an aesthetic has its danger, no doubt, the greatest being the dangers of wandering into wastes of sublime verbiage, and perhaps the "paroxystes" can hardly be held blameless in this respect. M. Nicolas Beauduin, their chief and the editor of their organ, *Les Rubriques Nouvelles*, has an enormous faith in his mission (which lures him into vivid hates, be it said); and there is a suspicion abroad that he is a great poet. "Nicolas Beauduin is one of the most fecund magicians of the word of this strong generation. He is the poet of cosmogonic drunkenness, of enthusiasm on the summits; an ardent, frantic joy, which knows no measure, lifts up this poetry of vertigo, and precipitates it into our souls with the tumult of a cataract."[2]

In book after book, *La Terre Mère, Le Chemin Qui Monte, Les Triomphes, La Divine Folie, Les Deux Règnes, Les Princesses de Mon Songe, Les Cités du Verbe*, all published within the last two or three years, M. Beauduin sings with that "heroic exaltation" which for him is sublime poetry. M. Beauduin has undoubtedly been greatly influenced by Verhaeren, and he claims kinship with Whitman; still, it is not my intention to analyse here his work – space will not permit – but to indicate an individuality. The poem I quote does not perhaps show off M. Beauduin's impetuous and ardent verse; but no matter; it is in his latest manner, over which there seems to have come a veil of tenderness.

to the current stature of the French poets he discusses. As Kenneth Cornell notes (*The Post-Symbolist Period, op. cit.*, p. 43), Rolmer published in numerous journals up until 1911, but became 'an object of ridicule' after he began to propagandize for his 'L'Ecole de la Grâce', and he is now forgotten.

[1] Nicolas Beauduin, *Nos Tendances*, in *Les Rubriques Nouvelles*, January, 1912. [Flint's note.]

[2] Jean Thogorma (Edouard Gerber), *Les Tendances nouvelles de la littérature* (1911).‡

Douceur suave et blancheur qui se fond,
Frais arc-en-ciel aux subtiles nuances,
Mon songe pur au songe se fiance,
Comme l'âme à l'amour dans notre moi profond.

Étends tes voiles, ma chère, ma blonde,
O mon automne aux ailes de velours,
O toi qui répands sur le monde
L'âme blonde
D'un dieu d'amour!

Le rêve du soleil plane encor sur les roses,
C'est un dernier sourire aux yeux lassés du ciel;
Mais dans la paix lumineuse des choses
S'exhale un avant-goût du bonheur éternel.
O mon âme lasse-ô ma tendresse –
Attends en paix dans le silence clair des mois,
Le cortège lointain des heures d'autrefois,
Au pas rose et fleuri d'allégresses.

Les oiseaux accablés par la ferveur du soir
Se taisent lentement comme ton coeur lui-même.
Écoute! Un dieu languide et noir
Vient se pencher sur ton front blême.
Regarde-le. Il tend, là-bas, vers les chemins
Où sanglotent des orgues d'ombre,
Le bouquet fané de ses mains
Qu'alourdissent des roses sombres.

Il espère, il attend, vaincu, dolent et doux,
La femme aux yeux d'or noir, offerts comme une cible;
Et tout mystérieux, il écoute, à genoux,
Le lent vol angoissant des amours impossibles.[1]

JEAN THOGORMA

M. Jean Thogorma is another "paroxyste," who holds that a poet has a divine mission. In the preface to his book, *Le Crépuscule du Monde*, he states that his ambition has been to evoke under its eternal and present form the struggle of life against itself, the conflict of Nature and of man, to sing pain and joy as a hero might feel them before the modern aspects of the abyss of the world.[2] Confronted with the great heaps and chaotic cliffs of brick and stone of our modern cities, he has had the giddiness of the gulf and the sensation of hell. He sees under the veil of civilization the most savage of barbarities. But despair and pain, necessarily begetting the aspiration to liberty and joy, he aspires to the conquest of both and of the vision of the celestial world beyond the world of appear-

[1] Nicolas Beauduin, 'Douceur suave et blancheur qui se fond', *Pan*, v, 2 (February–March 1912) 103–4.
[2] Jean Thogorma (Edouard Gerber). 'Préface', *Le Crépuscule du monde* (1910).‡

ances, beyond the world of fatality; yet, having attained to contemplation of the spectacle of heaven out in the silent vastnesses of space, he is forced to the knowledge that his happiness has been created from the impulse of his anguish, and, consequently, that he cannot enter definitely into the peace of the elect. To be worthy of happiness, therefore, one must install it in one's heart before seeking it elsewhere, and with the idea of the victory of the will over suffering one must put one's soul to proof. There is nobility in this, and M. Thogorma has found that the form best suited to its expression is the classic form of French verse.

He defends his practice in his *Lettres sur la Poésie*. Therein he says that the internal elements of the poem are thought and feeling. The principal external elements are:

> The rhythmic moment.
> The silent beat.
> The sonorous beat.
> The double sonorous beat.
> The rhythmic duration.
> The rhythmic period.
> The rhythmic cycle.[1]

The moment and the rhythmic duration are the minor rhythms: the period and the cycle, the major rhythms. The sonorous beat is the syllable which is pronounced (*sic*, accentuated?). The rhythmic moment is the succession of sonorous beats which are pronounced without any appreciable rest of the voice. The silent beat is the rest of the voice between two rhythmic moments. The double sonorous beat is the pause of the voice on the rhyme, which is placed at the end *or in the course of* certain rhythmic moments, i.e., the repetition at equal intervals, or having between them a common measure, of syllables of the same sonority. The rhythmic duration is a moment, or a succession of rhythmic moments, with a stoppage of the voice and of the sense, as:

> Derrière nous – au fond d'une antique poterne –
> S'ouvre – nue et déserte – une cour de caserne
> Immense – avec de vieux boulets ronds – dans un coin.
> — Albert Samain, *Le Chariot d'Or*.

This is a rhythmic duration of thirty-six syllables, comprising eight unequal moments of four, eight, two, four, eight, seven, three syllables. By the free use of the *enjambement*, M. Thogorma claims that his technique gives a traditionalist poet infinite liberties.[2] But he does not seem to see that these liberties really break up the traditional alexandrine,

[1] Jean Thogorma (Edouard Gerber), *Lettres sur la poésie* (1912).
[2] *Ibid.*‡

and form *vers libre*. Indeed, the definitions of his terms imply the *vers libre*. The type of the perfect traditional alexandrine – if there is any meaning in the word tradition as used by the traditionalist, which I doubt – is found in lines such as these:

> Oui, je viens dans son temple adorer l'éternel,
> Je viens selon l'usage antique et solennel.[1]

These lines have a movement which is not without charm; but the verse stops at the end of the line, and the rhythmic moment does not stride over (*enjamber*) from one verse into another, and, while retaining the outward aspect of tradition, yet kick tradition very vigorously out of the way. It is idle to talk of writing in rhythmic moments *in the course of which* a rhyme may occur; this phrase lets in the *enjambement*, which is the negation of the alexandrine (and of the heroic decasyllable, too, remember that). To squeeze the moments into the tight jacket of lines of twelve syllables serves no rhythmical or other purpose: it may hobble the true rhythm, and it tends to suffocate any music that may be got from the rhyme. M. Thogorma says nothing of the traditional cesura... It is only fair to add that he very rarely uses the *enjambement* himself, and that *Le Crépuscule du Monde* is a *rhythmic cycle* composed of *rhythmic periods* of sustained power. Here is one period:

> Je te hais d'une haine éternelle, ô Paris!
> A cause de la nuit dont ta splendeur est faite.
> – Pour les matins d'orgueil et les soirs de défaite
> Où ma douleur hurla dans chacun de tes cris;
>
> Pour mes tourments futurs et mes affres passées,
> Terre sans horizons, continents sans sommets,
> Babel des temps nouveaux, sois maudite à jamais;
> Je te hais à la fois par toutes mes pensées. –
>
> Sois maudite à jamais, dans les jours qui viendront
> Accroître ta puissance et ton ignomimie;
> Au feu de ma colère et de mon ironie,
> Jusqu'à la fin des temps je marquerai ton front.
>
> Pour ton orgueil infâme et ta luxure vile,
> Ta passion du lucre et ta frivolité,
> Tes maîtres corrompus et ta plèbe servile,
> Je te hais dans le temps et dans l'éternité!
>
> Maudits soient tes marchands comme tes courtisanes,
> Tes femmes d'une nuit et tes hommes d'un jour
> Dont les sombres travaux et les plaisirs insanes
> Avant qu'à la Beauté, ton horreur d'Amour.

[1] Thogorma.‡

Maudits soient tes amants et tes héros de fange,
Poètes de salons, cabotins ou croupiers,
Qui des mains de la vierge ou des regards de l'ange,
Arrachent tous les dieux pour les fouler aux pieds.

Maudite soit ton âme ignorante et vulgaire,
Sans idéal, sans foi, sans force, sans fierté,
Qui ne peut même plus, ce qu'elle a fait naguère,
Répandre sur le monde un rayon de beauté.

Maudits soient tes enfants dont la lèvre ironique
Raillant dès le berceau le sein qu'elle a pressé,
A tous les mots vivants, en parlant, communique
L'accent de je ne sais quel sarcasme glacé.

Et maudit soit enfin le baiser de tes femmes
Qui ne vaut même pas le prix qu'il est vendu;
Dans la fange dorée où se vautrent leurs âmes,
L'orgueil de mon amour n'est jamais descendu.[1]

FLORIAN-PARMENTIER AND "L'IMPULSIONNISME"

Having written, in 1904, an article, *La Physiologie Morale du Poète*, which caused him to be inundated with replies and letters from all over the world, M. Florian-Parmentier found himself, protesting, *malgré lui*, the head of a school, *L'Impulsionniste*. A review was started, *La Revue Impulsionniste*; the philosophy took a more and more definite shape; committees were formed in all countries;...the "Fédération Impulsionniste Internationale" was formed![2]

Impulsionnisme?...Life acts, organizes: there must then be something to move, to organize. Matter, the substance – that which exists by itself – of life; its essence – the individual being – is spirit. Life, considered as "being," is matter in activity; considered as "individuality," it is spirit, or soul: both interpenetrate and mingle in the rhythmic movement of life. The brain of man, which is probably the meeting-point of life-substance and life-essence, is substance, as "being" – essence, as spirit. Consciousness, the human individuality, is a natural phenomenon, deriving from the very essence of life; and the relation between human individuality and the total individuality – *il gran mar dell' essere* – is thought. But what is thought? Man-substance putting off momentarily his own individuality and becoming absorbed in the total individuality – meditation, ecstasy – is invaded by the infinite essence: that which he brings back from this incursion into the infinite is thought.

---

[1] Thogorma.‡

[2] The opening paragraph summarizes information from Florian-Parmentier's *La Littérature et la époque, op. cit.*, pp. 47–8. Information in the succeeding three paragraphs is drawn from pages 49–52 of the same source; it sometimes reflects a literal translation of important phrases.

The moment of contact between the infinite essence and the sensitive point (the human brain) has been termed *intuition*. The sensation of this phenomenon of intuition may be called the psychic instinct, and *impulsion* the beginning of activity, the particular fluctuation determined in certain organisms by the psychic instinct. The man whose sensitive system and cerebral organization are such that not only is he prone to meditation and knows the psychic instinct, but also feels the impulsion which urges him to fix his dreams, to realize his thought, is the Poet, the creator. His words are the attestation of essence by substance, individuality expressing itself as being, a mode of manifestation which can only be adequate to the vital essence: its rhythm can only be moulded on the rhythm of life.

Such are some of the affirmations of *Impulsionnisme*; but a philosophy does not consist so much in the statement of its principles as in their development.

M. Florian-Parmentier deduces from his philosophy an aesthetic wholly subordinated to inspiration, and in reaction against dilettantism and artificiality; and a prosody which can only be said to be personal. He insists that rhythms should be subordinated to inspiration, obeying the emotive movement, and not fixed and inadequate rules, but asserts that his result can be best obtained by combining with art the different types of regular verses. More interesting is his statement of the mystic effects he claims to get from rhyme-schemes. A poem whose rhymes, two by two, are the repetition of the same word, the meaning of which grows and enlarges, gives a thrilling impression of mystery. Words of masculine termination, rhyming regularly with others of feminine, translate a disordered state of mind, and describe excellently cataclysms or chaos. And so on.

The list of M. Florian-Parmentier's published works is too long to transcribe here. Besides being a philosopher and a poet, he is a novelist, a dramatist, a critic of all the arts, a literary historian, a painter, a musician and a sculptor; and as though all that were not sufficient for the activity of one man, still young, he has contributed to some two hundred and fifty different reviews and journals, French and foreign. I transcribe two sonnets from *Par les Routes Humaines*, "*poème d'intention si haute, de si grave et si pure inspiration*," as Pierre Quillard wrote in the *Mercure de France*. It tells of a spirit who, tired of eternity and infinite certitudes, desires and obtains incarnation. He mingles with humanity, and having been agitated by all the problems and subjected to all the humiliations, attains wisdom, dies, and enters into the Divine Essence. He has attempted to bring men to understand *la profonde simplicité de l'Infini*; to teach them to taste the sweet honey of the minutes, to enfranchise themselves from covetousness and strife:

The First Major Survey of the French Avant Garde

Au Coeur de la Cité

La Lumière luit dans les ténèbres, et
les ténèbres ne l'ont point comprise.

"Frères, je viens vers vous, amical et timide,
Osant à peine offrir les trésors que voici.
D'allégresse pourtant ma paupière est humide,
Tant d'avance me semble doux votre merci.

"Et – si grande est ma joie – enfin je me décide.
O merveille, voila pour vos yeux obscurcis
Le remède divin, grâce à qui s'élucide
Le problème qui vous donnait taut de soucis.

"Vos pauvres yeux s'usaient, dans l'ombre, mais qu'importe?
Le secret du bonheur, frères, je vous l'apporte;
Et vous l'aurez, ruisselant d'astres, mon trésor!"

Mais eux, se défiant des fables inexactes
Et voulant que l'on joigne aux paroles les actes,
Disent: "Va nous chercher tes femmes et ton or."[1]

[Flint concludes his discussion of Florian-Parmentier by quoting a second sonnet,
'L'or et les femmes, vous en savez les poisons...']

THREE MUSES: CÉCILE PÉRIN

Her first book, *Vivre* (1906), was almost entirely composed of minute
self-analyses, ardent with desire for happiness and fulfillment. Her
second, *Les Pas Légers* (1907) is lit up by the grace of her little daughter,
and emotional with the anxiety of motherhood. Alphonse Séché called
her "the muse of maternity." Unenslaved to art, she is essentially a
woman-poet and an instinctive singer, asking only emotion, passion and
sincerity. Her maternal joys, her love for her husband, Georges Périn,
...but would Elizabeth Barrett Browning have written this sonnet?

Jalousie

D'autres femmes ont ri dans tes yeux, je le sais.
D'autres ont murmuré les mots que je murmure,
Et tu gardes en toi, comme un trésor secret,
Le souvenir d'autres baisers, d'autres blessures.

Ce que je sais me fait souffrir. Ce que je sais!
Mais, mon ami, ce que j'ignore me torture.
Je voudrais te verser l'oubli total, et n'ai
Que mon amour à t'apporter comme une eau pure.

Je voudrais effacer de tes yeux tous les yeux,
Briser comme un miroir l'éclat mystérieux

---

[1] Florian-Parmentier, *Par les Routes humaines* (Paris, 1910).‡

133

Des souvenirs, au fond de ton âme ignorée;
Je voudrais aspirer ta vie en un sanglot,
Posséder ta jeunesse ivre, grave et sacrée...
– Et j'écoute en ton coeur résonner mille echos.[1]

[Flint, who was much taken by Mme Périn, quotes six other brief extracts and one complete poem, 'In Memoriam: A la mémoire d'Olivier de la Fayette'. In the course of these quotations he notes:][2]

Mme Périn willingly harks back to her childhood, its companions, the paternal roof, and the gardens and woods and fields of her country, Champagne. Her heart goes out in a great yearning for its spring, when the matutinal silver veils are on the meadows...[She is] a woman, too, with a dolorous heart, who sees with chagrin the slavery of her sex, so that there are tears in the eyes that smile at you kindly through the softly soughing branches of the trees...Not the least of her sorrows, *eheu fugaces*! is for time past and faces that will not smile again...A timid nightingale...

VALENTINE DE SAINT-POINT

Sensuous and ardent, loving life and the sea, with impetuosity, Mme Valentine de Saint-Point does not sing for the amusement of women who are prey to pity; nor for old men who no longer know the joy of desire, the value of pleasure; nor for lovers of order, to whom travel and struggle are the tares of life. No, she sings of pride for those young men whose youth is exaltation and desire; and to them she bequeaths:

...Mes émois à choisir
Afin d'en animer leurs multiples fantômes.

Si mon sang épuisé dans mon immense essor
A su les émouvoir, qu'ils gardent ma pensée;
Lorsque dans l'Univers je serai dispersée
Qu'ils me lisent le soir et m'écoutent encor.

Et trouvant en mes vers mon âme mise à nue,
Qu'ils rient de leur amante aux aspects enfiévrés,
Et vers l'ombre tendu murmurent enivrés:
"Cette femme, pourquoi, ne l'ai-je pas connue?"[3]

It is no small ambition, this, to desire the embraces, vicarious in body, actual in spirit, of all that is young and lusty in future generations.

Ronsard me célébrait du temps que j'étais belle.[4]

[1] Cécile Périn, 'Jalousie', *Variations du coeur pensif* (Paris, 1911).‡
[2] In the summary that follows, all ellipses but the last are my own.
[3] Valentine de Saint-Point, *Poèmes d'orgueil* (Paris, 1908), p. 14.‡
[4] Valentine de Saint-Point.‡

Regrets for irreparable beauty, but here a woman re-creates herself in art, expresses into the musical vehicle of verse all the white fire and the red blood of her:

> Je n'effeuillerai pas la marguerite, car il n'est pas de mesure à l'amour frénétique de mon impudique Amant. Je suis en lui comme une blessure, qu'il ne fermera, qu'en croisant ses mains sur ma nuque tandis que je lui serai une ceinture.
> Un peu, beaucoup, passionément, c'est assez pour les vierges pâles. Moi, je suis pâle sous la lune de l'attente, mais mon ardeur est en moi, sous ma peau, comme mon sang que nul ne voit et que seule je sens.[1]

. . . .

Cette femme...oh, she knows herself and her passions and her prides...But she lives in an interminable expectation, which she intensifies and prolongs with her shooting, her rowing, her swimming, in the exercise beneath the southern sun of her masculine sinews; and she has no desire to put an end to expectation, for she is of those whom no man may possess. *L'Orbe Pâle* is the chronicle in prose poems of a summer in solitude by the Mediterranean, every detail vivid, every emotion, every thought, every desire, every act, frankly given. The book is one cry of life. She hides nothing; and she knows that her masculine soul is biassed by the ruse of her feminine body, O Androgyne!

I consider *L'Orbe Pâle* (1911) to be the best of her poetical works, that in which she has been most personal. *The Poèmes de la Mer et du Soleil* (1905), though strong and vibrant, are too objective, too eloquent, conceived under the influence of Lamartine, who is a great-uncle of the writer. The *Poèmes d'Orgueil* of 1908 mark a further stage in the sensibility of the poet and in her craft, which is still obedient to "tradition." Three poems in this book contain Mme de Saint-Point as Electra, as Iphigenia, and as Antigone. Another, *Rêve Plastique*, is her masterpiece in the "traditional" form.

[Flint continues with a summary of 'Rêve Plastique', with extensive quotation. He concludes:]

Mme Valentine de Saint-Point is also author of three novels, *Trilogie de l'Amour et de la Mort: Un Amour* (1906), *Un Inceste* (1907), *Une Mort* (1910), wherein she has dared much; a play *Le Déchu* (Théâtre de Arts, May 28, 1909), and *la Guerre*, poème héroïque, and *La Soif et les Mirages*, poems (1912).

BERTHE REYNOLD

If we say of Mme Cécile Périn that she is all emotion, of Mme de Saint-Point that she is all passion, we may be allowed to say of Mme

---

[1] Valentine de Saint-Point, *L'Orbe pâle* (Paris, 1911), pp. 28–9. In an omitted portion following this, Flint quotes another poem from *L'Orbe pâle*, 'C'est l'éternelle histoire de fées', p. 10.

Berthe Reynold that she is all intellect. But the generalization is less true in her case, since to be all intellect is to be something less than a poet, and she is a poet, albeit overfond of allowing her emotion to suggest a theme for embroidery by her intellect; but the emotion is the prime mover:

> La Terre est l'astre où je m'émeus. O toute chose
> Vibre sur mes émois
> Son mystère sombre ou rose!
> Ou grandiose!
> Et je crois
> La merveilleuse voix
> Qui me hante,
> Et, sur le mode fabuleux,
> Je chante
> Au gré joyeux ou nébuleux
> De ma muse pathétique ou musarde,
> Allègre, grave ou hagarde![1]

In *Par les Chemins* (1908), her only book of verse so far, she has gathered together poems of all kinds: reflective, exhortative, parabolic, esoteric, descriptive, symbolic, dionysian – simple songs, sonnets, ballads, epigrammes and invectives. Whatever the kind may be, a woman, a personality, is speaking through the verses. That personality is, perhaps a little hypnotized by the accumulated poetic material of the centuries, but not always to its hurt; and it is now a tender-hearted, now a mocking, now a voluptuous, now an austere, now an angry, now a mysterious, and always – within its own limits – a free personality. I can only quote one short poem:

Nocturne

> La musique et les mots exquis
> retiennent l'étranger qui passe.
> (Lao-Tseu Tao Te King)

> C'est une nuit lunaire et le silence est beau.
> Les souvenirs du jour flottent dans ma pensée,
> – Blancs nénuphars sur le miroir profond d'une eau,
>
> Et je regarde au flot leur corolle bercée.
> De vous, comme d'un site aimé, je me souviens.
> Ce matin, sur des doigts s'inclina votre tête,
> Vous les avez baisés: ce n'était pas les miens!
> Pourtant de vous revoir j'avais le coeur en fête
> Et j'ai souri, songeant à l'adage naïf,
> Qu'il n'est point ici-bas sans épine une rose.
> Ah! puissent les démons de mon effluve actif

[1] Berthe Reynold, *Par les chemins* (Paris, 1908).‡

Ensorceler bientôt d'une métamorphose
Vos espoirs et vous prendre aux geôles de leurs rets!
Alors, sur l'horizon vous vous arrêterez,
Puis la terre, la mer, l'azur et mes paroles
Diront pour vous le chant de mes sirènes folles.[1]

It is not in the purely lyrical, but in the dramatic, form that Mme Reynold will find – has found – her way. She is the author of a number of plays, some of which have been produced, and one of which, *Les Moutons Noirs*, has had the unenviable fortune of having been billed for years (at the Odéon) and never staged. In desperation, Mme Reynold has printed it; and with the evidence of a good play in their hands, ironic critics are bombarding M. Antoine with their indignation. *Les Moutons Noirs* (evil destinies, evil thoughts) is a rustic tragedy; its scene is laid in Brittany. The form is prose; but Mme Reynold has allowed her peasants to speak their thoughts simply, without sophistication; and that and the tragedy following the hallucination of Alain Mériadeck – les moutons noirs – work the play up to a high lyrical pitch. *Les Moutons Noirs* is a poem.

TANCRÈDE DE VISAN

M. Tancrède de Visan is the theorist of *Symbolisme*. He was the first to show – in the prefatory essay to his book of poems, *Paysages Introspectifs* (1904) – the close relationship between the symbolist aesthetic and the philosophy of Bergson.[2] His later book of philosophical criticism, to which I have already referred, *L'Attitude du Lyrisme contemporain* (1911), developed this essay in a series of monographs on the most representative poets of the symbolist generation. It is a book to steep oneself in. M. de Visan is preparing a thesis on the same subject for his doctorship of letters. His book is to be awaited with pleasure, and even excitement.

As an epigraph to the poems in *Paysages Introspectifs*, M. de Visan has put these verses by Henri de Régnier:

> L'Aurore et le printemps, le couchant et l'automne
> Sont avec la forêt et le fleuve et la mer
> D'extérieurs aspects de ton soi monotone;
> Le verger fructifie et mûrit dans ta chair,
> La nuit dort ton sommeil, l'averse pleut tes pleurs,
> L'avril sourit ton rire et l'août rit ta joie,
> Tu cueilles ton parfum en chacune des fleurs,
> Et, tout n'étant qu'en toi, tu ne peux être ailleurs.[3]

[1] 'Nocturne', *Ibid.*
[2] Tancrède de Visan, 'Essai sur le symbolisme', *Paysages introspectifs* (Paris, 1904), pp. xxx–xxxii, xxxv–xl, xliv–l, lxxi, and *passim*.
[3] *Paysages introspectifs*, *op. cit.*, unnumbered p. 1.

They describe exactly the *état d'âme* in which M. de Visan has constructed his grave, reflective and intellectual poems. Intellectual, indeed, despite his own desire: "Ah! pouvoir tout sentir, toujours, avec tout nous!..." He had in mind, when writing his book, the mystics who, through the transparencies of their soul, perceived heaven reflected by the objects around them. Solitary, enthusiastic and pure, sheltered from the world, yet knowing its joys and sorrows, they attained an acuity of vision which showed them the real behind nature, the living idea beyond the material form. M. de Visan aspired to be like these. He has not altogether succeeded, he knows that: perhaps because he is too well trained in too many methods, which trammel his emotion and his inspiration, and have made it impossible, as he avows, to chant in any other fashion than a regular measured strain. This book must be looked upon as the book of his youth, conceived under the fascination of what I have called elsewhere the *concrete* symbol (the use of which obscured too much of the symbolist poetry), and marred here and there by doctrinal intentions. But when M. de Visan is content to let his emotion dictate the aspects of the surrounding landscape, then he attains a charm of grave utterance that is moving and fine. That beneath this utterance may lurk the concrete symbol is of no consequence:

Regrets

> Oh! qu'elle est là-bas!
> – Jules Laforgue

Tu vis comme autrefois, ô tourment de ma chair,
Au bord de ma mémoire, et ton visage clair
Effleure encor ma lèvre au cristal des fontaines!

Ton geste familier m'apparaît à travers
L'embrun de mon exil d'enfant, où tu conquiers
Le méplat incertain des aurores lointaines.

Mais l'automne a mûri les raisins du verger,
Tu ne reviendras plus, ô Psyché, vendanger
La grappe fraternelle où mordaient nos deux bouches.

Le faune du bassin garde son air moqueur,
Et j'écoute parfois son rire dans mon coeur;
Mais l'orage a cassé le fifre qu'il embouche.

Tu m'as cherché longtemps près des magnolias
Fleuris de blanc, où certain soir tu délias
La gerbe d'or de tes cheveux sur mes épaules.

Mais ton âme est toute [*sic*] autre et mon rêve a changé,
Tu ne comprendras plus mes larmes d'affligés [*sic*]
Je n'irai plus te voir baigner le long des saules.

Hélas, les jours ont fait notre esprit impuissant
A renouer les fils de cet amour naissant
Que le destin tissait d'après nos espérances.

Et nous voici réduits à regarder neiger
Nos flocons de bonheur semés dans l'air léger,
Selon la floraison des frêles remembrances...[1]

M. de Visan has contributed to many of the best French reviews, and is also author of *Lettres à L'Elue*, roman; *Colette et Berenice; Les Elégies et les Sonnets de Louise Labé; Le Guignol Lyonnais*, and of *Le Clair Matin sourit*, a book of poems, the fruit of many years, which will appear in autumn.

HENRI HERTZ

Mocking at life because it hurts him, M. Henri Hertz is the lineal son of Jules Laforgue, who cried: Un couchant des Cosmogonies! / Ah! que la Vie est quotidienne...But M. Hertz is less concerned with the cosmogonies, for he is healthier than Laforgue, and more concerned with life's dailiness. He is a bitter and ironical poet, wilfully enigmatic. You must follow him docilely into his reverie, and not grumble at the leaps he asks you to make; when you are at the end of your journey, you will, perhaps, be a little bewildered; but you will have a lasting impression of an acrid sorrow, a sharp scent of geraniums. Just as with Laforgue, just as with Tristan Corbière, you will be aware that you have been attacked by a piercing criticism of life, not the snarl of Diogenes, but the cry that comes from a man who would have men better, cleaner, more upright, less hypocritical, facing existence bravely as gods, supermen, if you will, and not as the wretched rascals and cowards that they are. In every generation, one poet at least will watch with sorrow in his heart and a twisted smile on his face, the human tragedy: Henri Hertz is that poet. Consider this poem:

Tu peux tirer ta guitare,
Trouvère,
Et tourner tes cils
E'exil
Vers
Les avatars
De ma richesse.
Laisse.
Je ne suis point la madone
Ni l'ange.
Range
Les soupirs que tu me donnes.

[1] 'Regrets', *Ibid.*, pp. 45–6. The words should read *tout* and *d'affligé*.

Mon mari part le matin
Chasser le daim.
J'entends la chaîne
Du pont
Qui peine
Sous le bond
De l'étalon.

Moi j'erre dans les salles
Que partage avec moi le vent d'Hiver.
J'erre
Dans les vals
Qui mendient sous ma fenêtre
Par le murmure des hêtres.

Je descends parfois dans les cours
Où sont les chenils, les étables, les fours.

Pourquoi, au lieu de prier, vais-je dans l'enfer
En fixant les lames des fers?

Mon amant Satan
M'attend.

Crispe ton écaille,
Trouvère,
Sur ma confidence,
Et que ta cadence,
Aille
De travers!

Satan m'emmene dans les fossés
Comblés d'eau
Et de crapauds;
Sur les glacis pelés,
Je m'y plais.
Assez!

Porte, porte ma damnation, mon plaisir
De château en château, sur ta lyre.
Va leur dire que la châtelaine
Est pleine
De démon.
Va, va, crie-le sur les monts.

J'entends le soir venir comme un sépulcre.
Mon mari ne rentre pas.
Les compagnes, tout bas,
Hurlent.

Cesse, trouvère, et va boire.
Cette nuit, tu pourras me voir.
A la lueur des torches, l'attendre.
Il rugira en mangeant des viandes
Et videra le lourd hanap.
Je serai tendre
En regardant mes bagues briller sur la nappe.

Viens à tâtons, en voleur,
Jusqu'à la porte bardée: tu entendras mes pleurs
Entre ses muscles ivres
Qui sentent le givre.

Tu entendras l'enfer
Craquer dans mes os.
Dans ses rots
Je laisserai tomber tes vers.

Il est tard.
Ralentis ta guitare
Et repose ta main.
Il est tard.
Songe au chemin.

Tiens, voici une fleur de l'été
Pour fleurir ta naïveté.[1]

M. Henri Hertz is the author of *Quelques Vers* (1906); and *Les Mécréants* (1909) mystère civil en 4 actes, in verse, wherein the irony and mockery that give pungency to his verses are applied to the setting forth of human beings and their appliances in action; it is a kind of satirical presentment of a nation in revolution. Revolution?... *Vous riez?...*

F.-T. MARINETTI AND "LE FUTURISME"

"We will sing the love of danger, the habit of energy and of temerity.

"The essential elements of our poetry are audacity and revolt.

"Literature having hitherto magnified pensive immobility, ecstasy and sleep, we will exalt aggressive movement, feverish insomnia, the step of the gymnast, the somersault, the smack in the face, and the blow of the fist.

"We declare that the splendour of the world has been enriched with a new beauty, the beauty of speed...

"The poet must expend himself with heat, vividness and prodigality, in order to augment the enthusiastic fervour of the primordial elements.

"There is no beauty except in strife. No masterpiece without an aggressive character. Poetry must be a violent assault upon unknown forces, summoning them to crouch before man.

"We are on the extreme promontory of the centuries!... Of what use to look behind us, since now we must needs break in the mysterious folding doors of the impossible! time and space died yesterday. We are living already in the absolute, since we have already created the eternal, omnipresent speed.

"We will glorify war – the only hygiene of the world – militarism, patriotism, the destructive gesture of the anarchists, the beautiful ideas that kill, the contempt for women.

"We will sing the great crowds agitated by work, pleasure, or revolt; the multi-coloured and polyphonic surf of revolutions in modern capitals; the nocturnal vibration of arsenals, and of dockyards, beneath their violent electric arcs; the gluttonous stations swallowing smoking serpents; the factories suspended to the

[1] Henri Hertz.‡

clouds by the threads of their smokes; the bridges leaping like gymnasts over the diabolical cutlery of sunny rivers; the adventurous liners that sniff the horizon; the great chested locomotives that paw the rails like enormous steel horses bridled with long tubes; and the gliding flights of aeroplanes, whose screw flaps like flags and the plaudits of enthusiastic crowds..."[1]

That is the poetical *credo* of M. F.-T. Marinetti, one electric with possibilities, its chief danger being rhetoric. But it is a creed to which its author has been faithful with all his courage. He has suffered for his faith in fines, prosecutions, arrests, imprisonments. The responsibility for the war in Tripoli has been attributed to him; he claims it as his, exulting that Italy is at last awakening from museum-sleep and hotel-keeping; his last book is *La Bataille de Tripoli*, vécue et chantée par F.-T. Marinetti, a series of prose poems: he has himself been under fire.

No doubt Italy needed its Marinetti; and to those who cry out against a great wind for its destructiveness, one must answer that great winds are the necessary sanitation of the earth. Degeneration? Rubbish! But by writing in French – which was forced on him by a French up-bringing – M. Marinetti has made of futurism a European problem (which must be remembered by those who talk of the conflict of languages: the European intellect speaks in French)...Read the futuristic programme again, and then ask yourself whether English poetry, too, has not need of the greater part of it?

M. Marinetti's poetical works are: *La Conquête des Etoiles, enorme visione oceanica in cui si svolge une lotta fantastica fra le onde in tempesta et le irraggiungibili stelle; Destruction*, poèmes lyriques; *La Momie Sanglante*, poème dramatique. I quote a poem, much mutilated, unfortunately, from *Destruction*:

La Chanson du Mendiane D'Amour

Je t'avais vue un soir, naguère, je ne sais où,
et depuis, haletant, j'attendais...
La Nuit gonflée d'étoiles et de parfums bleuâtres,
alanguissait sur moi sa nudité éblouissante
et convulsée d'amour!...
La Nuit éperdument ouvrait ses constellations
comme des veines palpitantes de pourpre et d'or,
et toute la volupté illuminante de son sang
rousselait dans le ciel vaste...
J'attendais ivre, sous tes fenêtres embrasées,
qui flambaient seules, dans l'espace;
j'attendais immobile le miracle suprême
de ton amour et l'aumône ineffable

---

[1] F. T. Marinetti, *Le Figaro*, 20 February 1909. Reprinted in *Archivi del Futurismo*, 1, Rome, ed. Marie Drudi Gambillo and Teresa Fiori, n.d., pp. 17–19.

de ton regard...
...Car je suis le mendiant affamé d'Idéal,
qui va le long des grèves,
quêtant l'amour et les baisers,
de quoi nourrir son rêve...

Une muraille se dressait,
implacable et hautaine comme le désespoir!...
J'attendais seul, et des étoiles par milliers,
et des folles étoiles semblaient jaillir de tes fenêtres
comme un vol d'étincelles d'une fournaise d'or!...
Ton [*sic*] ombre douce parut au creux des vitres,
semblable à une âme affolée qui s'agite,
en des prunelles agonisantes,
et tu devins pour moi la délirante proie,
là-haut, debout, tout au sommet
des tours fastueuses de mon Rêve!...
Mon Amour d'un grand geste brandit ses épées rouges,
dents étincelantes et prunelles crochues,
et monta farouchement vers ta splendeur tragique.

.   .   .   .

Je te suivis au fond de tes demeures...
Nous fûmes seuls, loin des foules humaines,
au seuil de l'Infini...et je sentis la suavité
des crépuscules sur la mer, quand l'on arrive
en des golfes violets, tout humides de silence!...
Nous fûmes suels et mon Rêve
chanta face à face à ton Rêve:

– "Oh! Baisse tes paupières langoureusement
sur la folie errante de ton regard.
Baisse tes paupières mystiques et lentes,
comme des ailes d'ange qui se replient.
Baisse tes paupières roses, afin que la flamme souple
de tes prunelles
glisse entre elles,
comme un soupir de lune aux persiennes mi-closes.
Baisse tes paupières et puis soulève-les encore,
et je pourrai alors me perdre en tes yeux,
me perdre à jamais en tes yeux,
comme sur les [*sic*] lacs assoupis, le soir,
parmi des frondaisons calmes et noires!...

– "Sois douce, car mon coeur tremble entre tes doigts,
sois douce! l'Ombre est attentive à nos ivresses;
le Silence se penche et nous caresse
comme une mère attendrie!...Sois douce!...
Pour la première fois, j'adore éperdument
mon âme et je l'admire de t'aimer ainsi
comme une pauvre folle...
J'adore mes lèvres, car mes lèvres te désirent...
Mon âme est à toi, mon âme est si lointaine et si bleue
qu'elle me semble une étrangère!...

Mon âme s'humilie devant toi,
comme une brebis mourante!...
Elle s'endort en frissonnant sous tes pieds frêles,
telle une prairie qui s'argente
sous les pas sournois de la lune...

. . . .

Mais la Luxure, hélas, nous guettait,
furetant insidieuse au ras de l'ombre...
La Luxure haletante rampait le long des murs!

. . . .

Par un geste sublime,
tum m'offris, délirante, ta nudité suave
comme on offre une gourde fraîche,
et j'abreuvai ma Soif immense, sur ton corps nu,
jusqu'au délire, pour y trouver l'immense Oubli...
Tremblante et affolée de vertige,
mon Ame se pencha sur ta beauté radieuse,
éperdument, comme sur un abîme
miroitant de parfums et de chaudes lumières!...
Tes yeux doucement s'alanguirent,
sous tes roses paupières,
– lampes voilées de tulle vaporeuse –
et m'inclinant parmi l'envol de tes cheveux,
je pris enfin ton Ame, toute ton Ame,
pieusement au bord des lèvres, comme une Hostie...
Quand je repartis vers la profondeur
des nuit blêmes,
ma gourde était vidée et mon coeur était noir!
J'eus soif et je bus
goulûment l'eau noire des fontaines...

. . . .

et puis je m'évadias [*sic*], hâtant mes pas, vers l'Inconnu.
Car je suis le mendiant qui va le long des grèves,
quêtant l'amour et les baisers de quoi nourir [*sic*] mon Rêve,
avec au coeur l'effroi mortel d'enlizer pour toujours,
par un grand Soir de lassitude et de néant,
ses pieds sanguinolents
dans la fraîcheur charnelle des sables, au bord des mers."[1]

M. Marinetti has written novels, among which *Mafarka le Futuriste* (the translation of which brought him prosecution in Italy and a triumphant acquittal); plays, books of criticism, pamphlets innumerable, and, in connexion with his review, *Poesia*, he has conducted an international inquiry on verse technique, *Enquête Internationale sur le Vers Libre*. M. Marinetti is the fautor of young artists; at his trial, he said that, being left by his parents with a competency, he conceived the

[1] Marinetti, 'Le Chanson du mendiant d'amour', *Destruction* (Paris, 1904), pp. 65–7, 69–70, 72, 73–4. The words should read *Ton, des, m'évadais*, and *nourrir*.

audace progetto di rinnovamente intellettuale ed artistico in Italia: quello di proteggere, incoraggiare ed aiutare materialmente i giovani ingegni novatori e ribelli che quotidianamente vengono soffocati dall'indifferenza, dall'avarizia, o dalla miopia degli editori...[1] "We stand upon the summit of the world, and once more we cast our challenge to the stars!"[2] I salute in M. Marinetti a life devoted to art.

I salute in the poets of France an inextinguishable vitality!

F. S. Flint.

[1] Marinetti.‡
[1] Marinetti, *Archivi, op. cit.*, 19. This is the concluding sentence in the founding manifesto.

A FRENCH ACCOUNT OF THE FRENCH CONTEMPORARIES: LETTRE DE FRANCE, II-V

In order to make good his intent to represent the *avant garde* (and hence, he felt, the French) in poetry as well as in fiction, painting, and other arts, editor John Middleton Murry obtained regular contributions to *Rhythm* from Francis Carco and Tristan Derème. The chief responsibility for reporting on French poetry rested with Derème, who contributed five columns headed 'Lettre de France' between June 1912 and February 1913. The author of *Les Ironies sentimentales* (1909), *Petits Poèmes* (1910), *Le Poème de la pipe et de l'escargot* (1912), and – later – *La Verdure dorée* (1922), Derème was in the tradition of ironic, sometimes comic, poets descended from Laforgue, Verlaine, and Corbière. He was a member of a loose association of poets known as *fantaisistes*, a group which included Carco, Henri Hertz, J.-M. Bernard, Jean Pellerin, Léon Vérane, and, much more distantly, Guillaume Apollinaire. A contributor to *Vers et Prose, La Phalange, La Cahier des poètes, Divan*, and *Les Facettes*, Derème was one of the first to take up the label *fantaisiste*,[1] and his *Rhythm* essays were among the earliest published comments urging attention to *fantaisiste* poets as a group.

His first two contributions to *Rhythm* established his individual perspective upon the poetic scene. The introductory essay (June 1912), is a general sketch of the dilemmas of a critic of contemporary poetry and a suggestion of Derème's own criteria for evaluation and selection. In an era in which some poets were stressing the traditional (as was the *École romane*) or the social and the cosmic (as were the *unanimistes*), Derème was emphatic in insisting upon the importance of the new or 'original' and the highly personal. 'Qu'un poème soit nouveau et m'émeuve et je dirai qu'il est beau: et même il suffit qu'il m'émeuve, car pour y réussir it [*sic*] faudra d'abord qu'il soit nouveau.'[2] Such an emphasis upon originality is one pole of the period's intense conflict between theoretical allegiance to tradition and the emergence of highly innovative techniques, and it has its significant echo in Pound's *Make It New*. Derème went so far as to say that *novelty* 'est une condition de l'emotion esthétique'[3] and he implied that he would apply this criterion in selecting the current poets he was to treat in his series of letters from France: Carco, Pellerin, Frène. In order to give a context through which to judge the originality and achievement of the poets he was to discuss, however, he devoted his second essay to a survey of current developments in France.

This column, 'Esquisse de la poésie française actuelle', appeared in the August 1912 issue of *Rhythm*, and thus with Flint's 'Contemporary French Poetry' (*The Poetry Review*, August 1912; see pages 86–145) it became one of two first authoritative accounts in England of current events in French poetry. It was much shorter than Flint's history, quoted very little poetry, and took a deliberately more partisan view of current developments. It treated, though briefly, many of the same nineteenth-century sources that Flint alluded to, and discussed as well *l'Abbaye* group (chiefly the *unanimistes*) and futurism. But even in its short space it took up three groups with which Flint in his 1912 survey did not deal directly – *les néo-classiques, romantisme*, and the *fantaisistes* – and named some 'independents' whom Flint did not treat at length, like Frène, Deubel, Salmon, Mandin, and Lauvaud. Derème highlighted the conflicting tendencies in French literature by ranging the groups on a scale from the highly traditional (Jean Moréas's Hellenists) to the complete libertarians: 'Ce qui caractérise le groupe de l'Abbaye, c'est son absolue liberté.'[4] (Futurism he simply

[1] Kenneth Cornell, *The Post-Symbolist Period: French Poetic Currents, 1900–1920* (New Haven, 1958), p. 150.

[2] "Lettre de France, I., Les Poèmes', *Rhythm*, II, 1 (June 1912) 32–3.   [3] *Ibid.*, 33.

[4] 'Lettre de France, II., Esquisse de la poésie française actuelle', *Rhythm*, II, 3 (August 1912) 115.

placed beyond the pale.) Thus the form of his discussion focused attention on an aspect of the conflict which T. E. Hulme elaborated in 'Romanticism and Classicism', probably slightly later. Derème also singled out in his essay three qualities in French poetry and criticism which were to become touchstones in England: the use of images, creation of a poetry of personal vision, and intense critical concentration upon the poetic text itself.

The use of images Derème specifically linked to the *unanimiste* poets associated through l'Abbaye: 'Ils n'écrivent pourtant pas des chapitres de économie politique; ils composent des poèmes, c'est-à-dire qu'ils expriment, comme les poètes de tous les temps, leurs sentiments ou leurs passions par le moyen d'images.'[1] In granting that these poets expressed social concerns by means of images Derème sounded very like F. S. Flint. Flint at the same time was writing of Jules Romains, one of the poets named by Derème, 'M. Romains is a great creator of images. He is the epic poet of modern life, aspiring always to the highest generalities.'[2] Both writers[3] are following (Flint to the point of paraphrase) the direction indicated by one of the prominent critics to support the *unanimistes*, Georges Duhamel. In *Propos Critiques* (published by Figuière in April 1912) Duhamel said of Romains:

'Son langage poétique vaut également par la notation, par l'image et par d'innombrables trouvailles qui semblent réunir les propriétés de l'image et de la notation...

L'image, plus que la notation, donne à la poésie sa valeur annonciatrice; elle rapproche parfois des éléments fort lointains et accoutume l'esprit à considérer d'un seul coup des idées dont le lien n'était point apparent. L'image est plus qu'un divertissement, plus qu'un jeu sensuel et brillant. Sond estin est plus haut et quand Jules Romains perçoit dans la nuit "Des couples noirs, ayant la forme des clochers..." il emplit son image d'un sens prophétique et livre encore plus à l'esprit qu'il ne confie aux sens.'[4]

The presence of Duhamel behind the briefer references of Derème and Flint is important, for it connects the comments in these London essays to a broader and more significant body of interpretation of the function of the poetic image. In the quoted passage, Duhamel suggested the metaphoric function of the image and noted its effectiveness in conveying a meaning that logical analysis alone would not develop. In this comment Duhamel showed his link with the earlier, symbolist view of the poet as a creator of meaning through the creation of new relationships. When he said that Romains, in so using the image, 'entrusts more to the "esprit" than he confides in the "sens" ', he underscored that the poet uses the language of sensory experience to communicate an abstract understanding, to share a nontangible comprehension or emotion, or to make accessible a direct intuition of the spirit that informs phenomena. In the latter two possibilities, of course, one approaches the veritable omnipresence of Bergson. This view of the image as metaphor does not necessarily go on, however, to imply that the new relationships reveal or create another aspect of 'the Absolute', in the mystical sense that both Mallarmé and Rimbaud (though very different) were inclined to feel. For the *unanimistes* whom Duhamel was discussing, the 'god-principle' arose out of the association of men,[5] and it was an altogether more

[1] 'Lettre de France, II., Esquisse de la poésie française actuelle', *Rhythm*, II, 3 (August 1912) 115.
[2] F. S. Flint, 'Contemporary French Poetry', *The Poetry Review*, I, 8 (August 1912) 383.
[3] Derème refers to Duhamel on p. 115 of this same essay; Flint borrows throughout his essay from *Propos Critiques*.
[4] Georges Duhamel, *Propos Critiques* (Paris, 1912), pp. 50–1.
[5] See for example, Duhamel, *op. cit.*, pp. 41–2; Jules Romains, *Puissances de Paris* (Paris, 1919; 1st pub. 1911), p. 153; B. Stoltzfus, 'L'Unanimisme', *La Revue des Lettres Modernes*, CXI–CXII (1965–6) 44.

social and temporal conception in origin than the mysterious and ineffable world that Rimbaud dimly perceived, or the radical creation out of *néant* that Mallarmé sought as the outcome of the poetic act. Duhamel, the *unanimistes* and many other poets of their decade, and the imagists of England all combined a retention of the idea of poet as metaphysically creative with a definition of Reality or the absolute altogether less otherworldly, altogether more firmly tied to the perceiving man rather than to a visionary seer, than that of their symbolist predecessors.

By his stress upon the 'valeur annonciatrice' and 'sens prophétique' which the image confers upon poetry, Duhamel implied a view of the lyric as a kind of instantaneous revelation, a transmission of a perception, impression or state of mind from poet to reader in a moment of swift comprehension. He also saw the image as fundamental to the kind of poetry then being written; far from a kind of baroque decoration, the image is a vehicle of meaning which gives both form and intellectual content to the poem as it evokes a sensual response.

A parallel view, also explicitly stimulated by the French *vers librists*[1] for whom Duhamel was one of the most aggressive proponents, was expressed by T. E. Hulme. At first, in 'A Lecture on Modern Poetry', delivered probably in early 1909 and revised into its present form in 1914, Hulme discussed combinations of images as the means of conveying a pre-existing but interior idea (or perception or emotion). He too saw a large part of the significance of the image in its use in a combination of logically disparate elements and in the resulting creation and communication of a new perception: 'Say the poet is moved by a certain landscape, he selects from that certain images which, put into juxtaposition in separate lines, serve to suggest and evoke the state he feels.'[2] Later, Hulme expressed an extended version of this theory, in which he suggested that the idea created in the poem might have no pre-existing object of which it was a representation. His language is very similar to Duhamel's, above:

'Very often the idea, apart from the analogy or metaphor which clothes it, has no existence. That is, by a subtle combination of allusions we have artificially built up in us an idea, which apart from these cannot be got at. As if a man took us on a rocky path and said look – and we saw the view, i.e. the analogy is the thing, not merely decoration...'[3]

Another restatement of French theories, represented by Duhamel and alluded to by Derème and Flint, of course, was T. S. Eliot's famous definition of the objective correlative in 1919: 'a set of objects, a situation, a chain of events which shall be the formula of that *particular* emotion; such that when the external facts which must terminate in sensory experience, are given, the emotion is immediately evoked'.[4] Here, like Hulme in 'A Lecutre', Eliot conceived the combination of images (*et al.*) as a representation of an intangible, interior, but pre-existing psychic phenomenon.

Neither Derème nor Flint themselves really anticipated the subsequent developments in England of the theory of the image though. Rather, they were transmitters; their references directed attention to the use of images by a group whose French theorists did anticipate English elaboration of imagistic theory. Derème himself had little personal sympathy with the *unanimistes*, and he saw their use of the image as a kind of saving grace among poets whose themes were dominantly social. (Flint, too,

[1] T. E. Hulme, 'A Lecture on Modern Poetry', *Further Speculations*, ed. Sam Hynes (Lincoln, 1962), p. 68.
[2] Hulme, 'Lecture', *op. cit.*, p. 73.
[3] Hulme, 'Notes on Language and Style', *Further Speculations*, *op. cit.*, p. 83.
[4] 'Hamlet and His Problems', *Selected Essays of T. S. Eliot* (New York, 1967), pp. 124–5.

spoke of Romains' use of images in the same breath in which he cited him as an epic poet in search of generalities.) Derème did not return to a specific discussion of the use of imagery when he turned to the poets with whom he sympathized far more – the personal lyricists and *fantaisistes*. Thus these accounts kept separate the two tendencies of attention to the image and intense personal lyricism. The imagist poets of England yoked the ideas juxtaposed in these essays together in single poems. Imagism became a way of expressing the intense vision of the individual, albeit in the 'objective' fashion of an image which presented the concept or emotion without reference to 'moi'.

It was precisely the open emphasis upon individual vision that Derème found significant in contemporary French work. 'Puis Jean-Jacques Rousseau ébranla toute la littérature; après lui, le romantisme brisa les chaines du *moi*, le symbolisme lui donna des ailes; aujourd'hui il règne en maître absolu.'[1] In fact, Derème felt, it was precisely the function of the poet to give the world an original conception of things. There is in his statement encouragement of the contempt that the most important English poets came to hold for the understanding of the mass of readers and for their experiment with highly obscure expression in an effort to capture the subtlest nuance of individual vision, while omitting direct, undistanced allusion to the writer himself. Derème, thus, is part of the milieu which gave rise to Pound, Eliot, H.D., Edith Sitwell and other figures in the tradition of the 'teens and 'twenties.

The lyric of individual vision, with its obscurity and allusiveness, demanded a special kind of critical approach, which rapidly developed in the next several decades under the name of the new criticism. To the extent that it relies upon the work and milieu of Eliot and I. A. Richards in England in the 'teens, this development is also rooted partially in the French recognition for the need for critical precision. In the comments in which he espoused the poet's function as the creator of an original interpretation, for example, Derème went on to describe the kind of criticism which this achievement necessitates. It is exactly that critical attention to the single text itself that became a touchstone and then a cliché of American criticism: 'Chacun juge par soi et la révolution cartésienne pénètre ainsi dans la poésie deux siècles après son entrée dans les sciences. M. Carco voit l'univers comme il l'entend. M. Vaudoyer écrit des vers réguliers parce que tel est son bon plaisir...Dès lors, plus de critique. Non, plus de critique qui distribue des bons-points et des *satisfecit*, mais une critique qui s'efforce de comprendre l'art de chaque poète et de démêler ce qu'il apporte d'émouvant et de nouveau.'[2] As Derème perceived, both the poetry and the criticism of the era must be seen in relation to the new definitions of the nature of human knowledge and its limitations. Both a poetry of personal vision and a criticism whose primary function is to articulate the formal structure of the poem in the belief that thus meaning will be implicitly articulated emerged in a world in which a simplistic faith in empiricism or common sense had been shaken by the growing awareness that the creative role of the poet is founded upon the creative role of human consciousness in perception itself.

Derème also considered the ancestry of modern schools in French symbolism and sketched an account of the neo-classical bent of one branch of French poetry. His comments on neo-classicism are so hostile that they do little to explain the Anglo-American inclusion of 'classicism' with the doctrine of the image and the espousal of the highly personal vision ('impression'). His notes on the heritage of French symbolism, however, do suggest some of the common forebears of both Anglo-American and French poets of the period: 'il apparait nettement que la situation poètique est

[1] Derème, 'Lettre, II', *op. cit.*, 119.
[2] *Ibid.*

actuellement dominée par les représentants de ce lyrisme qui a ses sources dans les livres de Charles Baudelaire, de Paul Verlaine, de Stéphane Mallarmé et de Tristan Corbière. Il n'est pas une poème de valeur à notre époque qui ne se ressent de l'atmosphère qu'ont criée Rimbaud, Laforgue, Samain, Moréas, Rodenbach, Guérin parmi les morts et, parmi les vivants, MM. Francis Jammes, Paul Fort, Henri de Régnier, Emile Verhaeren, Stuart Merrill, Vielé-Griffin, Gustav [sic] Kahn et le Maurice Maeterlinck des *Serres Chaudes*. Ceux-là sont tenus pour des maîtres et leur influence directe ou indirecte est profonde.'[1] Common in modern criticism, this account of influences in 1912 provided the names of poets which many Anglo-American writers were just beginning to read.

What is more, in paying homage to the dead, Derème also communicated an interpretation of what in their work remained significant. He stressed both the achievement of freedom of form and content and the perception of mystery – not within the mind or in the world beyond – but in the presence of temporal life. 'Ils ont rejeté à l'infini, aussi bien pour le fonds que pour la forme, les limites de la liberté poètique; ils ont apporté, ou du moins développé, affiné, aiguisé et rendu parfois comme maladif le sens du mystère en face de la vie et de la destinée.'[2] Thus he emphasized, first, the freedom of form that was a product of the symbolist *cénacle* and, second, the reconciliation of ideal conception and empirical experience that was actually part of the reaction against symbolism that occurred in the post-symbolist period. Both the abandonment of traditional metric forms in favor of an intrinsic rhythm and the attempt to render an ideal conception as an apotheosis of the implications of a material object became touchstones of Anglo-American poetry of the imagist period.

In the essays on individual poets which followed his general survey of current French work, Derème emphasized the *fantaisiste* poetry of sensitivity undercut by irony – a tone which Eliot at about the same time was capturing in 'Portrait of a Lady' and 'Mr. Apollinax'.[3] Like other Eliot poems, Derème's selections from Carco and Pellerin reflect a heritage of Corbière and Laforgue. The French *fantaisistes* thus helped to establish in London, as a hallmark of the modern poet, an ironic mode which recalled the ironists of the nineteenth century.

Most interesting, however, are the similarities between the descriptions offered for *fantaisisme* and those adopted by the imagists. In this connection, the most revealing essay is Derème's discussion of Francis Carco. Like the imagists, the *fantaisistes* were faulted for 'triviality', for failing to undertake a sufficiently profound poetic enterprise. They confined themselves, for the most part, to the exact conveying of the nuance of an immediate experience, or as Derème wrote in 'Poètes Nouveaux', 'Ils usent d'un langage précis pour exprimer des émotions parfois imprécises et connaissent le sens des mots qu'ils emploient et le manière de les lier pour en former des phrases.'[4] Moreover, they emphasized concision, Derème said; they sought perfection in presenting a narrowly limited poetic object, and they carefully sought the precise word to convey a vivid impression in a few lines. The sources of this art were also in many ways the same as the sources of imagist art: impressionist pictorial technique and Japanese haiku. In writing of Francis Carco, Derème specified: 'Sa manière rappelle à la fois l'impressionnisme pictural et la méthode des poètes japonais, écrivains de

1 Derème, 'Lettre, II', *op. cit.*, 114.
2 *Ibid.*
3 'Portrait of a Lady', for example, was written in 1910, after Eliot had been reading Laforgue and in the same year that he began his stay in Paris. The poem, thus, is an outgrowth of the same milieu which gave rise to the *fantaisiste* ironists.
4 *Rhythm*, II, 9 (October 1912) 228. See page 156 of this volume.

haikais...qui d'un petit pinceau tracérent de grandes choses'.[1] And in the manner of the haiku poets, Derème believed, Carco conveyed an intangible emotion by the most concrete and specific kind of poetic diction: 'sa poésie est, avant tout, concrète; elle hait l'abstraction et, par une sorte d'intuition, épouse si étroitement la forme et la matière des choses, qu'elle donne l'impression d'être une *poésie physique*...'[2] In practice, this meant that Carco avoided the direct description of a 'state of soul' and chose instead to render his inner feeling by the precise and selective description of the objects or milieu which gave rise to the feeling. What Derème praised in Carco's poetry sounds like a list of the qualities of the imagist movement, for which, indeed, the rationale was being shaped in the weeks immediately after his essay on Carco appeared in October 1912. The poetry itself, which includes both rhyming verse and prose poems, has most affinities with some poems of the earlier stages of imagism – with, for example, For Madox Ford's 'In the Little Old Market-Place', which Pound regarded later as more nearly impressionist than imagist. The Carco selections which appeared in *Rhythm*, however, while impressionist in selection of visual detail, are rigorous in finding an external correlative for an emotional state. By no means all the *fantaisistes* suggest a French predecessor to imagism, but it is fair to say that many poems by Carco in these years would not have seemed out-of-place had they appeared in *Des Imagistes*.

LETTRES DE FRANCE

II. ESQUISSE DE LA POÉSIE FRANÇAISE ACTUELLE*

En 1832, dans la préface d'*Albertus*, Théophile Gautier écrivait en parlant de lui-même: "*Cependant, si éloigné qu'il soit des choses de la vie, il sait que le vent ne souffle pas à la poésie...*" Il est permis de se demander s'il penserait aujourd'hui d'une autre manière et l'on sait que les poètes de tous les temps ont déploré, et assez justement, l'hostilité ou l'indifférence du public envers leurs ouvrages. Toujours, les écrivains se reportent par la pensée à des époques antérieures qui prennent à leurs yeux l'aspect de paradis à littérateurs, car d'un état social ce qui subsiste seulement ce sont les oeuvres de l'esprit, et les civilisations disparues nous donnent l'aimable illusion de ne s'être souciées que de lettres, d'arts et de sciences: c'est ainsi que si nous songeons au siècle de Louis XIV nous ne voyons que des écrivains, des artistes, des savants, des politiques et des amateurs et nous ne pensons pas qu'il y avait alors une foule grouillante qui vendait du drap au Marais, à Bourges ou à Bayonne, qui buvait du vin blanc, le dimanche, sous les treilles ou rentrait le foin, les soirs de Juin, dans les prairies provinciales et se préoccupait assez peu des tragédies de Jean Racine et ne savait même pas que Descartes eût disserté de la Méthode.

Ce phénomène historique n'est nullement fait pour servir les écrivains

[1] *Rhythm*, II, *op. cit.*, 229. See page p. 157.
[2] *Ibid.*, 230. See page 158.
* *Rhythm*, II, 3 (August 1912) 113–19.

qui respirent encore; la foule, avec un sourire narquois, leur montre leurs aînés qui règnent sur les siècles de jadis ou de naguère. *"Quelle étrange manie,"* dit M. Baliveau à Damès, le jeune poète, dans *la Métromanie* de Piron,

> *"Quelle étrange manie! Hé, dis-moi, misérable!*
> *A de si grands esprits te crois-tu comparable?"*

M. Clément Vautel, de la sorte, a pu l'autre jour dans *le Matin* reprocher à MM. Jammes, Paul Fort et Verhaeren de n'être pas aussi imposants que Victor Hugo, Lamartine et Musset; mais c'est mal faire que de mettre en balance des hommes encore occupés à composer leur oeuvre avec des poètes chargés d'un siècle de gloire et de comparer Victor Hugo tel qu'on le voit en 1912 à M. Francis Jammes tel qu'il apparait dans la même année. Quand Victor Hugo avait l'âge de MM. Jammes et Fort il était loin d'être universellement admiré; on le traitait assez volontiers de *vandale* et de *fou furieux* et l'on opposait à son soleil levant ces pauvres lampions qu'étaient Raynouard, Lemercier et Etienne,[1] car il s'est trouvé dans tous les temps des critiques pour préférer Pradon à Racine et Jean Aicard à Paul Verlaine. Que l'on veuille bien attendre cent ans et l'on reprendra le parallèle. Mais les jeunes poètes peuvent aujourd'hui répondre avec leur frère de *la Métromanie* :

> *"Ces maîtres même avaient les leurs en débutant,*
> *Et tout le monde alors put leur en dire autant."*

Si on laisse dans le tourbillon de leur vaine renommée et de l'encens populaire ou mondain qui les environne MM. Rostand et Richepin qui intéressent plutôt le chapitre de la publicité ou des accessoires de théâtre que celui des lettres, il apparait nettement que la situation poétique est actuellement dominée par les représentants de ce lyrisme qui a ses sources dans les livres de Charles Baudelaire, de Paul Verlaine, de Stéphane Mallarmé et de Tristan Corbière. Il n'est pas un poème de valeur à notre époque qui ne se ressente de l'atmosphère qu'ont criée Rimbaud, Laforgue, Samain, Moréas, Rodenbach, Guérin parmi les morts et, parmi les vivants, MM. Francis Jammes, Paul Fort, Henri de Régnier, Emile Verhaeren, Stuart Merrill, Vielé-Griffin, Gustav [*sic*] Kahn et le Maurice Maeterlinck des *Serres Chaudes.* Ceux-là sont tenus pour des maîtres et leur influence directe ou indirecte est profonde. Ils ont rejeté à l'infini, aussi bien pour le fonds que pour la forme, les limites de la liberté poètique; ils ont apporté, ou de moins développé, affiné, aiguisé et rendu parfois comme maladif le sens du mystère en face de la vie et de la destinée.

---

[1] Cf. Albert de Bersaucourt, *Les Pamphlets contre Victor Hugo.* (Paris, 1912) [Derème's note.]

Derrière ces écrivains parvenus à la gloire, bataillent les troupes des jeunes poètes.

M. Gabriel Vicaire écrivait,[1] parlant de la poésie et des poètes en 1893 *"Jamais pareille confusion ne s'était vue, ce qui n'est pas pour déplaire à ceux que ne trouble pas outre-mesure le sentiment de l'ordre et de la règle,"* et sur ce point il semble que depuis dix-neuf ans rien n'ait changé. Il n'y a plus d'écoles; il y a beaucoup de manifestes et de doctrines, mais si un poète a trois disciples, il faut crier au miracle et les théoriciens même sont les premiers à ne suivre pas leurs propres théories.

Pourtant, si l'on observe scrupuleusement leurs inclinations, les poètes, malgré leur impatience de tout frein, peuvent être rangés en quelques groupes parmi lesquels le groupe de l'Abbaye et le groupe néo-classique attirent d'abord l'attention aussi bien par leur valeur que par le bruit qu'ils mènent.

Ce qui caractérise le groupe de l'Abbaye, c'est son absolue liberté. Ses protagonistes, MM. Romains, Duhamel, Arcos, Vildrac et Chennevière, encore qu'influencés par Walt Whitman et Verhaeren, ont résolument mis sous leurs semelles toute tradition, toute loi, toute autorité et par conséquent toute mesure. Leur poésie est libre aussi bien dans sa pensée que dans son aspect.

Quelle est donc, outre la liberté, la qualité commune de ces esprits? C'est que le même spectacle les captive et c'est la vie sociale, *La présence humaine*, comme dit M. Duhamel qui est le critique, le Sainte-Beuve ou le Du Bellay du groupe, mais la présence humaine à l'état pur, considérée en soi, la simple contiguïté des individus à la fois dans le temps et dans l'espace avec ses conséquences, voilà l'objet de leurs méditations et de leur art. Pour eux, comme pour le vieux Grec, l'homme est un être qui vit en société. Ils n'écrivent pourtant pas des chapitres de économie politique; ils composent des poèmes, c'est-à-dire qu'ils expriment, comme les poètes de tous les temps, leurs sentiments ou leurs passions par le moyen d'images; mais leur lyrisme sociologique, plus voluntaire que spontané, en général trop viril pour être tendre, à la fois barbare et scientifique, apocalyptique et systématique, tantôt largement lucide et tantôt obscur et bégayant et, à certaines pages, étranglé d'une angoisse profonde qui n'est pas sans beauté, donne l'impression d'une force sourde et redoutable, constitue une forme rude et pesante et assez nouvelle de la poésie et qui est comme l'aboutissement de l'oeuvre de M. Verhaeren.

Les néo-classiques, eux, sont calmes et mesurés. Leur table est

---

[1] *Revue Hebdomadaire-févier*, 1893. [Derème's note.]

encombrée de règles exactes et de balances minutieuses. Ce sont hommes de goût et l'on sait qu'être homme de goût consiste à plaire non seulement à soi-même mais à certains morts révérés, à Jean Racine, par example, et quelquefois à l'abbé Delille. Ce sont des hommes d'ordre qui veulent rester dans ce qu'ils appellent la tradition française: pour ce faire, il [sic] chantent sous la bannière de Jean Papadiamantopoulous-Moréas, qui fut sujet hellène, pasticheur assez heureux qui usa son porte-plume et sa vie à traduire les pensées des autres dans la forme d'autrui.

On pourrait leur objecter, peut-être, que la tradition n'exige qas [sic] que les poètes se transforment en copistes des chefs d'oeuvre nationaux, que c'est aussi une tradition en France – et ailleurs – que d'innover; que La Fontaine, esprit classique s'il en est, a crié:

"*Il nous faut du nouveau n'en fût-il plus au monde!*"

et que Villon, Ronsard, Corneille, Racine, Rousseau et Hugo, dans l'histoire de lettres, font plutôt figure de révolutionnaires que d'élèves dociles des maîtres passés. A quoi nos poètes répondraient qu'ils innovent prudemment.

Leur langue, dont l'élégante sécheresse et la précision mécanique ne sont pas sans analogie avec la creuse perfection des vers de Voltaire, ne dédaigne pas d'exprimer par moments une manière de chaude sensualité dont on pourrait trouver l'origine dans les poèmes d'André Chénier. Mais-ce sont des écrivains très raisonnables, très sages, trop discrets pour oser se donner licence d'être profondément originaux.

En deçà des néo-classiques bavardent les innombrables élèves de M. Dorchain, poètes sans existence propre qui voient le monde à travers les lunettes du romantisme, recommencent inlassablement les oeuvres anthumes et posthumes de Victor Hugo, Vigny, Lamartine et Musset, n'ont pas encore lu Verlaine et ne soupçonnent pas que M. Jammes existe.

Au delà des poètes de l'Abbaye, c'est le futurisme éclatant, bariolé, illuminé d'éclairs de M. Marinetti qui rêve, au moins en théorie, d'anéantir le passé et de brûler les musées et les bibliothèques.

Mais, entre l'Abbaye et le Néo-classicisme, au centre du tableau, se trouvent ceux que j'appellerai *les Fantaisistes* (MM. Carco, Pellerin, Vèrane, etc....) et *les Indépendants* sans programme commun (MM. Frène, Puy, Deubel, Salmon, Mandin, Spire, Lavaud, Périn, etc....) qui édifient le monument poètique de l'époque et dont je ne définirai pas aujourd'hui le lyrisme me promettant de consacrer mes prochaines lettres à la critique de leurs ouvrages.

Si nous jetons un rapide coup d'oeil sur la France actuelle, nous voyons que la poésie politique n'existe plus; il ne convient pas de s'en étonner si ce n'est qu'en des époques profondément troublées que purent éclore *les Invectives* de Claudien,[1] *les Discours* de Ronsard, *les Tragiques* d'Agrippa d'Aubigné et *les Châtiments* de Victor Hugo. La poésie didactique et la poésie épique sont depuis longtemps défuntes ou plutôt il faudrait dire qu'elles n'ont jamais vécu chez nous. La poésie moralisatrice et pédagogique est morte elle aussi comme une pauvre chandelle depuis que Nietzsche a soufflé et personne aujourd'hui n'oserait plus écrire l'*Ode sur l'Amour-Propre* comme Lamotte-Houdar ni même *la Conscience* comme Victor Hugo.

La poésie actuelle est une poésie lyrique; son mode essentiel est l'expression du *moi*. Je sais bien que les poètes, même qui semblent le plus détacher de leur propre personne, n'ont jamais parlé que d'eux-mêmes; que les personnages de *Phèdre* ne sont que les divers aspects de l'âme racinienne et que les poèmes qui composent *Emaux et Camées* sont si peu distincts de Gautier qu'ils représentent la partie la plus intime du ciseleur, je veux dire sa pensée. Mais les poètes, jusqu'au siècle dernier, mettaient une certaine pudeur à dévoiler leurs sentiments particuliers; "*le moi est haissable*" disait Pascal, ils ne se laissaient deviner qu'a travers des fictions et sous des termes généraux. Pourtant, de loin en loin et comme par éclairs, la poésie personnelle s'était laissé entrevoir. François Villon s'était hardiment mis en scène, et plus tard les indépendants du XVIIe siècle, Théophile et Saint-Amand. Puis Jean-Jacques Rousseau ébran la toute la littérature; après lui, le romantisme brisa les chaines du *moi*, le symbolisme lui donna des ailes; aujourd'hui il règne en maître absolu. Dans les livres, le mot le plus employé est le mot *je*.

Chacun parle de soi, et c'est très bien ainsi; car si chacun le fait originalement, chacun nous livre une conception neuve des choses. Chacun parle *directement* de soi; on exprime un sentiment nu sans l'envelopper d'une anecdote ou d'un récit comme faisaient jadis Lamartine et naguère Coppeé. On n'écrit plus, non plus, de sonnets sur Cléopâtre ou sur les troubadours et rares sont les mains qui ouvrent encore la porte de ces magasins de décors que l'on nomme l'antiquité ou le Moyen-Age.

Chacun juge par soi et la révolution cartésienne pénétre ainsi dans la poésie deux siècles après son entrée dans les sciences. M. Carco voit l'univers comme il l'entend. M. Vaudoyer écrit des vers réguliers parce que tel est son bon plaisir. M. Arcos écrit des vers libres parce que cela lui plaît. Plus de règles. Dès lors, plus de critique.

---

[1] Le protégé de Stilicon et non pas notre excellent collaborateur M. Claudien. [Derème's note.]

Non, plus de critique qui distribue des bons-points et des *satisfecit*, mais une critique qui s'efforce de comprendre l'art de chaque poète et de démêler ce qu'il apporte d'émouvant et de nouveau.

III. POÈTES NOUVEAUX*

Henri Fabre, le naturaliste, celui que Darwin appelait *l'observateur inimitable* et qui apporte à l'exposition de ses souvenirs entomologiques une simple bonhomie qui n'est pas toujours dénuée de malice et qui rappelle, avec plus de cordialité et moins de sèche élégance, les spirituelles finesses dont Fontenelle assaisonnait ses causeries astronomiques, – Henri Fabre a écrit que la *mante religieuse* est un insecte beaucoup moins célèbre que la cigale parce qu'elle ne mène pas grand tapage. "Si le ciel, dit il, l'eût gratifiée de cymbales, première condition de la popularité, elle éclipserait le renom de la célèbre chanteuse." Et ces paroles me font songer à quelques écrivains – MM. Francis Carco, Jean Pellerin, Léon Vérane, Claudien, etc.... – qui travaillent sans secouer les cymbales du scandale et de la réclame, sans publier de tumultueux manifestes et qui n'estiment pas indispensable d'avertir la presse s'ils partent pour les bains de mer ou changent de veston.

Ils usent d'un langage précis pour exprimer des émotions parfois imprécises et connaissent le sens des mots qu'ils emploient et le manière de les lier pour en former des phrases.

Un tel éloge peut, en certains pays, paraître ironique ou naif. Il ne l'est guère chez nous où l'on voit louer et congratuler tels faiseurs de livres qui n'ont cure de la syntaxe et dédaignent l'orthographe. Dans la boutique de leur malheureux éditeur, s'entassent par leurs soins volumes sur volumes et de ce vain amas de papier imprimé ils se construisent un piédestal et s'élévent ainsi dans l'admiration du populaire, mais ne montent si haut, comme chante Claudien d'Alexandrie, que pour tomber d'une chute plus lourde.

Les poètes dont je parle sont plus sobres, car rien n'engage à la concision (M. Rémy de Gourmont l'a déjà noté) comme l'abondance des idées. Ils sont le souci d'enfermer une impression en quelques lignes et d'être brefs pour serrer plus étroitement leur pensée et toucher à la perfection; et quand on lit leurs ouvrages, il faut – suivant le conseil du vieux Guez de Balzac parlant de Malherbe – peser les mots et non pas les compter.

Une âme lyrique qui se manifeste à travers un visage pâle et rasé et des complets impeccables: c'est Francis Carco. Il chante les petits cabarets et les visages de la nature. Il a publié deux recueils: *Instincts* et *la Bohème et mon Coeur*; et ni les bars aveuglants et tumultueux de

* *Rhythm*, II, 9 (October 1912) 228–31.

Montmatre [*sic*], ni *la lumière stridente* des music-halls et ni les fêtes et le luxe de la Côte d'Azur n'ont pu emousser sa belle ferveur; et quand je le vois danser dans l'amertume de cette époque, en secouant comme une joyeuse oriflamme sa riche fraîcheur et son inaltérable jeunesse, ou que je songe à son énergie souriante, si rare parmi nos poètes trop souvent imbibés de larmes ou infestés d'un sentimentalisme flasque, je pense, en le trouvant si différent du milieu où il propage ses chants, que "vers les iles Chélidoines, comme écrivait St. François de Sales, il y a des fontaines d'eau bien douces au milieu de la mer."

Le poète maintenant se réfugie dans les paysages; il les regarde, les sent, les goûte et les peint avec passion par petites touches vives et minutieuses qui évoquent les larges ensembles. Sa manière rappelle à la fois l'impressionnisme pictural et la méthode des poètes japonais, écrivains de haikais, Bashô, Onitsoura, Bouçon, Tchiyo et les autres qui d'un petit pinceau tracérent de grandes choses. Je citerai ce fragment:

> "L'ombre du clocher noir entre dans la boutique,
> Un lilas, débordant les grilles d'un jardin,
> Se balance et je vois luire et trembler soudain
> Des foullis [*sic*] bleus, la route et l'auberge rustique.
>
> Des pigeons, mollement arrivés sur le vent,
> Tournent dans l'azur pâle en éployant leurs ailes..."[1]

et celui-ci:

> "Matin gris, paresse ingénue...
>   Sur l'horizon,
> Les vieux noyers de l'avenue
> Et le toit bleu de la maison.
> Le vent berce les feuilles rousses
>   D'un peuplier.
> On dirait qu'à brusques secousses
> Il pleut soudain dans l'air mouillé..."[2]

Ne sent-on pas dans ces quelques vers,[3] dans ces paysages de quelle nature sont ce calme et cet abandon et quelle sourde vigueur y fermente?

Francis Carco a essayé de traduire par des rhythmes et des images les inclinations les plus profondes d'un coeur humain, les tendances cachées et comme instinctives par quoi se manifeste cette volonté de vivre qui est comme la lampe et la clé de nos actions. Objet des plus importants que se puisse proposer un artiste, si c'est sur ce désir d'être

---

[1] Francis Carco, 'Province', *La Bohème et mon coeur* (Paris, 1950; first published, 1912), p. 96.
[2] Carco, 'Impression', *La Bohème et mon coeur, op. cit.*, p. 98.
[3] Voir en outre le poème très characteristique cité par M. John Middleton Murry dans le dernier No., p. 123. [Derème's note.]

que s'épanouissent tous nos sentiments, toutes nos idées, comme d'une même terre jaillissent mille plantes – rose, fenouil, menthe, orchidée, ciguë – vigoureuses ou étiolées, précieuses ou communes, salutaires ou vénéneuses. C'est ce souci d'évoquer les secrètes assises de la sensibilité qui transparaît aussi bien dans les proses *d'Instincts* que dans les poèmes de *la Bohème et mon coeur*. Mais que l'on ne croie point que pour chanter les choses les plus générales, le poète ait dû se servir, comme le conseille Buffon, des termes les plus généraux et, par conséquent, les plus abstraits. Il n'en est rien; sa poésie est, avant tout, concrète; elle hait l'abstraction et, par une sorte d'intuition, épouse si étroitement la forme et la matière des choses, qu'elle donne l'impression d'être une *poésie physique*, beaucoup plus faite pour agir sur la sensibilité que pour émouvoir l'intelligence.

Francis Carco peint des décors (salles de bar, arbres, prairies, etc. ...), mais il les peint comme il les voit, c'est-a-dire que délaissant le réalisme photographique, il nous livre seulement ses sensations les plus vives en face de l'object et, de la sorte, nous met dans son état d'âme par la seule évocation du milieu qui à conditionné son sentiment. Voici, en exemple, une courte prose:[1]

Le Boulevard.–La fraîcheur vive du boulevard pourri d'automne. Les larges feuilles des platanes dégringolent. C'est un écroulement imprévu et bizarre dans la lumiére croisée des lampes a'arc [*sic*]. Il tombe une petite pluie menue, serrée, que le vent incline parfois sur les visages. La nuit est parfumée de l'odeur des feuillages gâtés: elle sent encore l'ambre et l'oeillet, la poudre, le fard et le caoutchouc des imperméables."[2]

Il n'y a là, comme on a pu voir, pas un mot direct sur la pensée intime du poète. Son sentiment nous est traduit par le décor, ou plutôt par ce qu'il a retenu du décor: parfums des voluptés passées, feuilles qui tombent, pluie sur les lampes, automne.

Il se voue simplement et sans arrière-pensée à la joie de vivre, au bonheur de respirer, de regarder les teintes du soleil dans les feuilles des hêtres ou d'écouter verlainiennement le bruit de l'averse "par terre et sur les toits." Il n'est plus qu'une sensibilité extrêmement fine qui réagit au moindre souffle. On comprend dès lors l'importance que prend dans sa poésie la question de la pluie et du beau temps et qu'il consacre un poème à exprimer sa confuse et vive émotion devant un feuillage mouillé.

On s'étonnera de ce que cette poésie, que l'on devine pénétrée d'une belle et noble joie, prenne assez souvent un aspect mélancolique et mineur et que ce poète s'abandonne parfois à la tristesse, lui qui chante

[1] Voir aussi 'Aix en Provence', *Rhythm*, No. 1, p. 20. [Derème's note.]
[2] Carco, 'Le Boulevard', *Instincts* (Paris, 1924), p. 12. The correct phrase is *à arc*.

délibérément: *Carpe diem,* comme Horace et signerait volontiers cette tannka qu'écrivit, il y a douze siècles, le japonais Tabibito: "Puisque c'est un fait – Que tous les hommes vivants – Finessent par mourir – Mieux vaut être gai – Pendant qu'on est de ce monde." Mais il convient d'analyser cette tristesse et de noter que le poète a peut-être pour elle un penchant aussi vif que pour le bonheur. Triste ou gaie, une émotion est toujours une ivresse nouvelle, une richesse inattendue pour ces coeurs avides de sentir. On connait les vers de La Fontaine:

> "J'aime le jeu, l'amour, les livres, la musique,
> La ville et la campagne, enfin tout: il n'est rien
>   Qui ne me soit souverain bien
> Jusqu'au sombre plaisir d'un coeur mélancolique."

Oui, tout est digne d'être aimé *dans la maison de Jupiter,* comme disaient les stoïciens; tout est beau pour le poète dans la vie "vivante," passionnée, intense, héroïque que Frédéric Nietzsche préférait à la vie banalement et platement heureuse; et d'ailleurs si les coups du sort sont trop rudes, le poète retrouvera sa belle vivacité pour chanter non sans ironie ni symbole:

> "Et puis laisse pleuvoir s'il pleut...
> Sois philosophe à ta manière,
> Choisis ta meilleure bruyère
> Pour la fumer au coin du feu."[1]

Tel est cet écrivain allègre et lyrique qui nous montre par sa poésie mobile et concrète que l'on peut avoir une conception sérieuse et même tragique de la vie sans pour cela abandonner le sourire.

TRISTAN DERÈME

NOTE. – J'ai, dans ma dernière *Lettre,* groupé un certain nombre d'écrivains sous l'oriflamme de *l'Abbaye,* faute d'une enseigne qui exprimât les tendances communes que l'on trouve dans leurs livres. Mais je ne vourdrais pas que l'on en déduisît que ces auteurs ont tous appartenu à *l'Abbaye de Créteil,* fondée en Octobre, 1906, par le peintre Albert Gleizes et les poètes Alexandre Mercereau, Henri-Martin Barzun, René Arcos et Charles Vildrac, phalanstère d'artistes muni d'un atelier d'imprimerie où chaque membre s'engageait a'fournir plusieurs heures de travail par jour. – Le groupe initial se divisa par la suite en deux parties: l'une où l'on trouve MM. Mercereau et Barzun; l'autre s'unit à MM. Romains et Chennevière.

T.D.

---

[1] Carco, 'Mars', *La Bohème et mon coeur, op. cit.,* p. 116.

IV. JEAN PELLERIN*

M. Jean Pellerin est un curieux écrivain. C'est un poète jeune et tendre
et dont les vers sourient avec grace:

> Quand mon fil se cassera sous
>   Les ongles de la Parque,
> Quand ma bouche aura les deux sous
>   Pour la dernière barque,
>
> Où serez-vous? Dans le jardin
>   Où je devrai descendre?
> Que serez-vous? Charme, dédain,
>   Douce chair – ou bien cendre?[1]

Mais à sa tendresse s'ajoute et se mêle une délicieuse ironie. "L'ironie,"
dit M. Rémy de Gourmont, "est une clairvoyance. C'est pourquoi elle
ne semble jamais prendre rien tout à fait au sérieux, car ce qui a une
face triste a une face comique, et c'est dans le mélange des deux sensations qu'elle trouve ses teintes troubles." Elle est l'apanage de ces
esprits rares qui goutent leurs sentiments avec ivresse mais qui ont la
pudeur et le bon gout et aussi la force et l'intelligence de ne les prendre
pas au tragique. C'est que, depuis Heine, Corbière et Laforgue, il
semble un peu outrecuidant de prendre avec pompe et romantisme
l'univers à témoin de nos joies et de nos déconvenues. C'est une politesse
très moderne que d'assurer au lecteur que les malheurs qui nous
déchirent n'ont au fond qu'une minime importance et d'ensevelir un
sanglot sous des sourires comme un oiseau mort sous des roses. On
n'oserait plus guère aujourd'hui écrire "Les Nuits" de Musset; mais on
composerait volontiers, si l'on pouvait, "La Nuit d'Avril," comme a
fait M. Pellerin:

> Je ne me suis pas fait la tête de Musset;
> Je tartine des vers, je prépare un essai,
> J'ai le quart d'un roman à sécher dans l'armoire.
> Mais que sont vos baisers, ô filles de Mémoire!
> Vous entendre dicter des mots après des mots,
> Triste jeu!
>   Le loisir d'été sous les ormeaux,
> Une écharpe du soir qui se léve et qui glisse...
> Des couplets sur ce bon Monsieur de la Palice
> Qui répète un enfant dans le jardin couvert...
> Ce crépuscule rouge, et puis jaune, et puis vert...
> Une femme passant le pont de la Concorde...
> Le râle d'un archet pâmé sur une corde,

---

* *Rhythm*, II, 11 (December 1912) 322–5.
[1] Jean Pellerin, 'En Marge d'une vielle mythologie, IV', *Le Bouquet inutile* (Paris, 1923), p.
    120. Punctuation of the last line differs in the book publication.

La danse, la chanson avec la danse, un son
De flûte sur la danse entraînant la chanson,
Le geste d'une femme et celui d'une branche...
Ah! vain mots, pauvres mots en habit du dimanche...
Ah! vivre tout cela jusque à l'epuiser!
Muse, reprends mon luth et garde ton baiser.[1]

Ce poème (et en particulier son avant-dernier vers: "Ah! vivre tout cela jusques à l'épuiser") éclaire pour nous cet esprit qui est, sous un certain aspect de la famille de Laforgue:

"Que la mort ne nous ait qu'ivres-morts de nous-mêmes!"

de Racine:

"Et sans penser plus loin, jouissons de la vie
Tandis que nous l'avons."

de Ronsard:

"Vivez si m'en croyez, n'attendez à demain;
Cueillez dès aujourd'hui les roses de la vie."

et, plus loin, de Catulle avec son:

"Vivamus, mea Lesbia, atque amemus."

et d'Horace, avec le "Carpe diem" dix-neuf fois centenaire. Au banquet de la vie, non pas infortuné, mais heureux convive, c'est un poète subtil et délié qui se réjouit qu'on l'ait invité à la fête du monde et de la lumière. Son esprit scintille de cette gaîté dont La Fontaine a esquissé la définition: "Je n'appelle pas gaîté, disait-il, ce qui excite à rire; mais un certain charme, un air agréable qu'on peut donner à toutes sortes de sujets, même les plus sérieux." Il aime la vie sous toutes ses formes et chérit ses impressions personnelles autant que ses souvenirs les littératures classiques. Il écrit à la moderne. ("Il faut écrire à la moderne," disait déjà Théophile) et [*sic*] ne craint pas de noter ce dialogue aux vers un peu amers qui sentent la folle antithèse et la parodie et ou l'on trouvera, traitée d'une façon qui ne sent ni la déclamation ni le ton doctoral, la tristesse poignante des départs et de la jeunesse expirante:

Nous n'entendrons plus ta chanson,
Marchande..."Belles fraises."
Ni ta trompette à l'aigre son,
Doux rempailleur de chaises.

[1] Pellerin, 'La Nuit d'Avril', *Le Bouquet inutile, op. cit.,* pp. 61–2. Punctuation differs slightly throughout. Ironically, the only line in the 1923 edition which substantially differs is the one Derème singled out for favorable comment. It reads instead: 'Ah! vivre tout cela, le vivre et l'épuiser!...'

> – Prépare l'omelette au lard,
> Je vais plier les nappes.
> – Oh! ces écharpes de brouillard
> Sur mon quai de Jemmappes.

> – Où sont les restes du pâté?
> – Où tes rires, faunesse?
> – J'ai perdu ma passoire à thé
>   – J'ai vécu ma jeunesse.

> ...Nos premières heures d'amants,
> Ses baisers d'étourdie,
> Rêve...– Deux déménagements
> Valent un incendie.[1]

Il ne redoute pas davantage de mêler, en un décor féerique, et d'une manière inattendue et charmante, les siècles antiques aux civilisations modernes. Il écrira, avec un joli sourire:

> Puisque le maréchal-ferrant
> Ressemelle Pégase...[2]

ou ces deux stances imprévues ou l'on peut voir périr le héros de Chateaubriand et entendre encore le cri fameux que rapporte Flavius Joséphe, ce cri que Laforgue a raillé dans un jour de colère:

> "Les dieux s'en vont; plus que des hures!"

et que nous allons écouter:

> Jeanne lutte avec un huissier,
> Et le poète Chose
> Récite chez le Financier
> Sa Ballade à la Rose.

> Les dieux s'en vont – s'en vont au trot;
> Jeanne se décourage;
> Et le dernier Abencérage
> Est mort dans le Métro.[3]

C'est en lisant une telle poésie que l'on sent la justesse des remarques que M. Emile Zavie a épinglées aux pages délicates de son roman, "Une Idylle": "...nous ne savons point non plus," écrit-il, "ce que nos fils garderont de nous; mais peut-être reconnaîtront-ils que notre époque vit fleurir un genre littéraire qui en vaut bien un autre, un genre ou le

---

[1] Pellerin, 'Bohême, I', *Le Bouquet inutile, op. cit.*, pp. 123–4. There are minor differences in punctuation between this version and that cited.
[2] Pellerin, 'Familières, v', *Le Bouquet inutile, op. cit.*, p. 36.
[3] Pellerin, 'Bohême, II', *Le Bouquet inutile, op. cit.*, p. 124. There are minor differences in punctuation between this version and that cited.

sentiment ne s'étale point, ne fait pas de gestes ni de tirades et que les hommes d'aujourd'hui furent élevés à l'école d'ironie; ils diront que, dans ce siècle d'arrivisme pratique, il y eut encore quelque enthousiasme sous la blague, de l'émotion sous nous sourires et du courage sous nos vestons anglais." On ne peut caractériser d'une manière plus judicieuse la tournure d'esprit de quelques écrivains qui réléguent au fond des vieux tiroirs le morne dégout, l'ennui de vivre,

> "La honte de penser et l'horreur d'être un homme,"

l'appétit du néant cher à Leconte de Lisle et à quelques centaines d'ajusteurs de strophes, admirables d'ailleurs ou ridicules et plus ou moins imprégnés des doctrines de Schopenhauer et des bouddhistes. Les poètes dont je parle aiment la vie avec tout ce qu'elle a de mystérieux, de charmant et de tragique, la vie comme elle est, tout simplement. M. Jean Pellerin est l'un d'entre eux. C'est un lyrique fantaisiste, spirituel et gracieux, mais qui applique sa fantaisie, son esprit et sa grace à l'expression de sentiments profonds qui font de sa poésie une oeuvre émouvante et belle.

V. ROGER FRENE*

Il y a des poètes – ils sont assez rares d'ailleurs et Jean de Lafontaine est l'un d'entre eux – qui ont composé des vers ailés et légers comme des abeilles. Roger Frène n'est pas de ceux-là et sa poésie pacifique, robuste et solidement équilibrée, a quelque chose de physique, de quasi matériel qui n'est pas sans une originale et forte beauté. C'est ainsi qu'il écrira, parlant de l'automne :

> Mais parmi la splendeur pesante de tes phases
> Quand tu répands partout les forces de l'été,
> Je goute seulement les profondes extases
> Que donnent les couleurs de ta maturité.

ou bien :

> Ainsi su promenais presqu'ivre ton regard,
> Et tes sens savouraient la splendide matière
> Devant cette vallée ou d'un grêle brouillard
> Montait l'adieu des rossignols à la lumière.

ou encore :

> Tu contemplais, penché sur le sommet d'un mont,
> Tout le déroulement fastueux et fècond
> D'une grasse campagne à peine imaginaire.

* *Rhythm*, II, 13 (February 1913) 414–18.

ou enfin:

> Et tu rythmais ce livre aux remous enfiévrés
> Ou ta jeunesse peint avec des mots dorés,
> Dans l'ivresse joyeuse et la fraîche musique,
> Le resplendissement de l'univers physique.

Ces quelques citations que je cueille dans les deux volumes de Roger Frène: "Paysages de l'ame et de la terre" et "Les Sèves originaires, suivies de nocturnes," font sentir mieux que toutes dissertation la tournure d'esprit du poète et sa façon de contempler les choses. On se rend compte, lorsqu'il chante:

> Dans un vers lent, matériel
> Et plein d'une riche substance
> Comme un pesant rayon de miel,
> J'aime que la lumière danse...

qu'il a parfaitement pris conscience des moyens naturels qu'il emploie pour traduire ses émotions et qu'il est parvenu à mettre en pratique le précepte gravé au fronton du temple de Delphes et qui était de se connaître soi-même.

Il est permis de se demander quelle secrète et profonde inclination traduit cette poésie. La lecture des ouvrages de Roger Frène ne laisse bientôt aucun doute à ce sujet. Son but, c'est de donner et de se donner l'impression ou l'illusion de vivre de la vie générale du monde et de se rattacher à une chose immortelle ou, du moins, infiniment durable: l'existence de l'univers.

> Avec docilité je subis le mystère
> D'être comme un reflet des aspects de la terre;
> Ainsi qu'un arbre plie et courbe dans le vent,
> Je m'abandonne au souffle du destin mouvant...
>
> Je me compare à l'herbe, aux sources, aux ramures,
> Aux rivières tour à tour claires ou impures,
> Traîneuses des bleus ciels d'été, des graviers noirs,
> Reflêtant le rivage et le jour et le soir,
> Aux près, aux champs, aux bois, aux vallons ou je passe;
> Je chante la nature et sa robuste grâce;
> Les gouttes, les ruisseaux m'augmentent en chemin...
>
> Pareille à la forêt innombrable et vivante
> Qui, ravageant le sol d'une racine ardente,
> Se nourrit de la terre et transforme sa chair
> En beaux rameaux épais ou frémissent les airs,
> Fais que mon oeuvre éclate en strophes bien nourries...

Il faut voir là, non pas une félicité béate et superficielle, mais l'épanouissement magnifique, dans le panthéisme, de l'instinct le plus profond, la volonté de vivre et de grandir. C'est que le poète a gouté

La vielle volupté de rêver a la mort,

comme dit Stuart Merrill; volupté terriblement amère et désespérée et qui laisse à la bouche un gout de néant; émotion à laquelle il n'est point donné d'échapper pour peu que l'on médite sur les mystères de la destinée et de la vie. Tout la suscite en nous:

> Le café, les liqueurs, le feu des cigarettes
> Dans le cerveau l'insinuent doucement,
> C'est elle que je presse avec ton corps charmant...

et Roger Frène fait dir par le squelette qui, pendant un dialogue d'amour apparait en écartant les branches, "une rose a la mâchoire, un nid d'oiseau dans chaque main":

> Je suis au fond du vin qu'on boit et de l'amour,
> Dans la plus noire nuit et dans le plus beau jour.

Mais le poète s'est édifié une philosophie qui par certains aspects ne manque pas de rappeler la doctrine stoïcienne. Que l'on se souvienne de la parole de Marc-Aurèle: "Considère sans cesse que c'est par un changement que tout se produit et accoutume – toi à penser qu'il n'y a rien que la nature universelle aime tant que de changer les choses qui sont, pour en faire de nouvelles qui leur ressemblent. Tout ce qui est, est pour ainsi dire la semence de ce qui doit naître." (On trouve la même pensée dans Schopenhauer, "Die Welt als Wille und Vorstellung.") N'est-ce pas ce qu'exprime aussi Roger Frène:

> Les branches faneront bientôt comme nos ailes,
> Murmurent tous ces migrateurs ensoleillès,
> Et rendant notre corps aux formes éternelles
> Nous nous endormirons et serons rèveillès.

Devant le déroulement des saisons et les triomphes alternès de la vie et de la mort, devant les forces de l'été toujours renaissantes après l'hiver mortuaire, le poète, laissant de coté les vaines et romantiques imprècations à l'adresse de la nature impassible, a eu comme l'intuition de la vie éternelle de l'univers avec ses phases, ses exubérances et ses torpeurs. "Représente-toi sans cesse, disait Marc-Aurèle, le monde comme un être animé, composé d'une seule matière et d'une âme unique. Vois comment tout se conforme à son seul sentiment; comment tout se fait par son unique impulsion; comment tout est la cause co-opérante de tout ce qui se produit; enfin quels sont l'enchaînement, la solidarité mutuelle de toutes choses." C'est l'impérissable problème de l'univers. On se rappelle ce que M. Maurice Barrès en a écrit dans "Le Jardin de Bérénice": "Il était dans le tempérament de ce petit être sensible et résigné de considérer l'univers comme un immense rébus. Rien n'est plus judicieux, et seuls les esprits qu'absorbent de médiocres préoccupations cessent de rechercher le sens de ce vaste spectacle. A combien d'interprètations étranges et émouvantes la nature ne se prête-t-elle pas, elle qui sait à ses pires duretés donner les molles courbes de la beauté."

Mais le monde n'est plus tout à fait un rébus pour notre poète, qui n'a d'ailleurs que peu de gout pour les choses mystérieuses (parce qu'elles sont trop dèchirantes pour son âme, avide de certitude, qui ne trouve point dans le doute le mol oreiller qu'y rencontrait Montaigne) et s'il laisse de côté l'inexplicable but de la vie universelle à laquelle il participe, il ne veut du moins pas avoir la moindre hèsitation sur la réalité de ce but; et, loin de se rebeller, comme fit Schopenhauer, contre les volontés secrètes de la nature, il s'abandonne à la destinée non pas avec résignation, mais avec joie, avec confiance, "en un grand geste heureux."

> Nous bénissons ta loi, Dieu des métamorphoses
> Et du sourire universel,
> Qui fais reverdir l'arbre et délacer les roses!
> Sur ton passage sensuel
> Penche l'enivrement magnifique des choses.

Il est prêt a reprendre l'hymne de Cléanthe d'Assos ou à s'écrier avec le vieil empereur philosophe: "Tout ce qui t'accommode, ô monde, m'accommode moi-même. Rien n'est pour moi prématuré ni tardif, qui est de saison pour toi. Tout ce que m'apportent les heures est pour moi un fruit savoureux, ô Nature! Tout vient de toi, tout est dans toi, tout rentre dans toi. Un personnage dit: Bien-aimée cité de Cecrops! Mais toi, ne peux-tu pas dire: O bien-aimée cité de Jupiter!" N'est-ce pas ce que plus tard écrira Nietzsche: "Ma formule pour la grandeur de l'homme est *amor fati*; ne vouloir changer aucun fait dans le passé, dans l'avenir, éternellement; non pas seulement supporter la nècessité, encore moins la dissimuler – tout idéalisme est un mensonge en face de la nécessité – mais l'aimer." Et n'est-ce pas cet amour de la nature, cette fusion de l'homme dans la nature, cet abandon de notre fugitive et pauvre volonté à une volonté plus vaste, plus durable et grandiose, n'est-ce-pas, ce retour à la nature, ce qu'ont chanté les grands écrivains de tous les temps: Rousseau, Molière, Lafontaine, Virgile, Lucrèce?

Combien l'aspect de toutes choses change, considéré de ce point! Ecoutons Roger Frène:

> Comme il sent la flore blanche
> Bruire un moment,
> Le Faune courbe une branche

Qui vers lui gazouille et penche
Et la baise doucement;

Cent fois, j'ai vu ce bois dense
S'éclairer ainsi;
J'ai connu la renaissance
Des êtres, l'éveil immense
Des champs dans l'air adouci;

J'entendis cette fontaine
Que gorge l'azur
Gronder dans sa rive pleine,
Les ramiers gémir leur peine
Au murmure morne et pur;

Mais aujourd'hui tout s'éclaire
D'un charme inouï,
Mon âme visionnaire,
Du printemps, grace et mystère,
N'avait pas encore joui.

Tel est ce poète grave et parfois majestueux qui ayant longuement médité sur la mort ne nous apporte point des pages d'épouvante, de terreur et de découragement, mais nous donne une belle leçon d'optimisme, de ferveur et de confiance dans la vie.

TRISTAN DERÈME

THE MOVE TOWARD CLASSICISM

When John Middleton Murry noted in this essay a French swing toward classicism, he was – as with his support for Bergson – once again in the forefront of British writers who were introducing French ideas in England. The ground was not totally unprepared for such ideas. As early as the series *Patria Mia* and *Through Alien Eyes* in *The New Age* in 1912 and 1913, Pound had clearly revealed that his anti-Semitism had more native origins than the reactionary influence of the *Action française*. T. E. Hulme in 'A Tory Philosophy' in *The Commentator* (April–May 1912) had already distinguished the romantic and classic attitudes as antithetical approaches to both art and politics, and had cited Charles Maurras and Pierre Laserre of French reactionary circles as authority for use of the terms in such a way.[1] And Murry himself, as F. A. Lea has noted, first made a break from Bergson to classicism a month earlier, in May 1913, in a review of Julien Benda's novel *La Chute* for *The Blue Review*.[2] For Murry the *Action française* and other aspects of French political and literary reaction did not prove a deeply shaping influence, although his novel, *Still Life* (1916), was modelled on Benda's *La Chute*.[3] His essay calling attention to the 'classical renaissance' in France and attempting to link the *fantaisistes* to that current is, however, an important indication of the early stages of an influence that was to mark English literature. Murry's conclusion, that classicism is a valuable corrective to the romantic tendency, a reliable guide to 'putting things in their place', was reiterated throughout the second and third decades by critics as divergent as Hulme, Pound, Eliot, and Aldous Huxley.

FRENCH BOOKS: A CLASSICAL REVIVAL*

John Middleton Murry

There are perhaps two reasons why the younger generation of French writers is given to collective introspection and absorbed in speculation upon tendencies. The first is the economic fact that one of the easiest and least costly methods of procuring copy for a *revue jeune* is to conduct an *enquête*; the second is that for better or worse the French logical mind is prone to develop a mania for literary classification and a disregard for the essential characteristics of the subject matter of the classification – literature. Consequently, it is very difficult to derive any real information from so extensive an inquiry as that of MM. Picard and Muller ("Les Tendances Présentes de la Litterature Française." Basset, 3 fr. 50). Even if the classification into grandiose schools, *Unanimistes, Paroxystes* and the like, is admitted by the writers themselves, the labels tell us nothing, for they are concerned with the accidents rather than the essentials of literature; much as though we decided to base our own literary criticism upon a division of modern Poets into those who eat

[1] T. E. Hulme, 'A Tory Philosophy', in *The Life and Opinions of T. E. Hulme* by Alun Jones (London, 1960), p. 189.
[2] F. A. Lea, *The Life of John Middleton Murry* (London, 1959), p. 38.
[3] *Ibid.* * *The Blue Review*, i, 2 (June 1913) 134–8.

bacon and eggs for breakfast and those who do not. Chaotic classification is a delusion and a snare. More satisfactory, because more restricted and definite, is the inquiry conducted by M. Emile Henriot in *Le Temps* ("A Quoi rêvent les Jeunes Gens?" Champion, 2 fr.); yet even here, if we consider the replies as a whole, the result is negative. The young French writers of to-day have completely broken with Symbolism; and if the contributors to M. Henriot's symposium are unanimous in affirming that there is no "new school," they are unanimous no less in denying the gods of the nineties.

The desire for novelty at all costs is no longer characteristic of young French literature; and the generation which expressed this desire in *vers libre* and sought its models in America, in Germany, in Flanders, in any country save France itself, is past. It is true that any evolution from the artistic position taken up by Mallarmé was of itself doomed to sterility; but other causes than a mere aesthetic impossibility have been at work. It would be difficult to overestimate the literary importance of the foundation of the political organisation, *L'Action Française*, with its royalist and Catholic programme and its watchword "France for the French." The immediate cause of the *Action Française* was the Dreyfus trial, and though English opinion was practically unanimous in supporting Dreyfus and condemning anti-Semitism, there can be little doubt that on purely nationalist grounds the French agitation against Dreyfus was justified. A French nationalist policy, such as that adopted by the *Action Française* demands that France should remain a Catholic country and that its government should not rest in the hands of naturalised Jews or other aliens. Although it may seem that the growing popularity of such a party has no immediate connection with the literary tendencies of modern France, the connecting link is supplied by two individuals, Maurice Barrès and Charles Maurras. Catholic in their sympathies, nationalist in their politics, classical in their literary descent, Maurice Barrès as the creative artist, Charles Maurras as the critic, enjoy an influence which becomes every day more widespread. From Charles Maurras descends the most powerful of the younger critical groups to-day, that of the *Revue Critique*. The political programme of the *Action Française* is translated into literary terms. Alien influence must be excluded from French literature; a return to the truest French tradition, to Racine, Pascal, Lafontaine, Stendhal, to Villon and to the Pléiade, must be exacted by the new criticism. We have only to compare Charles Maurras' latest book, "La Politique Religieuse" (Nouvelle Librairie Nationale, 3 fr. 50), in which the Catholic anti-alien policy is argued with the author's accustomed purity of style and language, with "Les Disciplines," by M. Henri Clouard (Rivière, 3 fr. 50), the chief critic of the *Revue Critique*, to see how close is the connection between the classical renaissance in politics and in literature. The authority of M. Maurras is quoted again and again in M. Clouard's book; the very sub-title, "La Necessité littéraire et sociale d'une renaissance classique" reads like a phrase of the master's. The burden of the argument is pure Maurras. Romanticism must be forgotten, and the German prophets who preached it rejected for the true French tradition. "An imagination," says M. Clouard, "can very well be happy and brilliant, a point of view picturesque, a sentiment beautiful. But if you substitute them for analysis and experience where there are no other possible intermediaries between man and reality, you are mistaken and deceived on every hand." Analysis and experience – they are the old characteristics of French classicism and the ideals of the renaissance in France to-day.

It is symptomatic that a recent number of the *Revue Critique* was entirely devoted to Stendhal, in whom the analytic genius of French literature reached perhaps its highest development; while soon after *Les Marches de Provence* devoted a whole number to the consideration of *fantaisie et fantaisistes*. The *Fantaisistes* form a new school of French poets, with this striking difference from the generality of schools, that they have no programme or propaganda, no pseudo-philosophical theory of life on which to wreck their poetry. "Fantasy" in the sense in which the *Fantaisistes* use it for their watchword is a quality of temperament and not an aesthetic dogma; it is the faculty of analysing experience with an irony that verges on cynicism and an introspection that verges on egotism. In short, "fantasy" has always been an eminently French quality, in spite of the fact that its literary expression has been borne down for centuries by foreign influences, Spanish in the seventeenth century, English in the eighteenth, and German in the nineteenth. The terrible irony of Villon, the titanic imagination of Rabelais – these are the purely French products of fantasy. Jules Laforgue was a genius of the same mould. To this essentially French tradition many of the most significant of the younger generation attach themselves, P. J. Toulet, Tristan Derème, Francis Carco, Jean-Marc Bernard, Jean Pellerin, to name the most significant; and to this tradition belong three slender books of poetry, "Le Poème de la Pipe et de l'Escargot," by Tristan Derème, "Chansons Aigres-Douces," by Francis Carco (Collection des Cinq), "Sub Tegmine Fagi," by Jean-Marc Bernard (Editions du Temps Présent, 3 fr. 50). The title of M. Carco's book applies to all three; they are all bitter-sweet. There is a delicate irony and a wonderful perfection of form in all, and underneath there seems to lurk a profound malaise. I am not here concerned to detach the individuality of these three poets; but rather to emphasise their common quality. Here is poetry that is sure at least of its own ground, and sure of its essentially French spirit. It is poetry that does not thrust a theory of the universe into a lyric, nor disdain a perfection of form which is the birth-right of French poetry. Though as yet the *Fantaisistes* have no great body of work to their credit, they have at least this recommendation to our serious consideration, that they do not thunder before they have learned to speak, while they have jettisoned the preposterous cargo of "-ismes" under which young French poetry has laboured for twenty years. M. Derème has the secret of a real poetry when he writes:

> Ma vie en silence s'écoule[,]
> C'est pour peu d'hommes que j'écris[,]
> Car si je chantais pour la foule
> Je pousserais bien d'autres cris.
>
> Des deux poings défiant les astres
> Je clamerais à grand fracas
> Et ferais crouler les pilastres
> Et les balustres sur mes pas [;]
>
> .   .   .   .
>
> Et peut-être dans mon vieil âge
> Pourrais-je voir sur mon perron
> Un laurier bercer son feuillage [...]
> Mais à quoi bon? mais à quoi bon?[1]

There has lately been too much conscious "shaking fists at the stars" in French poetry, and the time has come for a classical revival after the anarchy and cosmopolitanism of recent years. A classical revival does not involve denying the last century and a half. Romanticism is in the French blood now as it is in ours. A classical revival means putting things in their place. In the pregnant phrase of M. J.-M. Bernard, Romanticism is but an element of literature; classicism is a principle.

---

1 *Tristan Derème*, 'Que mes poèmes soient étranges...', *Le Poème de la pipe et de l'escargot* (Paris, 1920), pp. 8–9. The sixth line of the quoted extract shows the reading *grands* in the 1920 edition.

MODERN FRENCH POETRY: POUND'S FIRST IMPORTANT VIEW

Ezra Pound recounted his 'Approach to Paris' in 1913 as an envoy's report of decisive foreign advances in the art of poetry. He had met the literary men of Paris in the cafés, he said, and he had felt himself at the center of Western literature. 'Thinking with good cause that Paris is always at least twenty years ahead of all other "worlds of letters"... [French intellectuals] deem with almost equal warrant that if an original mind appear in any other country he will be driven to Paris to get his first recognition', Pound wrote. 'This may not be the case, but it is near enough to go by.'[1] His respect for Paris was equalled only by his hopes for America, he said: 'There are just two things in the world, two great and interesting phenomena: the intellectual life of Paris and the curious teething promise of my own vast occidental nation.'[2] Nonetheless, he had no illusions that his journeys had brought him into really intimate contact with France; he had not 'come into Paris'[3] as he had fully entered the life of London, and he knew that his report on French poetry was selective and even governed in part by the accident of acquaintance. 'I do not pretend to any exhaustive knowledge of the writers of France. I have browsed about among their books and come upon matter of interest.'[4] But for London – in which there were but 'a few with whom one can talk', 'one man with a passion for good writing', 'one notable poet...and, perhaps, a half-dozen young men who want really to come at good writing'[5] – even a preliminary report from Paris could be the start toward a new era of English 'poetic glory'.[6] 'The voyager can but tell his private adventures', Pound declared; 'so be it'.[7]

The next essays in the series show that Pound's 'private adventures' at this time already concerned problems of constructive design in poetry. This theme, which reappears inconspicuously in four of the seven essays, gives the series an historical importance in English poetics, even beyond its significance in the transmission of French influence. Pound in his second article praised de Gourmont's poetic 'rhythm-structures' – not simply his rhythms. These structures are made up of homogeneous poetic units, he said, and possess analogy with 'a geometrical pattern made up of homogeneous units'. But he hastened to add – in phrases that anticipated his later willingness to seek formal excellence in representational as well as non-representational paintings – that he could equally praise rhythm-structures made up of 'units which differ among themselves'. The decision to use either symmetrical or asymmetrical structure in a poem is 'a matter of music...perhaps as complicated as any problems of musical construction'. And, Pound suggested, as part of his decisions about form, the poet must consider to what extent he can apply 'principles of pictorial design' and 'the laws or conveniences of "musical" rhythm' to poetry. The significance of de Gourmont to English poetry, Pound emphasized, was what his work suggested about rhythmic design, about 'a new principle of grouping'.

From such stress upon the importance of the formal grouping of poetic units in poems by Remy de Gourmont to praise for the poetry of Jules Romains in the third

[1] Ezra Pound, 'The Approach to Paris, I', *The New Age*, n.s. XIII, 19 (4 September 1913) 551–2. This introductory essay to the series is not reprinted in this edition, but the most interesting comments are summarized here. Further comments on the importance of the series as a whole appear in the General Introduction, pages 25–8.
[2] *Ibid.*, 552.   [3] *Ibid.*   [4] *Ibid.*
[5] *Ibid.* The 'few' with whom Pound talked at this time included Wyndham Lewis, H.D. and Richard Aldington and, probably, T. E. Hulme; the 'one man with a passion for good writing' was almost certainly Ford Madox Ford; and the 'notable poet', Yeats.
[6] Pound, 'The Approach to Paris, II', *The New Age*, n.s. XIII, 20 (11 September 1913) 577.
[7] 'The Approach to Paris, I', *op. cit.*, 551.

article – though apparently an abrupt change of topic – is but the extension of a pattern. Romains applied new ideas of grouping to social units, and devoted much of his poetry to presenting new structures of reality as he felt they were embodied in combinations and assemblies of men. That it was the formal concern which attracted Pound, and not the social, is clear from the excerpts from Romains Pound quotes in his third essay. The concept of the individual is not 'a reality pure and simple', but one among many possible ways of conceiving the units of social structures, Romains felt; but the poet who sought to show that familiar and unfamiliar ideas about the formal units of society are at least equally 'real' was treated as an 'abstracteur', he lamented. Pound cited this statement; and only months later he was deeply involved in the defense of non-representational art, maintaining that such art could often embody the reality of an emotion with greater truth than works of art which represented objects as people conventionally see them.[1] In fact, he came to argue, the pure arrangements of forms could be a 'certitude', an expression of a reality in itself.[2]

Some anticipation of this attitude toward form is implicit in the comments Pound quoted from Romains' *Puissances de Paris*. Groups, Romains argued, are in an early stage of evolution; their basically 'abstract' formal qualities – their lack of limit, their fluidity, their ability to interpenetrate, and their intermittent life – are apparent even in the early simple structures, which now exist.[3] And the poet, when he gives voice to these forms, is revealing previously unperceived structures of life: one can learn from these undeveloped groups 'the essential forms of life'. The statement has its co-incidental echo in Ernest Fenollosa's declarations, in the manuscript Pound received a few months later, that 'primitive metaphors...follow objective lines of relation in nature herself' and that the truth of forms, including verbal forms, is founded on 'identity of structure' in the natural world.[4] Clearly several influences, among them Romains, acted almost simultaneously to accelerate Pound's interest in exploring the possibilities of abstract form.

The *Puissances de Paris* was not a widely quoted text in London; Romains' poetry was far better known. Thus Pound's selection of this text for the most extended quotation of the series reveals the direction his interests had already begun to go. An interpretive comment on Romains' 'Ode to the Crowd Here Present' is equally revealing. He directs attention to the moment when the poet-narrator experiences an intensity that enables him, in some kind of fusion of the consciousness of the poet and the being of the crowd, to voice his own vision as the thought of the crowd; at this moment, Pound said, the poet became a crater or 'vortex'. The meaning of the metaphor is closer to those it later possessed in 'vorticism' than is a subsequent use in a letter to William Carlos Williams, often cited as the first appearance of the word in Pound's writing.[5]

---

1 See, for example, the argument in Ezra Pound, 'Edward Wadsworth, Vorticist', *The Egoist*, I, 16 (15 August 1914) 306.
2 Ezra Pound, 'Vorticism', *The New Age*, n.s. XVI (14 January 1915) 277.
3 The word 'abstract', throughout this period, had both descriptive and pejorative uses. Romains objected to being called an 'abstracteur' when the use of the word implied that his poetic view was fanciful and not true to essential reality. Pound could endorse 'abstract form' as a means of directing attention to essential structures of reality and could feel that such form embodied more of the 'real' than did a casually imitative painting of, for example, a realistic landscape.
4 Ernest Fenollosa, *The Chinese Written Character as a Medium for Poetry, with a foreword and notes by Ezra Pound* (London, 1936), p. 26.
5 For example, William C. Wees in 'Ezra Pound as a Vorticist', *WSCL*, VI, I (Winter–Spring 1965) 63, regards the letter to Williams in December 1913 as Pound's first written use of the word.

There were a few other passing indications that Pound's interests were shifting from primary attention to economy and exactitude of diction to a greater emphasis on form. He praised the *unanimistes* for their efforts at 'simplification of structure' and risked the opinion that 'the next great work may be written' in the fashion of Henri-Martin Barzun's 'poems like orchestral scores'. And he several times suggested an analogy between the 'wave length' of rhythms in verse and new conceptions of wave-form in sound or radioactivity.[1] Much of the series, however, continued the emphases usually connected with Pound's imagist period. He repeatedly stressed that assonance and other 'resolutions of sound' could be more suitable than rhyme. He praised Romains, Duhamel, Vildrac, Jouve, Arcos, and Chennevière for their 'strict, chaste, severe' qualities of syntax, Tailhade for the presentative method, Spire for restraint. He lauded Vildrac for his skill at narrative poetry, and extolled Francis Jammes at length for his skill at 'rendering his own times in terms of his own times'.

The last two topics show Pound in a curious lapse of judgement. He defended both Vildrac and Jammes against the charges of sentimentality, and he hinted that the latter – who, he said, 'does not repeat himself' – should be considered the best living French poet. Since Jammes was one of the more prolix and sentimental of the important poets of the day, those assertions seem particularly puzzling. Other evaluations seem to have been affected by Pound's concern for realistic rendering. He acknowledged the achievements of Rimbaud in form, with particular reference to his use of the prose poem, but Pound did not show any real sympathy with his poetry. Paul Fort, on the whole, received more acclaim for his prose rhythms – in poems that present the empirical world – than did the subtle resonances of Rimbaud's hallucinatory visions. The same concern with the realistic detail is apparent in Pound's discussions of the two satirists, Corbière and Tailhade. Pound's deepest knowledge, at this time, clearly lay with the symbolist *cénacle* poets. He had real acquaintance with the poets of *unanimisme*, and he made passing, if slightly patronizing, reference to Apollinaire and Claudel, but he had not the grasp of the whole French poetic world that Flint had. In the days ahead he would seek a new aesthetic which was the equal of his French contemporaries in its experiment with new possibilities in abstract form. For the present, however, Pound was primarily concerned to bring to English poetry the naturalness of subject matter and the excellences of rhythm and diction that had been the achievement of the poets of the symbolist *cénacle* and the fruit of the first years in which symbolism began to yield a new drive for precision.

THE APPROACH TO PARIS

Ezra Pound

II *

For the best part of a thousand years English poets have gone to school to the French, or one might as well say that there never were any English poets until they began to study the French. The Plantagenet princes despised the northern jargon, and their laureates sang Provençal. Chaucer began our tradition with adaptation and translation and he

[1] The references to the *unanimistes* and Barzun appear in the seventh essay; one of the more extended references to analogy between poetic rhythm and scientific waves is contained in essay two.
* *The New Age*, n.s. XIII, 20 (11 September 1913) 577–9.

did better than Chrétien de Troyes and in this manner English became a respectable speech...The history of English poetic glory is a history of successful steals from the French. It is, I dare say, the right of domination; Shakespeare is more to be prized than Ronsard; and yet the assiduous Pléiade had made all the experiments and provided the Elizabethans with all the technique that had not been left them by earlier adapters from the Language of "Oc," or from that of "Oil," from the North French or from Provençal – or from, perhaps, the thin stream that came straight from Italy and a rather inefficient jet from the Latin. The great periods of English have been the periods when the poets showed greatest powers of assimilation;...Even the 'nineties were fed upon the traditional exotic, and the work of that period shows virtues new in London, but already well known to the readers of the early Gautier. Lionel Johnson alone would seem to have reached the polish and fineness of 'Emaux et Camées" in those few poems of his where he seems to be moved by emotion rather than by the critical spirit.

.   .   .   .

There are two ways of being influenced by a notable work of art: the work may be drawn into oneself, its mastery may beget a peculiar hunger for new sorts of mastery and perfection; or the sight of the work may beget simply a counterfeiting of its superficial qualities. This last influence is without value, a dodge of the arriviste and of the mere searcher for novelty.

The first influence means a new keenness of the ear, or a new flair for wording, or a deeper desire for common sense if the work is what is properly called classic.

The present day English versifier...might do worse than look once more to the Mt. St. Geneviève and its purlieus.

M. Remy de Gourmont (b. 1858, etc.) is the author of "Le Latin mystique" and many other works – among them "Le Livre des Litanies" now part of "Le Pèlerin du Silence." I suppose M. De Gourmont knows more about verse-rhythm than any other man now living; at least he has made a most valuable contribution to the development of the strophe. It seems to me the most valuable since those made by Arnaut Daniel, but perhaps I exaggerate.

> Fleur hypocrite,
> Fleur du silence.

he begins, setting the beat of his measure.

> Rose couleur de cuivre, plus frauduleuse que nos joies, rose couleur de cuivre, embaume-nous dans tes mensonges, fleur hypocrite, fleur du silence.

Rose au visage peint comme une fille d'amour, rose au coeur prostitué, rose au visage peint, fais sembleant [*sic*] d'être pitoyable, fleur hypocrite, fleur du silence.

Rose à la joue puérile, ô vierge des futurs [*sic*] trahisons, rose à la joue puérile, innocente et rouge, ouvre les rets de tes yeux clairs, fleur hypocrite, fleur du silence.

Rose aux yeux noirs, miroir de ton néant, rose aux yeux noirs, fais-nous croire au mystère, fleur hypocrite, fleur du silence.

.   .   .   .

Rose topaze, princesse de légendes abolies, rose topaze, ton château-fort est un hôtel au mois, ton donjon marche à l'heure et tes mains blanches ont des gestes équivoques, fleur hypocrite, fleur de [*sic*] silence...[1]

And so it runs with ever more sweeping cadence with ever more delicate accords...I cannot..., for the benefit of those deaf to accords, go over the strophes quoted and point out every resolution of sound and every repetition subtler than rhyme. If a man is incapable of hearing this litany I cannot help it...

To my mind, M. De Gourmont has given us the procession of all women that ever were; you may say that he has not. In "Fleurs du jadis" he has given us the pageant of modern Paris, with this same shadowy suggestion, this same indirectness.

Je vous préfère aux coeurs les plus galants, coeurs trépassés, coeurs de jadis.

.   .   .   .

Jonquille, Narcisse et Souci, je vous préfère aux plus claires chevelures, fleurs trépassés, fleurs de jadis.

.   .   .   .

Nielle un peu gauche, mais duvetée comme un col de cygne,

Gentiannelle, fidèle amante du soleil, Asphodèle, épi royal, sceptre incrusté de rêves, reine primitive induite en la robe étroite des Pharaons,

Nielle, Gentiannelle, Asphodèle, je vous préfère à la grâce des vraies femelles, fleurs trépassés, fleurs de jadis.[2]

I give one strophe entire to illustrate the wave-length of his rhythm. And this is no slight matter if we consider that the development of the Greek verse-art came with the lengthening of the foot or bar.

His strophe is here slightly longer than in the litany of the rose:

Pivoine, amoureuse donzelle, mais sans grâce et sans sel,

Ravenelle, demoiselle dont l'oeil a des fades mélancolies,

Ancolies, petit pensionnat d'impubères jolies, jupes courtes, jambes grêles et des bras vifs comme des ailes d'hirondelle,

[1] Remy de Gourmont, 'Litanies de la rose', *Le Pèlerin du silence* (Paris, 1917), pp. 151–2, 162. The correct words are *semblant, futures* and *du*.
[2] De Gourmont, 'Fleurs de jadis', *Le Pélerin du silence*, pp. 165–6, 168.

Pivoine, Ravenelle, Ancolie, je vous préfère à des chairs plus prospères, fleurs trépassés, fleurs de jadis.[1]

I have given, perhaps, enough to indicate the form and the convention of these poems...

[In the intervening comments Pound alludes to de Gourmont's sources in medieval litanies, speaks of his ability to write in new wave-lengths, and quotes 'Jeanne' from *Les Saintes du Paradis* (*Divertissements*, pp. 65–6).]

The quotations which I have given are to be considered, not in themselves, but as parts of the rhythmic structure.

A rhythm-structure may be built up of parts which are homogeneous or of parts which differ among themselves. As the general reader is probably more accustomed to think in terms of design than in terms of rhythm one may make comparison with another art: thus, it is quite easy to think of a geometrical pattern made up of homogeneous units. It is very difficult to think of a picture made up of homogeneous units (unless they were very minute in comparison with the size of the whole).

It is also easy to think of a design made up of half a dozen kinds of unit arranged symmetrically.

. . . .

Because I praise these rhythm-units of M. De Gourmont and because they happen to be homogeneous, or very nearly so, I do not wish to appear hostile to rhythm-structures composed of units which differ among themselves. I do not hold a brief either for symmetrical or for asymmetrical structure; these things are a matter of music; they are perhaps as complicated as any problems of musical construction... The problem of how far principles of pictorial design can be applied, by a sort of parallel, in verse, is a problem like any other. The problem of how far the laws or conveniences of "musical" rhythm can be applied to word-rhythms is a problem like any other.

. . . .

And lastly, the artist may find these poems provocative, by which I mean that they may stimulate his old habits of perception, or they may even bring into being new modes of perception. He may begin to think about rhythm in slightly different manner; or to feel sound, or to gather up sounds in his mind with a slightly different sort of grouping. He may, it is true, imitate M. De Gourmont, but such imitation is scarcely more than a closer sort of study of the original. Such study may be more "provocative" than a casual reading, and therefore of value to the artist, so long as it does not impede him in his task of making new and original structures.

[1] De Gourmont, 'Fleurs de jadis', *op. cit.* pp. 167–8.

For those who seek refreshment in the arts, a new principle of grouping is far from negligible. It is far from a casual matter.

III*

[Following some remarks about his previous column, Pound enters a discussion of 'Monsieur Romains, Unanimist'.]

My first impression of Romains' work was that he erred towards rhetoric, but then I began with his prize ode, "To the Crowd Here Present" ['L'Ode à la foule qui est ici'], a possibly bad beginning. It is good rhetoric if that is what one wants. I said as much to M. Vildrac, and he told me Romains was very important. "Il a changé le pathé-tique."

...Nothing short of my inherited conscience could drive me into taking the slightest notice of M. Romains' new pathétique...[but] it is part of my job to know what it consists of...

As for his style, or at least his syntax, I grant that it is "strict, chaste, severe," and on these grounds worthy of approbation; but these qualities of language would seem to be marks of a group.

There would seem to be a certain agreement between the styles of Romains, Duhamel, Vildrac, Jouve, Arcos, Chennevière, and a few others, though Romains may have been the prime mover for their sort of clarification of the speech...

Let one not be alarmed!
I do not expect to divulge, in fifty pages, an aesthetic, a metaphysic, the origins of tragedy and the development of the race.
It will be enough if I present certain succinct affirmations.[1]

So begins M. Romains in the preface to "L'Armée dans la Ville." At least here is something to go by. He says... "The individual is merely an entity; yet an entity admitted for so many centuries that it passes for a reality pure and simple. By a pleasant irony the poets who wish to dissipate this illusion get themselves treated as "abstracteurs."[2] At the end of "Puissances de Paris" he says:

* *The New Age*, n.s. XIII, 21 (18 September 1913) 607–9.
[1] Jules Romains, 'Préface', *L'Armée dans la ville* (Paris, 1911), p. vii.
   'Qu'on ne s'effraye pas!
   Je ne compte pas exposer, en cinquante pages, une esthétique, une métaphysique, l'ori-gine de la Tragédie, le développement de l'Humanité.
   Il me suffira de présenter quelques succinctes affirmations.'
[2] *Ibid.*, p. xi.
   'L'individu n'est qu'une entité. Mais une entité admise depuis tant de siècles qu'elle passe pour une réalité simple et naïve. Par une plaisante ironie, les poètes qui veulent dis-siper cette illusion et revenir à la nature se font traiter d'abstracteurs.'

"There are to-day many men ready to recognise that man is not the most *real* thing in the world. One admits the life of combinations greater than our bodies. Society is not merely an arithmetical total or a collective designation [. . .] Man did not wait for physiology to give him a notion of his body [. . .] In the same manner it is necessary that we should know the groups that englobe us not by exterior observation but by organic consciousness. Alas! it is not sure that the rhythms wish to have their nodes in us who are not the centres of groups. We can only become such. Let us hollow out our souls, deep enough, emptying them of individual dreaming, let us make so many ditches to them that the souls of groups will of necessity flow there.

.   .   .   .

"I believe that the *groups* are at the most moving period of their evolution. . . One can learn the essential forms of life more easily from a mushroom than from an oak.

"[. . .] We have the great good fortune to be present at the beginning of a reign. . . It is not a progress, it is a creation. . .

"Already our ideas on *the being* (l'être) are correcting themselves.

.   .   .   .

"Thus one ceases to believe that *limit* is indispensable to beings. Where does the Place de la Trinité begin. The streets mingle their bodies. The squares isolate themselves with difficulty. [. . .] A being has a centre, or centres in harmony; a being is not compelled to have limits. Many exist in one place. . . a second being begins without the first having ceased. [. . .] Only individuals with ancestors possess affirmative contours, a skin which makes them break with the infinite.

"Space belongs to no one. And no being has succeeded in appropriating a morsel of space to saturate with its unique existence. All intercrosses, coincides, cohabits. [. . .] A thousand beings are concentric. One sees a little of some of them.

"How can we go on thinking that an individual is a thing which is born, grows, reproduces itself and dies? That is a superior and inveterate manner of being an individual. But groups! They are not precisely born. Their life makes and unmakes itself, as an unstable state of matter, a condensation which does not endure. They show us that life is, at the origin, a provisory attitude, a moment of exception, an intensity between abatements, nothing continuous, nothing decisive. [. . .] To make [life. . .] durable, that it should become a development and a destiny, that it should be clearly marked off at two ends by birth and death, a deal of habit is required. [. . .]"[1]

.   .   .   .

I have given, I think, enough in this translation to make his poems intelligible. I have shown by his own words what they mean by the new pathétique.

In "Un Être en Marche" M. Romains presents us a being already possessed of some general consciousness and of an intermittent life, a being with some habit of life, with even fixed habits of life, a being known humorously as "The Crocodile,". . . "A being out for a walk" treats of the procession of school-girls, pension de jeunes filles, first

---

[1] Jules Romains, 'Réflexions', *Puissances de Paris* (Paris, 1919; 1st pub. 1911), pp. 143–53. For copyright reasons, I have omitted parts of Pound's translation. My omissions are shown by bracketed ellipses or by a line of dots. The original of Pound's translation appears in the Appendix at the end of the book. In that quotation I have included, in brackets, sections quoted and translated by Pound but not included in this publication of his essay. See pages 318–19.

shuffling in the hall, preparing to set out, traces of individual life still present...[Then:]

> Les plus petites filles marchent en avant
>   Pour attendrir l'espace;
> La pension caresse avec leurs pieds d'enfants
>   La rue où elle passe.
>
> Elle grandit d'un rang à l'autre, sans surprise,
>   Comme une rive en fleurs,[1]

He then turns his attention to the street: –

> La rue a besoin d'un bonheur.
>
> .   .   .   .
>
> La rue aime la pension de jeunes filles...
>
> Pour son air de petite foule neuve et peinte;
> Pour sa façon d'aller comme le vent [sic] la pente,[2]

A troop of soldiers passes and the pension

> ...continue à sourire[;]
> Elle disperse l'invisible
> Avec le bout de ses ombrelles.[3]

Despite one's detestation of crocodiles, M. Romains makes us take interest in his particular crocodile, in its collective emotions, in the emotions of its surroundings.

> Elle monte en wagon; les jupes
> Escladent les marchepieds;
>
> .   .   .   .
>
> La pension s'effraye [sic] un peu,
> Car le train a plus d'âme qu'elle;[4]

They go out into the country[,]...over a still field and into a wood. They enter a village. They find a solitary fisherman, and the author unburdens himself of a little theorising to the effect that each man thinks that he is alone and that the world is about him.

> Inconscient et familier
> Comme le brouillard d'une pipe.[5]

...The "Poème Epique" ends with the crocodile put to bed. It is possibly the nearest approach to true epic that we have had since the middle ages.

[1] Jules Romains, Poem II, *Un Être en marche* (Paris, 1910), p. 10.
[2] Poem III, *Ibid.*, pp. 12–13. The reading in the original edition is *veut*.
[3] Poem IV, *Ibid.*, p. 18.
[4] Poem VI, *Ibid.*, p. 23. The reading in the original edition is *s'effraie*.
[5] Poem XV, *Ibid.*, p. 67.

The author has achieved a form which fully conveys the sense of modern life. He is able to mention any familiar thing, any element of modern life without its seeming incongruous, and the result is undeniably poetic...

[Pound then observes that 'Poème Lyrique', which makes up the second part of *Un Être en marche*, seems to him confusing and subjective, but he quotes several lines from this part of the volume.]

Turning to "Odes et Prières" I find that the odes leave me as unmoved as when the first time I read them...However much I may lose in my deafness to the odes, I find with the beginning of the prayers a new note. I find the words of a man curiously and intently conscious. In the second prayer to the couple we read:

> Je ne te voyais pas dans l'ombre des tentures,
> O nous! Je n'essayais pas même de te voir;
> Je me disais: "Nous sommes seuls! Nous sommes moi."
> Et l'air était gonflé de notre solitude.[1]

From here his consciousness moves out in ever widening and ever vivifying circles, to the family; to the group, to his house about him; to the street and to the village.

> Ma peau frisonne à cause de toi, groupe amer!
> .   .   .   .
> Il n'y a pas ici que nous deux, ma maison?
> Vois! mon âme s'allonge, remue et vacile
> Comme la flamme dans la lanterne fendue.
> .   .   .   .
> D'autres dieux sont entrés, d'autres, plus grands que toi.[2]

And to the street he prays:

> Tu seras divine au lieu d'être immense.
> Arranche-toi [*sic*] rudement à la ville
> Comme un lézard à la poigne d'un homme;[3]

The opening of the second prayer to the village would be poetry even if it were not *unammisme* [*sic*]:

> La fin du jour est belle et j'ai couru longtemps;
> La bicyclette osseuse a purchassé les routes;
> .   .   .   .
> O village inconnu qui me tiens dans le soir,
> Dis-moi pourquoi je suis joyeux, pourquoi je ris,[4]

---

[1] Jules Romains, 'Seconde prière au couple', *Odes et prières* (Paris, 1923; 1st pub. 1913), p. 97.
[2] 'Deuxième prière à un groupe', p. 109; 'Quartième prière à la maison', *Ibid.*, p. 121.
[3] 'Prière à un rue', *Ibid.*, p. 126. The reading in the original is *arrache-toi*.
[4] 'Deuxième prière à un village', *Ibid.*, p. 131.

...And he shows a knowledge that is not limited to his own peculiar pantheon in the verse beginning:

> Je ne veux pas murmurer un seul nom,
> Ce soir; je ne veux pas tenter les ombres;[1]

If one retain any doubt as to Romains' deed to Parnassus, this poem should serve for proof.

Whatever we may think of his theories, in whatever paths we may find it useless to follow him, we have here at last the poet, and our best critique is quotation.

IV*

[Pound begins his fourth column on French poetry by contrasting the attitudes in Jules Romains' 'Ode à la foule qui est ici' and Charles Vildrac's 'Gloire'. He suggests that Vildrac's poem is 'Nietzschean' and 'pre-unanimist', a portrait of the author disillusioned with the experience of controlling a crowd, and he indicates he does not know whether Vildrac accepts the label *unanimiste* or not. In contrast, Pound says, Romains affirms in his poem that the poet is able to merge with the crowd-unit. To demonstrate his point, Pound quotes about forty lines of Romains' 'Ode', in a mixture of the original French and an approximate translation. His outline traces the course of the poem from the opening, in which the poet feels himself living in the light of the crowd:

> O Foule! Te voici dans le creux du théâtre,
> Docile aux murs, moulant ta chair à la carcasse;
> Et tes rangs noirs partent de moi comme un reflux.
>
> Tu es.
> Cette lumière où je suis est à toi.

There follow lines in which the poet becomes the source of the crowd's voice – an event Pound interprets as the poet becoming a 'vortex':

> Écoute! Peu à peu, la voix sort de ma chair:
> Elle monte, elle tremble et tu trembles.
>
> .   .   .   .
>
> Elle est en toi l'invasion et la victoire.
> Les mots que je te dis, il faut que tu les penses!

As a result of the poet's giving both thought and words to the crowd, he becomes co-extensive with the crowd-soul: 'Foule! Ton âme entière est debout dans mon corps... / Ta forme est moi.' Finally, as he completes the outline of the ode, Pound quotes Romains' conclusion – the crowd, the possession of the poet while it lasts, is also a momentary god whose sign will remain with the individuals who separate as the crowd dissolves:

> Tu es mienne avant que tu sois morte;
> Les corps qui sont ici, la ville peut les prendre;
> Ils garderont au front comme une croix de cendre
> Le vestige du dieu que tu es maintenant.[2]

[1] 'Quatrième prière à plusieurs dieux', *Ibid.*, p. 143.
* *The New Age*, n.s. XIII, 22 (25 September 1913) 631–3.
[2] Jules Romains, 'Ode à la foule qui est ici' (first delivered in the Théâtre de l'Odéon in 1906), *Odes et prières* (Paris, 1923), pp. 163–7.

As an 'antistrophe' or 'counterblast' to this philosophy, Pound cites some thirty-five lines of Vildrac's 'Gloire'. The central figure of the poem is a man who had dominated crowds by his voice and who had believed his power endured in the hearts of individuals after the groups had dispersed. The poem recounts his discovery that his influence did not survive his departure and that the crowd responded as freely to some other who was skilled at 'making grimaces':

> Il se dressait devant la foule
> Et connaissait l'enivrement
> De la sentir soumise à sa parole ...
>
> .   .   .   .   .   .
>
> Et même, il vit une foule,
> Une foule comme les siennes
> Qui se pressait, ivre et séduite,
> Autour d'un autre
> Habile à faire des grimaces.

As a result of this experience, the man returned to seeking out people 'un à un'.[1] Pound breaks off his summary at this point, although Vildrac goes on to stress in the last fifteen lines that the man was preserved in the memory of his friends as a result of their solitary association with him.]

However far these compositions may be from "poetry" it cannot be denied that they contain poetical lines, and the latter poem is convenient to quote as it gives us, I think, a fair clue to M. Vildrac's attitude.

...If M. Vildrac were merely a writer with a philosophy of life slightly different from that of M. Romains I would not trouble to read him, but M. Vildrac is an artist. He is at his best, I think, in short narrative sketches such as "Visite" and "Une Auberge" (both in "Livre d'Amour,"...).

[Pound then provides in stanza form an English prose version of some sixty-eight lines of Vildrac's 'Visite'. The poem begins with a daydreaming man who remembers a frequent and neglected promise to visit a humble friend. Moved by his inner feeling, he goes out in the snow to pay the call:

> Il se vêtit à la hâte,
> Il sortit de sa maison,
> Et s'engagea dans la neige
> Vers la maison de cet homme.

When he arrives, however, the visit is attended by uneasy and unspoken questions, for the man and his wife assume their guest has come for some purpose beyond renewed friendship:

> Ces gens hélas, ne croyaient pas
> Qu'il fût venu à l'improviste,
> Si tard, de si loin, par la neige,
> Seulement pour sa joie et leur joie,
> Seulement pour tenir une promesse;

---

[1] Charles Vildrac, 'Gloire', *Livre d'amour suivi des premiers vers* (Paris, 1959; 1st pub. 1910), pp. 62–4.

It is only when he rises to leave that they understand the motive of the call and seek to detain him:

> Alors se fit une détente,
> Alors ils osèrent comprendre:
> Il n'était venu que pour eux!
>
> .   .   .   .   .   .
>
> Quelqu'un était enfin venu!

He promises to return, but he fixes the scene carefully in his memory, for as he turns away he deeply suspects that he will never come again:

> Il regarda bien chaque objet
> Et puis aussi l'homme et la femme,
> Tant il craignait au fond de lui
> De ne plus jamais revenir.[1]

Following his translation Pound comments:]

I have been told that this is sentiment and therefore damned. I am not concerned with that argument... The point is that M. Vildrac has told a short story in verse with about one fifth of the words that a good writer of short stories would have needed for the narrative. He has conveyed his atmosphere, and his people, and the event. He has brought narrative verse into competition with narrative prose without giving us long stanzas of bombast.

M. Vildrac had given us a more serious story in "Une Auberge," I think he has written two lines too many; I mean the last two lines of the poem; but he has achieved here some of his finest effects, in such lines as: "Mais comme il avait l'air cependant d'être des notres!"

The poem begins:

> C'est une auberge qu'il y a
> Au carrefour des Chétives-Maisons,
> Dans le pays où il fait toujours froid.

There are three houses there:

> Et la troisième est cette auberge au coeur si triste
>
> .   .   .   .
>
> C'est seulement parce qu'on a soif qu'on entre y boire
>
> .   .   .   .
>
> Et l'on n'est pas forcé d'y raconter son histoire.[2]

[Pound continues to summarize the poem, quoting in French the account of a man eating:

> Il mange lentement son pain
> Parce que ses dents sont usées;
>
> .   .   .   .   .   .

[1] 'Visite', *Ibid.*, pp. 74–7.
[2] 'Une Auberge', *Ibid.*, p. 35.

> Quand il a fini
> Il hésite, puis timide
> Va s'asseoir un peu
> A côté du feu.

And then the narration of an encounter between the man and a child:

> Et voilà qu'elle approche tout doucement
> Et vient appuyer sur la main de l'homme
> La chair enfantine de sa bouche;

> Et puis lève vers lui ses yeux pleins d'eau
> Et lui tend de tout son frêle corps
> Une pauvre petite fleur d'hiver qu'elle a.

Pound continues with the quotation of eleven lines spoken by the tavern's 'douloureuse femme' and concludes with the first two lines of this last stanza:

> "Et malgré sa jeunesse, malgré mon lit si froid,
> Malgré mes seins vidés, mes épaules si creuses.
> Il est resté tout un jour pour m'aimer, il m'a aimée.
> Et cette petite fille-là est née
> De l'aumône d'amour qu'il m'a donnée."[1]

The final two lines, unquoted in his essay, are the ones Pound called 'two lines too many'.]

To some these very simple tales of M. Vildrac will mean a great deal, and to others they will mean very little. If a person of this latter sort dislikes the choice of subject he may do worse than to consider the method of narration. Mr. D. H. Lawrence can do, I dare say, as well, but M. Vildrac's stories are different; they are, I think, quite his own.

As to the method of verse, if the reader's ear be so constituted that he derives no satisfaction from the sound of

> Et il vit son regard s'éteindre
> Dès qu'il fut un peu loin des autres.[2]

One cannot teach him by theory to derive satisfaction from this passage, or from the assonance of ensemble and entendre, drawn at the end of their lines, or from half a hundred finer and less obvious matters of sound.

...I, personally, happen to be tired of verses which are left full of blank spaces for interchangeable adjectives. In the more or less related systems of versification which have been adopted by Romains, Chennevière, Vildrac, Duhamel, and their friends, I do not find...an excessive allowance of blank spaces, and this seems to me a healthy tendency.

. . . .

[1] 'Une Auberge', *op. cit.*, pp. 36–8.
[2] 'Gloire', *Ibid.*, p. 63.

I am aware that there are resolutions of sound less obvious than rhyme. It requires more pains and intelligence both to make and to hear them. To demand rhyme is almost like saying that only one note out of ten need be in melody, it is not quite the same. No one would deny that the final sound of the line is important. No intelligent person would deny that all the accented sounds are important. I cannot bring myself to believe that even the unstressed syllables should be wholly neglected.

I cannot believe that one can test the musical qualities of a passage of verse merely by counting the number of syllables, or even of stressed syllables, in each line, and by thereafter examining the terminal sounds.

God, or nature, or the Unanim, or whoever or whatever is responsible or irresponsible for the existence of the race has given to some men a sense of absolute pitch, and to some a sense of rhythms, and to some a sense of verbal consonance, and some are colour-blind, and some are tone-deaf, and some are almost void of intelligence, hence we are lead to believe that it would be foolish to expect to move the hearts of all men simultaneously either by perfection of musical sounds, either articulate or inarticulate, or by an arrangement of colours or by a sane and sober exposition in wholly logical prose.

Those who are interested in ritual and in the history of invocation may have been interested in M. De Gourmont's litanies, those who are interested in a certain purging of the poetic idiom may be interested in the work of such men as Vildrac and P. J. Jouve.

v *

M. Laurent Tailhade..., the author of "poèmes Aristophanesques[,]" writes in accordance with a tradition of speech which has no need of clarification.

> Täglich geht sie dort spazieren,
> Mit zwei hässlich alten Damen –

wrote Heine with his eye very much on the object.

> Carmen est maigre – un trait de bistre...

wrote Gautier. I think this sort of clear presentation is of the noblest traditions of our craft...It is a practice of speech common to good prose and to good verse alike. It is to modern verse what the method of Flaubert is to modern prose, and by that I do not mean that it is not equally common to the best work of the ancients. It means constatation of fact. It presents. It does not comment. It is irrefutable because it does not present a personal predilection for any particular fraction of the

* *The New Age*, n.s. XIII, 23 (2 October 1913) 662-4.

truth. It is as communicative as Nature. It is as uncommunicative as Nature...It does not attempt to justify anybody's ways to anybody or anything else...It is open to all facts and to all impressions.

> Sur le petit bateau-mouche,
> Les bourgeois sont entassés,
> Avec les enfants qu'on mouche,
> Qu'on ne mouche pas assez.[1]

The presentative method does not attempt to "array the ox with trappings." It does not attempt to give dignity to that which is without dignity, which last is "rhetoric," that is, an attempt to make important the unimportant, to make more important the less important. It is a lie and a distortion.

The presentative method is equity. It is powerless to make the noble seem ignoble. It fights for a sane valuation. It cannot bring fine things into ridicule. It will not pervert a thing from its true use by trying to ascribe to it alien uses.

It is also the scourge of fools.

> Les femmes laides qui déchiffrent des sonates
> Sortent de chez Érard, le concert terminé
> Et, sur le trottoir gras, elles heurtent Phryné
> Offrant au plus offrant l'or de ses fausses nattes
> Elles viennent d'ouïr Ladislas Talapoint,
> Pianiste hongrois que *le Figaro* vante.[2]

This is what is called "rendering one's own time in the terms of one's own time." Heine wrote in this manner, and so did Catullus, and so for that matter did Aristophanes for whom M. Tailhade names the present volume.

. . . .

He is, one finds, full of tricks out of Rabelais and out of Villon, and of mannerisms brought from the Pléiade. He is a gourmand of great books; he is altogether unabashed and unashamed.

> Entre les sièges où des garçons volontaires
> Entassent leur chalants parmi les boulingrins,
> La famille Feyssard, avec des airs sereins,
> Discute longuement les tables solitaires.
>
> La demoiselle a mis un chapeau rouge vif
> Dont s'honore le bon faiseur de sa commune,
> Et madame Feyssard, un peu hommasse et brune,
> Porte un robe loutre avec des reflets d'if.[3]

---

[1] Laurent Tailhade, 'Bacarolle', *Poèmes aristophanesques* (Paris, 1904), p. 15.
[2] 'Place des victoires', *Ibid.*, p. 20.
[3] 'Diner champêtre', *Ibid.*, p. 13. Pound's quotation shows minor variations in punctuation from that used in the 1904 text.

He is equally vivid in his –

Quartier Latin

Dans le bar où jamais le parfum des brévas
Ne dissipa l'odeur de vomi qui la navre
Triomphent les appas de la mère Cadavre[.]
Dont le nom fameux jusque ches les Howas.

Brune, elle fut jadis vantée entre les brunes,
Tant que son souvenir au Vaux-Hall est resté[.]
Et c'est toujours avec bocoup [*sic*] de dignité
Qu'elle rince le zinc et détaille les prunes.[1]

The Louvre itself is versified with no less aptness –

Ces voyageurs ont des waterproofs d'un gris jaune
Avec des brodequins en allés en bateau;
Devant Reubens, devant Rembrandt, devant Watteau,
Ils s'arrêtent, pour consulter le *Guide Joanne*.[2]

When M. Tailhade parodies the antique [he] is considerably more than a parodist. He writes to his subject and the "snatches of ancient psalmody" are but a pa: cf the music. The cadence and the rhymes are sufficiently ridiculous, and these also are a mockery. That is to say, he is a satirist, he does not imitate a form merely for the sake of imitating …Tailhade enjoys himself as Cervantes enjoyed himself with the "Diana" of Montemayor. It is a pleasing and erudite irony such as should fill the creative artist with glee and might well fill the imitator with a species of apostolic terror.

Par example, this ballade "de la parfaite admonition," how uncomfortable for those writers who think that a derivative mysticism is valid excuse for bad verses.

Ballade

Voici venir le Buffle, le Buffle des buffles! – le Buffle. Lui seul est buffle et tous les autres ne sont que des boeufs. Voici venir le Buffle, le Buffle des buffles – le Buffle!

Le verbe sesquipédalier,
Le discours mitré, la faconde
Navarroise du Chevalier,
A Poissy comme dans Golconde,
Essorillent le pleutre immonde.
Mais, loin de tout bourgeois nigaud,
Hurle ta palabre féconde:
Sois grandiloque et bousingot.[3]

[1] 'Quartier latin', *Ibid.*, p. 18. The misprinted word is *beaucoup*.
[2] 'Musée de Louvre', *Ibid.*, p. 19.
[3] 'Ballade casquée de la parfaite admonition', *Ibid.*, p. 97. The prose sentences preceding the quoted lines appear as an epigraph to the poem in the 1904 edition.

II

DE RÉGNIER

[Pound next turns to Henri de Régnier, whom he compares to the 'vase-painters', and he expresses a high regard for the 'souplesse de rhythme' of the 'Odelettes'. He then quotes two excerpts from that nine-poem sequence:]

> Un petit roseau m'a suffi
> Pour faire frémir l'herbe haute
> Et tout le pré
> Et les doux saules
> Et le ruisseau qui chante aussi;
> Un petit roseau m'a suffi
> A faire chanter la fôret.[1]

These lines and the rest of this odelette have long been recognized as M. De Régnier's declaration of his intent. Almost any of the poems of this sequence would serve to show his method of rhyme, and of the blending of rhyme-sounds, as par example:

> Si tu disais:
> Voici l'Automme [*sic*] qui vient et marche
> Doucement sur les fueilles sèches,
> Ecoute le heurt de la hache
> Qui, d'arbre en arbre, dans la forêt
> Sape et s'ébrèche;
> Regarde aussi sur le marais
> Les oiseaux tomber, flèche à flèche,
> Les ailes lâches.[2]

The author is, I suppose, the last of the Parnassiens, or at the least the last one who counts. His melody presents nothing that is any longer new or startling. The perfection of his melody will interest none save the lovers of melody...If his work has the beautiful fineness it is of no importance – save to the lovers of beauty.

> J'ai feint que les Dieux m'aient parlé;
> Celui-là ruisselant d'algues et d'eau,
> Cet autre lourd de grappes et de blé,
> Cet autre ailé,
> Farouche...[3]

. . . .

...It is fairly obvious that there exists in Paris a numerous and clamorous younger generation who consider M. De Régnier a back number.

[1] Henri de Régnier, 'Odelette, I', *Les Jeux rustiques et divins* (Paris, 1911; 1st pub. 1897), p. 217.
[2] 'Odelette, VI', *Ibid.*, p. 237.
[3] Henri de Régnier, introductory poem, *Les Médailles d'argile* (Paris, 1911; 1st pub. 1900), p. 2.

It is equally obvious that there are among the English writers many who have not attained to any standards more recent than those employed by this author...

[Pound inserts here a digression on the nature of the serious critic and the role such a person should be able to play in evaluating innovations by poets like De Régnier.]

As touching innovations in the specific art of metric, I think De Régnier has given us little that we might not have had from the author of lines, "Sopra un basso rilievo" or of the "Ultimo canto di Safo". Still he has given us something. On the other hand, there would be a great advance in the standard of English verse writing if the poets north of the Channel would learn to write with such limpidity of syntax as De Régnier uses in his passage about the centaur:

> Il s'avance de quelques pas dans les roseaux,
> Flaira le vent, hennit, repassa l'eau.[1]

Nevertheless, I do not believe that any man should need two thousand odd pages to say that he delights in gardens full of statues and running water and that Greek mythology is enchanting.

. . . .

It would seem as if the French versifiers had become so engrossed in matters of craftsmanship as to forget that the first requisite of a work of art is that it be interesting... It is certain that the method of constatation drifts off imperceptibly into description and that pages of poetic description can have no interest save for those particularly interested in the things described, or for those interested in language as language.

III

CORBIÈRE

But all France is not Paris, and if anything were needed to refute these generalities it could be found in the work of Corbière. Tristan Corbière is dead, but his work is scarcely known in England...

Because his versification is more English than French, because he was apparently careless of all versification, I think that his one volume will lie half open on the tables of all those who open it once. They said he was careless of style, etcetera! He was as careless of style as a man of swift mordant speech can afford to be. For the quintessence of style is precisely that it should be swift and mordant. It is precisely that a man should not speak at all until he has something (it matters very little what) to say.

[1] 'Le Vase', *Les jeux rustiques et divins*, p. 117.

> Je voudrais être alors chien de fille publique[,]
> Lécher un peu d'amour qui ne soit pas payé;

Or earlier in the same poem:

> Ah si j'étais un peu compris! Si par pitié
> Une femme pouvait me sourire à moitié,
> Je lui dirais: oh viens, ange qui me consoles!...
> . . . .
> ...Et je la conduirais à l'hospice des folles.[1]

Or again by way of encouragement.

> Couronne tes genoux!...[et nos têtes dix-cors;
> Ris! montre tes dents!...] Mais...nous avons la police,
> Et quelque chose en nous d'eunuque et de recors.[2]

These scraps are from his Parisian gasconadings, but even in Paris he looked the thing in the eye and was no more minded...to soothe the world or the world-of-letters with flattery than he would have been to deceive himself about the state of the Channel off his native village, . . .

He "stands," as the phrase is, by his songs of the Breton coast, and the proper introduction to him is "La Rapsode Foraine," or the song in it, to St. Anne.

> Mère taillée à coups de hache.
> . . . .
> Bâton des aveugles! Béquille
> Des vieilles! Bras des nouveau-nés!
> Mère de madame ta fille!
> Parente des abandonnés!
> . . . .
> Des croix profondes sont tes rides,
> Tes cheveux sont blancs comme fils...
> . . . .
> Fais venir et conserve en joie
> Ceux à naître et ceux qui sont nés.
> Et verse, sans que Dieu te voie,
> L'eau de tes yeux sur les damnés![3]

[1] Tristan Corbière, 'Sous un portrait de Corbière en couleurs fait par lui et daté de 1868', *Les Amours jaunes*, éd. définitive (Paris, 1912; 1st pub. 1873), p. 19. All apparent ellipses in the second passage quoted are part of the original punctuation.

[2] 'Féminin singulier', *Ibid.*, p. 24. Pound did not include the bracketed words. Apparent ellipses are part of the punctuation in the original.

[3] 'La Rapsode foraine et le pardon de Sainte-Anne', *Ibid.*, pp. 193, 194, 196. Ellipsis in the third quoted stanza appears in the original.

...The note of the sea is in the sound of his

Au Vieux Roscoff

Trou de filibustiers, vioux [sic] nid
A corsaire!...
Dors: tu peux fermer ton Oeil borgne
Ouvert sur le large, et qui lorgne
Les Anglais, depuis trois cent ans...[1]

...And Corbière himself is most capable of defining those qualities of the national literature which least attract one.

Ne m'offrez pas un trône!
A moi tout seul je fris,
Drôle, en ma sauce juane [sic]
De *chic* et de mépris.
Que les bottes vernies
Pleuvent du paradis...[2]

He is more real than the "realists" because he still recognises that force of romance which is a quite real and apparently ineradicable part of our life, he preceded and thereby escaped that spirit or that school which was to sentimentalise over ugliness with a more silly sentimentality than the early romanticists had shown toward "the beauties of nature."

...I feel at present as if I had found another poet to put on the little rack with Villon and Heine, with the poets whom one actually reads...

VI*

When I began these articles I had no intention of proclaiming that M. Jammes was the most important writer in France. I don't know that I shall do so even now...for he completely escapes from all computation and from the adjectives of magnitude.

. . . .

M. Jammes is a part of our normal life; he is not the least bit less a poet. We read his books of verse. It is as if he entered our room. He speaks in a normal tone. He produces a conversation...He comes again. He "drops in," as we say in my country. He gets the habit of "dropping in." He usually says something, and gradually we perceive a man of "original mind." (If I am permitted that cliché.)

[1] 'Au vieux Roscoff', *Ibid.*, p. 262. The misprinted word is *vieux* in the definitive edition.
[2] 'Bohéme de chic', *Ibid.*, p. 25. The misprinted word is *jaune* in the definitive edition.
* *The New Age*, n.s. xiii, 24 (9 October 1913) 694–6.

I think M. Jammes can touch nothing without making that thing his own...It is, I think, the great gift. At least it is "style" in the fine sense...It is the manner of Montaigne. It is, with both these men, naturalness and humanity.

They tell me "Verhaeren is the greatest poet," etcetera, but much of Verhaeren is what I have called elsewhere "Symtomatic." [*sic*] That is, it is a sort of barometer. It is based on an economic condition. M. Jammes has based his work upon our nature as humans, and the economic condition is but one symptom of this nature.

This author delineates as clearly as Laurent Tailharde [*sic*], but he does so without irritation...Next to exasperating "Le Muffle" there are few things more delightful than to watch someone else do it well. And yet there are things beyond this. M. Jammes compares himself to a donkey –

> J'aime l'âne si doux,

which does not mean "I love the donkey," but "I like the donkey walking about the holly trees. He waggles his ears, and is on guard against bees; and he carries the poor people and the sacks full of barley. He goes near the ditches with a little halting step. The lady with me thinks he is stupid because he is a poet, etc."[1] This poem is not very important. Let us turn to another –

I was going to Lourdes by rail, beside a mountain stream, blue as air. The mountains seemed tin in the sunlight, and they were singing, "Sauvez! Sauvez!" in the train. There was a crowd crazy, excited, all over dust and sunlight.

There are cripples, and a priest in a pulpit covered with blue cloth, and the women who every now and again sing "Sauvez."

And the procession sings –

> ...Les drapeaux
> se penchaient avec leurs devises en or.
>
> Le soleil était blanc sur les escaliers,
> dans l'air bleu, sur les clochers déchiquetés,
>
> Mais sur un branchard [*sic*], portée par ses parents,
> son pauvre père tête nue et priant,
>
> et ses frères qui disaient: "ainsi soit-it" [*sic*],
> une jeune fille sur le point de mourir.
>
> Oh! qu'elle était belle! elle avait dix-huit ans,
> et elle souriait; elle était en blanc.

[1] Pound paraphrases the first five couplets of Francis Jammes's 'J'aime l'âne...', *De l'Angelus de l'aube a l'Angelus du soir, 1888–1897* (Paris, 1911; 1st pub. 1898), p. 12.

Et la procession chantait. Les drapeaux
se penchaient avec leurs devises en or.

Moi je serrais les dents pour ne pas pleurer,
et cette fille, je me sentais l'aimer.

Oh! elle m'a regardé un grand moment,
une rose blanche en main, souriant.

Mais maintenant où es-tu? dis, où es-tu?
Es-tu morte? je t'aime, toi qui m'as vu.

Si tu existes, Dieu, ne la tue pas:
elle avait des mains blanches, de minces bras.

Dieu ne la tue pas! – et ne serait-ce que
pour son père nu-tête qui priait Dieu.[1]

You will see that the author does not sentimentalise. He portrays a situation full of feeling, or emotion, and, if you like, of sentiment. He distorts nothing. He does not try to make the thing any more pathetic than it was...As for being sentimental, you might as well call "Steve" Crane sentimental. You might, if you like, say that the next poem is irony. Yet, is it precisely that? It is simple and adequate statement. The author does not *forbid* you to add to it. It is simple and adequate statement –

La Jeune Fille...

The young girl is white; she has green veins on her wrists, inside her open sleeves.

One does not know why she laughs. She cries out all of a sudden, and this is shrill.

Est-ce qu'elle se doute
qu'elle vous prend le coeur
en cueillant sur la route
    des fleurs?

On dirait quelquefois
qu'elle comprend des choses.
Pas touours. Elle cause
    Tout bas[.]

"Oh, ma chère! oh! là là...
...Figure-toi...mardi
je l'ai vu...j'ai rri[.]" . Elle dit
    comme ça.

Quand un jeune homme souffre[,]
d'abord elle se tait:

[1] 'J'allai à Lourdes...', *Ibid.*, pp. 22–4. The misprinted words are *brancard* and *soit-il* in the original.

elle ne rit plus, tout
étonnée.

Dans les petits chemins
elle remplit ses mains
de piquants de bruyères
de fougères.

Elle est grande, elle est blanche,
elle a des bras très doux.
elle est très droite et penche
le cou.[1]

Finis. Richard of St. Victor who was half a neoplatonist, tells us that by naming over all the beautiful things we can think of, we may draw back upon our minds some vestige of the unrememberable beauties of paradise. If we are not given to mystical devotions we may suspect that the function of poetry is, in part, to draw back upon our mind a paradise, if you like, or, equally, one's less detestable hours and the outrageous hopes of one's youth. However that may be, I get a distinct pleasure when M. Jammes writes –

J'ai vu, dans de vieux salons, des tableaux flammands,
où, dans une auberge noire, on voyait un type
qui buvait de la bière, et sa très mince pipe
avait un point rouge et il fumait doucement.[2]

...I get a vision of the old château-inn at La Tour, near Marueil, where I lunched slap in the middle of a Rembrandt. It is not M. Jammes' picture; he is talking of a Dutch merchant; but my picture is near enough; he gives me his, and he gives me back my own. I have the pleasures of comparison, and mine is like enough for me to know that his is reliable...

[Pound goes on to comment on his reaction to 'Le Paysan...' and to compare Jammes to Laurent Tailhade and Henri de Régnier. He notes that it is difficult to represent all facets of the French poet because he 'does not seem to repeat himself', then alludes to a poem in a second major collection, *Le Deuil des Primèveres*. He then summarizes as follows:]

It might be claimed by one's adversaries that Francis Jammes is for the most part only a *causeur* in verse...I think, however, that a man reading Jammes about A.D. 2500 might get a fair idea of our life, the life of A.D. 1913.

[In the remaining third of the essay Pound in a long analogy compares Jammes' work to a gallery of pictures, then turns to a discussion of those of his books which appeared

[1] 'La Jeune fille...', *Ibid.*, pp. 107–8.
[2] 'J'ai vu, dans de vieux salons...', *Ibid.*, p. 143.

after 1900. He gives most emphasis to 'Existences', a novel or collection of scenes in verse, which was published in *Le Triomphe de la vie* in 1902. Pound regards this composition as fully successful, a capturing of 'the life of every small town in France', and laments that English and American poets are unable to do the same for provincial life in their own countries. In his concluding comments he notes that soon after the publication of 'Existences' Jammes returned to Catholicism, but he refrains from discussing those later verses in the context of a survey of contemporary French poetry.]

VII*

[For his final column in the series, Pound treats very briefly six other French poets and provides a seventh unit of summary and evaluation. He begins his discussion with Rimbaud, whose poems (like 'beautiful forms made by chance') Pound believes prefigure accomplishments later poets have achieved by their own hard labor, rather than through straightforward imitation of Rimbaud. 'Tête de Faune' represents precisely the kind of beauty he is at that moment seeking, Pound says, but in order to value the excellence of the French poem he believes he has had to learn a desire for that kind of beauty on his own. Nonetheless, Pound notes, Parisians did know Rimbaud's work, and contemporary critics should take account of his pre-existence when they evaluate the achievements – whether in conciseness, prose-poetry, or a literature of vision – of the current poets of France. In a second section Pound provides a perfunctory nod at Verhaeren; he is, in 'Les Pauvres' and the Flemish volumes, 'a very fine poet', and elsewhere 'just a hopeless rhetorician'. Besides, Pound implies, he is already well known in England, for 'everybody writes of Verhaeren'.]

3.

And there is M. le Prince des Poètes, Paul Fort, with a delicate, ironical and kindly temper...One must read Fort aloud or hear him so read. He is delicacy and charm, and he is much more civilised than we shall ever care to be and he is what they call "The Last Bohemian."

To exhibit Paul Fort to a foreign public by means of criticism! It would be like trying to exhibit butterflies with a threshing machine.

Ce soir, on vend des fleurs sur le Pont au Change. L'air[,] par bouffées, sent la tubéreuse et la poussière. C'est demain Sainte-Marie. Une heure dorée coule au fond du ciel occidental et sur les quais, et jette un éclat fauve au milieu de la foule. On voit le mouvement trouble de la plac [*sic*] du Châtelet.[...][1]

.   .   .   .

It is natural as that...

I do not know that he has given a name to his system of metric. We shall probably adopt the Greek system of quantitative verse in English

---

* *The New Age*, n.s. XIII, 25 (16 October 1913) 726–8.
[1] Paul Fort, 'Sur le Pont au Change', *Ballades françaises*, *VIᵉ série: Paris sentimental* (Paris, 1902). The poem appears in *Poètes d'aujourd'hui*, I, ed. A. Van Bever and Paul Léautaud (Paris, 1910), p. 88. Later in his essay Pound cites this anthology, which is clearly the place of his first acquaintance with many of the figures he has discussed.

before we try this subtle combination of accords. Also the Greek system is probably more germane to the nature of our speech.

I shall not preach Paul Fort in these islands for I do not think these islands want him . . . It is the function of the art-critic to bring his public, as expeditiously as possible, to those works of art in which they may take pleasure.

[Pound then notes that Paul Claudel is currently attracting a great deal of attention, but defers any further comment until he has had the chance to read more deeply in 'his prose as well as his verse'.]

5.

Among the men who are neither old nor young, André Spire is well worth attention. He has learned not to slop over. The quality of his charm is perhaps best presented by quotation . . .

> Mère, le printemps aux doigts tièdes
> A soulevé l'espagnolette
> De mes fenêtres sans rideaux.
> Faites taire toutes ses voix qui montent
> Jusqu'à ma table de travail.
>
> Ce sont les amies de ma mère
> Et de la mère de ton père,
> Qui cause de leurs maris morts,
> Et de leurs fils partis.
>
> Avec, au coin de leurs lèvres,
> Ces moustaches de café au lait?
> Et dans leurs mains ces tartines?
> Dans leurs bouches ces kouguelofs?
>
> Ce sont des cavales anciennes
> Qui mâchonnent le peu d'herbe douce
> Que Dieu veut bien leur laisser.
>
> Mère, les maitres sensible
> Lâchent les juments inutiles
> Dans les prés, non dans mon jardin!
>
> Sois tranquille, mon fils, sois tranquille,
> Elles ne brouteront pas tes fleurs
>
> Mere, que n'y occupent-elles leurs, lèvres,
> Et leurs trop courtes dents trop blanches
> De porcelaine trop fragile!
>
> Mon fils, fermez votre fênetre.
> Mon fils, vous n'êtes pas crétien![1]

---

[1] André Spire, 'Dames Anciennes'.‡

In the earlier work "Et Vous Riez," he writes with a deal more eagerness; with a rather fine, embittered impatience, first with his literary friends because they persist in concerning themselves exclusively with their craft, instead of attempting to uplift the proletariat; second, with the proletariat because it won't let him civilise it, and won't civilise itself in three weeks.

[Pound calls the poem an account of the journey of a 'modern Faust' who seeks to establish an 'equitable social order'. He then quotes the following passage:]

> Les sombres militants, plus tristes que moi-même.
> Ils m'ont dit[.]
>
> .   .   .   .
>
> Assemble les oiseaux...
> Et chante leur.
> Mais tenter d'exalter ces hommes sans désirs,
> Ce peuple qui se traîne!
> Tu n'as donc pas encore regardé ses yeux vides?
> Viens avec nous,
> Rythme-nous des injures pour fouetter son dos mou.
> Par crainte de nos coups il lèvera la tête,
> Et, nous le lancerons contre ceux qui l'oppriment.
>
> Il n'a pas relevé a tête.
> Il a gémi:
> "A quoi bon ces grands cris sur mes épaules lasses.
> Mes yeux regarderont tousjours [*sic*] mes pieds trop lourds.
> J'ai cru longtemps, j'ai cru me posséder un jour.
> Mais, chaque fois qu' un peu de sève m'est donnée,
> L'un de vous me la prend, pour s'en faire homme. [...]"[1]

I think Spire is honest and that he writes from himself. Among the younger men Jouve seems to me to show promise and Apollinaire has brought out a clever book.

6.

M. Henri-Martin Barzun has an idea that we should write poems like orchestral scores with a dozen voices at once...People do read orchestral scores. I suppose one could learn to read five or ten lines at once or at least to imagine that the five or ten sounds represented in the different lines were all going on at once. There are in this plan both opportunities and dangers...One might represent the confusion of metropolitan life where too much does certainly happen all at once. M. Barzun offers a mode of synthesis that is not to be despised. Of

---

[1] André Spire, 'Au Peuple', *Versets* (Paris, 1908), pp. 21–2. The misprinted word should be *toujours*.

course there are any number of objections. If you insist in being all apperception and all sorts of apperception at once you are in danger of paralysing thought; of bringing all your other faculties to a standstill. Art is, at least to some extent, selection. . .

M. Barzun's "Hymne des Forces" moved me, although I thought it rhetorical. It seemed to me significant that the voice of the mass should have come so near to being coherent. M. Barzun is nowhere near being content with the book above-mentioned. The polyphonic method will be·justified when a great work is presented through it. In the meantime there is no use blinding oneself to the fact that the next great work may be written in this manner. . .

7.

It is not possible for me to discuss all the fifty-three authors contained in Van Bever and Léataud's [*sic*] anthology. There are a host of younger writers who will doubtless receive fitting recognition at the hands of Mr. Flint. My intention at the outset was to write in conversational tone of my personal adventure; of such French poetry of to-day as had seemed of interest to one as easily bored as I am.

[In an intervening two paragraphs Pound implies that he has been attacked for not showing in this series enough respect for French artists. Pound defends himself by affirming that 'intelligent respect' based on sound artistic standards does not require an attitude of constraint. He continues:]

My contention was that Paris is rather better off for poets than London is, or if you like, "that Paris is twenty, at least twenty, years ahead of the other worlds of letters.". . .

Dante defined poetry as a composition of words set to music. . . The art of music which still remains to the poet is that of rhythm, and of a sort of melody dependent on the order and arrangement of varied vowel and consonantal sounds. The rhythm is a matter of duration of individual sounds and of stress, and the matter of the "word melody" depends largely on the fitness of this duration and stress to the sounds wherewith it is connected.

In determining the relative state of art in Paris and in London, one would consider rhythm, word melody, and the composition of words, of words that is, considered as language not as sound.

As to rhythm, I doubt if there is in England at the time of this writing, anyone whose rhythm and word melody are comparable to those of Remy de Gourmont or of Paul Fort, or of De Régnier in the "Odelettes." I think there is no one who writes English as well as De Régnier writes French, or whose work has the quality of seeming so *modo pumice expolitum.* Neither have we a satirist comparable to Laurent Tailharde [*sic*], nor yet a poet who delineates his time as clearly as does Francis Jammes.

Nor, for that matter, can I see about me any young man whose work is as refreshing as Romains'. It is true that there are a few writers who are attempting a simplification of structure, somewhat like that attempted by the crowd gathered about "L'Effort Libre"; but for the most part both writers and critics in England are so ignorant that if a man attempt these finer accords and simplicities there is hardly anyone who can tell what he is up to. Neither do I believe that the excellences referred to will appear in English writing until at least twenty years after their respective appearances in France. And with that I rest my case.

A QUARTERLY REPORT ON FRENCH POETRY:
1913–14

F. S. Flint's 'French Chronicle' was distinguished by the systematic nature of his report on genuinely current French work and by his extended attention to the debate on classicism, the *unanimiste* coterie, futurism, and the *fantaisistes*. In addition, Flint accorded early appreciation to contemporary poets like Claudel, Apollinaire, and Péguy. The importance of a quarterly account as systematic and extensive as this one, replete with bibliographies and undistorted by any deliberate intent to propagandize for a particular poetic ideology, is not to be underestimated. Part of its impact lay in the column's availability, for it appeared in *Poetry and Drama*, which in 1913 was London's most widely read little magazine (a position it shared with *The Egoist* in the following year). Harold Monro edited *Poetry and Drama* in conjunction with his operation of the Poetry Bookshop, an institution which served as a London meeting room for lectures and poetry readings and which was one of the reliable places to obtain recent *avant garde* work. Consequently, information which appeared in Flint's column was assured of reaching most of the steadily growing number of British literary figures who tried to keep up with current events in the Parisian poetic world. In the last half of the second decade several currents of French and British poetry appear to show parallel development from similar roots, rather than horizontal borrowing. The 'French Chronicle' in 1913 and 1914 is the most extensive periodical source of the French background which is part of the foundation of the poetry of both countries in those years.

A case in point is the decisive influence of Rimbaud in both England and France during and after the war. The publication of Paterne Berrichon's *Jean-Arthur Rimbaud, le Poète* and the *Oeuvres de Arthur Rimbaud*, edited by Berrichon with a famous preface by Paul Claudel (both in 1912), caused an upsurge of attention to Rimbaud in France. Apollinaire, particularly, was drawn to his work, and he helped to build Rimbaud's high reputation among the dada poets at the end of the war.[1] Flint drew attention to the rising interest in Rimbaud at length in the 'French Chronicle' for June 1913, and he referred to both of the Berrichon volumes.[2] Flint emphasized Rimbaud's role as poet-seer (the role which Edith Sitwell was to stress) and he gave a more sympathetic and probably more accurate estimation of his influence on contemporary poets than did Pound. (It may be significant that Pound's slightly condescending observation that Rimbaud should not be overlooked came only about two months after Flint's discussion in the June 'French Chronicle'.)

In his comments on the romanticism–classicism controversy (March 1913), Flint carefully reflected the range of meanings French critics had given to the word. In France, *classicism*, for some, meant political and ethical attitudes which were closely connected to a reverence for tradition and a belief that limit, restraint, and closely controlled form are needed to enable men – and poetry – to reach the highest possible standard. This was the view of the *Action française* – Maurras, Lasserre, Clouard, *et al.* – and it was reflected in T. E. Hulme's assertion: 'Man is an extraordinarily fixed and

---

[1] Kenneth Cornell, *The Post-Symbolist Period, op. cit.*, notes that Rimbaud received one of the highest ratings in a poll on the literary merit of poets of interest in *Littérature* in December 1920.

[2] Coincidentally, Edith Sitwell quoted extensively from Berrichon's Rimbaud biography in preparing her essay for the introduction to Helen Rootham's translations of *Les Illuminations*, and she noted in her autobiography, *Taken Care Of* (London and New York, 1965), p. 32, that she felt her childhood resembled that of Rimbaud.

limited animal whose nature is absolutely constant. It is only by tradition and organisation that anything decent can be got out of him...The classical poet never forgets this finiteness, this limit of man.'[1] But there was also a more general French use of the term which helps to explain the sense in which H.D. and Richard Aldington, and imagism itself, belonged to a classical movement in English verse, beyond the obvious fact that the poets of the group rendered Greek and Latin verse into English. For P.-J. Jouve, Flint pointed out, the word *classicism* meant economy, naked expression, and the absence of artifice and rhetoric – precisely the qualities espoused by imagism. For Henri Ghéon, Flint said, the word meant 'perfect equilibrium' in the work of art. Thus English poets could find in France as much support or inspiration for their divergent uses of the term classicism as they did for their interest in the concept.

Flint's treatment of the *unanimiste* coterie, like his handling of classicism, emphasized achievements close to the interests of imagism as a sustained movement. Consistently (as in the essay for June 1913), Flint called attention to the qualities of diction in *unanimiste* poetry rather than to the thematic concerns with essential structures of reality that Pound discovered there.[2] Following a perceptive evaluation of the achievements of Jules Romains, Flint quoted one of his poems and praised: 'No rhetoric, no eloquence; a style stripped of everything that is merely verbal, a simplicity of diction that is itself an appeal.' He discovered another of the qualities of imagism, its objectivity, in the work of P.-J. Jouve. Of Jouve's *Présences* Flint interpreted: 'Finally, you will be able to project your own life by means of the images of all that is around you; that is, you eliminate yourself, and leave these *presences* to bear witness to you.' Flint returned to a discussion of the poets associated with Romains and *unanimisme* in the essays for December 1913, and September and December 1914.

Despite the fact that Flint's own tastes in poetic form never led him to abandon conventional syntax, his comments on Marinetti and H.-M. Barzun in the *Poetry and Drama* special issue on futurism (September 1913) suggested the possibility of a poetry that is structurally abstract and divorced from normal representation. He expressed reservations about Marinetti, but he asked: 'what is the use...of logical syntax in poetry? Why should we have so absolute a respect for the integrity of words?' And he went on to discuss Barzun's 'simultaneous dramatic poem' and to quote his belief that 'the lineal, monodic, consecutive poetry of the past is doomed'. Thus Flint once again called the attention of London poets to possibilities for innovation that lay beyond his own interests and range as a poet.

The techniques of some of the *fantaisiste* poets, whom Flint treated in two installments in March and June 1914, lay closer to his own interests and those of some other imagists.[3] In his first essay on the subject, Flint awkwardly linked Paul Fort to the *fantaisiste* movement, suggested Walter de la Mare for an English parallel, and corrected his earlier omission in 'Contemporary French Poetry' of comments on the work of André Salmon. Then in the second essay of the two he provided extended quotation from poetry by Francis Carco, Tristan Derème, and others associated with the 'fantastic' (and ironic) tone and imagery. Flint himself had a more sober and less detached approach. The *fantaisiste* poets he quoted so copiously, however, added their own imitation of Laforgue to the interest in that poet which was developing in the second decade in London. Once again, the thorough presentation of the current scene

---

[1] T. E. Hulme, 'Romanticism and Classicism', *Speculations: T. E. Hulme, op. cit.*, pp. 116, 120.

[2] See 'Modern French Poetry: Pound's First Important View', pages 172–4. Pound also alluded to the 'purging of the idiom' achieved by Romains and his associates, although he gave new ideas about form greater attention.

[3] For correlations between the work of some *fantaisiste* poets and early imagist verse, see 'A French Account of the French Contemporaries', pages 150–1, 157–9.

in Paris served indirectly to increase British acquaintance with the nineteenth-century figures who were to appear so large in the poetry of the years beyond the war. One did not need to go to Paris to absorb French interest in the image, in 'classical' attitudes, in non-syntactical form, and in the ironies of Laforgue and the visions of Arthur Rimbaud.

FRENCH CHRONICLE I–VIII

F. S. FLINT

I. MARCH 1913

It would prevent misunderstanding, I think, if I began this French chronicle with a definition. In the *Irish Review* of October last, a certain Mr. Bodkin quarrelled with me for calling the article published in the *Poetry Review* of last August "Contemporary French Poetry", for, he said, "the really great poets of the age, such men as Paul Fort, René Ghil, A. Ferdinand Hérold, Gérard d'Houville, Francis Jammes, Camille Mauclair, Stuart Merrill and Henry Spiess are for the most part unmentioned" in my pages; all these writers are "contemporary in any possible significance that may be given to the word"; and the only explanation of my studied omissions must be that I consider them already out of date. Wonderful! And Hérold, Mauclair, Merrill, Spiess and Gérard d'Houville (who is not a man, but Mme Henri de Régnier) are great poets! We should be chary of the word *great*. Victor Hugo was great and...*bête comme l'Himalaya*. A man may be a good poet, an exquisite poet, even, and you will do him a disservice by calling him great. Let us keep the word for the poet whose work adds a new and important province to literature. Then from the mess of names above, only those of Paul Fort and Francis Jammes will emerge. But it is not Mr. Bodkin's uncertainty as a critic that is my concern at the moment. A poet, I submit, is a contemporary of the generation in which he fought his youthful battle, of the generation in which he formed part of the literary *movement*. Having won consideration and reached the apex of his achievement, the *classical* period of his art, he no longer moves forward, but turns on himself, producing mature, perhaps perfect work, but work which still reflects the aesthetic of the period when he flung himself with ardour into the literary combat. Such men are Vielé-Griffin, Verhaeren, Paul Fort, Francis Jammes.

It was "the contemporary movement in French Poetry" that formed the subject of M. Charles Vildrac's third lecture on Modern French Poetry at the Grafton Galleries in November last. The first two lectures were devoted to "Paul Verlaine, his character and influence," and "Art and Academic Art in the work of modern writers – Moréas, Verhaeren, Régnier, Maeterlinck, Jammes, Paul Fort." N. Vildrac said the right thing about each of these poets, and his remarks were illuminated by the very wonderful reading of M. Jacques Copeau, one of whose missions in life is to read poetry to people who will listen. But in the third lecture, M. Vildrac could only find, as representing the "contemporary movement," MM. André Spire, P.-J. Jouve, Luc Durtain, and Henri Herz [*sic*] (whom he mentioned in passing) and Duhamel, Romains, Arcos, and Chennevière, the author of a dramatic poem, *Le Printemps*. At the end of this lecture M. Vildrac fled from the room, and M. Copeau read half a dozen poems from the lecturer's *Livre d'Amour*, the book that brought him fame. Now, I have a great admiration for the strength, virility, and intellectuality of the group of poets whose names are Duhamel, Romains, Arcos, Vildrac, and Chennevière; they are as powerful a group as any in France to-day; but I think that M. Vildrac was not acting fairly and impartially in allowing an English audience to believe that these poets alone made the "Contemporary Movement in French Poetry." His answer, I know, will be: But they alone at least have brought new elements into French poetry; and this may be true; yet there are other good poets: and we should have been told of them.

Those who wish for information about the literary movement in France to-day should get M. Emile Henriot's book, *A quoi rêvent les jeunes gens* (enquête sur la jeunnesse littéraire), (H. & E. Champion, no price). Therein may be found a fairly accurate estimate, in the words of the men concerned, of what is going on, and an indication of its direction.

From M. Henriot's inquiry, one word seems to stand out more than any other, the word *classicism*. Every group uses the word. Even M. P.-J. Jouve, replying as a *unanimiste* (he is not one, by the way), means *classicism* when he speaks of their "need for economy" which "impels them to seek for the most naked expression, that which is most devoid of artifice and rhetoric, that which is most exactly *glued* (Flaubert's word) on the the initial *entrevision* of the mind."[1] But, as M. Henri Ghéon points out in his book, *Nos Directions*, there are two utterly opposed solutions of the problem of classicism. There is that which consists in setting up as an example to be followed an acknowledged classical period – in France, the seventeenth century – and which finds favour in those writers who look for inspiration to the ideals of the now defunct *Ecole Romane*, founded by Jean Moréas with Charles Maurras,

---

[1] Flint here gives a paraphrased translation of the response of P.-J. Jouve to the question 'Existe-t-il, à votre sens, une "jeune école littéraire"?' from Emile Henriot, *A Quoi rêvent les jeunes gens* (Paris, 1913), p. 41. Kenneth Cornell, in *The Post-Symbolist Period, op. cit.*, p. 126, has pointed out that material in this book first appeared serially in *Le Temps* between 23 April and 4 June 1912. The date is important, for Pound, H.D. and Aldington were in Paris in late April and early May 1912, and were carrying on the early discussions which led to imagism. The language with which Jouve describes his drive for economy in poetic diction is strikingly like that used to describe the goals of imagism.

Raymond de la Tailhède, Maurice du Plessys, and Ernest Raynaud. Their journals are *la Revue Critique des idées et des livres, l'Action française* and *les Guêpes*. Their sponsors in this *enquête* are MM. Eugène Marsun [*sic*], Henri Clouard, and Jean-Marc Bernard. They all owe a great deal of their driving force to M. Charles Maurras, the wonderful limpidity of whose style is in itself an argument in their favour. But there is another classicism, defined by M. Ghéon as "that perfect equilibrium which is the end of an art and its supreme victory," – and "what was once classical cannot become so again". I find in the answer of M. Jacques Copeau some admirable words on this subject. "For my part," he says, "I am very pleased that the aspirations of the day are connected with that fine word 'classicism' – provided that you do not make of it merely a literary label, but that it designates an attitude of the will, a quality of the mind; provided that nothing human, nothing living is excluded from it, nor that notion of research and invention, in default of which culture is sterile; if in short, to be classical is to bring a sentiment to its fulfilled expression, to the supreme point of its perfection, of its style, from whatever depth it may come, from whatever obscurity it may emerge, from whatever region of being, however unfrequented, it may be born."[1] It will be part of my task, no doubt, as the year goes on, to say more about French classical tendencies; but if I were asked now where their finest expression was to be found, I think I should answer, In *La Nouvelle Revue Française*, of which M. Copeau is the director;...any corrective needed may be found in *La Revue Critique des Idées et des Livres*.

I have four books that are classical in M. Ghéon's sense; they represent the perfect equilibrium of the art of their respective authors: Francis Vielé-Griffin and *La Lumière de Grèce*, Emile Verhaeren and *Hélène de Sparte (Nouv. Rev. Franç.*, 3.50 both), Paul Fort and *Vivre en Dieu (Figuière*, 3.50), Francis Jammes and *Les Géorgiques Chrétiennes (Mercure de France*, 3.50).

La Lumière de Grèce is in three parts, *Pindare, Sapho*, and *La Legènde ailée de Bellérophon Hippalide*. Like all the rest of M. Vielé-Griffin's work, these poems are written in free rhythms – free, that is, from regard for a conventional form, but absolutely in servitude to the poet's sense of movement; and the rhythm, or, in its stead, the assonance, is used to mark the rhythm. The dialogues in which Pindar and Sappho are made to speak their hearts and the legend of Bellerophon are full of passages of a very rare beauty. M. Vielé-Griffin is what the French call a *métèque*, i.e. a foreigner turned Frenchman, in this case an American; and it is a pleasant speculation that the creator of Yeldis owes his

[1] Flint translates several sentences of the answer of Jacques Copeau in Henriot, *op. cit.*, p. 46.

exquisite lyrical gift to an ultimate English extraction. M. Vielé-Griffin takes three characteristic moments in Sappho's life: in the first, Mnécédicé asks Sappho why she does not take a husband:

> L'amour est désir, Mnécédicé,
> grain semé, fleur d'avril;
> si l'amour possédait, Mnécédicé,
> que désirerait-il?
> Il désire et n'a pas, Mnécédicé ma prude,
> l'amour espère et craint:
> il est incertitude;
> il doit craindre de perdre
> ce qu'il croit posséder une heure,
> sinon il n'est plus le désir,
> Mnécédicé, ma fleur.[1]

In the second, Sappho repulses the love of Alcaeus, in whom she admires the hero and not the man. The third episode is Sappho's death. The winged Legend of Bellerophon is as admirable a story as it is possible to conceive in verse.

It is disconcerting that, after having celebrated the Tentacular Towns, the Tumultuous Forces, and the Multiple Splendour of the modern world, after having sung the Whole of Flanders, M. Emile Verhaeren should turn to Greece for a subject, the homecoming of Helen to Sparta, where she finds, not the peace of the rest she had expected in the arms of Menelaus, but the tormented desire of her half-brother, Castor, and the illicit love of her niece, Electra, turning her haven into a place of disquietude and anguish. Castor kills Menelaus and is in turn slain by Electra, as he stoops to quench his thirst after the deed; and Pollux, who had stewarded for Menelaus while that king was besieging Troy, remembers the words of his father Zeus:

> Tu seras maître
> Et règneras dûment sur les peuples domptés.[2]

But Helen refuses to share the kingdom offered to him by the popular voice; she is tired, and beaten by the desire she feels around her; and, in the last scene, amid the rut of nature, satyrs, naiades, baccantes proclaiming their dementia towards her, she implores Zeus to annihilate her, for even the earth would burn her dead flesh. Zeus answers:

> Il te fallait saisir l'adversité rebelle
> Pour en tordre la force et la suprême ardeur:
> Mais tu n'étais que femme et si ta chair fut belle
> Ton front n'imposa point l'orgueil de sa splendeur;[3]

[1] Francis Vielé-Griffin, 'Sapho', La Lumière de Grèce (Paris, 1912), p. 66.
[2] Emile Verhaeren, Hélène de Sparte (Paris, 1912), p. 103.   [3] Ibid., p. 130.

and, with a clap of thunder, he takes her up to heaven. I do not know how this play was received at the Châtelet. It is hardly a good play, since it turns on an anticlimax, the homecoming of Helen, with a weak central figure, a weatherwise and weary Helen; and, although the passage from *Les Villes Tentaculaires* by way of *La Multiple Splendeur* and *Les Rhythmes* [*sic*] *Souverains* to *Hélène de Sparte* is easy to follow, I am not sure that, in the end, either the glory of Helen or that of a great poet has been well served.

"Vivre en Dieu" is to be a poet (*Entendez-moi bien: dieu? je veux dire un tel homme qu'il peut rêver sa vie d'un bout a l'autre bout*), and in the case of Paul Fort, a Prince of Poets. Every book that he publishes seals the appropriateness of that choice by the French poets. Mallarmé was a wise and lofty prince; and his disciples received the law from him in his quietude and seclusion. Verlaine was unwise, and, in his life, ignoble: his disciples followed him from café to café; his law was the caprice of the moment and the absinthe: *tout est bel et bon qui est bel et bon, d'où qu'il vienne et par quelque procédé qu'il soit obtenu*; but at the back of that caprice was a vivid appreciation of good poetry. Léon Dierx, third in the dynasty of princes, was a noble figure-head, who had but few dealings with the poets, his subjects. But Paul Fort is with them, of them, and for them, their friend, comrade and defender. Here is a passage characteristic of the man. Returning from Ferté-Milon, where he had been to watch the Birth of Spring, he reflects on the worthlessness of friendship:

Et gardons-la, cette fierté, gardons-la bien. Repoussons l'amitié, ce fantôme aux cent mains. J'ai dit, je fais deux pas et rencontre, ô douceur! content de me revoir, un cher poète en pleurs.

Je le console un brin – de toute ma tendresse. "Dis-moi ta peine." On va, bras dessus, bras dessous. "Hier elle est partie, je n'ai plus de maîtresse. Qu'avez-vous vu là-bas?" "Je n'ai rien vu du tout."

"Vous savez que sur vous, Spiess fait des conférences." "Où donc?" "Fribourg, Genève"..."Eh mais, vive la France!" "Je ne sais qui doit en faire aux Etudiants. Amusant ce voyage? Vous avez l'air content."

"Oui, là! je suis content. C'est même ridicule...Viens, nous la chercherons ta Laurette adorée! Figure-toi, mon cher, j'étais désespéré." "Pourquoi?" "Rien. J'avais pris un mal de crépuscule."[1]

Alone in a railway carriage with the recollections of a holiday and the melancholy of a return, he gives way to despondency; but the chance encounter of a friend, and hey! all is gone. He is like a sensitive mercurial thermometer with a recording attachment; he registers every change of

[1] Paul Fort, 'Le Regret', *Naissance du Printemps a la Ferté-Milon*, in *Ballades françaises*, *XIVe série: Vivre en Dieu* (Paris, 1912), pp. 115–16.

temperature...of temperament; in doing so, he makes poetry of all the incidents of his life. They go through his brain, and come out clothed in raiment of fantasy, of delicious humour and gaiety, or of tragedy. He is full of laughter; but it is that fine laughter which is not far from tears. In the poem called "Vivre en Dieu" he is grave and brave before the problem of life.

After "Vivre en Dieu" and the series of poems entitled *La Naissance du Printemps à la Ferté-Milon,* in this volume, Paul Fort publishes the third chapter of his poetical autobiography, *L'Aventure Eternelle* (the first chapter appeared in *L'Aventure Eternelle* and the second in *Monthéry-la-Bataille*). I wish to quote one passage from this third chapter:

> Ce que je dois à Moréas ne peut-être dit en paroles. J'avais une âme obscure et lasse. Quasiment il en fit la folle
> Fée des feux libres dans l'éther. "Aérez, aérez les mots! Qu'ils soient de ces flammes légères dansant plus haut que les flambeaux."
> Ce que j'appris de Moréas fut mon secret. Non pas pour lui, puisque vivant – mon maître! hélas! il savait tout comme aujourd'hui.[1]

"Aérez les mots!" Paul Fort's case is one of those wherein the influence of Moréas has not been pernicious – the influence of a stylist on an original poet. Each succeeding book that Paul Fort now publishes shows a growing clarity of style, or, to use his own – Moréas's – words, his poems are more and more *ces flammes légères dansant plus haut que les flambeaux.*

What are we to say of *Les Géorgiques Chrétiennes*? M. Francis Jammes is a fervent Roman Catholic. "At the threshold of this work," he says in a prefatory note, "I confirm that I am a Roman Catholic humbly submissive to all the decisions of my Pope, H. H. Pius X, who speaks in the name of the True God..." He lives a pastoral life at Orthez in the Basses-Pyrénées. His poetry hitherto has been cherished for three things: its simplicity, its sincerity, and its spontaneity, and for the scents of field and wood that seemed to emanate from his verses. And these verses were not made with a mechanical beat; they were at times deliciously awkward; they stammered: they did not always rhyme; the final syllable would evoke a trembling echo, an assonance, and that was all; sometimes, however, they were as melancholy and as sustained as the long sigh of the wind in an aspen-tree. But now:

> Maintenant il me faut du calme pour écrire[,]
> Car ma barbe blanchit autour de mon sourire.
>
> J'entreprends dans mon âge mur ce grand labeur.
> Il est le fruit que donne au bel Eté la fleur.[2]

[1] Paul Fort, 'La Aventure éternelle, Livre III', in *Ballades françaises, XIVe série: op. cit.,* p. 134.
[2] Francis Jammes, 'Chant I', *Les Géorgiques Chrétiennes* (Paris, 1914; 1st pub. 1912), p. 30.

And this "great labour" is the writing of the Christian Georgics, in seven books, composed of couplets like the two quoted, each making a complete statement, ending in a full stop – a form so restricted that its only use would seem to be for the rhyming of maxims and epigrams; but M. Jammes, in his ripe age and his conviction of grace, has deliberately chosen it as a vehicle for the conveyance of his most earnest beliefs and his message, raising a mountain in the path of his genius, to make his work more worthy. *Les Géorgiques Chrétiennes* are a monument to his faith.

Needless to say, however, *Les Géorgiques Chrétiennes* are not georgics; they are not a treatise on husbandry; they might have been called eclogues, but there would have been no challenge in that word. The seven books describe the life and labours of a simple, pious peasant folk, that exists perhaps only in the imagination of the poet. Passages of the flattest prose – breathing-spaces, no doubt – alternate with passages of real beauty; and it is as a whole that the book will finally be judged.

Two of the greatest influences in France, at the present time, are Francis Jammes and Paul Claudel, both Catholics. In *A quoi rêvent les jeunes gens*, their names are invoked eleven and twelve times respectively. Their most fervent admirers, no doubt, are on *l'aile gauche de l'armée littéraire contemporaine*, as M. J.-M. Bernard puts it in *La Revue Critique* of January 10. He himself is on *l'aile droite* – generalissimi, Maurice Barrès (seventeen times) and Charles Maurras (fourteen times). But M. Claudel is also much in favour with *l'aile droite*; you will find his praise by that wing both in the book cited and in the same number of the same review, and also in M. Bernard's Anthology, *Pages politiques des poètes français*. In truth, M. Paul Claudel, as a great poet, whose humanity is all-embracing, appeals to all the literary sects, except that to which M. Maurice Boissard of the *Mercure de France* belongs; and what is that? To some, M. Claudel has restored the sense of veneration; to others, he is a great lyric poet, whose seduction it is impossible to avoid; others he has taught how to think usefully and nobly, how to tear themselves from the consideration of their easy pleasures and ephemeral pains; to others, he is the most considerable dramatic poet of the time.

I have of the works of Claudel these volumes: *Théâtre* (première *série*), vol. I, *Tête d'Or*, first and second versions, vol. II, *La Ville*, first and second versions, vol. III, *La Jeune Fille Violaine* and *l'Echange*, vol. IV, *Le Repos du septième Jour*, *L'Agamemnon d'Eschyle* and *Vers d'Exil*, and three philosophical essays under the title *Art Poétique* – all these five volumes are published by the *Mercure de France* (3.50). I have also *l'Otage*, drame, and *l'Annonce faite à Marie*, mystère en quatre actes et un prologue – these two published by *la Nouvelle Revue Française* (3.50). But there are other works which I have not seen yet: *Cette Heure qui est entre le Printemps et l'Eté,* cantate à trois voix (*N.R.F.,* 10 fr.), *Connaissance de l'Est,* prose pieces (*M. de F.,* 3.50); and *Partage de Midi,* drame, *Cinq grandes odes suivies d'un processional pour saluer le siècle nouveau,* and *Hymnes.* These latter are out of print or have not yet appeared in book form. In his essay on Paul Claudel (*M. de F.,* December 16, 1912, January 1, 1913), M. Georges Duhamel, poet and critic of poetry for the *Mercure de France,* one of the most intelligent of the younger French writers, and one whose judgments are always interesting – we can ask no more of a judgment – M. Georges Duhamel says that Claudel's works should be read in this order: *Connaissance de l'Est, l'Otage, l'Echange, l'Annonce faite à Marie*; then, by comparing the latter with *la Jeune fille Violaine,* which is a kind of first version, you will be prepared to compare, each with the other, the two versions of *Tête d'Or* and *La Ville.* The *Odes, Hymnes, Partage de Midi, Repos du septième Jour* and other works may next be read; but, finally, *Art Poétique,* which is an introduction to M. Claudel's whole work, but that kind of introduction which must be read last of all.

Although the bulk of M. Claudel's work is dramatic in form, none of his dramas had been produced before the end of 1912, when M. Lugné-Poé played *l'Annonce faite à Marie* at the Théâtre de l'Oeuvre. It was, I have been told by a friend who was present, a revelation...

[Flint goes on to quote at some length from two contemporary reviews of *L'Annonce faite à Marie.*]

For Claudel, *I am, I breathe, I make a verse* are identities; into the mouth of Coeuvre (*La Ville*) in whom may be divined more than one trait that belongs to Claudel himself, are put these words:

O mon fils! lorsque j'étais un poète entre les hommes,
J'inventais [*sic*] ce vers qui n'avait ni rime ni mètre,
Et je le définissais dans le secret de mon coeur cette fonction double et réciproque
Par laquelle l'homme absorbe la vie, et restitue[,] dans l'acte suprême de l'expiration,
Une parole intelligible.[1]

And this cadenced speech, this *parole intelligible,* pours forth with the changing speeds of dramatic necessity, of which its beat has the strength; it is easy to see therefore why Claudel's lyricism broke the bondage of the alexandrine. It is moreover a lyricism that amplifies speech by the constant creation of new metaphors, new images – this, indeed, being the sign-manual of all great poetry.

The conflicts in Claudel's plays have no fixed relationships to any determinate time and place; they may be said to have the dimensions of

[1] Paul Claudel, *La Ville, seconde version, Oeuvres complètes,* VII (Paris, 1954), p. 228.

an absolute. It is true that the time and place of *l'Echange* would appear to be the America of to-day; that *l'Annonce faite à Marie* takes place in a "Moyen-âge de convention," and *l'Otage* is apparently an historical drama of the French Revolution. But the characters in these plays emerge from the time and space allotted to them and become universal, the mouthpieces of the great sentiments and the great passions that have agitated humanity for all time. And this is even more so in the other dramas. Who could assign a time and place to *Tête d'Or*, or to *La Ville*, or to *Le Repos de septième Jour*? The characters, too, are creations worthy, I think, to be mentioned with Shakespeare's finest: Simon Agnel, Coeuvre, Besme, Avare, Louis Laine, Thomas Pollock, Georges de Coûfontaine, Toussaint Turelure, Anne Vercors, Jacques Hury; and the women: the princess in *Tête d'Or*, Lala, Marthe, Lechy Elbernon, Violaine, Mara, Sygne de Coûfontaine: they are distinct; they remain in one's memory. And this characterisation is intensified rather than weakened by the lyricism with which Claudel invests each personage – a lyricism that is often the speech of their creator himself.

I wish to close these notes on Claudel by quoting from a noble passage of M. Duhamel's essay:

"The God of Claudel! I discern him in all these dramas, as we find the same supernatural figure of Christ in all the pictures of Rembrandt. The images that Claudel offers us of the divine person proceed, all of them, from the same absolute model; but in the latter he has an angry bearing, while in Claudel he is mansuetude and sovereign compassion.

"I must confess to a secret and fervent delight in this God of *l'Otage*, for this God, of whom Badilon, "le gros homme chargé de matière et de péchés," is the humble and imperious advocate:

O mon enfant, quoi de plus faible et de plus désarmé
Que Dieu[,] quand Il ne peut rien sans nous? – *L'Otage*, p. 122.
Dieu n'est pas au-dessus de nous, mais au-dessous.
Et ce n'est pas selon votre force que je vous tente, mais selon votre faiblesse. –
    L'Otage, p. 136.

"Who would refuse his admiration for such a conception of God? Who can disregard the sublime moral value of such a faith?...How I admire this human God who *is* according to the measure of men's honouring of him, who needs, in order to be great, the greatness and the generosity of men!"[1]

These notes are inadequate, I know; but a work of art comes to us first as *sensation*; *appreciation* follows after; and the greater the artist, the harder will it be to express our appreciation, since we must meditate at length on a new interpretation of life. M. Duhamel's essay is a very able and maturely considered exposition of Claudel's art and philosophy; and the reader will find in that essay what I have been unable to give

[1] Flint here translates two pages from Georges Duhamel, *Paul Claudel* (Paris, 1913), pp. 44–5.

him here. But he must first of all read Claudel's own works. (*Note*: M. Duhamel's essay has just been published as a book by the M. de F., 2.50.)

The fourth series of M. Remy de Gourmont's *Promenades Littéraires* (*Mercure*, 3.50) opens with 92 pages of his "Souvenirs du Symbolisme." Why were they not 346 pages, the whole book? However, here is what M. de Gourmont remembers of Stéphane Mallarmé, Paul Verlaine, Jean Moréas, Villiers de l'Isle Adam, the groups that formed round Anatole Baju, René Ghil and Gustave Kahn, and lastly a short history of *Le Mercure de France*. M. de Gourmont's criticism is one of the most satisfactory that I know; it always seems as though, once he has spoken, there is nothing more to be said. And this is true, because, from his point of view, he sees with absolute clearness and amazing penetration. To say anything fresh, you must change the point of view, and then you get a new truth, which does not necessarily displace the old. And this book is M. de Gourmont's journalism, made up of his articles contributed to *Le Temps* and elsewhere; yet what could be more satisfying than the following about Mallarmé? – "The obscurity of some of his verses was held up to him as a crime, no credit being given for all the limpid part of his work, and no attempt being made to grip the fact that, by the logic of his symbolist aesthetic itself, he had been led to reject all but the second term of the comparison. Classic poetry, so clear on that account, and so monotonous, expresses both. Victor Hugo and Flaubert united them in one complex metaphor. Mallarmé severed them once more, and only allowed the second image to be seen, that which served to throw light on and poetise the first."[1] And so on. It is these qualities of clarity of expression and perfect comprehension – the two paired are not so monotonous, I assure you – that make M. Gourmont's *Deux Livres des Masques* so valuable a document in any consideration of the symbolist art – and these souvenirs the indispensable appendix to the *Masques*. The other essays in the book bear witness to M. de Gourmont's wide and amazing culture. His wisdom is a thing to rejoice in.

[Flint notes that 'This chronicle has dealt exclusively with *les maîtres*; in my next I will return to *les jeunes*' and concludes with a list of new French books which he plans to discuss in later columns.]

II. JUNE 1913

Arthur Rimbaud was born in 1854; he began writing at the age of fifteen; he burned his manuscripts at the age of nineteen; he died at thirty-seven. Endowed with the faculties of a man of genius, this lad,

[1] Flint translates from Remy de Gourmont, 'Stéphane Mallarmé', *Promenades littéraires*, *IV* (Paris, 1912), pp. 6–7.

says M. Claudel, appeared in France, "comme Jeanne d'Arc," at a time of disaster and of material and moral dejection. His story is the strangest in literature. M. Paterne Berrichon's book, *Jean-Arthur Rimbaud, le Poète* (*Mercure de France*, 3.50), gives the outward course of that story, the biographical details, until Rimbaud's disappearance from the world of letters. He puts events into their right connection with documents, deals with the legend of illicit relationship with Verlaine, and supplies a textual commentary on Rimbaud's work. For all this, those who admire Rimbaud's work – all those who know it – must be grateful to M. Berrichon; in fact, his book is indispensable. But the real story of Rimbaud is not biographical at all; the events of his life are the outward manifestations of the inner conflict: the escapes from Charleville to Paris; the extenuating tramps between those two towns; the drunkenness, the responsibility for which M. Berrichon lays to the charge of Rimbaud's companions; the suffering in Paris; the relationship with Verlaine and its lamentable end, – these are just the noise which a caged spirit made against its incomprehensible bars. The true story of Rimbaud can only be told by men like Claudel. I think his Preface to the *Oeuvres de Arthur Rimbaud – vers et prose – revues sur les manuscrits originaux et les premières éditions, mises en ordre et annotées par Paterne Berrichon* (which the *Mercure de France* has published in a fine, well-printed volume at 7 fr.) brings out the real Rimbaud, the "mystique à l'état sauvage, une source perdue qui ressort d'un sol saturé," a seer an austere spirit. How the dust, the dirt – earthly, moral, human – the vermin vanish! And Rimbaud appears like an angel from a suit of rags, a terrible angel. On the death-bed in Marseilles, to which he had been brought from Africa with a leg to be amputated, he dreamed aloud. He had renounced literature at the age of nineteen to dream; perhaps he had renounced dreaming simply to live; he finishes his life in a dream. "He says now," relates his sister, "strange things, very softly, in a voice which would delight me, if it did not pierce my heart. What he says are dreams, yet it is not at all the same thing as when he had the fever. You would say, and I believe, that he did it purposely." Sometimes he asked his doctors whether they could not see the extraordinary things he himself perceived; and he described his impressions marvellously. But there was something in his case which they did not understand. There is something in his case which we shall never understand; we may grope and meditate. Happy if we are ever so fortunate as Sainte Chantal (quoted by M. Claudel): "At the dawn of day, God gave me to enjoy, almost imperceptibly, a little light in the highest, supreme point of my mind. All the rest of my soul and its faculties did not participate: but it only lasted about half an Ave Maria." In *L'Histoire d'une de ses folies*, Rimbaud says:

J'inventais la couleur des voyelles! – *A* noir, *E* blanc, *I* rouge, *O* bleu, *U* vert. – Je réglais la forme et le mouvement de chaque consonne, et, avec des rhythmes instinctifs, je me flattai d'inventer un verbe poétique accessible, un jour ou l'autre, à tous les sens. J'en réservai la traduction.

Ce fut d'abord une étude. J'écrivais des silences, des nuits, je notais l'inexprimable. Je fixais des vertiges. – *Une Saison en Enfer.*[1]

In the four years of his literary life he absorbed all the styles, and invented new; then his vision transcended language, and he wrote no more. But French poetry, from his advent onwards, radiates with his energy.

This edition of Rimbaud's works bears witness to the awakening in France of an interest in the printed book, as such. Good printing is in honour. The publications of Georges Crès, of the *Nouvelle Revue Française*, and this new series of the *Mercure de France*, in which has also appeared a volume of Verhaeren, are examples. The volume, *Oeuvres de Emile Verhaeren*, contains (for 7 fr.) the matter of two of the volumes of the ordinary edition: *Les Campagnes Hallucinées, Les Villes Tentacularies – Les Douze Mois, Les Visages de la Vie*. The greatest European poet of our time is Verhaeren. I have said it before, and each time I renew contact with his work I am forced to repeat it. He is not perfection – that is one of his merits; and it is affecting to picture him hovering over the poems in this volume correcting them – Jupiter correcting his lightning! But the old Verhaeren is still there, nevertheless – the hallucinated spectator of the desolation of the country-side and of the omni-absorbent towns; the tender-hearted poet of *Les Douze Mois*. Surely no more touching thing has been written about the poor than his poem for February, *Les Pauvres*, with the mournful beat of its first line –

> Il est ainsi de pauvres coeurs,

repeated in every stanza, the last word being changed; and with its protest, marked by the change of rhythm of the last stanza:

> Il est ainsi de pauvres gens,
> aux gestes las et indulgents
> sur qui s'acharne la misère
> au long des plaines de la terre.[2]

As one of his critics (whom I must not quote here too often, for fear of those who carp), M. Duhamel, says, Verhaeren was the first to see

---

[1] Arthur Rimbaud, *Une Saison en Enfer*, édition critique (Paris, 1941), p. 68.
[2] Emile Verhaeren, 'Les Pauvres', *Les Douze Mois* (1895), in *Oeuvres* (Paris, 1912), pp. 215–16.

things in a certain way; what is more important, to see certain things, and to express what he thus saw with exactly suitable words and rhythm; and Verhaeren was an initiator because he gave speech to a whole category of emotions which were never before so completely and so consciously experienced. What a sinister menace there is in these *Campagnes Hallucinées*, for instance! Never once does the poet allow the sunshine and the beauty of growing things to distract him from his contemplation of the cancerous evil which is eating into and poisoning the life of the country-side. It is a picture bitten into the copper with the most corrosive of acids; it is a picture of universal corrosion – of men and morals, of field and village. And the winds in Verhaeren's poems! You feel them searching into your bones; the grit of them is in your nostrils, between your teeth, and your skin is loathsome to the touch with it. Then there is the Verhaeren, contemplator of the town; …but a book must be written, one that will replace the dull book of M. Stefan Zweig.

The influence of these two poets, Verhaeren and Rimbaud, extends over many of the young French poets of the twentieth century, who, according to M. H.-M. Barzun (I noticed his *Hymne des Forces* last year), may be divided into two groups.

First, there are the *intuitives* – analysts, subjective, *lyrical* – whose aspiration it is to realise the poetical sum of the acutest sensations and the subtlest correspondences of the present. Principal among these are: Jules Romains, Charles Vildrac, Georges Duhamel, René Arcos, Théo Varlet, Paul Castiaux, Henri Herz [*sic*], Luc Durtain, and P.-J. Jouve. These poets are said to be continuing the *lyrical expression*, with its homocentric image and notation, of Rimbaud, Laforgue, Verlaine, and Mallarmé.

Next, there are the *visionaries* – synthetists, objective, *dramatic*; they are: Louis Mandin, Guillaume Apollinaire, Fernand Divoire, Jean de Bosschère, Georges Polti, Pierre Jaudon, Sébastien Voirol, R. Canudo, A.-R. Schneeberger, Claude-Amayrol-Grander, Tancrède de Visan, Alexandre Mercereau, and H.-M. Barzun. These poets are said to be following Paul Adam, Verhaeren, and Claudel in the creation of the *dramatic chant*, be rhythm, idea, and universalised conflicts.

I give M. Barzun's own words. He makes these distinctions in an article called *Du Symbole au Drame*, which appears in the second number of a review he has founded, *Poème et Drame* (*Figuière*, 6 vols. a year), for the defence of the second group and for the illustration of the ideas contained in his *Ere du Drame, essai de synthèse poétique moderne* (*Figuière*, 2.50). He also defines the "new beauty" as the beauty of crowds and of all the different forces of modern life.

M. H.-M. Barzun finds his athletes, pioneers, poet-pioneers of the "new beauty" in every country of the world: a German phalanx has proclaimed "la grande poésie mondiale"; ten Italian athletes have torn the great Roman nation from the frequentation of its tombs. In Spain, Russia, Austria, and Bohemia isolated voices call and answer one another; while in England an English "pléiade" has arisen – I do not know where.[1]

Still, as regards France, M. Barzun's division may, I think, be accepted as real. The definition of the aims of those on each side, like all definitions of that nature, is arbitrary. The poets of the first group, for instance, owe quite as much to Verhaeren, Paul Adam, and Claudel as do those in the second group. Yet not one of those who have been called *intuitive* would wish to see himself ranged with those termed *visionaries* (Orphic dramatists, according to Guillaume Apollinaire); and vice versa, I dare say. There is evidence even of a great deal of bad feeling between *intuitive* and *visionary* (the words are not mine, I repeat): two camps, in fact, and open warfare. Meanwhile, works will be produced; and it is by works, not faith, that a poet will live.

[Flint goes on to discuss in some detail books by two minor 'visionary' poets: Alexandre Mercereau's *Paroles devant la vie* and Louis Mandin's *Ariel esclave*.]

Verhaeren stands at the fountain-head of what may be called the *social* poetry of to-day – Futurism, M. Barzun's Dramatism, Whitmanism, and Unanimism. But Unanimism owes its value purely to the personality of its creator, M. Jules Romains. Without that personality Unanimism, as a creed, would not move us one whit; it is the subtlety of M. Romain's notations of the actions and interactions on himself of the group-forces that are the gods of Unanimism that calls for our admiration. M. Romains is one of the most powerful and original of the younger French writers: twelve volumes, none of them negligible, since 1904, poems, novels, a play in verse, and two prose books are there to vouch for his calling; and in them may be traced the gradual unfolding of a writer who bids fair to become a master. In verse, *La Vie Unanime*, rough-hewn and strong, violently new in feeling, *Le Premier Livre de Prières*, M. Romains's private meditations before the different groups, *Un Être en Marche*, a long study in complex emotions; and, in prose, *Le Bourg Régénéré* a tale of "la vie unanime," doctrinal and yet full of interesting notations, *Mort de Quelqu'un*, a study, in the form of a novel, of the social effect of the death of an obscure man – lead up to, but do not allow us to anticipate, the odes of *Odes et Prières* (just published,

[1] For the amusement of the inside circle, Flint here alludes elliptically to the formation of imagism.

Mercure de France, 3.50) and the novel, *Les Copains* (*Figuière*, 3.50). It is as though M. Romains, having climbed the steep, rugged, often obscure mountain-paths of his consciousness, had emerged into the loneliness, the clear air, and the simplicity of the summit; had been overwhelmed by the melancholy of his loneliness; and then, remembering men in the towns below, he had laughed. The Odes owe nothing to the *Unanime*, except their distance from it. But perhaps my image has led me too far. Still, there is an open-hearted laughter in *Les Copains*. Every one who is not afraid of life and words should read this book. M. Romains has amused himself in writing it, and has poked a little fun at himself and at one or two of his contemporaries; it is a farce – but a joyous farce – with an undercurrent of unanimism, unnoticeable to those who are ignorant of the previous books. You will like the book for its humour, its style, its humanity, its story, and its fresh imagery. M. Romains has an inimitable way of describing ordinary situations so that the sensations seem entirely new: they are indeed new; he recreates them. See, for instance, his description in this book of cycling, alone and in company, or of the journey of the old man to Paris in *Mort de Quelqu'un*. As for the Odes, M. Romains seems to have been driven to meditate in solitude. They are the most intimate of his poems. All the minute psychological analysis of *Un Être en Marche* tells you little of its author; you are aware of a powerful directive intelligence and a wonderfully receptive sensorial system – of the qualities and the powers of a poet; but the Odes come from the man himself. You share his heart and its sorrows, his mind and its preoccupations; the group only interrupts the meditation with its cry. No rhetoric, no eloquence; a style stripped of everything that is merely verbal, a simplicity of diction that is itself an appeal:

> Le Sable du chemin
> Luisait cruellement;
> Une chaleur amère
> Fourmillait par mes membres.
>
> Je faisais à quelqu'un
> Des réponses polies.
> Il y avait deux mois
> Qui je voulais mourir.
>
> L'espace de la terre
> Semblait se contracter;
> L'horizon montagneux
> Me serrait comme un casque.
>
> Il y avait deux mois
> Déjà que nuit et jour
> J'inventais des raisons
> Pour différer la mort.[1]

[1] Jules Romains, 'Ode V', 'Livre premier', *Odes et Prières* (Paris, 1923; 1st pub. 1913), pp. 23–4.

With these Odes are reprinted the Prières of *Le Premier Livre de Prières* and the fine "Ode à la Foule qui est ici." In this book, therefore, may be seen three stages of one thought.

M. P.-J. Jouve's book, *Présences* (Crès, 3.50), is the work of a poet closely akin in spirit to M. Romains, and the latter's influence upon him is visible; but he is too intelligent – too ferociously intelligent, as readers of *Les Bandeaux d'Or* will know – not to free himself eventually from that. Presences? If you are sitting in a room, quiet and alone, you suddenly become conscious of a mysterious correspondence between yourself and the objects surrounding you. You are alive in the midst of an entanglement of forces. You may cultivate this sense of your place in a changing scheme of things until not a moment of your day will pass, not a movement, wherever you may be, will be made without its corresponding evocation in your mind of the mute and yet powerful participators in your existence. Finally, you will be able to project your own life by means of the images of all that is around you; that is, you eliminate yourself, and leave these *presences* to bear witness to you. When you have gone so far, the poetry in which you have been rendering your sensations will be difficult to understand, and men will cry out on you. That is, I think, what has happened to M. P.-J. Jouve. He has been so intent on the mute companions of his existence that he has forgotten the critical spectator to whom every artist who wishes to be understood unconsciously refers. M. Jouve has been too original, too eager to give the "most naked expression" of an absolute impression; and he has not supplied the necessary links between the new and the old. You therefore feel, in reading his book, that you are in the presence of a poet who will satisfy you fully, and who yet never satisfies you, except with one or two poems, such as "Amour" and "Heures du Matin." But you are aware that in *Présences* is a whole mass of sensations, of keen observations, of emotions that have not had a fair chance in their passage through M. Jouve's selective intelligence and before his determination not to be led into imitation of what has been written in the past. Hence, as always when you attempt wholly to reject the stereotyped, leaving only the new, M. Jouve's hermeticism. But the "Hymne à un Enfant" and the series of poems called "Heures du Matin" already mentioned, have not this fault. The "Hymne" has other faults, but it is nevertheless a fine study of a child's psychological growth; and there are sun and air and movement in the "Heures du Matin." M. Jouve will not, however, go back to this manner. Rather should one expect and hope to see from him a fusion of the qualities of observation, "atmosphere," and clarity of these poems with the emotional and psychological qualities of "Amour" and "Retour"; in fact, these two poems do very nearly fulfil one's hope of him.

A Quarterly Report on French Poetry: 1913–14

[Flint next comments on Georges Duhamel's play *Dans l'ombre des statues*.]

You and I could make the discoveries of which M. Vildrac tells us in his *Découvertes* (*Nouv. Rev. Française*, 3.50), if we had the...heart to. All you need do is to go into the streets. You will meet children, and see what they see, feel what they feel. You will find men who are only too glad to be glad, only too happy to be good to one another. The world will seem to you an extraordinary complex of generosities. But, before you go into the street, it will be well to examine yourself to see whether you have within you what you are setting out to find. Otherwise, your search may be fruitless. You will, perhaps, evoke the hidden malice of men. But these discoveries come naturally to the author of the *Livre d'Amour*:

> Mais si l'on avait assez d'amour.[1]

One must have enough love.

M. Vildrac has transposed Wordsworth's "Reverie of Poor Susan," a poem made for him to translate, but made badly. Possibly, M. Vildrac would agree with Wordsworth that "all good poetry is the spontaneous overflow of powerful feelings," but he would not allow that natural goodness of heart and sympathy excuse bad workmanship. His "Pauvre Susanne" is better than Wordsworth's; M. Vildrac has made a poem out of Wordsworth's doggerel verses. It is too long to quote – unfortunately, because it contains a good lesson; but it begins like this:

> Il y a une grive au coin de la rue. Depuis trois années qu'elle est là, dans une cage, cette grive change au petit jour une chanson de prisonnier, une chanson pour elle toute seule.[2]
>> At the corner of Wood Street, when daylight appears,
>> Hangs a Thrush that sings loud; it has sung for three years.

No, no, no!

These short prose pieces (prose poems, but the phrase is somewhat discredited) may seem slight, but they bring you into contact with a personality whom you cannot help liking; a man is speaking to you without emphasis, soberly, but with little trills of emotion. I am sure that those who have read the *Livre d'Amour* with pleasure will find in *Découvertes* the qualities that pleased them in the former book.

There is the accent of a poet in M. Henri Herz's [*sic*] last book of poems, *Apartés* (*Phalange*, 2 fr.); but his voice is the voice of one who steps out of the drama and daily spectacle of life in order to deliver an

---

[1] Charles Vildrac, 'Paysage', *Livre d'amour* (Paris, 1959; 1st pub. 1910), p. 48.
[2] Charles Vildrac, 'La Pauvre Suzanne', *Découvertes* (Paris, 1913), p. 83. The prose poem is dedicated, significantly, to Roger Fry.

"aside," and you do not always follow him. A naive despair at the agony and death of each day; a still more naive astonishment that dawn should break once more; then despair again that the illusion of rebirth should be dispelled by contact with a topsy-turvy world, – these are attitudes. If it were not for his inability to accept men and manners as they now are, he might take his tongue out of cheek (it being there really to prevent its crying out too loudly some of M. Herz's more intimate secrets), and his ironical gibes at what should be our virtues would become songs of gladness. There is a singer in M. Herz; but a bitter singer, who hovers behind a kind of cosmic disquietude. His rhythms are very cunning and supple; they are not encased within any ready-made form. He has the gift of imagery; and he has learned from Laforgue the trick of sudden juxtaposition of the sublime with the commonplace, by which one is made to criticise the other...ironically. M. Herz's poetry is a criticism of life in both senses of the word – the principle of being and the interaction of beings. I place *Les Apartés* by the side of his *Mécréants* and his *Quelques Vers*, three volumes which have not yet wholly revealed a poet.

To be carried away at the age of twenty when all the world was looking towards him with confident expectancy of what his fine, ardent, generous mind would bring forth – and to be mourned thereafter by all the best spirits of his time, this has been the fate – unenviable, enviable – of Henri Franck, one of that phalanx of young Frenchmen whose wide culture seems to have acquired a more deeply human substance under the noble influence of Whitman. During the last two years of his life – years of sickness – he composed his poem, "La Danse devant l'Arche" (*Nouv. Rev. Français*, 3.50), breaking through, to do so, the habits of abstract thought which his philosophic training had imposed upon him. This poem is the poem of his youth and his enthusiasm, of his hope in life, and his friendship. There is no prescience of death in it, but an eager looking-forward into a wonderful future and a Biblical indignation at the abuses of the time. Henri Franck had an intellect in which were blended the best qualities of the French and Jewish mind, as they are to be found in André Gide and Spinoza. "Aimant tout, excellant en toutes choses," says Mme de Noailles in the Preface to this book; "Henri Frank manque ici-bas à toutes les nobles causes qui l'eussent sollicité, car ses aptitudes égalaient sa curiosité." In composing his poem, he found a sensibility which promised rich realisations. His prose (the articles printed at the end of this book) had already become the effective instrument of a penetrating intelligence.

M. Guy-Charles Cros must be happy in *Les Fêtes Quotidiennes*, his second book of poems, for in the chorus of voices which have welcomed it was that of M. Remy de Gourmont, and praise from M. Remy de Gourmont is worth having. He says: "Nothing but chance attracted me towards *Les Fêtes Quotidiennes* of Guy-Charles Cros – nothing, not even the name of his father (the friend of Verlaine, author of the famous *Hareng Saur* and inventor of the phonograph), and I may assure him that it is his poetry alone which has made upon me so profound an impression that I am as though tormented by it. I do not know whether it is admirable for all, but it is admirable for me, and that suffices me. This little volume has seemed to me for the last two days poetry itself. I revel in it; I see myself in it; I find myself in it; I have lived these emotions. It is a miracle, and it is the natural effect of an ingenuous sensibility. True poetry is known by this sign, that one believes that it has been written for you alone, that you are its hero, and I understand women who give way to it, and cry, 'But that is I!' That is the reward for having been sincere...You who do not know, let your initiation to poetry be through *Les Fêtes quotidiennes*" (*Vers et Prose*, tome xxx).[1] I add nothing to that, except that, in the *Mercure de France*, M. Jean de Gourmont said: "Ce livre, admirable, clôt le symbolisme: c'est la dernière, la suprême larme verlainienne."

I have said little hitherto of the innumerable French reviews, which are the forcing-frames of the literature of France. First, the *Mercure de France* – but everybody reads the *Mercure de France*. M. Remy de Gourmont has published therein (March 16, April 1) thirteen remarkable sonnets in prose, of which number xi is:

Je parlerais des yeux, je chanterais les yeux toute ma vie. Je sais toutes leurs couleurs et toutes leurs volontés, leur destinée. Elle est écrite dans leur couleur, dont je n'ignore pas les correspondances, car les signes se répètent et les yeux sont un signe.

J'ai tiré autrefois l'horoscope des yeux, les yeux m'ont dit beaucoup de secrets, qui ne m'intéressent plus, et je cherche en vain celui des yeux que j'ai découverts, un jour d'hiver. Je le cherche et je ne voudrais pas le trouver.

Ni sous les paupières, ni entre les [*sic*] cils, dans l'iris clair où se mire le monde des formes, des couleurs et des désirs, je ne voudrais pas le trouver. J'aime mieux le chercher toujours,

Non comme on cherche sous l'herbe une bague tombée du doigt, mais comme on cherche une joie que la vie a façonnée lentement pour vous dans le mystère des choses.[2]

The two best purely literary monthly reviews are *La Phalange* and *La Nouvelle Revue Française*; the criticism in both is informed and penetrat-

---

[1] Flint translates from Remy de Gourmont, 'Poésie', *Vers et Prose*, xxx (July–September 1912) 183–4.

[2] Remy de Gourmont, 'XXIIIᵉ Lettre à l'Amazone: Sonnet XI', *Mercure de France*, CII (1 April 1913) 574–5. The misprinted word is *leurs*.

ing; the literary contents always of a high, exceptional quality. In the *Phalange* I note (January) *Friedrich Hebbel, raconté par lui-même*; (February) *Les Séjours du Symbolisme*, by Henri Herz [*sic*]; *Remy de Gourmont à cinquante-cinq ans*, by Jean Florence; *Les Chansons Populaires du Ghetto*, by Raymond Geiger, with twenty-five songs, translated; (March) *Soirs de Flandre*, poems by Emile Verhaeren; *La Renaissance lyrique actuelle et la Tradition*, by Henri Herz.

In *La Nouvelle Revue Française* (January and March) *L'Esthétique des Trois Traditions* (i.e., *classique, catholique, monarchique*), by Albert Thibaudet ("the shrewdest, the subtlest, and the most cultivated of those who are not with us," says M. Henri Clouard in *La Revue Critique des Idées et des Livres*); (February) poems by Emile Verhaeren; (March) by Vielé-Griffin, *Le Geste de Saül*; by Paul Claudel, *Cantique de la Pologne*; Valery Larbaud's novel, *A.-O. Barnabooth: Journal d'un Milliardaire* (from February); (April) *Charles Blanchard*, an essay by Léon-Paul Fargue, on Charles-Louis Philippe, followed by an extract from *Charles Blanchard*; and by André Gide, *Les dix romans français que...*, to wit: *La Chartreuse de Parme, Les Liaisons Dangereuses, La Princesse de Clèves, Le Roman Bourgeois, Manon Lescaut, Dominique, La Cousine Bette, Madame Bovary, Germinal*, and...*La Marianne*, "de Marivaux, que je rougis de ne connaître pas encore." In this review, also, the articles by Henri Ghéon on new books of poems.

La Revue Critique des Idées et des Livres: political, royalist; literary standpoint, "classical"; its attitude, belligerent; the number of March 10 was devoted entirely to Stendhal, 144 pages. Between M. Henri Clouard in this review and M. Albert Thibaudet in *La Nouvelle Revue Française* an interesting debate on classicism and romanticism.

Two of the smaller – the "younger" – reviews which I always read with pleasure: *Les Bandeaux d'Or* – MM. Paul Castiaux, Théo Varlet, P.-J. Jouve, René Arcos, G. Chennevière, Luc Durtain: a belligerent attitude, too; in fact, the most interesting work being done at the present time is strongly partisan. *L'Effort Libre* – MM. J.-R. Bloch, Ch. Vildrac, Ch. Albert, Léon Bazalgette (the translator of Whitman), André Spire, P.-J. Jouve Henri Herz [*sic*], René Georgin: a valiant review devoted to the uplifting of life and art. Then there are *L'Indépendance*, in which you may read MM. Francis Jammes, Paul Claudel, Georges Sorel (the syndicalist philosopher), Henri Clouard; *Le Temps Présent, La Renaissance contemporaine, L'Île Sonnante, Les Horizons, Les Cahiers du Centre* (number for February to March, *La Jeunesse de Proudhon*, by Daniel Halévy, 150 pages), *L'Essor, Le Beffroi. Le Thyrse, Flamberge* (Belgian these two), and *La Flora*, wherein M. Lucien Rolmer, armed against ugliness, fights for grace in art. There are many others.

I have not mentioned *Vers et Prose*, the important anthological quarterly of MM. Paul Fort and Alexandre Mercereau, which carries the purest literature of France to the four corners of the world; and now fast on its heels comes the first number of another anthological quarterly, M. Nicolas Beauduin's *La Vie des Lettres* (176 pp.), whereof the first number (April) contains the names of the Comtesse de Noailles, Henri de Régnier, Emile Verhaeren, F. Vielé-Griffin, André Gide, J.-H. Rosny Aîné, Han Ryner, Pierre Mille, Pouchkine, Byron, Rossetti, Walt Whitman (translated), C. Mauclair, William Speth, T. de Visan, Auguste Aumaître, Philéas Lebesgue, and Nicolas Beauduin. M. Beauduin, besides a series of poems, called *Le Poème des Trains*, contributes an "Essai de Synthèse," on *Les Directions de la poésie contemporaine*. M. Beauduin, once more, finds the finest lyrical expression of to-day in "paroxysme," which proceeds from "un état riche de la personne." M. Beauduin is very much at the mercy of his own temperament; but so are many other French poets. Happily, I am only a spectator; and I may, therefore, watch with equanimity the interchange of blows between them – which is at least a sign of life.

III. SEPTEMBER 1913

[The following essay was included in the special futurist number of *Poetry and Drama*. In an introductory statement Flint noted: 'M. Marinetti's work is not really within my province; but he writes in French and his books are published by French publishers, so that my chronicle...may, without too much strain, include a discussion of futurism.']

Futurist?...Futurism!...Every *creative* poet (a pleonasm this) is a futurist in one sense. But in its restricted sense, *futurism* = F. T. Marinetti (to use his own notation); and I do not think that Marinetti has any following in France. I notice that a French poet, M. Guillaume Apollinaire, the author of *Alcools* and the defender of the cubists, signs the last manifesto, "L'Antitradition Futuriste," which is referred to elsewhere in this quarter's "Varia." I am afraid that M. Marinetti's later manifestoes on the technics of futurist literature are likely to ruin futurism. Here (condensed and somewhat rearranged) are a few of his dicta – or, rather, the commandments dictated to him by the screw of his aeroplane:

1. *Syntax must be destroyed* by placing substantives in the order of their birth.
2. *The verb must be used in the infinitive*, so that it may adapt itself elastically to the substantive...The verb in the infinitive alone can give the sense of the continuity of life and the elasticity of the intuition perceiving life.
3. *The adjective must be abolished*, so that the naked substantive may retain its essential colour (the adjective, which suggests a nuance, being incompatible with dynamic vision, since it supposes a stoppage, a meditation).

4. *The adverb must be abolished* (it preserves a tedious unity of tone in the phrase and holds the words together).

5. *Each substantive should have its double* (i.e. the substantive to which it is joined by analogy, e.g. crowd-surf, square-funnel, door-tap). Aerial speed having multiplied our knowledge of the world, perception by analogy is becoming more and more natural to man. "Like," "such as," "as," "similar to" must therefore be suppressed. Better still, the object must be blended directly with the image it evokes by giving the image foreshortened in one essential word.

6. *No more punctuation*...To accentuate certain movements and indicate their directions will be employed the mathematical signs × + : — = > < and the musical signs.[1]

And there is much more of a long manifesto: images must be orchestrated by placing them with a *maximum of disorder*; the "I" in literature must be destroyed; interest in human psychology must be replaced by the *lyric obsession of matter*; the weight and odour of objects must be given; and so you are led on to *wireless imagination*, or absolute liberty of images or analogies expressed by unbound words without the conducting wires of syntax and *with no punctuation*, and to the *mechanical man with replaceable parts*. But these are things which can too easily be flung back at M. Marinetti, and I doubt whether he himself really believes in the mechanical man, despite his statement that by intuition we "shall break down the seemingly insuperable hostility separating our flesh from the metal of motors." Here is an extract from a fragment of one of M. Marinetti's latest works:

Bataille

Poids + Odeur

Midi 3/4 flûtes glapissement embrasement toumtoumb alarme Gargaresch craquement crépitation marche Cliquetis sacs fusils sabots clous canons crinières roues caissons juifs beignets pains-à-huile cantilènes échoppes bouffées chatoiement chassie puanteur cannelle
fadeurs flux reflux poivre rixe vermine tourbillon orangers-en-fleur filigrane misère dés échecs cartes jasmin + muscade + rose arabesque mosaïque charogne hérissement   + savates mitrailleuses = galets + ressac + grenouilles Cliquetis sacs fusil canons ferraille atmosphère = plombs + lave + 300 puanteurs + 50 parfums pavé matelas détritus crottin charognes flic-flac entassement chameaux bourricots tohubohu cloaque.[2]

Moreover, it appears from a later manifesto that there was "nothing categorical" in M. Marinetti's declaration that the adjective must be suppressed and the verb used only in the infinitive. The adjective may

---

[1] This quotation is a translation and paraphrase of excerpts from 'Manifesto della Letteratura futurista' of 11 May 1912. See F. T. Marinetti, *Zang, Tumb, Tumb* (Milano, 1914), pp. 192–3.

[2] The Italian version of the poem, 'BATTAGLIA. PESO + ODORE', is reprinted in *Zang, Tumb, Tumb, op. cit.*, pp. 217–25.

serve as a signal regulating the speed of the analogies. But the verb in the infinitive is indispensable to a dynamic and violent lyricism, because, having the form of a wheel, adaptable as a wheel to all the coaches of the train of analogies, it constitutes the speed itself of style. The verb in the infinitive is in itself a denial of the period, and prevents the style from stopping and resting at any determined point. While the infinitive is round and rolling as a wheel, the other forms and tenses of the verb are triangular, square, or elliptic. M. Marinetti is also undertaking a typographical revolution, which shall abolish the idiotic and nauseous conception of the book of the past, with its ornaments, colophons, initials, and mythological vegetables. He is against what is called the typographical harmony of the page, which is contrary to the flux and reflux of the language on the page. If necessary, he will use on the same page inks of three or four colours and twenty different characters, *italics* for a series of similar, rapid sensations, *heavy* for violent onomatopoeia. He also has in mind a free, expressive orthography. Poets began by running their lyric ecstasy into the mould of a series of equal respirations, with accents, echoes, and a jingling of bells or rhymes predisposed at fixed distances (traditional prosody). Later, poets persuaded themselves that the different moments of this lyrical ecstasy should create their appropriate respirations, of unforeseen and very different lengths, with an absolute liberty of accentuation. Thus they invented naturally the *vers libre*; but they still preserved the order of syntax, so that their lyric ecstasy might run into the mind of the listener by the logical canal of the conventional period. Now M. Marinetti no longer wants the lyric ecstasy to place the words in a certain order before they are sent forth by means of the respirations invented by futurist poets. Thus he has *words at liberty*. Furthermore, the lyric ecstasy should freely deform and remodel words by cutting them down or lengthening them, reinforcing their centres or their extremities, augmenting or diminishing the number of vowels or of consonants. You will have thus a new *orthography*, which M. Marinetti calls a *free expressive orthography*. This instinctive deformation of words corresponds to our natural bent towards onomatopoeia. It does not matter if the word becomes equivocal. It will blend better with the onomatopoeic chords or résumés of noises, and will permit the futurist poet to attain very soon the *psychical onomatopoeic chord*, or the sonorous abstract expression of an emotion or of pure thought. How the aims of futurist poetry differ from those of music I cannot say, unless it be that M. Marinetti has marked out as his province, as he seems to suggest, all the cacophonies of nature. He has said in another manifesto that the futurist poet will, by obeying his commandments, be able to use all the onomatopoeias, even the most cacophonous, that reproduce the innumerable noises of matter in movement. People may laugh at M. Marinetti; but if they will take the trouble to consider his theories without prejudice – it is very stupid to have literary prejudices – they might profit; and the beginning of the poetic art that is to fit in with the future mind, modified by machinery, might be made. Without going so far as M. Marinetti, we may ask ourselves what is the use, for instance, of logical syntax in poetry? Why we should have so absolute a respect for the integrity of words? Whether poetry will not finally develop into a series of emotional ejaculations, cunningly modulated, and coloured by a swift play of subtle and far-reaching analogies? Are we not really spellbound by the past, and is the *Georgian Anthology* really an expression of this age? I doubt it. I doubt whether English poets are really alive to what is around them. And, to betray myself completely, whether, perhaps, it is worth while being so alive. It is a question to consider and thresh out. There are so many old emotions to which we cling that it is legitimate to pause before we set out to transform ourselves into the fiends M. Marinetti would have us be, although it may be admirable to be a fiend.

But the French poet most confident of the future is M. Henri-Martin Barzun, the editor of *Poème et Drame,* in the May number of which he has published an *art poétique d'un idéal nouveau.* He is not, he says, founding a new school, but is formulating the aesthetic of a new *era,* the "era of drama." According to M. Barzun, the lineal, monodic, consecutive poetry of the past is doomed. It is impotent to express the multifarious life of our globe, and, whether neo-classic or *vers libriste,* its form is effete and inadequate. To take its place, M. Barzun has invented the *simultaneous dramatic poem.* The *vers libre* was a reform in *length;* the simultaneous poem will be a reform in *depth.* Like the chords in music, the voices of the world heard by the poet all around him and combined by poetic inspiration will be harmonised on a scale of verbal tones; the effects of rhyme, assonance, alliteration, echo, and other embellishments used in the symbolist aesthetic, will be heard and felt *up and down* the scale during the progress of the poem; and as the trained listener hears a symphony and disengages the different instruments and motives, so the voices in the simultaneous poem will be heard together as harmony and understood separately as sense; the listener must train himself to this; the printed poem will have the same value as the musical score. The whole poem will be a dramatic expression of the life of this planet, quintessentialised by the genius of the poet. Such, it seems to me, is the main outline of what M. Barzun proposes to do; but until he has published his new book, *L'Universel Poème, orphéide, en VII épisodes (voix, rythmes, et chants simultanés),* it will be impossible to say how far he can carry his ideas into practice. If their realisation is possible, then poetry will become an art as rich as music, and still more complex, since, in addition to sound and emotion, it will deal with thought. It will also become, like music, an art requiring performers, or, for private enjoyment, a gramophone record: few will ever, I imagine, learn to read and enjoy the "score." But for a complete statement of M. Barzun's aesthetic, you must consult his essay, which, though confused and turbulent, is full of ingenious remarks.

[Flint concludes the column with a list of the important contents of ten French little magazines or literary reviews and acknowledges other books of French verse recently received.]

IV. DECEMBER 1913

Until recently the whole of the lyrical works of Paul Claudel have been almost inaccessible – scattered in reviews or printed only in rare and highly-priced editions; and the publication now by the *Nouvelle Revue Française*, at 3.50, of the *Cinq Grandes Odes suivies d'un Processional pour saluer le Siècle nouveau* immediately precedes, it is to be hoped, as cheap and as well-printed editions of *Cette Heure qui est entre le Printemps et l'Été, cantate à trois voix,* and of the various hymns and other lyrical poems. Paul Claudel's work is for the world, not for the shelves of bibliophiles.

And yet the world would have some difficulty in finding its way through these five Odes: *Les Muses, L'Esprit et l'Eau, Magnificat, La Muse qui est la Grâce,* and *La Maison fermée.* In *La Muse qui est la Grâce,* I read:

Les mots que j'emploie,
Ce sont les mots de tous les jours, et ce ne sont point les mêmes!
Vous ne trouverez point de rimes dans mes vers ni aucun sortilège. Ce sont vos
  phrases mêmes. Pas aucune de vos phrases que je ne sache reprendre!
Ces fleurs sont vos fleurs et vous dites que vous ne les connaissez [*sic*] pas.
Et ces pieds sont vos pieds, mais voici que je marche sur la mer et que je foule les
eaux de la mer en triomphe![1]

And in the same Ode again:

Que m'importent tous les hommes à présent! Ce n'est pas pour eux que je suis fait,
mais pour le
Transport de cette mesure sacrée!...
Que m'importe aucun d'eux? Ce rythme seul! Qu'ils me suivent ou non? Que
  m'importe qu'ils m'entendent ou pas?[2]

The difficulty is the difficulty presented by genius...Paul Claudel is undeniably a great poet in every sense; and in these five Odes the

[1] Paul Claudel, 'La Muse qui est la Grâce', *Cinq Grandes Odes,* in *Oeuvres complètes,* I (Paris, 1950; 1st pub. 1913), p. 117. *Connaissez* should be *reconnaissez.*
[2] *Ibid.,* p. 116.

intoxication of his vision of the universe, of his certainty, lifted him above methodical composition. The development of his thought does not proceed by a logical dovetailing of phrases, but by the accumulation of images and rendered visions:

O Grammairien dans mes vers! Ne cherche point le chemin, cherche le centre! mesure, comprends l'espace entre ces feux solitaires!

Que je ne sache point ce que je dis! que je sois une note en travail! que je sois anéanti dans mon mouvement! (rien que la petite pression de la main pour gouverner). – *Les Muses*, p. 24.[1]

In his book, *Études*, M. André Rivière [*sic*] has said of these Odes: "A secret thought, the same right to the end, weighs in the heart of the poem, carrying it along by its simple presence, without ever completely unveiling itself. It remains close and dark. But it persists. And though I may not be able, at the last line, to express this thought, at least I have understood it, *taken it with me*. From time to time only, as beneath a rough and tossing sea one catches sight of a rock, the idea under the fluctuation of the images is revealed. It is there, and I am about to seize it. But immediately a new wave of visions rolls up, and it is submerged."[2] And he adds that the puissant undulation of these Odes translates joy in its utmost fulness and generosity. M. Claudel, aware of the difficulty of his Odes, has in this new edition added Arguments; but they do not explain the poems any more than a chart explains the sea. No, you must plunge into them again and again; each time you will emerge with some new pearl. As I have explained before in Claudel's own words... [e.g. in the first essay of this series], the verse-form Claudel uses for preference has neither rhyme nor metre (it has measure and balance), and it is the act of breathing that regulates the length of a verse:

O mon âme impatiente, pareille à l'aigle sans art! comment ferions-nous pour ajuster aucun vers? à l'aigle qui ne sait pas faire son nid même?
Que mon vers ne soit rien d'esclave! mais tel qui l'aigle marin que s'est jeté sur un grand poisson,
Et l'on ne vois rien qu'un éclatant tourbillon d'ailes et l'éclaboussement de l'écume!
Mais vous ne m'abandonnerez point, ô Muses modératrices. –

Les Muses, p. 17.[3]

Claudel's genius, it will be seen, needs freedom and wide spaces wherein to unfold its wings. The narrow Alexandrine, as witness his

[1] 'Les Muses', *Ibid.*, pp. 58–9.
[2] Flint here translates from Jacques Rivière, 'Les Oeuvres lyriques de Claudel', *Etudes* (Paris, 1911), pp. 123–4. He mistakenly identifies him as 'André' Rivière.
[3] 'Les Muses', *Cinq Grandes Odes, op. cit*, ., p. 55.

Vers d'Exil, would have encaged it, but – *la petite pression de la main pour gouverner,...ô Muses modératrices!*

Ainsi un poème n'est point comme un sac de mots, il n'est point seulement
Ces choses qu'il signifie, mais il est lui-même un signe, un acte imaginaire, créant
Le temps nécessaire à sa résolution[,]
A l'imitation de l'action humaine étudiée dans ses ressorts et dans ses poids.[1]

Claudel has a Biblical grandeur. "Savez-vous," said Charles-Louis Philippe to MM. Georges Le Cardonnel and Charles Vellay when they were conducting their "Enquête," "Savez-vous que nous avons un grand génie égal à Dante? C'est Claudel!"

[In a three-page section Flint discusses the formation of the Théâtre du Vieux Colombier and responds to the article "The Crisis of the French Theatre" in the June 1913 issue of *Montjoie*. He then supports his contention that there is much to admire in current French theater by the following extended comments on the recently published poetic dramas of P.-J. Jouve, Georges Duhamel, René Arcos, and O.-W. Milosz.]

M. Pierre-Jean Jouve's play, *Les Deux Forces* (Effort Libre, 2.50) seems to have been influenced in style by the work of Claudel. The two Forces? – the force of passion and the economic force of the world? It is not clear. An engineer (Sériès) finds in the satisfaction of his passion for a woman (Mme Mégard) a strength of will and a largeness of conception lacking in him till then. "Par une après-midi d'avril," says the banker Durker, "beau soleil, bon vent, joie de vivre – dans le silence des bureaux, un homme sent s'ébaucher en lui le commencement d'un surhomme."[2] In the joyous certainty of this new impulse, he enlarges the plans, timidly conceived at first, of the docks that are nearing completion, after ten years' work; and he carries through his new projects against all objection and all opposition – opposition of his financial colleagues and their financial enemies, of his own engineers, of his workmen, who strike. "Par sa joie," says his mistress, "mon corps devenait les chantiers, les bureaux, les banques de la ville, et, plus loin que les trains, d'autres bureaux et d'autres banques, des foules sur le devant des Bourses, des rues, des champs, des maisons hautes, des grands trajets dans la mer."[3] The subject-matter of the play is modern; you are the whole time amidst an ambience created by the presence of machinery and the instruments of modern industrial life; groups coalesce, break apart, grow and diminish according to the disposition of the psychological forces engaged in action; and these forces and

[1] 'Les Muses', *Ibid.*, p. 59.
[2] P.-J. Jouve, *Les Deux Forces.*‡
[3] *Ibid.*‡

groupings interest the author more than individual characterisation. But the effect is not artificial and the play is perfectly human. In the preface to *L'Armée dans la Ville*, M. Romains says: "Every dramatic work sets groups in motion. The isolated individual, who dominates many lyrical poems, has no place in the theatre. That which we call a 'scene' in a play is nothing but the precarious and ardent life of a group. An act is a combination of groups. The spectator sees them following each other, opposing, penetrating and begetting each other. Or, rather, he has not yet learned to see them. Of all the groups, the couple is the only one that dramatists have seized in its original unity and nature. Beyond this, they have represented only more or less necessary encounters of individuals."[1] M. Jouve is one of the younger men of to-day who understand this. One occasionally seems to catch the Claudelian accent in this play; but, on the whole, M. Jouve can only be said to have gone to the school of Claudel and to have profited by what he learned there – a perfectly legitimate thing to do. Where the emotion works up to lyrical intensity, a balance begins to be felt in the periods, which take a versicle form:

Puisque l'amour que j'ai eu s'inscrit dans une grande oeuvre de pierre, au milieu du monde!
Puisque je l'ai quitté, cet amour...comme la chair séparée par le couteau quitte la chair![2]

Elsewhere there is balance, but over longer periods, the advantage of this form as against a strict and restricted verse-form being that it gives a wide series of gradations from prose to verse.

M. Duhamel's *Combat* confronts us with a country at the mercy of a river that, overflowing, spreads rot and disease everywhere, material and moral; – shows it too well, indeed; you smell the mist and feel the dampness in your bones. There seems no hope in any one. But the certainty of his approaching death inspires the consumptive son of the principal [*sic*] landowner of the district to stir his father and friends from their lethargy, and to build a dike as a protection against the waters. He dies alone, neglected, at the moment of victory over the river, the whole country-side, old and young, men and women, having rushed, in a race with the rising flood, to fill the last breach with stones and rubble. *Le Combat* is the struggle first with the moral influence of a periodical calamity, and then with its cause; the welfare and destiny of a people are at stake. It is an illustration of one of M. Duhamel's theories (and herein may be detected the influence of Claudel) that the

---

[1] Flint translates from Jules Romains, 'Préface', *L'Armée dans la ville* (Paris, 1911), p. x.
[2] Jouve, *Les Deux Forces, op. cit.*‡

interest of a play should be in the drama itself, and it should owe nothing to contemporary events or particular localities. *Le Combat* is written in unrhymed verse, but not in *vers libre*. The preface of M. Romains, from which I have already quoted, says also that "great dramatic art demands verse. Prose is an imperfection, a licence, so much less beauty." *L'Armée dans la Ville* is, as I have pointed out elsewhere, written in blank verse, the length of the line in the periods being determined by the intensity of the emotional moment. So, too, *Le Combat*. I note one interesting and, it seems to me, effective experiment. Gérard, the consumptive who rouses the country to combat the river, makes a speech to the peasants wherein he tries to get them to understand his project. He begins slowly; the length of the line is seven syllables; as he warms up to his subject the length of the lines passes from seven, to eight, nine, ten, eleven, and at last to twelve syllables, the ringing Alexandrine; the speech gaining in speed and eloquence meanwhile. *Le Combat* is soberly written, with no romantic fustian, the language always being adequate to the situation. M. Duhamel has himself said that "the error of the romantic theatre and of the contemporary theatre consists in the use of lyrical language from the beginning of the drama, and in circumstances that do not warrant it. Lyricism should spring naturally from the action, and at the moment it appears it should respond to the need of the spectator, duly prepared; it should fill a void. It is much less difficult to put into the mouth of a character a fine poetic passage than to make him say exactly the words suggested by the *pathos* of the moment...Therefore, a resultant, never a preconceived, lyricism."[1] But I think that M. Duhamel's *Dans l'Ombre des Statues* indicates that his destiny lies in what is known as prose. Prose? I have had all the emotions of poetry out of such prose as may be written in imaginative literature. The distinction between prose and verse has begotten the illusion that there is a distinction between prose and poetry. Poetry is a quality of words put together at the behest of the emotions and the imagination, irrespective of forms, the establishment of which has been due to a natural human desire to lay down rules and laws whereby effects once obtained may be repeated. They have been repeated – alas!

M. René Arcos's *poème dramatique*, *L'Île Perdue*, is in prose. "Les cinq actes se passent dans une île que l'imagination peut situer parmi les îles de la Polynésie." Thither has fled a band of utopians, leaving behind them a country angry beneath the rule of an unassailable despot. Rather than remain behind and destroy, they wish to be free to build anew in a region where life is easy and virginal and the sun abets. But they

---

[1] Cf. similar remarks by Duhamel in *Paul Claudel* (Paris, 1913), p. 101.

cannot root out their interest in the country of their birth; a passing ship sets them sighing and pondering; someone has even sent a message home against their mutual compact, violating so the conditions under which they had been granted land by the ruler of the island. Only Timon, the idealist, is unmoved – steeped and eloquent in his dreams of a new becoming and a victory – "tracer le meilleur homme dans la meilleure vie." His words banish their newly awakened, unavowed, and hardly conscious longing to return. But the message home has been sent by Laure, his betrothed, to her brother, Philippe Corme, a man violent and pitiless in his hatred of the king: and Corme arrives. He has killed the tyrant, and has come to recall the exiles; the work of reconstruction awaits them at home. But they put him off; they have started a new life here; why should they return to the old cares and responsibilities? Philippe is angry; he calls them cowards and renegades. Soon the debate resolves itself into a struggle between Timon, the master-mind of the community, and Philippe, and finally Timon, feeling that he has no support in his friends, tires and gives way. As they depart, he blows up the house they had been building and dies beneath the ruin.

Like the other writers in this group, M. Arcos has sought the highest expression of a general sentiment. His characters are not drawn for themselves, but for the attitude they each represent; they are not dependent on contingencies of time and place. The conflict between the idealism of Timon and the spirit of practical politics in Corme is felt and foreshadowed from the first in the presence of Laure. The scenes between Laure and Timon and between Corme and the community and Timon reach a high pitch of poetic passion.

But perhaps the most completely satisfying of the four dramatic works before me is M. O. W. Milosz's *Miguel Mañara, mystère en six tableaux* (*Nouvelle Revue Française*, 2.50). In the other three, you feel that the technician or the philosopher is in the foreground; in M. Milosz's work, the poet. Don Miguel Mañara Vicentelo de Leca, M. Milosz says, is "the historical Don Juan of whom the Romanticists made Don Juan Marana." If that is so, Don Juan has been most horribly maligned, for he seems to have been a noble scoundrel, and not at all the heartless lecher that Molière and Mozart paint. Indeed, M. Milosz's Don Juan is, fundamentally, not very different from Mr Shaw's; the external differences are of course enormous. Don Miguel Mañara drags about with him a vast boredom.

Car le temps est long; car le temps est terriblement long, Messieurs, et je suis las étrangement de la chienne de vie que voilà. Ne point gagner Dieu, c'est vétille, à coup sûr,

mais perdre Satan, c'est douleur grande et ennui vaste, par ma foi.
J'ai traîné l'Amour dans le plaisir, et dans la boue, et dans la mort;
je fus traître, blasphémateur, bourreau; j'ai accompli
tout cela que peut entreprendre un pauvre diable d'homme,
et voyez! j'ai perdu Satan. Satan s'est retiré de moi.
Je mange l'herbe amère du rocher de l'ennui.
J'ai besogné Vénus avec rage, puis avec malice et dégoût.
Aujourd'hui je lui tordrais le cou en bâillant.[1]

But he meets Girolama Carilo, and for a while the darkness is dispelled:

Vous avez allumé une lampe dans mon coeur:
et me voici comme le malade qui s'endort dans les ténèbres
avec le charbon de la fièvre sur le front et la glace de l'abandon dans le coeur,
et puis qui se réveille en sursaut dans une belle chambre
où toutes choses baignent dans la musique étale de la lumière...[2]

She dies, and the Spirit of Heaven tells him to rejoice. He carries his sorrow to a monastery, and, growing in grace, works a miracle. He dies soon after with verses from the Psalms on his lips and the voice of the Spirit of Heaven in his ears. M. Milosz's *Miguel Mañara* is a sombre piece of work, but very fine and very moving. The language, imagery, and rhythm are those of a poet.

I have two books of verse that have pleased me for the same and for opposite reasons: *Les Servitudes*, by Philéas Lebesgue, and *Alcools*, by Guillaume Apollinaire (*M. de F.*, 3.50 each): there is poetry in both, but in the first it springs from contact with simple, natural things; in the second, from a complex of culture and phantasy. M. Lebesgue sings his family, his native village, its animals, trades, work, dreams, and... his escapes therefrom; M. Apollinaire, all the subtle fancies, images, symbols that his mind weaves into the stuff of his emotions; his portrait by Pablo Picasso is given as a – cryptic – frontispiece; he has suppressed all punctuation in his verses; he is exotic, deliberately artificial, and willingly obscure. But both are poets, M. Lebesgue appealing to the brain through the heart; M. Apollinaire to the heart through the brain. Quotation will show their qualities and their differences. First from M. Lebesgue:

Tu as vieilli, ma Mère, et quand je vois tes rides,
Ton dos courbé, tes bras amaigris, ta pâleur,
Je sens monter, du fond de ma poitrine aride,
Jusqu'à mes tristes yeux une averse de pleurs.

[1] O. V. de L. Milosz, *Miguel Mañara*, in *Oeuvres complètes*, III (Paris, 1957; 1st pub. 1912), p. 18.
[2] *Ibid.*, p. 37.

La noblesse des traits usés affirme encore
Que tu fus belle en ton printemps, et ton regard
Atteste une vertu que notre époque ignore,
Quelque chose dont l'or ne peut acheter l'art.[1]

Or, from "In memoriam patris":

Je suis venu m'entretenir, ce soir,
Avec ton image éternelle;
Dans la grand'salle, où l'âtre vide est resté sans feu,
Où le dernier tison n'a plus une étincelle,
En face du fauteuil où tu ne songes plus,
Je suis venu m'assevoir; [sic]
Je t'ai parlé de tout mon coeur silencieux;
Je t'ai revu
Pensivement penché sur le livre ouvert,
Et la main droite à ton front nu;
Je t'ai parlé: tu n'as pas répondu![2]

But these clipped quotations are doing M. Lebesgue an injustice. From M. Apollinaire's "La Maison des Morts":

Arrivé à Munich depuis quinze ou vingt jours
J'étais entré pour la première fois et par hazard [sic]
Dans ce cimetière presque désert
Et je claquais des dents
Devant toute cette bourgeoisie
Exposée et vêtue le mieux possible
En attendant la sépulture.

Soudain
Rapide comme ma mémoire
Les yeux se rallumèrent
De cellule vitrée en cellule vitrée
Le ciel se peupla d'une apocalypse
Vivace.

Et la terre place à l'infini
Comme avant Galilée
Se couvrit de mille mythologies immobiles
Un ange en diament brisa toutes les vitrines
Et les morts m'accostèrent
Avec des mines de l'autre monde.[3]

And then the poet and the dead march off to the strange inconsequent adventures that one has in dreams – a curious, remarkable poem. *La Synagogue* is a poem of a kind that seems new in French:

[1] Philéas Lebesgue, 'Tu as vieilli', *Les Servitudes* (Paris, 1913), p. 9.
[2] 'In memoriam, II', *Ibid.*, p. 19. The misprinted word should read *m'asseoir*.
[3] Guillaume Apollinaire, 'La Maison des Morts', *Alcools* in *Oeuvres poétiques* (Paris, 1956) p. 66. The word should be *hasard*.

Ottomar Scholem et Abraham Loeweren
Coiffés de feutres verts le matin du sabbat
Vont à la synagogue en longeant le Rhin
Et les coteaux où les vignes rougissent là-bas.

Ils se disputent et crient des choses qu'on ose à peine traduire...

Parce que pendant le sabbat on ne doit pas fumer
Tandis que les chrétiens passent avec des cigares allumés
Et parce qu'Ottomar et Abraham aiment tous deux
Lia aux yeux de brebis et dont le ventre avance un peu...[1]

Les Servitudes and *Alcools* should be read by all who are interested in contemporary French poetry.

I wish to recommend, too, the work of M. Luc Durtain, who is one of the band of admirably intelligent young men gathered round *Les Bandeaux d'Or*. M. Durtain has published three books: *Pégase* (Sansot, 3.50), a volume of light, witty poems; *L'Étape Nécessaire* (Sansot, 3.50), in which he has flung pell-mell all the impressions of his formative years – a necessary stage, but memorable, and recorded in many a profound page; and *Manuscrit trouvé dans une Île*, just published (Crès, 3.50), five *contes*, that reveal mastery and...good masters; read *Complices*. M. Durtain should be watched. He promises some extraordinarily good work.

[Flint concludes the column with a list of important contents of recent French literary magazines and acknowledgments of books of French verse received since the appearance of his previous column.]

V. MARCH 1914

Poètes Fantaisistes. I. – It seems that we have no words in English for "fantaisie" and "fantaisiste." "Fancy" and "fanciful," "fantasy" and "fantastic" do not convey the same sense. One could not, for instance, – at least, I would not – call Mr Walter de la Mare a "fanciful" or "fantastic" poet; yet he is the most truly "fantaisiste" living poet we have. However, my care at the moment is to present a few French "poètes fantaisistes," let the English label be what it may.

First, chief and undoubted "prince" of these is M. Paul Fort, who has just published a *Choix de Ballades Françaises*, consisting of nearly six hundred closely printed pages and representing only about one-seventh of his whole work; and immediately following this selection the fifteenth volume of his "Ballades Françaises," *Chansons pour me Consoler d'être Heureux* (Figuière, 6 fr. and 3.50). But M. Fort is not only a "fantaisiste"

---

[1] 'La Synogogue', *Ibid.*, p. 113.

poet. Like them, he is gay and bantering only to become sad; sad to become gay; he is lucid and ironical; but he is tender; he has moments of disillusionment; but any next moment life may offer him a motive for intoxication. There is no other living poet who is so entirely a poet. You fear with each volume of his that appears that he publishes too much; but doubt is soon dispelled: his work is always poetic; often it is pure poetry, without qualification: and it is poetic because, even when he is least inspired, his speech is a poet's speech. Applied to any other writer, the word "poetic" might mean that he had presented merely some of the external aspects of poetry. But with Paul Fort emotion and its translation into imagery are so instantaneous – and simultaneous – that he never seems to quit the plane of poetry. M. Remy de Gourmont said of him that he was "une sensibilité toujours en éveil." M. Paul Fort cannot walk down a street without encountering all the incidents and accidents of a poem. "Recommencer toujours à vivre," he quotes from Guyau as an epigraph to one of his poems; "tel serait l'idéal de l'artiste: il s'agit de retrouver, par la force de la pensée réfléchie, l'inconsciente naïveté de l'enfant." But Paul Fort needs no effort of thought to recover that artlessness; it is always with him, behind the poet, behind the artist, behind the man. And no other French poet has the command of his language that Paul Fort has; his poems are rich in word and idiom; they are intensely French. They are also superbly rhythmical. His poems are printed in their prose form, he says, in a note – which is a re-edition of the prefatory note to the *Roman de Louis XI.* of 1898 – to *Chansons pour me Consoler d'être Heureux*, to prove the "superiority of rhythm over the artifice of prosody. It has been said that I 'sacrifice' my books to 'the cause' of this truth, which – if it were once recognised – would very much help to relieve our poet's craft, would endow it with much more liberty, much more suppleness, and would allow of infinitely more personal discovery (*fantaisie*) in the traditional forms of French poetic language, which would be rejuvenated thereby. Thus the poet would be less inclined to think in fine lines: the expression of his thought would be translated directly into fine musical strophes, which to my mind are the characteristic of true poetry."[1] French critics have been at pains to show that M. Fort is in reality a very traditional poet, and that, granted certain licences of rhyme, elision, assonance, *et aliorum*, his poems conform to tradition. Be that as it may, M. Paul Fort's range is astonishing. His *Choix de Ballades* contains "Hymnes, Chansons, Lieds, Elégies, Poèmes Antiques (Hymnes Héroïques, Eglogues et Idylles, Chants Paniques), Poèmes Marins, Odes et Odelettes, Romans, Petites Epopées, Fantaisies à la Gauloise, Complaintes et Dits, Madrigaux et

[1] Paul Fort, 'Prèface', *Chansons pour me consoler d'être heureux* (Paris, 1913).

Romances, Epigrammes à moi-même." And each of these headings needs
the kind of commentary given by M. Louis Mandin in his *Etude sur les
"Ballades Françaises"* to enforce its full significance. Nor can I, in a
Chronicle of this kind, do more than refer you to his books. But before
I pass on to other poets, I should like to quote two of Paul Fort's poems,
the first from *Chansons pour me Consoler d'être Heureux,* for its movement
and its melancholy.

La Voix des Boeufs

Grande voix des boeufs dans le soir, alors que, champ par champ, la terre sombre
en ce gouffre où meurt l'espoir des sillons privés de lumière,

clames-tu la mort ou la vie? Cependant la lune est sans voiles. Un sillon rêveur te
dédie, grande voix des boeufs, aux étoiles.

Quel bruit fait cortège à leur voix, quand les boeufs rentrent dans l'étable? Des
millions d'épis à la fois se bercent au ciel admirable.

Ah! tout n'est que silence enfin! L'on entendrait mourir les dieux: du monde
énorme est-ce la fin? La voix des boeufs est dans les boeufs

qui sort, au contact du matin, des étables vers l'aube fine et les droits sillons
argentins lèvent. – Et tinte une clarine.

Le calme solaire à présent. Les troupeaux, en un mol murmure, seuls animeront
l'air dormant sur le sommeil de la Nature.

Loin des moissons, dans les pâtures, avec douceur ils reprendront leur majesté devant
l'azur, au profil vaporeux des monts.

Le calme est tombé plus profond. Un vent soudain couche l'herbage. Des frissons
rident les fanons, montent jusqu'aux mufles qui bavent,

jusqu'à ce Cri remplissant tout, les monts avec leurs bois sauvages, les quatre
plaines jusqu'au bout, la voûte du ciel noir d'orage –

O voix des boeufs, hymne du soir aux heures où la terre sombre à l'abîme, entraînant l'espoir des sillons pris du froid des ombres,

clames-tu la mort de la Vie? Cependant la lune se lève...La glèbe en rêve te
dédie, grande voix des boeufs, au seul Réve![1]

The second from *Île de France* (perhaps only Frenchmen can appreciate
to the full M. Fort's local poems):

La Petite Rue Silencieuse

(Senlis)

Le silence orageux ronronne. Il ne passera donc personne?
Les pavés comptent les géraniums. Les géraniums comptent les pavés.
Rêve, jeune fille, à ta croisée. Les petits pois sont écossés.

[1] Paul Fort, 'Les Voix des boeufs', *Chansons pour me consoler d'être heureux, op. cit.,* in *Anthologie
des ballades françaises 1897–1917* (Paris, 1917), pp. 264–5.

Ils bombent ton blanc tablier que tes doigts roses vont lier.
Je passe de noir habillé. Un éclair au ciel t'a troublée,
jeune fille, ou c'est donc ma vue? Tes petits pois tombent dans la rue.
Sombre je passe. Derrière moi les pavés comptent les petits pois.
Le silence orageux ronronne. Il ne passera donc personne?[1]

and there is

Gonesse Au Couchant

Gonesse embroche le soleil!...J'écris seulement ce que je vois. Rose est la page,
sous la tonnelle, où glisse l'ombre de mes doigts.

Gonesse embroche le soleil avec la lance de son clocher. Ce que je vois de ma
tonnelle est toujours vrai[,] sans vous fâcher.

Attendez...sous la vigne vierge, qu'aperçois-je? une oie embrochée, de fleurs de
flammes toute léchée, dans la cuisine de l'auberge!

Astre alléchant, oie délectable, Gonesse embroche deux soleils. Ma page est rouge
sur la table. Buvons un coup de vin vermeil.[2]

La Fantaisie is no new thing in France. M. Alphonse Séché declares in
Les Caractères de la Poésie Contemporaine (Sansot, fr. 3.50), that it is "one
of the most peculiar, the most constant traits of French poetry, a
characteristic which might be said to be one of the essential marks of
our national genius...*La Fantaisie* – in France, at least – is distinguished
by restraint and good taste. It is not sentimental acrobatics, any more
than it is word-juggling. Half-serious and half-humorous, often gay, it
can be sad on occasion. But, by nature, *La Fantaisie* loves frankness and
ease; sometimes it wears the costume of the dandy, at others the picturesque habiliments of Bohemia...Young and spruce, somewhat boastful,
ready with words, graceful in gesture, bantering, lackadaisical..."[3] I
cannot follow M. Séché any farther; he allows his vein to run away
with him (and since this book has been sent to us, it may be said now
that, while presenting a true enough picture of the poetic activity of
France to-day, it does so without distinction in its appraisal). Charles
d'Orléans, Villon, Ronsard, Du Bellay, La Fontaine, Nerval, Gautier,
Banville, Verlaine, and above all – forgotten, overlooked by M.
Séché – Laforgue, Rimbaud, Corbière, and M. Paul Fort himself: this
seems to be the lineage of the younger Fantaisistes. There is a large
number of them: André Salmon, Tristan Klingsor (Leclère), Alexandre

[1] Paul Fort, 'La Petite rue silencieuse', *Île de France* (Paris, 1908), in *Anthologie des ballades
françaises, op. cit.*, p. 165.
[2] Fort, 'Gonesse au couchant', *Île de France, op. cit.*, in *Anthologie des ballades françaises, op. cit.*,
pp. 165–6.
[3] Flint here translates from Alphonse Séché, *Les Caractères de la poésie contemporaine* (Paris, 1913),
pp. 11–12. The first part of the statement is quoted in *Vers et Prose*, XXXV (October–
December 1913) 7.

Mercereau, Guillaume Appollinaire [*sic*], Fernand Divoire, Henri Hertz, André Spire, Louis de la Salle, Max Jacob, Jean-Marc Bernard, René Bizet, Charles Perrès, Claudien, Fagus, Francis Carco, Tristan Derème, Jean Pellerin, Paul-Jean Toulet. . .

M. Tristan Leclère (Klingsor) is a musician, an art-critic and a delicious poet. The hundred poems of *Schéhérazade* (1903), in which he says:

> En rêvant de la princesse Grain-de Beauté. . .
> Je mêle Samarcande et le Quartier Latin,
> Et j'ai toujours peur de voir au coin d'une borne [*sic*]
> Ou bien au bout d'un vers
> Un Haroun Al-Rachid coiffé d'un haut-de-forme,[1]

have all the flavour of those other exquisite poems of Mardrus's *Mille et Une Nuits*, of which they are avowed imitations, but imitations that owe their charm to the delightful fancy of a modern French poet. Again, the whole carnival of the "Fête Galante," the Harlequinade, the Fairy Tale and the Folk Song sweep through the pages of *Le Valet de* [*sic*] *Coeur* (1908); M. Leclère loves to take the refrains of the old songs and put new embroidery upon them. I regret that a moment's parsimony prevented me from buying his *Poèmes de Bohème* (1913), of which I have been unable to obtain a review copy. M. Francis Carco's description of M. Leclère's art (in the volume of *Vers et Prose* referred to later on) could not be bettered. "M. Tristan Klingsor (Leclère)," he says, "has created smiling and slender masterpieces out of nuances. He wears irony like a mask, and his personages, however motley they may be – arrant serenaders, amorous rogues, and dandies of Bohemia – have less grace than he. He crowns a skeleton with roses, and the beautiful legends he tells us are noisy with tears declarations and vows. The nightingales of Apain enchant Kings' daughters. Scaramouche beguiles the fairest and Cupid laughs shamelessly in the wings."[2] But M. Leclère has also the malice, the mockery and the salacity of the Gaul; and, it must be added, his tenderness, his sentimentality, and his melancholy. He is preparing a new book of poems, *Humoresques*, from which the following:

> Je m'assieds dans l'herbe bleue:
> Qu'il est joli le trèfle blanc;
> La fille embrasse le galant
> Et l'amour danse tout autour d'eux;
> Qu'il est joli, le vieil enfant!

[1] Tristan Klingsor (Léon Leclère), *Schéhérazade* (Paris, 1903), p. 50.
[2] Flint here translates from Francis Carco, 'Les Poètes Fantaisistes', *Vers et Prose*, xxxv (October–December 1913) 10.

Où est le temps où moi aussi
Je faisais l'amoureux,
Le temps de Berthe et de Lucie
Et de la femme du marchand de Dreux;
Où est le temps des coeurs tremblants;
Et de ma barbe noire et de vos blonds cheveux,
Où est le temps?

Derrière la haie les galants s'en vont
Et l'amour à leurs trousses sourit;
La jeune heibe bleue tremble dans le vent
Et moi, qui reste seul, je me morfonds
A regarder le trèfle blanc
Et tirer sans répit les poils gris
De mon menton.[1]

M. André Salmon has published *Poèmes* (1905), *Les Féeries* (1907), and *Le Calumet* (1910). It has been said of him that, since Banville, no one has used more wit in the service of lyrical poetry; there is a technical – modern – difference only in the following example:

Mister Clown assis sur un tambour
Fume la pipe,
Il est lugubre avec humour,
Mais sa lippe
Divertit Dolorès, la danseuse de corde,
Et ce leur est un sujet de discorde.

Pourtant, huissier hippique à l'oeil loyal,
Cet excellent mossieur Loyal,
Dans ses mains grasses a trois fois frappé.
L'orchestre polonais y va d'un air huppé
Et Dolorès sur la corde s'élance,
Lors il se fait un grand silence.

Et Mister Clown assis sur son tambour
Suit du fond des tristes coulisses
Sa vie, sa foi, son âme, son coeur et son amour
Qui glissent
Et tourbillonnent dans la lumière
Selon les lois mathématiques
Dont s'émerivelle le vulgaire,
Ahô yes! les jolis yeux [*sic*] du Cirquè!

Voici que ces [*sic*] amours se posent
Le jambe en l'air, en maillot rose,
Et Mister Clown, homme précis, constate,
En bien considérent la pose,
Que son amour, sa foi que rien ne peut abattre,
Sa vie, son coeur, son âme tiennent dans le chiffre 4.[2]

[1] Tristan Klingsor (Léon Leclère), 'Humoresques, III', *Vers et Prose*, xxxv (October–December 1913) 43–4.
[2] Andre Salmon, 'Cirque', *Les Féeries* (Paris, 1907), pp. 40–1. The words should be *jeux* and

But M. Salmon is not always witty, funambulesque; he can be bitter, profound, imaginative, moving. He is – or was – a nocturnal poet:

> J'aime les nuits de mi-carême,
>   Les cigares, l'or dispensé [*sic*],
>   Une écharpe, un miroir glacé,
> Et les violons de Bohème.
>
> J'aime le feu, j'aime l'alcool
>   Et sur tes mortels yeux d'idole,
>   Autour des cils en auréoles,
> La jaune malice du khol.[1]

He has strange encounters in nocturnal taverns with criminals and prostitutes; the streets outside are full of adventure; and on the blue curtain of tobacco smoke in his lonely reveries he contemplates the unfolding of unworldly dramas. An exotic poet, he has seen and put into his poetry all the variegated and much-mixed life of Europe; sometimes, by a complication of the mind, dream and reality mingle:

> Un soir, près de Fingal ou bien près de Moscou,
> J'ai vu trois déserteurs menant par une corde
> Viviane la fée au chapeau de lilas
> Que suivaient tristement Elisabeth la Sainte
> Et la reine Esclarmonde en robe de jacynthes [*sic*];
> Je me souviens des vins que je bus ce soir-là.[2]

And much more could be said of M. André Salmon.

Here is another poem by M. Guillaume Appollinaire [*sic*], whose *Alcools* I reviewed in December last:

Monparnasse [*sic*]

> O porte de l'hôtel avec deux plantes vertes
> Vertes qui jamais
> Ne porteront de fleurs
> Où sont mes fruits. Où me plantè-je
> O porte de l'hôtel un ange est devant toi
> Distribuant des prospectus
> On n'a jamais si bien défendu la vertu
> Donnez-moi pour toujours une chambre à la semaine
> Ange barbu vous étes en réalité
> Un poète lyrique d'Allemagne

ses in lines 20 and 21. There are minor differences in punctuation throughout and four final lines in the 1907 edition, but in all other respects Flint's citation conforms to the printed original.

[1] Salmon, 'Ma Béatrice', *Le Calumet*, édition définitive (Paris, 1920; 1st pub. 1910), pp. 75–6. In the definitive edition the reading of the second quoted line is *dispersé* and there are minor differences in punctuation.

[2] Salmon, 'Le Voyageur', *Le Calumet*, op. cit., p. 48. The word should be *jacinthes*.

Qui voulez connaître Paris
Vous connaissez de son pavé
Ces raies sur lesquelles il ne faut pas que l'on marche
    Et vous rêvez
D'aller passer votre Dimanche à Garches
Il fait un peu lourd et vos cheveuz sont longs
O bon petit poète un peu bête at trop blond
Vox yeux ressemblent tant à ces deux grands ballons
Qui s'en vont dans l'air pur
A l'aventure[1]

[Flint briefly notes some recent books he has not seen, because 'the pockets *minimorum poetarum* are not always well lined', then goes on to mention René Bizet and to quote his poem 'Trois Negres sur un Bateau'.]

There remains, then, of the list given above a little band of poets who really constitute the "fantaisiste" group: Claudien, Fagus, Francis Carco, Tristan Derème, Jean Pellerin, Paul-Jean Toulet (and M. Jean-Marc Bernard, and one or two others). They name each other in their verses, or dedicate their poems to each other. They form a small school therefore. But their work, published in plaquettes or in reviews, is not easy to obtain. A series of volumes, called *La Collection des Cinq* (Coulanges, Marseille, subscription only), is in course of publication which will make access to them easier. Two volumes have already appeared: *Au Vent Crispé du Matin*, by Francis Carco, and *La Flûte Fleurie*, by Tristan Derème. These will be followed by *Mauvais Chemins*, Claudien; *Contrerimes*, P.-J. Toulet; *Familières*, Jean Pellerin. And an anthology of "fantaisistes" poems, with a preface by Francis Carco, occupies one half (70 pages) of the last number of *Vers et Prose*, tome xxxv. But, as I have no more space, I must return to these poets in my next article.

[The chronicle ends with Flint's usual acknowledgment of books recently received and an abbreviated list of titles of reviews received.]

VI. JUNE 1914

Poètes Fantaisistes, II. – The poems and prose pieces in M. Francis Carco's *Au Vent Crispé du Matin* have been selected from his three previous plaquettes, *Instincts* (prose poems), *La Bohème et mon Coeur*, and *Chansons Aigres-Douces*, a new series, *Détours* (prose poems), being added thereto. The whole makes up a volume of 87 pages. The "fantaisistes" are not torrential. He has also published in the *Mercure de France*, Jan. 16th–Feb. 1st, a novel, *Jésus-la-Caille*, in which prostitutes, male and

---

[1] Guillaume Apollinaire, 'Montparnasse', *Il y a* (Paris, 1925), pp. 91–2. The poem was written in 1912 and published in *Vers et Prose*, xxxv, *op. cit.*, 21.

female, and their bullies speak their slang. "Tiens! vise mon oeil. Le plus mariole y verra nib..." And he has in preparation a volume of short stories and one of criticism.

.   .   .   .

As for his poetry, I have turned over the pages to find a poem that I could quote; but there is little to choose between one poem and another. The influence of Verlaine is apparent (as is that of Rimbaud in the Proses). Perhaps this poem will do:

> Des saules et des peupliers
> > Bordent la rive.
> Entends, contre les vieux piliers
> > Du pont, l'eau vive!
>
> Elle chante, comme une voix
> > Jase et s'amuse,
> Et puis s'écrase sur le bois
> > Frais de l'écluse.
>
> Le moulin tourne... Il fait si bon[,]
> > Quand tout vous laisse[,]
> S'abandonner, doux vagabond,
> > Dans l'herbe épaisse!...[1]

M. Tristan Derème's book, *La Flûte Fleurie*, offers more scope for comment. He tells you that he loves to live:

> loin des cours où Dorchain tourne sa manivelle...
> Car j'ai quitté les toits, les livres, les musées,
> pour la mer et les prés où fume la rosée [*sic*].[2]

And again:

> Je dirai pour l'instruction des biographes
> que ton corsage avait quarante-deux agrafes,
> que dans tes bras toute la nuit j'étais inclus,
> que c'était le bon temps, que je ne quittais plus
> ta chambre qu'embaumait un pot d'héliotrope.
> Duhamel animait son héroïque *Anthrope*,
> Pellerin habitait Pontcharra et Carco
> quarante-neuf, quai de Bourbon, Paris. Jusqu'au
> matin, je caressais tes jambes et ta gorge.
> Tu lisais *Chantecler* et *le Maître de Forge*;
> Tu ignorais Laforgue, estimant qu'avec art
> écrivaient seulement Botrel et Jean Aicard.
> Pourtant dans Aurignac embelli de ses rêves,

---

[1] Francis Carco, 'Des saules et des peupliers...', *Au Vent crispé du matin* (Paris, 1913), p. 62. The poem was originally published in *La Bohème et mon coeur* (1912).
[2] Tristan Derème, 'Terrible passion, voici que tu m'exiles...', *La Flûte fleurie* (Paris, 1913), p. 16. The last three words of the quotation should read *fument les rosées*.

Frène, pâle et barbu, méditait sur *Les Sèves*
et Deubel, revêtu des velours cramoisis,
publiant au *Beffroi* ses *Poèmes Choisis,*
déchaînait dans les airs le tumulte des cuivres.

Et j'aimais beaucoup moins tes lèvres que mes livres.[1]

Happy M. Derème, with his pipe, his woods and meadows, his friends,
his mistress, his irony, and his wounded heart! And if all other record
of him is lost except *La Flûte Fleurie*, posterity will reconstruct him thus:
his poets were Laforgue, Mallarmé, Villon, Tailhade, Verlaine,
Jammes; his friends were Francis Carco, Léon Vérane, Jean Pellerin,
and so on; his mistresses were...many. He was fond of queer rhymes
like cornac–tu n'as qu', d'où ce–douce, malgré que–grecque, mimosa–
nouais à; of German rhymes: siffles–buffles, flûte–insolite, mire–
ramure; and of "consonances": pupitre–pâtre, fraîches–ruches,
sources–écorces; and of assonances that have the effect of delicate
rhymes. He painted pictures:

Lorsque tu étais vierge,
(le fus-tu? le fus-tu?)
Nous dînions à l'*Auberge
de Caniche Poilu.*

C'était une bicoque
sous un vieux châtaigner;
tonnelle pour églogue,
lavoir et poulailler.

Buis sec à la muraille,
et rosiers aux carreaux...
A travers une paille
tu suçais des sirops.

Guinguette au toit de chaume,
mur d'ocre éclaboussé...
Un grand liseron jaune
fleurit sur le passé.[2]

And he decorates his melancholy with so many leaves and flowers that
one lays aside *La Flûte Fleurie* with regret.

Fumerai-je au soir de ma vie
une pipe en bois de laurier?
Nous voilà vieux, ma pauvre amie,
j'ai eu vingt ans en février.

Nous avons lu beaucoup de livres
et crayonné bien des feuillets,
et jadis blonds comme des cuivres,
nos rêves sont de blancs oeillets.

[1] 'Je dirai pour l'instruction des biographes...', *Ibid.*, p. 44.
[2] 'Lorsque tu étais vierge...', *Ibid.*, p. 46.

Et tout cela n'est pas peu triste;
Mais dans l'ombre où nous défaillons
enfin l'ironie oculiste
ouvre boutique de lorgnons.

Des lièvres dansent aux pelouses,
et dans la chambre mon espoir.
Maintenant j'attends que tu couses
une rose à ton jupon noir,

et que le rire ensevelisse
sous des guirlandes de clarté,
notre rêve, ce vieil Ulysse
que les sirènes ont tenté.[1]

As for M. Jean Pellerin, all I know about him is that he has made, *en marge d'une vieille mythologie*, some amusing puns:

On plaisantait Jupin, là-haut
– Joyeux propos de table –
Diane criait "T'as Io, t'as Io!"
Calembour détestable.

Sur tous, Vénus le harcelait...
Le maître à la pécore
En regardant Mars, dit: "Encore
Un peu de ce filet?"[2]

But he offers this excuse:

C'est vrai j'aurais pu devenir
Fabricant d'élégie [*sic*].[3]

I do not know enough about the work of M. Fagus or M. Claudien to speak of it with competence. M. Fagus contributes regularly amusing "Ephémérides" – notes and comments on actualities – to *La Revue Critique*. He is also the author of *Ixion* (1903) and of *Quelques Fleurs* (1906). For both poets, see *Vers et Prose*, tome xxxv. So, too, for examples – eighteen poems – of the work of M. Paul-Jean Toulet. M. Toulet does not seem to have yet published any of his poems in book form. He is the most impeccable of this group of "fantaisistes" poets. He writes little poems in eights and sixes, and each is like an exquisite, fantastic, ironic cameo. I have read these eighteen poems over and over again, and I still turn to them with predilection. M. Toulet uses words so imaginatively that they are refined into something more than mere vocabulary:

---

[1] 'Fumerai-je au soir de ma vie...', *Ibid.*, p. 103.
[2] Jean Pellerin, 'Intermède', *Le Bocquet inutile* (Paris, 1923), p. 119. The poem differs slightly throughout in both punctuation and word order in the posthumous collected edition.
[3] 'Quotidiennes', *Ibid.*, p. 37. The last word of the quotation appears as *d'élégies...* in the collected edition.

he recreates them; each poem is a word. "Aérez les mots," said Moréas to M. Paul Fort. M. Toulet's words have a diaphanous beauty that gives to his poems an immaterial quality. These, as often as not, are the records of moments – a fancy, an impatience, a sudden emotion that for the moment thrills the senses. M. Toulet is careful not to go beyond this impulse. Here is one poem:

> Vous qui revenez du Cathay
> Par les Messageries,
> Quand vous berçait à leurs féeries
> L'opium ou le thé,
>
> Dans un palais d'aventurine
> Où se mourait le jour
> Avez-vous vu Boudroulboudour,
> Princesse de la Chine,
>
> Plus rose en son noir pantalon
> Que nacre sous l'écaille?
> Et cette lune, Jean Chicaille,
> Etait-elle au salon
>
> A jurer par la Fleur qui bêle
> Aux îles de Ouac-Ouac
> Qu'il coudrait nue, – oui! dans un sac –
> Son épouse rebelle
>
> ...Et plus belle, à travers le vent
> Des mers sur le rivage,
> Que l'or ne brille au paon sauvage
> Dans le soleil levant?[1]

M. Toulet is a poet who has stepped out of the "Arabian Nights," and he sees with the lucid irony and he wears the mocking smile of modern Paris.

M. Henri Clouard, the knight-herald of modern French classicism, has said of the last poem by M. Derème, quoted above, that the wisdom which was forming in it has since sprung, fully armed, from the head of M. Jean-Marc Bernard, author of *Sub Tegmine Fagi* (*Temps Présent*, 3.50). M. Bernard's wisdom is the wisdom of Horace, *aequam memento...*: *rebus in arduis*, a little irony will deflate all emphasis, and, *in bonis*, will preserve the mind's equilibrium:

> ab insolenti temperatam
> laetitia...

or of FitzGerald's Omar, which he translates creditably. So M. Bernard wanders round the Dauphiné – he is another *poète champêtre* – with

---

[1] P.-J. Toulet, 'XLIV, Vous qui retournez du Cathai...', *Les Contrerimes* (Paris, 1929; 1st pub. 1921), pp. 57–8. The quoted poem differs greatly from the version in the collected edition, particularly in the last three stanzas.

Virgil's Eclogues, or Horace's Odes, or Lucretius, or Catullus in one pocket, and Parny, or Charles d'Orléans (in his own edition), or Villon, or François de Maynard, or Mathurin Régnier, or Scarron, or La Fontaine in the other. (At least, it pleases one to imagine that he carries his poets with him.) And in the inns he courts the pretty girls who wait on him, or – not often – parodies Mallarmé or M. de Régnier, or simply drinks wine with a friend and listens to the light babble of a mistress, whose memory he will keep...in some future poem. Unfortunately, M. Bernard has not written the poem he should have written for me to place here. I gather it – unquotably – turning over the pages of his *Livre des Amours*, in *Sub Tegmine Fagi*; and transcribe another piece:

> Des chèvres près de ton ruisseau,
> Prairie, et toi qui nous accueilles.
> Le doux frémissement de l'eau
> Qui se marie au bruit des feuilles.
>
> Et, là-bas, dans le chemin creux,
> Entre les branches de tes saules,
> Cette enfant, au rire joyeux,
> Dont on ne voit que les épaules...
>
> Aussi rentrant à la maison,
> Ce soir, tout pleins de cette idylle,
> Nous trouverons dans ton gazon
> La trace des pas de Virgile.[1]

We hear the echo of no bad masters in M. Bernard's poems, avers M. Clouard, meaning no modern masters; and he adds that in this gay awakening of "fantaisiste" poetry there may be a new victory of the mind – over the rhetoric of romanticism, over the complications of symbolism.

I have four books of criticism and appreciation for which a word must be said: *Prétextes, réflexions sur quelques points de littérature et de morale*, by André Gide; *Promenades Littéraires, Ve série*, by Remy de Gourmont; *Préférences*, by Paul Escoube (M. de F., 3 fr. 50 each); and *Figures d'Evocateurs*, by Victor-Emile Michelet (Figuière, 3 fr. 50): four different personalities, four different methods. M. Gide's reflections are the notes on his own art of letters suggested to him by the work of other writers, or rather they are an account of certain reactions on his artistic sensibility. He has no opinions; but he has an admirable literary sense, guided by sanity and insight. One can but assent to all he says of Villiers

---

[1] Jean-Marc Bernard, 'A ma prairie', in *Livre des bergeries et des jeux* of *Sub Tegmine Fagi*, *Oeuvres*, I (Paris, 1923), p. 61. The poem is dated July 1911.

de l'Isle Adam (one of M. Michelet's évocateurs), for instance, or of *vers libre* (p. 120), or of the Limits of Art, or of Influence in Literature, or of...but the whole book solicits one. M. Gide's passion is art: "J'attends toujours je ne sais quoi d'inconnu, nouvelles formes d'art et nouvelles pensées, et quand elles devraient venir de la planète Mars, nul Lemaître ne me persuadera qu'elles doivent m'être nuisibles ou me demeurer inconnues."[1] No lapidary formulas, then, but taste, touch (metaphors from our physiological life), and M. Gide's own culture – the first two formed by the other and at its service – are at play in this book. And, at the end, are some souvenirs of Oscar Wilde that are a masterpiece of narration. M. Gide's theme is art; M. Remy de Gourmont's, men and their ideas. He accepts nothing without investigation; and often his investigations lead him to a conclusion that is different from common opinion (as with the "Bonhomme," La Fontaine). He delights in little known literatures, old books, a mediaeval romance like that of the poet Guillaume de Machaut and his Peronne d'Armentières; he discusses Flaubert, de Vigny, the art of Stendhal, the "grandeur and decadence of Béranger," Balzac and Sainte-Beuve, Mallarmé, the Art of Gardens (according to the Abbé Délille) – anything, indeed, connected with literature and worthy of his notice, the only limits to his range, apparently, being those of time and printed matter. Every one of the twenty-two essays in this book is written with grace, easy knowledge, and perspicacity, and together they form a series of causeries that is both pleasurable and profitable to follow. But M. de Gourmont's reputation is a consecrated one. M. Paul Escoube's "Préférences" are Charles Guérin, Remy de Gourmont, Stéphane Mallarmé, Jules Laforgue, and Paul Verlaine. M. Michelet's "Evocateurs," are: Baudelaire ou le Divinateur douloureux, Alfred de Vigny ou le Désespérant, Barbey d'Aurevilly ou le Croyant, and Villiers de l'Isle Adam ou l'Initié. Here again two different methods, or, if you like, two other men. M. Escoube establishes his preferences on a solid documentation and a thorough knowledge of his texts. He follows the literary evolution of his subjects step by step, interpreting, throwing into relief significant phrases and passages, until the exposition is complete. Two of the essays in this book – those on Remy de Gourmont and Jules Laforgue – are exhaustive treatises, luminous, and written with perfect comprehension. M. Michelet, on the other hand, is concerned with the soul of his "Evocateurs," and its mystic and occult relationships with the soul latent in the universe. He seeks to distinguish their real life from their apparent life, and by this distinction to interpret their works. If M. Escoube is illuminating, it is the illumination of texts – light thrown on

---

[1] André Gide, 'Lettres à Angèle, VI', *Prétextes, suivi de nouveau prétextes* (Paris, 1953), p. 61.

the workings of the intelligence. If M. Michelet is illuminating, it is the inner illumination of the mystic that carries a torch into further darkness.

M. A. van Bever, in conjunction with the *Mercure de France*, has undertaken the publication of an *Anthologie de la Poésie Française des origines jusqu'à nos jours*, of which the first volume, *La Poésie Française du Moyen Age, XIe–XVe siècles*, complied by M. Charles Oulmont, has just appeared (*M. de F.*, 3.50). M. Van Bever (who with M. Paul Léautaud, is the editor of that super-excellent and model anthology, *Poètes d'Aujourd'hui*, which is the indispensable work of reference for the symbolist period) knows his subject well, and he justifies this new publication by the statement that such an anthology of French poetry does not exist. The *Recueil des Poètes Français* of Claude Barbin (1692), besides being rare, is necessarily incomplete; the *Annales Poétiques* of Imbert and Sautereau (1778–1788, 40 vols.), also rare, are not to be relied on; while *Les Poètes Français* of Eugène Crepet (1861) is more or less a monument to Romanticism. There are no other first hand anthologies, and the lack of them and of the texts they bring as illustrations has impoverished French criticism and permitted the continued life of false views and counterfeit opinions. This anthology will therefore fill a gap and fulfil a need. Movements have been redetermined: writers grouped; texts collated with the originals. The labour must have been enormous, for M. van Bever says that no sincere manifestation has been overlooked, no figure allowed to remain obscure without an interrogation of its claims and credentials; "Nous avons tout vu, tout lu, tout interrogé, avec cette passion persuasive qu'inspire la connaissance des choses belles et mystérieuses. . ." The plan of this first volume, and apparently of those that will succeed it, is much that of *Poètes d'Aujourd'hui*: a short, sufficient notice of each poet, sources, editions, and works of reference, followed by a selection from the poet's work, with explanatory notes or translation, where necessary. M. Oulmont's introduction is somewhat lugubrious.

[Flint concludes with an unusually long survey of the contents of recent French reviews and a brief acknowledgement of books received.]

VII. SEPTEMBER 1914

. . . I sit here watching the North Sea roll in on to a flat sandy beach. . ., wondering what will be left of the poetic clans of France after the war. At home, in a pigeon-hole of my desk, is the last chronicle I wrote about them, unsuitable now. My principal theme was sincerity in writing; and all the books I had had before me, by chance, gave point to it. There were Emile Verhaeren's *Les Blés Mouvants*, and, since the poems were written, hell has flooded the countryside that was its background, and hideous outrage has been wrought on its *dramatis personae* (Verhaeren is now in London, I am told); *Les Divertissements* of Remy de Gourmont, who is, I believe, in Normandy, *waiting for news; Parler*, by Pierre-Jean Jouve (with the colours, undoubtedly); *Le Dessous du Masque*, by François Porché (with the colours); *Les Oeuvres de Barnabooth*, by Valery Larbaud (with the colours; his weekly articles to the *New Weekly* stopped at the first outbreak); *Choix de Poésies*, by Charles Péguy: what is Péguy doing, I wonder, that fine figure of exhortation to France, one of those who were creating a Jeanne d'Arc that would have been the inspiration of the French race?* Well, then, out of the lassitude that followed 1870, out of symbolism, was gradually being created in France, I am convinced, a literature that went back to France's healthiest sources, and forward to France's greater honour. There was to be in it no trace of the empty magniloquence of romanticism, or of the dreamy emptiness that was the worst fault of symbolism; there was to be in it a sincerity that would stand no shams either of impression or expression. The men who were making that literature, or preparing the way for it, are in the firing line; and we can only guess what that means, and cannot know what the result will be. The war may wipe out – will wipe out, indeed – some of the best brains in France. For that reason, I stand on the cliff here at night and curse the land opposite I cannot see. For that reason I have wished for a conscription that would have severed ties and paid no heed to slight physical defects.

I have at home a book called *Histoire Contemporaine des Lettres Françaises*, a bulky volume by Florian-Parmentier, just published. It is an account of all the schools, an attempt at a conspectus of the whole literary activity of France to-day – or, rather, it was yesterday; to-day, we are in the melting-pot, and to-morrow, where will all the *isms* be? Of the group of writers centred round the *Mercure de France* some have gone to the war, others, the old brigade of the symbolists, are, like Remy de Gourmont, waiting for news. So, too, with *Vers et Prose* and *La Phalange*. Then there is the mixed group represented by *La Nouvelle Revue Française*: one can only speculate. All the different *Cahiers*, which had for their object the regeneration of France in some way or other, stop while France fights for regeneration in other fields. As for the *revues des jeunes*, the young men are elsewhere. How they will all issue from the melting pot, nobody can tell. Charles Louis Philippe, who thought that France had come to a culminating point of civilisation in Anatole France, used

---

* The answer to my question has come too soon. Lieutenant Charles Péguy has been killed in action by a German bullet. [Flint's note.]

to say, "*Maintenant il nous faut des barbares.*" The barbarians have come indeed; they will certainly destroy certain over-refinements, and, in so doing, they will have done harm as well as good to French literature. It will be good to have the last relics of symbolism swept away; but it will be an evil thing if the *fantaisiste* poets of whom I have been writing – Klingsor, Apollinaire, Salmon, Cros, Carco, Derème, Pellerin, Bernard, Toulet – should have all the *fantaisie* knocked out of them. There is a group of young writers who will probably find new sources of inspiration in the emotions of the war – if they come through: I mean Jules Romains, Georges Duhamel, Georges Chennevière, Charles Vildrac, René Arcos, Pierre-Jean Jouve, Luc Durtain. Romains has already written a play, in verse, *L'Armée dans la ville*, which deals with an army of occupation in conflict with the inhabitants of a conquered country, and a short story, *La Prise de Paris*, describing, in soldiers' slang, the effect of an army on a town in riot. Both are exceedingly good work. The other writers have all that interest in men as human beings which a great conflict will bring out and strengthen. The self-styled "paroxystes," too, Nicolas Beauduin and "les poètes de l'*Arthénice*," who have, while making a great noise about it, given us hitherto little more than frantic asseveration, will perhaps have their excessive verbalism pruned, and will find new matter for exaltation. As for H.-M. Barzun and the writers he has grouped round *Poème et Drame*, "L'Ere du Drame" has come with a vengeance, and it is to be hoped that someone among them will find genius enough to crystallise it. But one must not make too much of these groups. They are obvious, and present themselves; there are others which may ultimately prove of greater importance; and there are the single writers, of no group at all, who will be more important still. There are also the masters who are *waiting for news*; the war may leave some stranded; others will be borne up by it...

VIII. DECEMBER 1914

It is curious that at this moment should appear an English translation of a book by a German on a great Belgian poet who has sought refuge in England: *Emile Verhaeren*, by Stefan Zweig, translated by Jethro Bithell (Constable, 30p net); and it is difficult, in reading it, to rid one's mind of the obsession of the flaming horror that is now Belgium. Yet it is a contribution to pure letters and to the contemplation of modern life – before the cataclysm; there is not in it even any of the favourite affectations of the Teuton; I do not believe that the word "culture" occurs once with its Prussian significance; it is careful; it is exhaustive; it is reverent; it is enthusiastic; and, in its English form, it is much more interesting than the French, which is dull (of the German original I know nothing): so dullness comes and goes with the transmutations of language. And if Stefan Zweig were asked, I believe he would answer that M. Verhaeren alone is sufficient justification for Belgium's separate existence: and German has answered German; and the right bank of the Rhine is theirs – if they can keep it.

However, few Englishmen know of the guest they have, and it is to those of them to whom it imports that they should know that this book is addressed: that it is written by a German, all the better – a poetic justice. England, as usual, has paid little attention to Verhaeren's work: an essay or so by Edmund Gosse, *Les Aubes*, translated by Arthur Symons, a few poems rendered – and rended – by Alma Strettel in "Poems by Emile Verhaeren" (1899), the poems translated by Mr Bithell himself in "Contemporary Belgian Poetry," and one or two odd articles, including an excellent one by Mr M. T. H. Sadler in *Poetry and Drama* – I think that is all. And yet, as Stefan Zweig says: "In Verhaeren's work our age is mirrored. The new landscapes are in it; the sinister silhouettes of the great cities: the seething masses of a militant democracy; the subterranean shafts of mines; the last heavy shadows of silent, dying cloisters. All the intellectual forces of our time, our time's ideology, have here become a poem; the new social ideas, the struggle of industrialism with agrarianism, the vampire force which lures the rural population from the health-giving fields to the burning quarries of the great city, the tragic fate of emigrants, financial crises, the dazzling conquests of science, the syntheses of philosophy, the triumphs of engineering, the new colours of the impressionists."[1] Nor is that all. Verhaeren has written poems of an infinite tenderness, in *Les Heures Claires* and *Les Heures d'Après-midi* especially. But, to return to my point, the English contribution to the Verhaeren bibliography is almost negligible, and this translation is the first complete exposition in English of Verhaeren's work. May it be read.

I confess that there is a large mass of Verhaeren's work that interests me very little: that, in fact, I am attracted by spiritual and not by cerebral adventures. There is a little poem by Nietzsche, for instance, in *Ecce Homo* that is for me the quintessence of poetry and worth more than volumes. I have never been able to care for Verhaeren's pentalogy *Toute la Flandre*, because – I may be wrong – its inspiration seemed rhetorical, that is, cerebral, to me. Therefore, I opened with some trepidation M. Verhaeren's last book, *Les Blés Mouvants*, in which he has returned to Flanders. But I was soon reassured. The book, I think, is one of his best.

A large part of it is occupied by seven "dialogues rustiques," which

---

[1] Stefan Zweig, *Emile Verhaeren*, translated by Jethro Bithell (Boston and New York, 1914), p. 9.

are separated from one another by descriptive poems. No attempt is made in the dialogues to reproduce the language of the peasant interlocutors; but M. Verhaeren, who lived among them (Heaven knows where they are all scattered to now), sought to be faithful to their ways and habits of thought; and so we have the passionate courtship of a pair of young lovers, brutal but healthy, the lament of two ancients on the passing of the old order –

> Comment ne point se plaindre ou ne se fâcher pas
> Depuis que l'on a peur de se lasser les bras
> Et de s'user les poings et de ployer l'échine,
> Et que l'on fait venir quelque grêle machine
> Qu'active un feu mauvais et qui bat le froment,
> Et le seigle, et l'avoine, et l'orge, aveuglément?
> Ce n'est plus le travail, mais c'en est la risée,
> Et Dieu sait bien pourquoi la grange et la moisson
> Flambent parfois et font crier tout l'horizon
> Dès que s'envole au loin quelque cendre embrasée –[1]

the cunning of two thankofferers; the jealousy of a man for his wife; the attachment of an old peasant to the earth he has cultivated

> D'une poussée et d'une haleine,
> Il m'arrive au printemps d'aller au fond des plaines,
>   Jusqu'à mon champ des Trois Chemins.
> Tout y est calme et je n'entends que l'alouette.
> Alors, sans la choisir, je prends entre mes mains,
>   Qui prudemment l'émiettent,
>   Une motte de terre où l'orge doit lever.
> Et quand je vois le grain qui me semble couver [*sic*],
>   Dans ce morceau de sol humide,
> Et par toute la pluie et par tout le soleil
> Fendre d'un filet vert son ovale vermeil,
> Je me sens si ému que j'en deviens timide.
> Que c'est beau, sous le ciel, un menu grain de blé! –[2]

The gardener and the shepherd who claims the knowledge and powers of a sorcerer, – and I copy this picture –

> Pourtant la plaine la plus belle
>   M'est toujours celle
>   Que font
>   Les dos mouvants de mes moutons,
> Quand ils vaguent, de l'aube au soir, en peloton,
>   Sur les éteules
> Et que l'ombre géante et tranquille des meules
> Au coucher du soleil s'étend sur leurs toisons –[3]

[1] Emile Verhaeren, 'Dialogue rustique, 2', *Les Blés mouvants* (Paris, 1918), p. 38.
[2] 'Dialogue rustique 5', *Ibid.*, p. 74. The misprinted word should read *couvé*.
[3] 'Dialogue rustique 6', *Ibid.*, pp. 97–8.

and, lastly, two young farmers who have learned modern ways and the
advantages of towns –

> Le vieil esprit des champs
> Comme le chaume a fait son temps;
> Armez-vous de pensers fermes et téméraires,
>   Comme nos toits et nos auvents
>   Se sont vêtus contre le vent
>   D'une armure de tuiles claires;
>   Sinon passez et taisez-vous
> Et laissez croire à ceux qui déjà vous méprisent
> Que l'ombre et le soleil et la pluie et la brise
>   Ne sont plus faits pour vous.[1]

M. Verhaeren does not take sides; his only desire seems to have been
to give you a picture of his country as he saw it. The old hatred of the
"tentacular towns" appears to have gone, however. His voice is calm,
and it is richer by more intimate accents. His vision is clear and without
hallucination. But he is still a great poet, and I see no reason to change
the opinion I have before expressed: that he is the greatest European
poet living; and in this I am at one with Stefan Zweig. May I suggest
that the next Nobel prize be given to Verhaeren? In many ways the
award would be apt.

M. Remy de Gourmont's preface to his "Divertissements" (M. de F.,
3.50) is so much the best commentary on his poems that I wish I could
quote it wholly. But this one paragraph I will translate, because of its
general application. "In this collection," he says, "there are very few
purely verbal poems, which are governed by the pleasure of directing
the willing troop of words, whose obedience, it will be seen, discouraged
me as I became aware of their excessive docility. Perhaps, it will even
be found that, in the end, I conceived the poem under too scant a form;
but that may be permitted to the author of the *Livre des Litanies*, which,
by the way, was refused admittance to a collection that he wished to be
representative of the sentimental rather than of the artistic life. It is
doubtless a misfortune for the poet when he comes to perceive that there
is more poetry, maybe, in a look or in a touch of the hand than he
could create with the cleverest and most perilous of verbal constructions.
It is a misfortune because it coincides with the depopulation of his life,
at the very moment when the faculty of the miracles of writing is on the
point of escaping him also, and because this comes with an overwhelming
sentiment of dissolution, in which he is only capable of writing down
useless dreams or sad intentions. But as this is a misfortune which puts
an end to all poetry, it is to be hoped that no very visible traces of it will

[1] 'Dialogue rustique 7', *Ibid.*, pp. 113–14.

254

be found here."[1] I wonder whether it is necessary for me to comment on that analysis of a stage in the psychology of a poet. M. de Gourmont himself has escaped in other directions. There are also in the same pre- face – and I hope that this dwelling on M. de Gourmont's preface is no reflexion on his poems – a few sane words on the liberation from the so-called classical versification. He proves, in fact – but can M. de Gourmont ever be said to prove anything? – he shows, he offers this for our reflexion, that, in the sense that Racine's versification is called classical, there never was a classical versification. The number of syllables may have been there all right, but that number was fixed on a defunct pronunciation: hence...but need one insist? M. de Gourmont is here sweet and reasonable; he always is; it is comforting, when one thinks of the baseness and abasement of those who write for print, to say to oneself, Well, there is Remy de Gourmont, and...others as well, of course. What has struck me most about M. de Gourmont's poems is their crystalline ring. This, I think, has been brought about by his choice of words with the consonants *r, l, p, f, b, v, t* in them, and the vowel sounds *a, ê, é, i, in, eille, oi, eu* – not an exact enumeration maybe, but approximate enough. Another noticeable thing, too, is that M. de Gourmont always writes with full knowledge: you are aware that, for him, each concrete word he uses is evocatory of ideas and other images he has not expressed or called up; that, indeed, he shows you the iri- descent flower of a wide and deep-rooted growth. The pleasure from his verse, therefore, is one of divination and contemplation. The emo- tion expressed has never that daring and nakedness which catches one up – rapture, in a word; but the emotion is genuine. M. de Gourmont says, in his preface – again! – that he has been sincere when it pleased him to be so, and that sincerity, which is scarcely an explanation, is never an excuse. But I undertake to say that M. de Gourmont is always sincere to himself: sincerity is good writing; and good writing is the expression of a real intellectual and emotional process. M. de Gourmont has always been a good writer.

In 1912, when I was collecting books and information for the notes on modern French poetry that appeared in our *Poetry Review*, I wrote to M. François Porché, asking him if he would kindly send me copies of his works. He replied some months later (when my notes were in print), in a letter of quiet regret for his habitual nonchalance that stood in the

---

[1] Remy de Gourmont, 'Préface', *Divertissements* (Paris, 1914), pp. 13–14. Flint's translation is less than smooth in places: e.g., 'Peut-être même trouvera-t-on que j'ai fini par concevoir le poème sous une forme trop dépouillée, mais cela était peut-être permis à l'auteur du *Livre des Litanies*, d'ailleurs rejeté d'un recueil qu'il voulait réprésentatif d'une vie de sentiment plutôt encore que d'une vie d'art.'

way of his ever being widely known. But he sent me his three books; and they have stood on my shelves ever since as a reminder of their author's modest courtesy; I like to look at them. They are: *A chaque jour* (1907), *Au loin, peut-être* (1909), *Humus et Poussière* (1911), published by the *Mercure de France*. M. Porché has now added to them *Le Dessous du Masque* (N. R. F., 3.50). Now, I have been talking of sincerity in writing, and I can broaden the discussion: there is artistic sincerity and human sincerity; a writer may have one or the other or both, the one being expression, the other feeling, without stereotype or imitation. No writer of any importance has ever had one without the other; and both are equally important. M. Porché has both; he is more human than artistic; and that is not to his discredit. His last book is one of the most humanly interesting and poignant that has come into my hands of late years; it has been born of an immense need to be sincere with himself, a need that the tragedies of life have forced upon him. Here is the preliminary poem to *Le Dessous du Masque*:

> La clé tourne, un pas glisse, et la chambre s'éclaire.
> L'homme en rentrant promène un regard circulaire
> Sur les murs, et sourit comme s'il échangeait
> Un doux bonsoir furtif avec le moindre objet.
> Dès la porte, il se plaît à goûter dans l'accueil
> D'humbles choses parlant par leur simple présence
> Comme un repos des mots où tout est médisance.
> Puis, laissant un à un sur les bras du fauteuil
> Tomber les oripeaux dont son coeur se déguise,
> Il soupire et s'assied pour rêver à sa guise.
> Sa véritable vie est dans ce court moment,
> Car son plus grand souci, son éternel tourment
> Fut toujours de gagner sur les tracas du monde
> Ce luxe d'être seul dans une paix profonde.
> C'est alors, s'il écrit, qu'il met son âme à nu,
> Et qui le cherche ailleurs ne l'aura point connu.[1]

In this new volume M. Porché speaks for the most part in a form that is admirably suited to his confession:

Vers et prose ou ni l'un ni l'autre: une ambiguïté qui surprend l'oreille, née de dissonnances entre les deux modes, une oscillation entre deux aimants...

Oui, sans hypocrisie et sans fausse honte, le complet aveu des choses de la chair, la plus incurable tristesse...

La souffrance, mais belle et fière: un sourire navrant plutôt qu'une grimace...

Jusqu'au désespoir, jusqu'au goût de la mort...[2]

M. Porché must henceforward be reckoned among the number of those French poets whose work one looks and waits for.

---

[1] François Porché, *Le Dessous du Masque* (Paris, 1914), unnumbered p. [9].
[2] Porché, 'Larmes de la volupté, II', *Ibid.*, pp. 69–70.

I cannot drop the word "sincerity" even now, for M. P. J. Jouve's book, *Parler* (Crès, 2.50), furnishes an example of another kind of sincerity, or, more accurately, of the same sincerity under another form. M. Porché gives a direct rendering of his emotions; but M. Jouve translates his emotions by means of an *immediate* expression of his sensations. The word "immediate" here has its primary meaning. Moreover, M. Jouve's whole will is bent on preventing any stereotyped sensation from moving him. He endeavours to perceive, to *feel*, the world anew, and always to state his experiences in terms of his own personality. The consequence of this determination to let nothing pass through him in any traditional sequence is that he is often obscure and hermetic where you are sure that, had he only vouchsafed a little more guidance, he would have given full satisfaction. You seem to be on the point of a revelation that rarely comes. If it were not that you knew from his critical notes in *Les Bandeaux d'Or*, from his play, *Les Deux Forces*, and from some of the poems in *Présences*, and in this book, *Parler*, that he is intelligent and a poet, you might be tempted to put his book down. M. Remy de Gourmont has pointed out some time ago, in *Le Chemin de Velours*, that a wholly new form of expression must be obscure, or, in other words, that the stereotype is a medium. The difficulty of Mallarmé's later poems is partly due to their having been written entirely without *cliché*. Every man, unless he is a poet, speaks to his fellow in forms of speech that have been consecrated by ages. Ignore these forms and invent new, you become unintelligible. Invent new, and add them to the common store, you are doing the ordinary work of a poet. M. Jouve's obscurity, however, as I have indicated, is due to a cause that is prior to speech: it is due to his rejection of the *cliché* of sensation. The only barrier between us and him, therefore, is our habits of thought and feeling. Of course, it may often have happened that, in the familiarity and unfamiliarity of his own sensations and their translation, M. Jouve has forgotten to supply necessary links. Yet, despite all this, one would rather receive a book like *Parler* than a hundred volumes of perfectly clear, perfectly elegant, and perfectly tiresome verses. They merely bore you: M. Jouve's work is always curious and interesting.

Once upon a time, there was a publication in an extremely interesting form, *Les Cahiers du Centre* (foreign annual subscription 7 fr., M. Buriot, 16, Boulevard Chambonnet, a Moulins (Allier); also from Figuière). These *Cahiers* used to appear each month, except August and September; but two or more numbers were often published together. Each "fascicule" thus constituted was devoted wholly to one subject – something connected with the sociology, history, sciences, art or literature of the region, which I will not attempt to delimit, that was the special province of the review. The amalgamation of two or more numbers permitted of the publication of studies that were works in themselves. In 1913, for instance, appeared a book by Daniel Halévy (double number, February–March) on *La Jeunesse de Proudhon*, and one by Maurice Mignon (double number also, November–December) on *Jules Renard, L'Écrivain, L'Auteur dramatique, L'Apôtre*. Other numbers for the year were: (January) *Des Vieux*, by Pierre Débeyre, sketches of peasant life; (April) *Le Paysan Berrichon*, by Hugues Lapaire; (May–June) *Le Député en Blouse*, by Ernest Montusès, a life of Christophe Thivrier, formerly Socialist deputy for Montluçon; (July) *Les Parlers du Nivernais d'après les travaux de l'Abbé J.-M. Meunier*, by Paul Cornu, a study of the *speech* in different localities of the Centre. This "local" literature is conceived in no local spirit, and it is a pity that we have had no similar movement of decentralisation in England.

In these *Cahiers du Centre* (February–March, 1914) was published an important and interesting book of criticism, *Quelques Nouveaux Maîtres*, by Daniel Halévy, author of *La Jeunesse de Proudhon*, mentioned above, and of a *Vie de Frédéric Nietzsche*, one of the best biographies of Nietzsche extant. This book is important because it brings together four French writers whose work is peculiarly representative of their time: Romain Rolland, Suarès, Paul Claudel, and Charles Péguy. There are also constant references in it to Maurice Barrès and Charles Maurras. A most profitable study could be made of the work and influence of these six men, and of the regeneration of France, of which they are the sign-manual. But, as this cannot be done here, I will say a few words about Charles Péguy, who has died on a battlefield in France.

Péguy was an example of the idealist who stands up frankly, honestly and bravely to the world, and gives it his opinion: insincerity hated him; cowardice feared him; hypocrisy avoided him in vain. His first work, a drama, *Jeanne d'Arc*, was dedicated "A toutes celles et à tous ceux qui seront morts pour tâcher de porter remède au mal universel," and to this work of "remedying the universal evil" he devoted his life. I cannot follow M. Halévy through the fine essay in which he analyses M. Péguy's psychological evolution step by step, illuminating his analysis by apposite illustration from the work of his author, whom he knows thoroughly, and by his own original comments. Charles Péguy was a pamphleteer with an extraordinary prose style. A friend of mine, just back from a stay in Germany, came upon the selection from Péguy's prose works (published by Grasset), the first book in French he had seen since his departure. He read half a dozen lines, and then cried out, "Good heavens! I have forgotten my French!" And, indeed, he was to be excused, because Péguy's prose style proceeds by a most complicated series of movements towards its predestined end; the inversions, the repetitions and the convolutions are all organic, however, and when once you have become used to their play, it is possible that you may also become fascinated by it. It is the style of a man having so much to say, and wishing to say it with so much force and accuracy, that he cannot leave any part of his conception unaccounted for in words; its movement has been compared to that of the waves of the sea; each new wave is similar to the preceding wave, but it goes a little further. However, it is not the prose writer but the poet in Péguy of whom I wish to speak especially at the moment – the mystic and religious poet. His first work, I have said, was a drama, *Jeanne d'Arc.* Péguy was a great revolutionary Christian poet. The Church, representing the formal religion of the rich, for him was nothing. His religion had to recreate the old grandeur of the human race: the man, the father, the artisan, the soldier. But I am again trespassing too far; M. Halévy is there for those who would go further.

Péguy's principal poetical works are the *Jeanne d'Arc* (1897); *Le Mystère de la Charité de Jeanne d'Arc* (1910); *Le Porche du Mystère de la Deuxième Vertu* (1911); *Le Mystère des Saints Innocents, la Tapisserie de Sainte Geneviève et de Jeanne d'Arc* (1912); *La Tapisserie de Notre Dame, Eve* (1913). He had published just before the war a volume, *Morceaux Choisis des Oeuvres Poétiques*, 1912–1913 (Ollendorff. 6 fr.), containing all the important poems, except the *Mystères*.

The style of Péguy's verse, differing from the prose, is very simple. In poems like *Les Armes de Jésus*, for instance, it has the simplicity of a catalogue; but such a catalogue of vehemence and fire and faith that one feels that its author was the living and passionate inventory of the world – his world – of good and evil. There are eight hundred and seventy-three duodecasyllabic lines in this poem, and it is an enumeration of the arms of Jesus and Satan. Yet the verse has such an accent, the voice is so authentic, that you find yourself at the end of the poem with the conviction that this is your religion, that you subscribe to these things, that these, being symbols, stand for your innermost notions of right and wrong, and that the difference between Péguy's symbols and your plain statement is only the difference between his riches and your poverty. Moreover, if he does not move you, you are not in a state of grace; and one may truthfully say that the state of grace among those who read poetry and those who pretend to be poets is very rare. We are, there is no doubt about it, part of the *arms of Satan* for the best part of our time, and, for that reason, we may be loth to give our admiration to a man to whom these things are real. What I want chiefly to bring out here is this, that a poet like Charles Péguy is not to be measured by the standards of a literary coterie or fashion; his poetry is the spontaneous and overflowing expression of a strong and original personality:

and, however much I may admire the exquisite and perfect rendering of some momentary emotion, when I read lines like these:

> Les armes de Jésus c'est sa croix équarrie,
> Voilà son armement, voilà son armoirie,
> Voilà son armature et son armurerie;
>
> Les armes de Jésus c'est sa face maigre [*sic*],
> Et les pleurs et le sang dans sa barbe meurtrie,
> Et l'injure et l'outrage en sa propre patrie;
>
> Les armes de Jésus c'est la foule en furie
> Acclamant Barabbas et c'est la plaidoirie,
> Et c'est le tribunal et voilà son hoirie;
>
> Les armes de Jésus c'est cette barbarie,
> Et le décurion menant la décurie,
> Et le centurion menant la centurie;
>
> Les armes de Jésus c'est l'interrogatoire,
> Et les lanciers romains debout dans le prétoire,
> Et les dérisions fusant dans l'auditoire;
>
> Les armes de Jésus c'est cette pénurie,
> Et sa chair exposée à toute intempérie,
> Et les chiens dévorants et la meute ahurie:
>
> Les armes de Jésus c'est sa croix de par Dieu,
> C'est d'être un vagabond couchant sans feu ni lieu,
> Et les troix croix debout et la sienne au milieu;
>
> Les armes de Jésus c'est cette pillerie
> De son pauvre troupeau, c'est cette loterie
> De son pauvre trousseau qu'un soldat s'approprie;
>
> Les armes de Jésus c'est ce frêle roseau,
> Et le sang de son flanc coulant comme un ruisseau,
> Et le licteur antique et l'antique faisceau;
>
> Les armes de Jésus c'est cette raillerie
> Jusqu'au pied de la croix, c'est cette moquerie
> Jusqu'au pied de la mort et c'est le brusquerie
>
> Du bourreau, de la troupe et du gouvernement,
> C'est le froid du sépulcre et c'est l'enterrement,
> Les armes de Jésus c'est le désarmement...[1]

I shall not deny my respect. It is here that one's conceptions of the kind of poetry that one would like to write oneself give way before the abounding spirit of a man.

You will find much to please you in M. Valery Larbaud's multi-millionaire, A. O. Barnabooth (*A. O. Barnabooth: ses oeuvres complètes;*

---

[1] Charles Péguy, 'Les Armes de Jésus', *Morceaux choisis des oeuvres poétiques* (Paris, 1914), pp. 35–6. The form used in the collection is *maigrie*.

c'est à dire un conte, ses poésies et son journal intime, N. R. F., 3.50), who spends his money and abandons the vulgar displays of it – yachts, mansions, motor-cars, women – in the search for reality and peace, which he finds in the arms of the humblest of his feminine friends. But he has many curious spiritual and physical adventures before he reaches that happy point – all set down with fidelity, and, may I say, vividness in his *journal intime*. There is also a certain Comte Putouarey; and the pair go through Europe together, and Barnabooth sees and renders everything so well, probing his friend and himself all the while, that his *journal* has become for me a most attractive document. There is a kind of European consciousness in its pages. Barnabooth takes his sick soul into every country in his search for quietude, and his knowledge of each (or is it M. Larbaud's) is remarkable. But my business is not really with the *journal* or the alertly ironical *conte*, *Le Pauvre Chemisier*: it is – if they can be dissociated – with Barnabooth's *poésies*. Here, indeed, is a modern emotion:

> Prête-moi ton grand bruit, ta grande allure si douce,
> Ton glissement nocturne à travers l'Europe illuminée,
> O train de luxe! et l'angoissante musique
> Qui bruit le long de tes couloirs de cuir doré,
> Tandis que derrière les portes laquées, aux loquets de
>   cuivre lourd,
> Dorment les millionnaires.
> Je parcours en chantonnant tes couloirs
> Et je suis ta course vers Vienne et Budapesth,
> Mêlant ma voix à tes cent mille voix,
> O Harmonika-Zug![1]

Or this again:

> A Colombo ou à Nagasaki je lis les Baedekers
> De l'Espagne et du Portugal ou de l'Autriche-Hongrie;
> Et je contemple les plans de certaines villes de second rang,
> Et leur description succincte, je la médite.
> Les rues où j'ai habité sont marquées là,
> Les hôtels où j'allais dîner, et les petits théâtres.
> Ce sont des villes où ne vont jamais les touristes,
> Et les choses n'y changent de place pas plus
> Que les mots dans les pages d'un livre.[2]

Barnabooth is a poet. I could fill this chronicle with lines of his that have moved me. I could almost quote his poetical works entire. I am sorry that he has retired to South America, and will nevermore write about

---

[1] Valery Larbaud, 'Ode', *A. O. Barnabooth: ses oeuvres complètes* (Paris, 1948), p. 35.
[2] 'Europe, IV', *Ibid.*, p. 90.

London as it should be done. Perhaps M. Larbaud will one day find some more of his poems?

[In concluding notes Flint announces the suspension of *Poetry and Drama* and hence the interruption (actually, the conclusion) of his 'French Chronicle'.]

ALDINGTON ON DE GOURMONT

Richard Aldington took the occasion of the reissue of Remy de Gourmont's *Le Latin mystique* (an anthology, with commentary, of medieval Latin poetry, published in 1892) to discuss one of the French symbolist *cénacle* poets most influential in England. The de Gourmont book contains the studies which shaped the collection of symbolist poems, *Litanies de la Rose* (1892), which was so highly praised and so influential for Ezra Pound.[1] Aldington himself, according to some testimony, knew of de Gourmont as early as his university days in 1911; other evidence suggests that he was introduced to the French poet early in 1912, shortly after meeting F. S. Flint.[2] In any case, he went on to produce a considerable number of commentaries on the poet or translations from his work, including *Remy de Gourmont: A Modern Man of Letters* (Seattle, 1928), and the two-volume *Remy de Gourmont: Selections from All His Works* (Chicago, 1928). During Aldington's tenure as literary editor, *The Egoist* was particularly hospitable to de Gourmont's work, and the translations published there include 'Tradition and Other Things' (see pages 275–9), 'Lautréamont' (see pages 289–93), and the novel *The Horses of Diomedes*.

Aldington's interest in this volume by de Gourmont connects both with his attraction to Latin literature and with his concern with the varieties of rhythm and form which de Gourmont derived from his Latin studies and incorporated in his own influential poetry.[3] For Aldington, 'classicism' meant primarily attention to the technical achievements in Greek and Latin, rather than the reactionary philosophical speculations about the nature of man by which the *Action française* intrigued Englishmen like Hulme and Wyndham Lewis. This essay, with its lament for the reproach into which Greek, he said, had fallen in England and its scholarly appreciation of the Latin verse itself, illustrates the nature of Aldington and H.D.'s branch of English 'classicism' and suggests that this interest was reinforced and extended by de Gourmont's similar concerns. It also is the occasion of an early statement of de Gourmont's significance in England; he is for many of the *avant garde* British poets, Aldington notes, 'the most fascinating literary artist now living in France'.

REMY DE GOURMONT'S *LE LATIN MYSTIQUE**

RICHARD ALDINGTON

The work of M. Remy de Gourmont has been probably more written about in *The Egoist* than in any other English periodical. That is because many of the younger people who are enthusiastic about litera-

---

[1] See Pound, 'The Approach to Paris, II', *The New Age*, n.s. XIII, 20 (11 September 1913) 577–9. See pages 175–8. See also John J. Espey, *Ezra Pound's Mauberley: A Study in Composition* (Berkeley, 1955).

[2] Alec Randall in *Richard Aldington: An Intimate Portrait* (Carbondale, Illinois), 1965), p. 115. Aldington to Amy Lowell, 20 November 1917. The manuscript is in the Harvard University Library.

[3] Glenn S. Burne, *Remy de Gourmont: His Ideas and Influence in England and America* (Carbondale (Illinois), 1963), pp. 112–15.

* *The Egoist*, I, 6 (16 March 1914) 101–2. Approximately two-thirds of the entire essay is published here. The omitted portions chiefly include quotations of Latin poetry and technical commentary on the translations.

ture feel that M. de Gourmont is the most fascinating literary artist now living in France. Perhaps that is too much to say, but at the same time it is difficult to find any other writer in France whose work is as interesting and beautiful as that of M. de Gourmont.

Le Latin Mystique is not a new book; it was first published by the "Mercure de France" over twenty years ago, and until recently many people must have regretted that it was out of print. The present edition is in a form which better suits the contents of the book. It may be most delightful, as Lamb thought, to read Shakespeare in the cheapest and most used editions, but this resuscitated Latin poetry reads more gracefully in good type on fine paper. Le Latin Mystique is a book for poets, perhaps for the better kind of connoisseur, and for people who are curious about poetry not read in schools, universities, the British Academy, Soho restaurants, the provinces and the Cabaret. That last sentence should make it apparent that Le Latin Mystique is a book of great merit, of learning without undue selfconsciousness, of poetry without pale purple hysterics, of great beauty without singularity. It is true that a large portion of these traits result from the poetry which M. de Gourmont has quoted through his pages, but then he has practically re-discovered it and his choice seems admirable. I do not pause to enquire whether there be further gems of poetry lying undisturbed in the 222 volumes in-4 of Migne's Patrologie latine and in the 500 other works M. de Gourmont mentions; they may be taken as read; and quite a number of people will read Le Latin Mystique with pleasure and without question.

In another article elsewhere I have written at some length on the question of the language and interest of the period during which the mystic Latin was written. It will be enough to say here that there can be no doubt that Latin, as a vital language, did exist without a break right down to the Renaissance and even afterwards. This Latin is, of course, not the idiom of Virgil and Cicero; its source, as M. de Gourmont tells us, was the Vulgate, its subject was Christianity in all its curiously divergent phases, and the period of its use lasts roughly over a thousand years. It is interesting also to observe how, at certain periods, and in the poetry of certain men – Ausonious for example – the lion of Christian zeal has lain down in perfect amity with the lamb of classic culture. M. de Gourmont, who will be a perfect companion for Lucian on the other side of Styx, cannot forbear giving up half a page to displaying the somewhat uncommon breadth of mind of Ausonius, who wrote on one page:

> "Sancta salutiferi redeunt solemnia Christi
> Et devota pii celebrant jejunia mystae..."

and on the next, opposite:

> "Cum dubitat natura marem faceret ne puellam,
> Factus es, o pulcer, pene puella, puer."

But, in general, it may be laid down as an axiom that the writers who are quoted in Le Latin Mystique were as a class hostile to Greek and Roman religions and sincerely devoted to their own particular heresy or orthodoxy, as it happened to be at the time.

It would be both instructive and tedious to trace the growth of this literature from Commodien in the third century to Thomas à Kempis. It will be more feasible to select a few authors. One of the most interesting is Saint Bernard (1091–1153), abbot, father of the church, and in general one of the most cultured men of the 12th century. To readers of Villon the poem "de contemptu mundi" of St. Bernard is extremely important. Along with the "Pianto de la Chiesa reducta a mal stato" of Jacopone de Todi and (so I am told) "Las coplas di Manriquez," St. Bernard's poem suggested to Villon his renowned ballades of the Ladies and Lords of old time, and the other "à ce propos en vieil françois." M. de Gourmont, who uses practically the words I have used above, brings this derivation out very well by his quotations...

．　　．　　．　　．　　．　　．　　．

In another poem St. Bernard has given a Christian turn to one of the beautiful commonplaces of all literatures. He reverses the advice of Omar, Catullus and Ronsard, and says:

> "Nec modo laetaris, quia forsan cras morieris:
> Cur caro laetatur, quae vermis esca paratur?"

(Take no delight to-day; for to-morrow you may be dead. Why should that flesh rejoice which is made ready as nourishment for worms?)

Conclusum est contra – Bernadum!

The rhymed rule of St. Bernard, with its command to study, is held by some to have aided in the preservation of learning in Europe between the 12th and 15th centuries. It may be translated thus: "Every hour thou shalt chant hymns and prayers and thou shalt love to keep silence. Beyond this thou shalt take pleasure in orisons and in reading, that nurse of the cloister." Will not some charming millionaire endow a few modern monasteries, celibacy optional, and every man to deal in his own religious poetry? For the barbarous days draw near to us, and soon you will seek from Cornwall to Sutherlandshire and find no books save novels and scientific tracts; the word "Greek" is already a reproach, and literature is in the hands of the dull and degreed or the avaricious or the duped and degraded devotees of singularity.

．　　．　　．　　．　　．　　．　　．

It is quite a hopeless task to try and give any general idea of the scope of this book; it is in itself so compact and so interrelated that one would need to quote a quarter of the whole thing to make a complete essay. The fact is that the whole literature is practically unknown to us, we have nothing to compare it with, no standards, no previous judgments to upset. Naturally everyone knows of the "Dies irae" and the "Stabat mater" and the "Veni, creator," and so on, but who ever thought of criticising these poems as poetry, and not as part of a religious service? Who, before M. de Gourmont, had been curious to discover the authors of these hymns and the prose pieces and litanies of the Roman Catholic services, and who has ever discoursed upon them at once learnedly and unpedantically, with appreciation untouched by religious prejudice? Are good Catholics allowed to know that eight centuries passed after the hymns of St. Ambrose were written – hymns which are still sung at the "hours" – before the "Dies irae" received its final form from Jacopo da Celano? Is it orthodox to rake over the records of origins of the "Stabat mater" and the "Dies irae," to show how they grew from litanies and séquaires, and were works of art, not works of "divine" origin? Is it orthodox to rake over the records of the Church and to tell the world how much the priest was entitled to fine his parishioners for various proceedings, now known as "unnatural vices"? Does not M. de Gourmont tell us that one Elian was condemned as a heretic by the council of Nicea, merely because he declared that "The Word entered in at the Virgin's ear"? And does not M. de Gourmont tell us even worse heresies, without turning a hair? In the end we shall see Le Latin Mystique placed upon the Index as a book unfit for the perusal of the faithful. Exquisite irony! at least it will be appreciated by the book's author, for he has invented several quite new species of ironic pleasure.

NEW FRENCH POETRY IN 1914

The selection of poems by Guillaume Apollinaire and Max Jacob, high praise of work by Blaise Cendrars, and the comparison of Luc Durtain with the modern sculptor who had been called cubist and post-impressionist show Richard Aldington's attraction toward an important tendency in English poetry in 1914 – the adoption of the diction and concepts of non-representational modern art. Both Apollinaire and Jacob were associated with the cubist tendency in French poetry. The absence of punctuation which pleased Aldington in the Apollinaire poems is part of this tendency in France, and one of the quoted poems, 'Rotsoge' appeared as part of 'A travers d'Europe' in *Calligrammes* (1918), the highly experimental volume in which Apollinaire often abandoned stanza form altogether in favor of the use of words in pictorial as well as aural arrangement.[1] Cendrars, whose 'Journal' Aldington singled out for special praise, was having difficulty getting his work published even in experimental Paris. Indeed, the 1914 issue of *Les Soirées de Paris* in which Aldington had read it was one of the first anywhere in which the editors had consented to include Cendrars' work.[2] This issue of *The Egoist*, thus, directed the attention of experimental London poets toward French work which was to receive wide emulation in Paris only during the growth of dadaism and surrealism after the war.

Aldington's own work, however, did not show experiment with non-representational forms. Indeed, one may conclude that he felt his allegiance to imagism implied a rejection of precisely that kind of experiment, for he had commented in the preceding issue that imagism 'casts us away from the "cosmic" crowd and it equally bars us from the "abstract art" gang...'[3] Accordingly, this same selection also treats several figures whose technique was somewhat more congenial to later imagist preferences – the poets loosely grouped round the Abbey, unanimism, or Whitman. Both Durtain and Jouve were associates of *unanimiste* Jules Romains, and André Spire was technically not far distant. Here, like Flint, Aldington stressed the poets' ability to render a mood 'exactly and effectively'. Finally, he referred to *fantaisisme* and *paroxysme*, to compete the panoply of French movements most frequently noted by British poets. Although the essay is short and directed toward exhibiting lesser-known poets, it is an accurate suggestion of many of the French tendencies which proved important in England.

SOME RECENT FRENCH POEMS*

RICHARD ALDINGTON

The French continue to write poetry, to criticise it, and what is almost more astonishing, to read it, in spite of the apathy of the British public. I do not wish to be unjust to any unknown persons, but I believe I am right in saying that practically the only men in England who have sufficiently omnivorous habits to read *all* the modern French poetry published are Mr. F. S. Flint and Mr. John Gould Fletcher. Whenever

---

[1] Guillaume Apollinaire, 'A travers d'Europe', *Oeuvres poètiques* (Paris, 1956), p. 201. The other poem of Apollinaire, previously uncollected, appears as 'Inscription pour le tombeau du peintre Henri Rousseau douanier', *Ibid.*, p. 660.

[2] Kenneth Cornell, *The Post-Symbolist Period, op. cit.*, p. 153.

[3] Aldington, 'Modern Poetry and the Imagists', *The Egoist*, I, 11 (1 June 1914) 202.

* *The Egoist*, I, 12 (15 June 1914) 221–3.

I meet Mr. Flint I say to him, "Well, I've read the latest thing from Paris you told me about the other day," and he says, "My dear child, did I tell you to read *that* old-fashioned book? However, I'm afraid I can't stop now, because I have six new Fantaisiste authors, two volumes of Apollinaire and thirty-two other books by representatives of sixteen different schools to review by Saturday."

You see, there is a great deal of poetry written in Paris nowadays.

I am afraid I haven't Mr. Flint's amazing energy, so that the knowledge I have of these new poets is somewhat scrappy and is practically all derived from the reviews they are kind enough to send me. I wish they would send me more (French poets, please notice). It is thus impossible for me to pretend to write critically on the subject; the best I can do is to reproduce certain of the poems printed this year which have interested me.

At the head I set this extremely fine poem by M. Luc Durtain.

Tonneins

Arc-boutant pouce et index aux tempes,
Une énorme proximité de main:
La paume, pareille à une voûte
Semble molle comme un nuage,
Avec creux, pentes, reflets bleus et rouges.
– Au-dessus, trou: le ciel.
– Au-dessous, l'herbe.
– Et tout cela porté
Par mon poilu avant-bras, colonne
Qui plonge dans la terre universelle.

J'écarte un peu la main: comme elle change!
Un digital fantôme s'étire
Quintuple hors de cinq autres et mêmes doigts
Qui eux offrent
Ceci de sûr: qu'ils sont opaques.

Je l'écarte encore, et la pose dans l'herbe
Ma puissance de droite, très concrète,
Complète, simple.
Au-dessus, entre les épis,
D'une demi-lieue de toits la ville domine la Garonne.
Plus haut, l'abîme
Informé d'une grande profondeur.

Je me regarde des pieds au sternum et me vois
Démesuré, car je forme
Tout l'horizon antérieur du monde:
Rien que mon pantalon rayé de noir
Boit le fleuve entier.

Vais-je, debout,
La ville m'atteignant au flanc,

268

Marcher géant. . . puis me sentir soudain (c'est
  justice)
Diminué au premier regard d'homme?
Ou bien,
Ici, tel le nouveau-né vénérable,
Resterai-je noué par l'ombilic à un dieu?[1]

Luc Durtain
(From "Les Bandeaux d'Or," Jan., 1914.)

I had an argument about this poem with a sculptor whose work might be called Post-Impressionist and is always called Cubist and is really neither. Really I have no idea what M. Durtain labels himself, or if he labels himself at all. He is certainly "modern" – like my sculptor – but none of the usual words seem to fit. But at any rate he has made an original poem out of a commonplace incident of real life. M. Durtain's book "Kong Harald" was reviewed last December in the "Mercure de France." Beyond that I know nothing whatever about him.

M. Guy-Charles Cros is a Fantaisiste – I think I am right in saying that, though I don't remember where I read it. He published some poems in the February number of the "Mercure de France."

Une Tristesse de Canapé

Une tristesse de canapé
embrume élégamment mon âme.
– Je reprendrai un peu de thé
à la prière de la dame.

Mais, Dieu, pourquoi ces creux propos,
pourquoi ces caquetages rares?
On serait si bien au repos
parmi ces bleus coussins épars.

Et que veut-elle absolument
que je lui mente avec tendresse?
– Nous serons, tout à l'heure, amants
si le désir trop fort t'oppresse. . .
Mais tais-toi encore un moment.[2]

Sur Les Quais

Grise la rue
et les maisons;
la Seine roule
un flot de boue. . .

---

[1] Luc Durtain, 'Tonneins', *Perspectives* (Paris, 1924), pp. 40–1. The book publication of the poems shows frequent changes from the periodical version cited here.
[2] Guy-Charles Cros, 'Une Tristesse de Canapé', *Mercure de France*, Vol. cvii (February 1914) 468.

Que fais-je ici ?
Pourquoi, d'ailleurs,
vouloir changer ?
Ah, je serais
plus mal ailleurs !

Mieux vaut rentrer.

Les gens qui passent
sont-ils plus gais ?
Ils n'ont pas l'air
de s'amuser.
– Dis donc, et toi ?[1]

Guy-Charles Cros
(From "Mercure de France," Feb., 1914.)

There is indeed a pleasant "fantasy" in his poems. M. Cros has admirably filled the gap left in French literature by the retirement of M. Laurent Tailhard [*sic*]. M. Cros is the poet of irony. He is slightly the poet of ennuie. He is probably a great man.

From "Fantasy" to "Paroxysm" – truly a large bound – from gaiety and ironic carelessness to serious Whitmanisms on the subject of loco-motion, labour and the new century. M. Beauduin is not without power, and in France he has succeeded in attracting a great deal of attention. Personally I dislike the length of his poems. I hate reading more than sixty lines of poetry on one theme. That is why I relish M. Cros' little pieces.

L'Ame du Siècle Neuf

Tout le siècle immense se dresse
Rouge de travail et d'ivresse.
C'est l'aube d'une ère de feu
Où tout l'humain s'érige et pressent Dieu.

Lutte, lutte sans trêve,
Le rêve fou s'ajoute au rêve,
L'espoir naît des autres espoirs,
Et le monde qui veut monter et non dêchoir,
Hors du chaos et du difforme,
Violemment déjà dresse sa face énorme.

Quelque chose gronde et flamboie ;
Et tes murs, Ô Paris, s'ouvrent pour le passage
Des siècles de science et des siècles de joie
Des nouveaus âges. &c.[2]

Nicholas Beauduin
(From "La Vie des Lettres," April, 1914.)

M. Beauduin has succeeded in rendering something of his age – but has he done it "in terms of the age" ?

---

[1] Cros, 'Sur les Quais', *Ibid.*, pp. 467–8.
[2] Nicolas Beauduin, 'L'Ame du siècle nuef', *La Vie des Lettres et des arts* (April 1914) 60.

I have had some little difficulty in selecting from poems to represent M. André Spire, whose works are the adornment of the "Effort Libre." M. Spire is one of the most invigorating of the writers of young France. Here are two admirable little impressionistic pieces by him.

Ligurie

Bleu de Prusse,
Avec des moutons,
La mer fuit devant le vent
Sous les nimbus qui galopent.
Dans le clos, sous les orangers,
Les poules, en troupe, picorent;
Le chat joue dans les artichauts.
Le barbet entre, gentil, gentil.
Le chat se rase, les poules fuient;
La fillette pose sa pioche,
Jette des pierres, tape dans les mains,
Et gallope derrière le chien
Qui derrière les poules galope.[1]

Provence

Le chant du coq,
La grande respiration de la mer
Et le ciel plein d'étoiles.
Eh bien! chante, poète!
Tu joins les mains.
Tu pries!
Toi aussi!
Et qui donc?
Quel dieu, parmi les dieux?

Mais non, tu ne pries pas.
Tu admire. [*sic*] Tu pleures.[2]

André Spire
(From the "Effort Libre," May, 1914.)

I have looked unavailingly for a poem to represent M. Georges Duhamel, M. Charles Vildrac and M. Romains. There seem to be none – at least in the reviews I have – which are not either too long or not quite worthy of their authors. One of M. Romains' novels has just been translated into English; M. Duhamel and M. Vildrac are becoming slightly known in England. They will readily forgive my not quoting them, I am sure, so that I can give space to other lesser known poets.

M. P.-J. Jouve has a very interesting personality. He renders a mood exactly and effectively, as witness this quotation from

[1] André Spire, 'Ligurie', *Le Secret* (Paris, 1919), p. 47. The 1919 edition gives the reading *poulets* in line 6 and *ses mains* in line 11.
[2] Spire, 'Provence', *Ibid.*, p. 11. The last line should read *Tu admires, tu pleures.*

RICHARD ALDINGTON

Paix de Vivre

Des chaleurs gonflent. Paix.
Rien ne démentira la clarté d'être.
Rien ne fuira. Tout est donné
Et contenu dans la limpidité humaine.
Que trille un oiseau précis!
Qu'il soit midi!
Qu'un enfant courant
Me fasse trembler d'air!
Que les confins du ciel
Eclatent douloureux!

Il n'est plus d'anxieuse joie
Qui soit perdue dans le vent.
Il n'est plus de jeunes yeux
Qui soient dénudés d'amour.

Dans les glissements de la rue,
Dans les repos vieux des toits,
Dans la croissance de l'arbre,
Et jusqu'en ces visages perdus,
Se révèle en meme temps
Une grace sans paroles,
Premier message de Dieu
Qui ne voudra plus mourir![1]

P.-J. Jouve
(From "Les Bandeaux d'Or," June, 1913.)

It is a matter of regret to me that I have no copies of "Les Soirées de Paris" by me at the present moment. From what I can hear this review, edited by M. Guillaume Apollinaire, is one of the most up-to-date and interesting of the French journals. Happily one or two of the other revues quote from "Les Soirées de Paris." I can take this poem from the notes in the March number of "Le Gay Scavior."

La Tombe d'Henri Rousseau

Gentil Rousseau tu nous entends
Nous te saluons
Delaunay sa femme Monsieur Queval et moi
Laisse passer nos bagages en franchise à la porte du ciel
Nous t'apporterons des pinceaux, des couleurs, des toiles
Afin que tes loisirs sacrés dans la lumière réelle
Tu les consacres à peindre comme tu tiras mon portrait
En face des étoiles[2]

Guillaume Apollinaire
(From "Les Soirées de Paris"?)

---

[1] P.-J. Jouve, 'Paix de Vivre', *Les Bandeaux d'Or* (June 1913).‡
[2] Guillaume Apollinaire, 'La Tombe d'Henri Rousseau', *Oeuvres poètiques d'Apollinaire* (Paris, 1956), p. 660. The title in the collected edition is 'Inscription pour le tombeau du peintre Henri Rousseau douanier'. The last line, as printed there, reads *La face des étoiles*.

It will be observed that M. Apollinaire has decided to dispense with punctuation, except in certain places. The result is rather pleasing, as witness this poem quoted by the "Mercure de France."

Rotsoge

Pour M. Ch.

Ton visage écarlate ton biplan transformable en hydroplan
Ta maison ronde où il nage un hareng saur
Il me faut la clef des paupières
Hereusement [*sic*] que nous avons vu M. Panodo [*sic*]
Et nous sommes tranquilles de ce côté-là
Qu'est-ce que tu vois mon vieux M.D....
90 ou 324 un homme en l'air, un veau qui regarde à travers
le ventre de sa mère. &c.[1]

Guillaume Apollinaire
(From "Les Soirées de Paris," April 15, 1914.)

The same number of this revue contains a poem called "Journal" by M. Blaise Cendras [*sic*]. I wish there were space to quote this remarkable piece of writing as well as the poem of M. Max Jacob of which I give the last few lines.

Les souverains d'Angleterre
Se rendent au Rialto
Plus tard se félicitèrent
D'avoir vu entre deux trains
Le printemps à Aix-les-Bains.
Je préfère au Rialto
Mon logement rue Rataud,
je régale d'un air de danse
Sur la flûte ou sur l'alto,
Je le dis sans outre-cuidance,
Mes voisins des hôpitaux
Et les colliers de jais que sont les hirondelles.[2]

Max Jacob
(From "Les Soirées de Paris.")

I regret that the typographical resources of *The Egoist* do not permit me to include any of the simultaneous poems of M. Barzun, M. Voirol and M. Divoire. These works may be studied in their journal, "Poéme et Drame."

By way of conclusion I ask pardon of all those French poets whose works I have omitted to mention in this short anthology. If they will send me their revues I will try and repair the omissions in some future number.

---

[1] Apollinaire, 'Rotsoge', *Calligrammes* in *Oeuvres poètiques, op. cit.*, p. 201. The two words should read *Heureusement* and *Panado*.
[2] Max Jacob.‡

DE GOURMONT AND THE CONCEPT OF
TRADITION

This essay by Remy de Gourmont, translated by Richard Aldington, is an important part of the active dialogue about the proper relation of the poet to tradition, a critical controversy which received its most important expression in T. S. Eliot's 'Tradition and the Individual Talent' in 1919. The essay is the more significant because it is the product of the author of *Le Problème du Style* (1902), a book which shaped major critical statements by Pound, Eliot, John Middleton Murry and Richard Aldington. Moreover, this essay was written upon commission for publication in English translation in 1915,[1] when the discussion of this subject was just getting underway, and its impact was extended by the fact that it appeared in London and Chicago in the same month.[2]

De Gourmont sharply separated himself from the tendency of the era's 'classicists' to minimize the importance of artistic originality. 'Tradition', he declared, 'is a great power opposing the originality of writers.' But this declaration was an attack, not upon the writer's sense of the living nature of the past, but upon slavish imitation. He went on to affirm that 'tradition is a choice and not a fact', or, in other words, that the artist's idea of the tradition is an expression of his aesthetic sensibility. For de Gourmont, the tradition was as wide as Europe ('Shakespeare, Dante...Byron... Goethe...Schopenhauer...') and the Latin Middle Ages were as contemporary as Flaubert. The denial of tradition for him would have been the refusal (in the name of conformity) to reconsider the elements of literary tradition anew in each generation: 'The true tradition of the French mind is the liberty of the mind.' But only in that sense could one deny participation in the literary tradition: 'You are, then you are also a tradition.'

All of these statements became commonplaces of Anglo-American criticism. Even if one confines the comparison simply to de Gourmont's most distinguished follower, T. S. Eliot, one may observe an implicit or explicit reshaping of all of these dicta in the single essay, 'Tradition and the Individual Talent'. Although the essay in its demand for the 'continual extinction' of the artist's personality went far beyond de Gourmont's acknowledgement of literature as inevitably traditional, Eliot too included a denunciation of facile imitation: 'Yet if the only form of tradition, of handing down, consisted in following the ways of the immediate generation before us in a blind or timid adherence to its successes, "tradition" should positively be discouraged.'[3] He went on to affirm that the poet must form a conception of the tradition that expresses his aesthetic choices 'he can neither take the past as a lump...nor can he form himself wholly on one of two private admirations...')[4] and to insist that the tradition is as extensive as 'the mind of Europe' changing through the centuries.[5]

Eliot's tradition seems at the outset a more elitist concept than de Gourmont's, for Eliot maintained that the tradition could be grasped only by the laborious development of an 'historical sense'. But another concept which de Gourmont made accessible to English critics serves to relate the two definitions more closely – the idea of sensibility. 'At bottom everything in literature is useless except literary pleasure,

---

[1] Glenn S. Burne, *Remy de Gourmont: His Ideas and Influence in England and America* (Carbondale, (Illinois), 1963), p. 144. Burne discusses de Gourmont's influence on Eliot's criticism on pp. 141–8.

[2] René Taupin stresses the impact of this essay in 'The Example of Remy de Gourmont', *The Criterion*, x, 41 (July 1931) 623.

[3] T. S. Eliot, 'Tradition and the Individual Talent', *Selected Essays of T. S. Eliot*, new edition (New York, 1967), p. 4.

[4] *Ibid.*, p. 5.   [5] *Ibid.*, p. 6.

but literary pleasure depends upon the quality of sensibility', de Gourmont wrote. The phrase suggests another important thread of influence, for Eliot developed the idea of sensibility in his essays on the metaphysical poets at about the same time that he formulated his views on tradition. What is more, the attempt to extend the 'quality of sensibility' in de Gourmont's critical world seems much like the effort Eliot envisioned in developing one's 'historical sense' – a sense that 'compels a man to write...with a feeling that the whole of the literature of Europe from Homer...has a simultaneous existence and composes a simultaneous order'.[1]

The influence of de Gourmont began to spread with the notices given him by Flint and Pound in 1913, and this essay significantly advanced his dissemination as a critic. Articles on him became frequent in 1915, as he himself came to be regarded, in the words of Richard Aldington, as 'an example of the tradition of European culture'.[2] An outpouring of essays on him followed his death in 1915, and his influence remained high throughout the rest of the second decade.

TRADITION AND OTHER THINGS*

REMY DE GOURMONT TRANSLATED BY RICHARD ALDINGTON

We must not boast too much of tradition. It is no great merit to place our feet exactly in the tracks which indicate the road; it is a natural tendency. Though it is not very wrong to give way to this tendency, it is better to attempt a new path. Necessarily, it becomes confounded here and there with the old. We must resign ourselves, but without arrogance. The deed is less meritorious than unavoidable.

Tradition is a great power opposing the originality of writers. That is why the present so strangely resembles the immediate past, which again resembles the preceding past. This subjection, which is always very oppressive, even in epochs of apparent literary innovation, tends to become a real yoke when the fashion is obedience to tradition. Hence the literary eighteenth century, hence the literature of the First Empire.

There is the continuous tradition and there is the renewed tradition. They must not be confounded. The seventeenth century believed that it was renewing the bond with antiquity. The Romanticists believed that they had rediscovered the Middle Ages. These discontinued traditions are more fertile when the period which is renewed is distant and unknown.

It seems then that to-day would be a propitious moment for renewing the seventeenth century. It is an illusion. The seventeenth century, with its appearance of distance, is infinitely near us. It has served as a part of

---

[1] Eliot, 'Tradition and the Individual Talent', op. cit., p. 4.

[2] Richard Aldington, 'Remy de Gourmont', *The Little Review*, II, 3 (May 1915) 11.

* *The Egoist*, I, 14 (15 July 1914) 261–2. A slight variant of this translation appeared in *Poetry* in the same month.

our education. It is known even to those who have not frequented it. We still breathe its atmosphere. Everything derived from it would savour of imitation.

The seventeenth century is relative to the renaissance in the position that we are to romanticism; the seventeenth century does not continue the renaissance, there are erasures, changes in taste; it does take up the renaissance again, but unconsciously and thanklessly. Does it not seem to us that romanticism understood nothing of its own work? We have attempted to refashion it with an unconsciousness comparable to that of the seventeenth century. The works of George Sand and of Alexandre Dumas seem absurd to us; we deny their genius, but we refashion them. We are as incapable of refashioning the novels of Balzac and of Stendhal as the seventeenth century was of refashioning Montaigne and Rabelais.

You take literary tradition as far back as the seventeenth century. Why? Is it from ignorance of the past? Do you know that our great literary centuries were the twelfth and thirteenth, otherwise good judges would not give the "Vie de Saint Alexis" for a tragedy by Racine? Come now, your tradition savours too much of the fools who put it into your head.

I like the seventeenth century so much that its most furious admirers will never succeed in disgusting me with it. But if I had to pick out a unique book I should take it from the nineteenth century.

Tradition – I find it everywhere. All the past can be a part of tradition. Why this and not that? Why the laborious mysticism of Bossuet and not the spontaneous irony of Voltaire?

Tradition is a long chain with alternate rings of gold and lead. You do not accept the whole of tradition? Then tradition is a choice and not a fact. Considered as a fact tradition is merely a mass of contradictory tendencies.

As soon as we choose we commit an act of arbitrary criticism.

The true masters of tradition are those who, like Saint-Beuve, have despised nothing, have wished to understand everything.

Do you believe that anyone who goes back no further than Flaubert and Baudelaire can possess a good literary tradition? I know such men and women, and they astonish me with the delicacy of their taste.

Tradition is sometimes nothing more than a bibliography, sometimes a library. Brunetière was a bibliography; Saint Beuve a library.

"The best French writer of the seventeenth century is Hélisenne de Crenne," I was informed by a woman who possessed a somewhat feminist erudition, and who, beside that, was a bibliophile.

People who say to me, "You are in the tradition of Montaigne," amuse me, for I am no great reader of the "Essais" – a fact of which I am almost ashamed. The greater part of the discoveries of professors on the formation and tradition of minds is of this sort. The traditional man cannot see analogous tendencies in two minds without thinking the later comer is an imitator of the earlier. School habits.

My tradition is not only French; it is European. I cannot deny Shakespeare, Dante, and Byron, who taught me what poetry is; nor Goethe, who enchanted my reason; nor Schopenhauer, who began my philosophic education: I cannot deny Nietzche, who gave a principle for my repugnance to spiritualist morality; I cannot deny Swift and Cervantes. And yet the two first books which opened the world to my soul were Stendhal's "Amour" and Flaubert's "Madame Bovary," found in a cupboard of the house!

A curate who taught me Latin during the war, when the schools were shut, revealed Molière to me. I have always been grateful to curates on that account. The remainder of the classics was matter for lessons and impositions. I *read* them much later in life. Such is my tradition.

What most strikes me in the young men of to-day is their docility. They learn what is taught them. In my time a professor had no authority. We recognised in him a mission for preparing us for a degree.

In the second class I took my rhetoric (old style); in rhetoric, my philosophy; in philosophy, verses. I was a boarder.

My knowledge of French literature came slowly. I preferred foreigners at first. When I was thirty I still knew nothing of the seventeenth century, whose pulpit-smell pursued me down to the day when I handled the old editions.

This kink in my mind, this scorn of anything taught, has caused me to be behindhand in certain things, in advance in others.

I have only enjoyed that which does not teach. This plunged me into the Latin of the Middle Ages.

I have never put foot in the Sorbonne except to look at pictures – Puvis de Chavannes – and, the last time, the frescoes of Mlle. Dufau. It is apparent how much I have been impassioned by the discussions of the teaching at the Sorbonne.

When I see a hand painted on a wall indicating a direction I instinctively look the opposite way. In the street I always walk against the crowd; I go where nobody goes. The voice crying "follow the crowd" makes me afraid.

I have often fought against my natural tendencies, often praised a state which was quite inaccessible to me; and several of my books are merely protests against myself.

For a long time I have had no aggressive opinions on anything, but, with the débris of my old convictions, interior principles have been formed in me with which I judge even those matters on which I am silent.

They are neo-classic; that is to say that they wish to be classic immediately, without passing through a flattening mill! Ronsard has been three hundred and fifty years becoming a classic and the Chanson de Roland eight hundred years.

We are always tempted to imitate what we love, when we do not love enough. Push love as far as admiration; admiration discourages.

The true "classics" of the seventeenth century, the models for all men of taste, are to-day forgotten. They were Patru, Balzac, d'Ablancourt. Boileau in his day was a breaker of dishes.

The punishment of the tribe of professors is that it is eternally destined to despise La Fontaine alive and to venerate him dead. The great classic poet was first of all a kind of Ponchon, who entered life with his hat over one ear and with a girl on each arm. He has the reputation of a Théophile, but la Bruyère, at that time, still hesitated between Théophile and Malherbe.

The true tradition of the French mind is the liberty of the mind. To discuss all questions anew, to admit none save those which can be resolved *à priori*, only to admit the best reasons and to consider as the best those which contain a principle of independence. To remember that no tradition is worth the tradition of liberty. To be oneself, to disregard those who speak to one in the name of a dogma, but not to be one's own dupe, and not to wish to impose on others that liberty of which the constitution of their brains renders them incapable.

Preferences! A good word to use in a matter of literary taste or even philosophical. It contains no negation, no dogmatism.

Yet some negations are necessary; there must also be a little dogmatism. Deny bravely what your taste does not relish. Affirm valiantly what you like. You are, then you are also a tradition.

And you are more complex than you imagine. However religious you are, be certain you are also slightly Voltairian. However positive you think yourself, you contain in yourself so much mysticism that you would be terrified if you could see everything clearly. Your admiration is for the great classics, but if you were quite sincere you would admit that nothing has so taken you as the beautiful works of romanticism.

At bottom everything in literature is useless except literary pleasure, but literary pleasure depends upon the quality of sensibility. All discussions die against the wall of personal sensibility, which is flesh on the inside and on the outside is a wall of stone. There is a way to turn it about, but this you do not know.

We have put art above everything and it must remain there in spite of those who wish to replace it by opinions. I put *Candide* and *René* into my sack. Take away your Voltairian blague and Chateaubriand faith; they have nothing to do with me.

The French tradition is so vast, so contradictory, that it lends itself to all tastes. A famous poet once told me that his master was Dorat. Why not? I might have liked Dorat myself if I had known him.

How heavy is the burden of this literary tradition, which goes (let us not pass the fourteenth century) from Emile Deschamps to Verlaine, across Villon, Rabelais, Ronsard, Montaigne, Malherbe, Corneille, Bossuet, Voltaire, Rousseau, Chateaubriand, Hugo, Saint-Beuve, Flaubert, and so many others.

It is chaos, a bog in the forest. We can no longer see the sky. Cut them! Cut them!

They have taken beforehand all my words, all my phrases, all my ideas. Oh, these obligatory ancestors! They bind me. They suffocate me. Far from drawing tighter the bonds of tradition we should release the brains which it binds. Bend your branches, great tree,

Flecte ramos, arbor alta,

What we need is less models and more of the free light of life which you hide from us.

NICOLAS BEAUDUIN AND A FRENCH
CORRELATIVE TO FUTURISM

Nicolas Beauduin, the editor of *Les Rubriques nouvelles* (1908–12) and the author of seven volumes of verse between 1908 and 1913, emerged in 1911 as the proponent of a new movement in French poetry: *paroxysme*.[1] Although he was a minor poet, his advocacy of paroxysm attracted widespread attention and formed one of the major currents in immediately pre-war France.[2] The central organ for the movement was the journal *La Vie des lettres*, which began in March 1913. Aldington's preparation of this essay for *The Egoist* is an indication, not of personal admiration, but of the importance in contemporary poetic theory of the views Beauduin expressed. 'The truth of it is', Aldington wrote, 'that the paroxystes are trying to do the right thing in the wrong way, and as most other people are doing the wrong thing in the wrong way, we have a certain sympathy with the paroxystes'.[3]

In terms of the development of English poetic theory, the most interesting content of this essay is its restatement of a number of principles which formed important slogans of futurism. Beauduin espoused an art of 'perpetual dynamism' and 'creative violence' and he called 'movement...the life and the great criterion of poetry'. He attacked the 'antique' and the 'Pastists', exalted the airplane, the dreadnought, the dockyard, and 'giant cities in construction', and indicated a preference for the battle-field over 'lettered solitude'. All these ideas had formed a part of the early (1909–11) stages of futurism, and by 1914 the poets and artists of *Blast* were defining themselves by their broadside attack upon these slogans. But ostentatious attack concealed some fundamental sympathies, and as British artistic theorists dissociated themselves from slogans like those restated by Beauduin, they also worked out some concepts of non-representational art similar to those of the futurists. Some of these more sophisticated ideas also appeared in the Beauduin essay. One of the basic concerns of both art and poetry, for example, was the creation of forms that communicated the *simultaneous* interaction of facts, shapes, or images, instead of suggesting a chronological, logical, or sequential order. Or, as Beauduin put it: 'we can already salute the coming of a new conscience, that of the modern man who "lives" simultaneously and daily in himself all the multiple "facts" of the globe'. Beauduin, like Marinetti and Pound, also recognized the imaginative achievements of modern science, and urged the poet to adapt some of the formal conceptions of science to literature: 'Science does not clip the wings of imagination, but increases, doubles its power.'

In other important respects, Beauduin represented some of the most decisive concerns of the post-symbolist period as a whole, in both France and England. He urged a poetry which eschewed both the decadence, the 'vague dreaming' and the idiosyncratic sensation of an allegorical symbolism and 'the servile copying of reality'

---

[1] Tracing the paroxyst idea back to Verhaeren in the 1890s, Florian-Parmentier noted that there had been no paroxyst movement since that time, but concluded: 'Et tout récemment, M. Henry Maassen publiait en Belgique une brochure initulée *La Poésie Paroxyste* pour signaler l'apparition d'un nouveau disciple: M. Nicolas Beauduin.' *La Littérature et l'époque, op. cit.*, p. 32. The author indicates the date of composition as October–November 1911.

[2] Cf. the judgement of Kenneth Cornell: 'His talent was far inferior to his theme...[but he] was a real force in his time.' *The Post-Symbolist Period, op. cit.*, p. 131. Beauduin's *paroxysme* figured prominently in such contemporary accounts of French literature as Emile Henriot's *A Quoi rêvent les jeunes gens* (Paris, 1913) and Jean Muller and Gaston Picard's *Sur les tendances présentes de la littérature française* (Paris, 1913).

[3] Richard Aldington, 'In the Arena', *The Egoist*, I, 15 (1 August 1914) 288.

of the empirical movements. Rather, he sought a poetry which achieved a *rapprochement* between the two, an art which 'enables us to express in a direct lyricism all the idealism of daily reality'. In this, as in his call for intuitive vision, Beauduin showed the debt to Bergson ubiquitous in the period.

In his criticism Beauduin was often hostile to the *unanimistes*, but his own theories showed, if not debt, some markedly similar concerns. He hoped to find in poetry a way 'to feel our individual me become greater in collectivity', for example, and he called upon the poet to be a 'superior consciousness of the will and aspirations of his time'. His poetry was also marked by the cosmic, almost religious themes common to several movements, among them *unanimisme* and H. M. Barzun's *dramatisme*. 'We know one thing only – life, the motion of our whole being towards life'; Beauduin wrote, 'to its appeals we respond with enthusiasm, and that is the secret of our "paroxysm"...' To such a statement, Wyndham Lewis's 'Our Vortex' – written after the French publication of Beauduin's theories but before the English appearance of this essay – seems almost direct rebuttal: 'The Vorticist does not suck up to Life. He lets Life know its place in a Vorticist Universe!'[1] By 1914, essays from French theorists were part of such a vigorous and often deliberately tactless debate about how poetry should be written.

THE NEW POETRY OF FRANCE*

Nicolas Beauduin Translated by Richard Aldington

Recent literary epochs were above all critical, destructive, insipid with dilettantism.

Up till now poets have hardly done anything except lament over ruins. They translated the anguishes and the last convulsions of a world which is now dead. To-day is the turn of enthusiasm, of tumult, of the violence of working days, of all the gladness of sonorous dockyards and of giant cities in construction – these sing and are exalted within us.

This is the hour of virile creations, of joyous audacities; this is the era of fertile affirmations. All great epochs were epochs of faith. Ours in its turn rises up towards a weighty belief in human significance.[2] To the anarchistic destruction of all order succeeds a keen desire to reconstruct life on a new basis. Smiling or agonised doubt has nothing more to attract us. We take no pleasure in mocking dilettantism. We have made

---

[1] Wyndham Lewis, 'Our Vortex, II', *Blast*, 1 (20 June 1914) 148.

* *The Egoist*, I, 16 (15 August 1914) 313–16. Aldington here translates an essay which is an amalgamation and abridgment of several of Beauduin's significant statements of position. The most important sources are two: Beauduin's response to a questionnaire by Jean Muller and Gaston Picard, published in *Les Tendances présentes de la littérature française* (Paris, 1913), pp. 34–46; and his essay 'La Poésie de l'époque', *Mercure de France*, CVII (16 January 1914) 278–9. The central question asked by Muller and Picard was: 'Dans quelle mesure la littérature actuelle, dans son ensemble, continue-t-elle, à votre avis, ou transforme-t-elle les grands *courants* littéraires qui se sont partagé le XIXe siècle: romantisme, naturalisme, Parnasse et symbolisme; dans quelle mesure s'y oppose-t-elle? Croyez-vous, d'autre part, que la nouvelle génération littéraire apporte des formules originales?' (pp. xxxix–xl).

[2] These two paragraphs paraphrase 'La Poésie de l'époque', *Mercure de France*, CVII (16 January 1914) 286.

our choice, and the sceptic does not seem to us superior to the believer.

We know one thing only – life, the motion of our whole being towards life; to its appeals we respond with enthusiasm, and that is the secret of our "paroxysm," that rich state of the person, knowing that the more we mingle with life the more we shall participate in its fullness.

Human reality always attracts us, responds to our intimate sentiments, increases our interior activity.

The human! To render man more complete! That above all is the art which possesses all our sympathies. Scepticism, elegant dilettantism, detached analysis, pure reason, the superior smile, egotistic irony are deeply repugnant to us. To all these different unhuman attitudes we prefer all which understands, which sympathises, which co-operates.

"To art for art's sake, that social nonsense" – I said in the "Mercure de France" for January 16th last – "which is born of a transcendent scorn for active and productive humanity; to art for truth's sake, which is and could only be a utopia, generous like all utopias, and always deceptive, the present lyric generation opposes art for the sake of life, and not art for the sake of the art of life, for that seems to us to be still the attitude of the aesthete and of the dilettante. Thus our art for life's sake is in perfect conformity with contemporary anti-intellectual philosophy – which is equally a return to life – and the other advanced arts which by their dynamic aesthetic – that of movement – also seek a more profound and direct reconciliation with reality.

["]The new poets do not separate art from life. For them life is not on one side and art on the other. The two are interpenetrated. An art which cuts itself off from the life of its time is a dead art, without ties with reality. Literature should plunge its roots into life; a literature uprooted from its epoch has no reason for existence; it is without significance, without human value. It is merely the jest of dehumanised aesthetes[."][1]

For this reason we have not shrunk from the epithets of "Paroxystes," of "Dynamists," of "Poets of movement," first of all because people have imposed them on us, and, secondly, because these denominations are not incorrect.

And since they have thus baptised us, what would be the use of insisting on that instinctive disgust we feel for labels because they are always limiting and arbitrary, and representative of the spirit of a clique. For a clique is merely "a position, a point of view," the exploitation of a formula.

We have no formula. Against the old art-gatherings we oppose a

[1] These two paragraphs Beauduin quotes from 'La Poésie de l'époque', *op. cit.*, 278–9. Except where indicated, most other material down to footnote 1, p. 284, is an abridgment of the response to Muller and Picard, pp. 35–42.

living art which strives to be the specifically modern expression of "the frenzy, the passion, the violent contrasts of our seething abrupt epoch." It is a poetry far removed from the discursive classic and romantic, from symbolist allegory. It is a new art which, without remaining in symbolism or the servile copying of reality, enables us to express in a direct lyricism all the idealism of daily reality.

We have no theories, and we do not want them. That which binds us is a similar manner of approaching contemporary society and the art of our epoch.

We have no conformity, but a sort of vital atmosphere, a similar desire for expansion beyond the annihilating bourgeousie; a similar need to know everything, to feel everything, to understand everything, and to love more.

Without disdaining the literatures called antique, we think that the present is of a more vital reality; the great currents which shake the modern world move us more profoundly than the study of the cataclysms of the past.

Whether our age be good or bad we wish to live in it. We do not disdain it; if it is full of sordidness it has also a fierce grandeur; its epic power is formidable.

Some people say to us: "Are you classics?" We reply that we know nothing about it, but that we consider that up till now no classicism has been retrospective. A classicism of imitation is false classicism. As to the famous classical discipline it has become in our days, alas, merely academic. We are barbarians then? We do not think so. But we admit that we should prefer to be young men marching towards a grander to-morrow than to be the sheepish decadents and the last of the race of a declining literature. We are alive, and we will not resign ourselves to death, even when elegant and perfumed.

We desire no codification. Codification into rules, definite crystalisation, are a synonym for death. Art always grows, it is a processus, a perpetual dynamism. We do not find it only in libraries but in that which surrounds us, in palpitating multitudes, those immense reservoirs of joyous energies.

Paroxysme, dynamisme, inspiration, movement, are for us synonyms, which we claim and which we make ours. Poetry is revealed to us with the grandeur of religion, and it gives to life an absolute value. We wish to find in it the great current of spiritual illusion so long interrupted, to steep our hopes in a sort of many-sided joy, to lose the sentiment of our littleness by participating in a higher truth, to feel our individual me become greater in collectivity, to be that collectivity itself with its appetitions and its unsuspected thirst for religious communion.

It is a fact. The "lyric revealer" wants to live not only with the intensity of individual existence, to participate in the greatest life, to rise always higher in the reality of being, but also to live with the life of universal existence. He wants to integrate the universe, not to disappear in it, to be annihilated; he wants to be incarnated in nature, to dominate it, and to be its supreme manifestation.

It is like the coming of a new God; it is man, not finding God outside himself, deifying himself.

Who does not perceive the possibilities of such a conception? Who does not perceive in it a new phase of infinite aspiration, inalienable in man, who takes it to the point of desiring to exhaust in the "paroxyst" fullness of a moment of his existence all that eternal life in which he believed formerly.

It seems useless to me to insist further on the eminently religious aspect of modern inspiration.

Rich with such a fervour and such a power of life, our poetry is freed from the circle of personal sensation in which the earlier symbolists delighted. It attains the oecumenical, intuitive, divine, continuous life. It also draws near to the living nation, no longer separating "the idea of art and the idea of a certain function and destination," and outside the labyrinths of decadent obscurantism it plunges into modern light.

Thus, if our epoch is that of intuition and of clairvoyant delirium – not that of vague dreaming and of unformulated aspiration – it is above all that of action. And the new poets had grasped this thoroughly, those who to Byzantinism, to the narrow, to the fetal have preferred lucid realisations, rich with significance and human value.[1]

For my part, however great, however pure, however thirsting for the absolute an artist may be, when I do not find a man in him I reject him. If he does not co-operate with the life of his time I have no use for him. He does not seem a complete writer to me. He is cut off from acting humanity. He is a juggler with cold symbols instead of participating in the communion of the living.

I want the poet to have a passion for an ideal, for a living ideal. Human indifference tells me nothing of value – the sentimental folding upon oneself, that is all. I want to see the poet in the centre of the real world, a medium for the nation, a superior consciousness of the will and aspirations of his time.

To this end we encourage certain friendly critics, who believe in the all-creative and saving power of the Word, and not in filling the rôle of an amuser, of the playboy of letters, of one who charms the langour of idle hours, who juggles with rhymes for the delectation of the bourgeois, or who combines for himself and a few abstracters of quintessence

[1] All but one sentence of the preceding six paragraphs is taken from 'La Poésie de l'époque', *op. cit.*, 280–1.

harmonies, shades, a play of long and short syllables with no thought except to satisfy an intellectual egoism. This is the art of the dehumanised, of the aesthete, still professed by certain rare sophists of poetry. These are also the counsels of certain bourgeois critics who attempt to extinguish every personal song, every virile, passionate voice. They show by this fear they have of true, individual art, whose creative violence always harasses them.

As to us, everything that does not tremble, everything which does not show flight, movement (movement which is the life and the great criterion of poetry, movement, "the demon" which reveals whether the work is that of one inspired or of a patient aesthete) is merely death, jewellery, eunuch's distraction, Brummagum goods, false art. Doubtless these stillborn poems can give an impression of ability and of knowledge in their craft, but what I do [*sic*] care about this conventional or falsely original artifice if it contains no human value, has no wings, does not live!

To all these painted mummies we prefer the lyric creations of a suffering soul, which hopes and desires; we prefer even the brute's cry of love or the death-rattle of the dying beast.

Sincerity, the gift of every human being to the God he sings, such is the actual will of the poet. The sun of each day, the earth of the living, daily enthusiasm, that is what we cry to the laggards who shut themselves in a hot-house in order to cultivate artificially rare flowers with venomous scents, without noticing the temperature outside, without knowing whether the wind is blowing or if the weather is stormy.

More than ever the world is advancing. Then let the poets not be in the rear of the column but the leaders of the file, the men of good will. Even to lettered solitude let us prefer the violent tumult of battlefields, the great vibration of the awakened collective conscience; let us be deaf to the sceptics, let us overthrow the painted corpses.

Take care you don't become ridiculous, certain very clean little old men will say. They will say that to us from the threshold of their door. But let us not wait for them, they will never come with us. Their ideal is too old, and they sterilise what they touch. They do not give themselves up. They have no gift of their own. Their soul sleeps, a cold discoloured husk. Under their hands the gold of life is changed into dried leaves. They delight in established classifications, traditional definitions. A new art which declares itself, which displaces plastic mythologies, annoys them; so does the paroxyste aesthetic, the poetry of movement, modern dynamism. [The following nine sentences are an abridgement of 'La Poesie de l'époquet', *op. cit.*, 281.] They do not perceive the rapid evolution of poetry, as overwhelming as material evolution. Owing to marvellous scientific discoveries in a few years, our moral and intellectual [overturning: *bouleversement*] has been complete. And the revelation of a new man, the machine man, the multiplied man, the bird man, has appeared to us.

The rapidity of mechanical evolution has created in us a state of anxious frenzy, of incessant mobility, of hope ceaselessly renewed, of permanent enthusiasm which places us at the antipodes of the "place of repose," which the mechanic calls "stable equilibrium."

The rhythm of the world has been accelerated at the same time that life has become enriched with new splendours. Our mentality is transformed. And we can already salute the coming of a new conscience, that of the modern man who "lives" simultaneously and daily in himself all the multiple "facts" of the globe.

To-day humanity vibrates in each one of us. The old conceptions of the multiple, of time, and of space are modified in our minds. The field of vision and of thought has been immeasurably increased.

"To the renewal of action," writes Professor Esch, "to the exaltation of human energies, to this courageous affirmation of existence, to the glorification of all the aspects and enthusiasms of contemporary life, in a word, to the moral grandeur of our time, a new art must respond. The particular and novel physiognomy of our age, the pulsation of innumerable lives, inventions, conquests, heroisms, and above all the amazing scope of technical life, ought, little by little, to produce a new beauty; not the classic beauty which is a static beauty, that is to say, immobile and fixed in an eternal attitude, and not romantic beauty which consists in the delight of the eye and of the ear, or in the mysterious resonances in the depths of the soul, but a living, dynamic beauty, a beauty in movement.

The romantics said that industry killed poetry: "Shame on the memory of Newton," cried Keats. "Because he has destroyed the poetry of the rainbow by reducing it to a prism." And Ruskin said that a "rich country is an ugly country," and that "the smoke of the factory is a leprosy which devours monuments, dishonours towns, and soils landscapes."

Therefore modern poetry will be partly a poetry resulting from effort, from the gesticulations, cries, tumults of contemporary life, beauty in action, no more contemplative; a barbarous and brutal beauty, perhaps, over which passes violent tremblings, strange vertiges, like the shivering of motors and the pantings of chimneys, and which will be animated with the exasperated rhythm of modern life.

This lyricism will be powerfully instinctive; it will have more persuasive eloquence, more movement, and as they have already said, it will bring "a new pathos."

In short it marks the coming of a new beauty, free, active, dynamic, which is opposed to the old theories of aesthetics which abhorred "movement which displaces lines." What is the new poetry as we conceive it: A movement of life in direct relation with all the other movements of universal life. The old divorce of science and art ceases; art and science are not only united but mingled; modern mechanism which seems ugly to the eyes of poets occupied with the forms of the past and femininely gracious reveries is at last magnified in odes to modern powers, to a vaster life, and to the solidarity of human efforts.

Many laggards will protest. Many will deny that the aspects of the modern world contain the elements of poetry. They deny the grandeur and the tragedy of manufacturing cities, of the conflicts between capital and labour, of economic strife, of great financial enterprises which alarm the Stock Exchange, Wall Street and the Bourse de Paris. They consider unworthy of art those formidable engines of civilisation, the super-dreadnought, the submarine, the modern express, the 100 h.p. racing automobile, the aeroplane, the mechanism of a Creusot, etc.

If we all thought in that way poetry would have to abdicate entirely, and the only true poets of the age would be the savants and the inventors. But happily the poets of paroxysm and of modern dynamism do not hurl their anathemas at science; they know that science opens great horizons, bears us to new countries where unknown flowers grow. Science does not clip the wings of imagination, but increases, doubles its power. It is the auxiliary of poetry. The Pastists desire to enclose us in the system of Ptolemy, or to make us accept the doctrines of Epicurus. They forget that the Odyssey like the work of Lucretius and the Commedia Divina represent the sum of the knowledge of their times.

Does anyone think that these robust geniuses would have ignored the scientific discoveries and the marvellous inventions of to-day?

As to us, before the aeroplane, that dream become a reality, that miraculous flying matter which bears our hopes towards an inconceivable end, we say: "O marvellous Bird, you are more formidable and more fabulous, O son of science, than all the old griffins, pegasus and hippogriffs of the ancient poets. You pass by a hundred cubits all that the most lyrical imaginations could have dreamed. You pass before us full of strange dizziness, but you do not terrify us. We know what you are, whence you come, whither you go, O Bird, born from the daily fire of a century of miracles, to-morrow you will be out-of-date, you are only an antediluvian of the future, and as such we regard you."

This is a materialist poetry: so say the retrogrades, the lovers of emptiness, the atheists of a living world, the deniers of human intelligence.

Who does not perceive the ineptitude of such an affirmation!

Materialist poetry! Let it speed with outspread wings towards the discovery of scientific marvels! Let it set out towards the future in search of the cities of God! Let man liberate himself to attain oecumenic life, and live in the universal and the omnipresent!

Materialist poetry! Let her fly over the new world, bristling with shaking factories, and electric towns where the human races are gathered to seek a religious revelation!

As Gaston Sauvebois recently wrote, it is a human, living poetry, a lyrical revelation which must initiate us to the superior conscience of modern times. As to myself, I think it will give a rhythm to European thought, and replace France at the head of the living nations for the greater good of humanity.

This vision of the world which I have personally exalted in La Cité des Hommes, L'Homme Cosmogonique, La Beauté Vivant has been expressed by others, by Mercereau in Les Paroles devant la Vie, by Pierre Hamp in Hymnes et Psaumes, by Divoire, Lebesgue, Gossez, Parmentier, Le Roux, Apollinaire, Hertz and Martinet in some of their poems.

Poets, we have wished to sing the hymn of these new times, to hurl our winged strophes in opposition to pastoral ditties, to gracious elegies and other flowers of decadence.

In doing this we have had within us the profound feeling that we are preparing the future and "contributing, according to our power, to something greater than personal glory."

LAUTRÉAMONT, VIA DE GOURMONT AND ALDINGTON

It was precisely through the impact of essays such as this one that Lautréamont began his rise to prominence in the years just before the war and became such a major foundation of the surrealist movement in the years immediately after it. He himself died in 1870, having published the first 'Chant de Maldoror' in 1868 and the 'Poésies' in 1870. Left in printed sheets, to receive their first publication in 1879, were five other chants. All six appeared in a new edition in 1890,[1] and Lautréamont gained a select following among the decadents or symbolists, among them Remy de Gourmont, who included this essay on Lautréamont in *Le Livre des Masques* in 1896. Then, through such intermediaries, Lautréamont was handed on to the post-symbolist and post-war generations. *Le Livre des Masques* itself began to receive substantial English attention after Flint, Pound and Aldington began to write of de Gourmont, especially in 1913 and 1914. Then in 1915 Aldington made it his business to do something 'in a small way to maintain the tradition of the arts and of a Europe above nationalism' by translating 'essays, articles, and poems by Gourmont [who was in failing health] for English and American periodicals, and to send him on the money'.[2] This Aldington translation of the Lautréamont essay appeared in *The Egoist* in August 1915, only about a month before de Gourmont's death.

By this time Lautréamont had attracted the attention of Apollinaire, Max Jacob, and Valery Larbaud in France.[3] As these three writers emerged to greater prominence in the post-war years, so too did the nineteenth-century poet they had brought forth before the war. This greater attention to Lautréamont was matched to some extent in England and America, although by and large greater interest in him did not significantly precede the impact of the surrealist movement.

LAUTRÉAMONT

Remy de Gourmont Translated by Richard Aldington*

He was a young man of furious and unexpected originality, a diseased genius, and, frankly, a mad genius. Stupid people go mad, and there remains in their madness a stagnant or agitated stupidity; but in the madness of a man of genius there is often genius: the form of the intelligence has been altered, not its quality; the fruit has been crushed in falling, but it has kept all its perfume, all the taste of its hardly over-ripe pulp.

Such was the adventure of the prodigious, unknown Isidore Ducasse, decorated by himself with the romantic pseudonym of "Comte de Lautréamont." He was born at Montevideo in April, 1846, and died at the age of twenty-eight, having published the "Chants de Maldoror"

---

1 'A Note on Lautréamont', *Maldoror (Les Chants de Maldoror)*, trans. by Guy Wernham (n.p., c. 1943), pp. vii, ix.
2 Richard Aldington, *Life for Life's Sake* (New York, 1941), p. 172.
3 'A Note on Lautréamont', *op. cit.*, p. x.
* *The Egoist*, I, 16 (15 August 1914) 308–9. Aldington gives no source, though he indicates he is the authorized translator. The essay in fact is one section of Remy de Gourmont's *Le Livre des Masques*, first published in 1896 and reissued in a sixth edition in 1911.

and "Poésies," a collection of thoughts and critical notes, somewhat less exasperated, and here and there somewhat too wise. Nothing of his short life is known; he seems to have had no literary relationships, and the names of the numerous friends apostrophised in his dedications have remained occult.

The "Chants de Maldoror" are a long poem in prose, of which only the first six cantos were written. It is probable that even if Lautréamont had lived he would not have continued the poem. As you read the book you feel his consciousness going and going – and when it returns to him, a few months before death, he writes the "Poésies," where, among very curious passages, is revealed the state of mind of a dying man, repeating – while disfiguring them with fever – his earliest memories, which for this young man were the teachings of his professors!

That is another reason for the surprise of the "Chants." It was a magnificent stroke of genius, almost inexplicable. The book is unique and will remain so, and from now onwards it will always be found in the list of those works, which, to the exclusion of all classicism, form the small library and sole literature admissible to those whose badly-constructed minds refuse the more obvious joys of the commonplace and of the conventionally moral.

The value of the "Chants de Maldoror" is not the result of the exercise of pure imagination. Ferocious, demoniacal, disordered or exasperated with pride in mad visions, it terrifies rather than seduces. Even in the unconscious there are influences possible to determine: "O Night-Thoughts of Young," exclaims the author in his "Poésies," "how much sleep you have cost me!" Here and there he is influenced by certain English novelists still read in his day – Anne Radcliffe and Maturin (whom Balzac admired), Byron, and also the medical reports on cases of eroticism and the Bible. He had certainly read widely, and the one author he never mentions – Flaubert – must always have been close to his hand.

This value which I want to qualify is, I think, produced by the novelty and originality of the images and metaphors, by their abundance, their sequence logically arranged in a poem, such as in the magnificent description of a shipwreck. Here all the strophes (though no typographical arrangement shows it) finish thus: "The distressed ship fires warning cannon-shots; but it founders slowly...majestically."[1] In a similar way the litanies of the Ancient Sea: "Ancient Sea, your waters are bitter...I salute you, Ancient Sea. – Ancient Sea, O great celibate, when you pace the solemn solitudes of your cold kingdoms... I salute you, Ancient Sea."[2] Here are some more images: "Like an

[1] Isadore Ducasse, Comte de Lautréamont, 'Chant II', *Les Chants de Maldoror; Poésies* (Lausanne, 1946), p. 101.   [2] 'Chant I,' *Ibid.*, pp. 27–32.

invisible angle of chilly cranes, deeply meditating, which, in the winter, flies powerfully across the silence." "Polype with the silken gaze." To qualify men he has expressions which suggest Homer: "Thin-shouldered men – ugly-headed men – a lousy-haired man – a jasper-eyed man – red-wanded men." There are others: "He sinks down again in his fierce attitude and continues to watch, with a nervous trembling, the hunting of the man, and the great lips of the shadow, from which flow ceaselessly, like a stream, immense dark figures, which swarm in the dismal ether, hiding with the vast amplitude of their bats' wings all nature and the solitary legions of polypes, gloomy at the aspect of these deaf, inexpressible fulgurations."[1] (1868. Let no one imagine that these phrases were devised for one of Odilon Redon's prints.) But what a story, what a theme for a master of retrograde forms, of fear, of the amorphous rumblings of beings almost come to birth – and what a book it would be!

Here is a passage characteristic of Lautréamont's talent and of his diseased mentality: "The bloodsucker's brother (Maldoror) walked slowly in the forest...At last he cried: 'Man, when you meet a dead dog turned up against a lock-gate which prevents the stream carrying it away, do not, like others, pick up the worms from its swollen belly and consider them with amazement, do not bring out your knife to cut them up, and say to yourself that you also will be no more than that dog. What mystery are you seeking? Neither I nor the four swimming paws of the sea-bear of the Boreal Ocean have been able to solve the problem of life...What is that on the horizon and who dares to approach me so fearlessly with oblique tortured leaps! His gaze, though gentle, is profound. His enormous eyelids play in the wind and seem alive. He is unknown to me. As I watch his monstrous eyes my body trembles...There is an aureole of blinding light about him...How beautiful he is...You must be strong, for you have a more than human face, sad as the universe, beautiful as self-slaughter...What!...It is you, toad!...fat toad!...unhappy toad!...Pardon me!...Why have you come to this world of the accursed? What have you done with your fetid viscous spots that you seem so sweet? I saw you when you came down from above! Poor toad! I was thinking then of infinity and of my own weakness...Since you appeared to me monarch of the lakes and swamps, covered with a glory which belongs only to God, you have partly consoled me, but my staggering reason is engulfed by such grandeur...Fold your white wings and cease to look up with those disquieting eyelids...!' "[2] The toad sits down on his hind legs (which

---

[1] 'Chant II', *Ibid.*, pp. 110–11. Aldington's translation is so bowdlerized that it bears little relationship to the original.

[2] 'Chant I', *Ibid.*, pp. 48–9.

resemble those of a man), and the slugs, the wood-lice, and the snails flee away at the sight of their mortal enemy; he takes up the parable in these terms: "Maldoror, listen to me. Notice well my face; calm as a mirror...I am only a simple dweller in the reeds, it is true, but, thanks to your contact, only taking what is good in you, my reason has grown and I can speak to you...I should prefer to have fixed eyelids, my body lacking arms and legs, to have murdered a man who was not you!... Because I hate you...Farewell! Do not hope ever to see the toad again in your wanderings. You have been the cause of my death. I depart for eternity to beg for your pardon."[1]

The physicians of the mad, if they had studied this book, would have placed the author among the persecuted ambitious: he sees in the world only himself and God – and God distresses him. But at the same time it might be asked whether Lautréamont were not a superior kind of ironist,[2] a man engaged by a preconceived scorn for mankind to feign a madness whose incoherence is wiser and more beautiful than reason. How many honest, pondered pages of good clean literature I would give for this one, for these shovelfuls of words and phrases beneath which he seems to have wanted to bury reason itself. They are taken from the "Poésies":

"Perturbations, anxieties, depravities, death, exceptions to moral or physical order, the spirit of negation, brutishness, hallucinations served by the will, torments, destruction, defeats, tears, insatiabilities, servitudes, hollow imaginations, novels, that which is unexpected, that which should not be done, the chimerical singularities of the mysterious vulture which watches the corpse of some dead illusion, the shelly obscurities of the bug, the terrible monomania of pride, the innoculation of profound stupor, funeral prayers, envies, treasons, tyrannies, impieties, irritations, acrimonies, aggressive petulant insults, insanity, spleen, reasoned terrors, strange inquietudes – which the reader would prefer not to undergo – grimaces, narrowness, the bleeding ropes with which we bring logic to bay, exaggerations, absence of sincerity, saws, platitudes, the sombre, the lugubrious, child-births worse than murder, passions, the clan of novelists of the court of assises, tragedies, odes, melodramas, extremes presented in perpetuity, reason hissed with impunity, the smell of damp chickens, longings, frogs, polypes, sea-fish, the desert simoon, all that is sonambulous, squint-eyed, nocturnal, sleep-bringing, noctambulous, viscous, seal-speaking, equivocating, consumptive, spasmodic, aphrodisiac, anaemic, one-eyed, hermaphro-

---

[1] 'Chant I', *Ibid.*, pp. 50–1. Aldington's translation is not altogether accurate.

[2] Here is an obvious example of irony: "You, young man, must not despair, for you have a friend in the vampire, in spite of your contrary opinion. If you count the parasite which causes the itch you will have two friends." [Lautréamont's note.]

dite, bastard, albino, paiderast, aquarium phenomenon and bearded woman, hours glutted with taciturn discouragement, demoralising syllogisms, filth, that which does not reflect like a child, desolation – that intellectual manchineel-tree – perfumed boils, the thighs of camelias, the culpability of a writer who rolls on the edge of nothingness and despises himself with gleeful cries, remorse, hypocrisies, vague perspectives which grind you in their imperceptible machinery, serious spitting on sacred axioms, vermin and their insinuating ticklings, prefaces mad as those of "Cromwell," of "Mademoiselle de Maupin." and of Dumas *fils*, senilities, impotencies, blasphemies, asphyxiations, suffocations, rages – before these foul charnel-houses, which I blush to name, it is time to react against that which sovereignly shocks and bends us."[1]

Maldoror (or Lautréamont) seems to have judged himself by making the enigmatic toad apostrophise him thus: "Your mind is so diseased that you do not realise it, and you believe that you are quite sane every time your mouth utters words which are senseless though full of an infernal grandeur."[2]

[1] Lautréamont, 'Poésies I', in *Les Chants de Maldoror; Poésies, op. cit.*, pp. 272–3.
[2] 'Chant I', *Ibid.*, p. 50.

ALDINGTON ON A FRENCH SATIRIST: TAILHADE

Aldington's attention to Laurent Tailhade undoubtedly reflects his interest in another writer who drew inspiration from classical literature, but it also may well owe something to suggestions both from Pound and from Remy de Gourmont. De Gourmont devoted a brief section of *Le Livre des Masques* (1896) to Tailhade and Pound directed a substantial part of an essay in his series 'The Approach to Paris' to a discussion of him. (Flint, in contrast, paid the French satirist little attention.) Two of Aldington's quoted selections correspond to passages cited by de Gourmont and Pound. Unlike Pound, Aldington did not carry his interest in Tailhade's satire into his own poetry; none of Aldington's verses of the pre-war and war years represent the sarcastic onslaught that characterized some work by both Pound and Tailhade.

This essay thus is important chiefly for its contribution to an English literary milieu hospitable to the anti-sentimental, ironic, and intellectual attitudes which were generally associated with a support for classicism. Further, one of Tailhade's basic themes, a scorn for the bourgeois, was certainly shared by Aldington and indeed formed a *sine qua non* for much of the English poetry of the second and third decades.

LAURENT TAILHADE*

RICHARD ALDINGTON

There are reasons for presuming that the poetry of M. Laurent Tailhade will not be widely read in England; he is a satirist; his work is not vast in bulk; and his French is not easy.

The English nation is too gentlemanly to admire satire; it is also too prosperous. *Punch* entirely reflects the national taste in this respect, and we are all unwilling to welcome anything more bitter, more disdainful or more obscene. The three qualities of bitterness, disdain and obscenity are essential to satiric writing – bitterness, which is a hatred of stupidity; disdain, which denounces its hatreds; obscenity, which satire uses to vilify its victims, to revolt us from meanness. On the whole the English do not like such writing, and fail to observe its value. Schools may admit the works of Aristophanes and Juvenal – with omissions – scholars dig into Petronius and Filelfo, poets admire Rabelais, but the English suspicion of satire prevents its proper appreciation. We may commend the mild scoldings of Swift and Pope, but satire in its real sense is entirely left to the more emotionalized Latins.

The power of M. Laurent Tailhade is his Latin quality. He may elect Aristophanes as his master – his great book is called "Poèmes Aristophanesques" – but his true kin is Catullus and Martial, the fierce Latin epigrammatists, whose works lack neither bitterness, disdain, nor obscenity. Rabelais is the true follower of Aristophanes. Aristophanes is diffuse, turgid, Cyclopean; and so is Rabelais. Catullus and Martial are concentrated, clear, orderly; and so is M. Laurent Tailhade.

* *The Egoist*, II, 10 (1 October 1915) 159–61.

He delights in formal accented verse, in artificial metrical constructions, like the ballade and the sonnet. His language, like that of Villon, is allusive and topical, but is used with Villon's sparseness and clarity. Perhaps Villon and Verlaine of all French writers have influenced him most. For them there was no playing with hatreds or loves; they are not of those "who were neither rebels nor yet of God's side, but for themselves alone"; they saw things clearly and made their choice – erroneously perhaps – but made it, and M. Tailhade is with them in this. He knows his likes and his dislikes perfectly well; he is not in the least afraid to voice his hatreds, and his speech is violent and direct. He calls a fool a fool, and if metrical exigencies permit he adds an opprobrious adjective.

This forbidding prelude is intended as some sort of a preparation for the "Poèmes Aristophanesques," and not as a warning against them. It also means that I regard M. Tailhade's "Poèmes Aristophanesques" as by far the most valuable part of his work. The "Poèmes Elegiques," beautiful as some of them are, I omit as not of vital interest to English readers. The latter poems are valuable to those deeply interested in the Symboliste movement; but it was the "Poèmes Aristophanesques" – and especially that section entitled "Au Pays du Mufle" – which inspired a great living French-man to write that M. Tailhade is one of the truest glories of contemporary French literature. Naturally it is not easy to present such an author adequately and agreeably, the more so since the difficulty of the French necessitates a close study on the part of the foreigner.

The "Poèmes Aristophanesques" are divided into several sections, with characteristic titles, like "In the Land of the Mugs (Mufle)," "Eighteen Familiar Ballades to Exasperate the Mugs," "Certain Variations to Displease Divers Folk." "Le Mufle," "the Mugs", the bourgeois, are M. Tailhade's chief butt, though he uses literary and political satire with the same freedom. In his "Ballade Prèmonitoire," set at the head of his book, he invokes his quatorzaines and his ballade, saying,

> Vous éffarez le Mufle ìvre de *cant*;
> Ce que j'écris n'est pas pour ces charognes.[1]

The English slang word "cant" will explain best to English readers the nature of the qualities which most arouse M. Tailhade's wrath.

Nearly every one of the poems in "Au Pays de Mufle" is a *chef-d'oeuvre* of irony and scorn, sometimes frivolous, sometimes merely contemptuous, but always effective. Take the first:

[1] Laurent Tailhade, 'Ballade prèmonitoire', *Poèmes Aristophanesques* (Paris, 1904), p. 5. The quotation is a variant from 'Vous effarez les snobs ivres de cant'.

Si tu veux, prenons un fiacre
Vert comme un chant de hautbois.
Nous ferons le simulacre
Des gens urf ("bloods") qui vont au Bois.

Les taillis sont pleins de sources
Fraîches sous les parasols;
Viels! nous risquerons aux courses
Quelques pièces de cent sols (sous).

Allons-nous-en! L'Ombre est douce,
Le ciel est bleu; sur la mousse
Polyte (the "johnnies") mâche du veau. &c.[1]

Apart from the admirable fooling of the poem by itself, it is a most amusing parody of Victor Hugo's "Un peu de Musique":

Si tu veux, faisons un rêve.
Montons sur deux palefrois;
Tu m'emmènes, je t'enlève.
L'oiseau chante dans les bois. &c.[2]

After Hugo's pompous romanticism this *blague* of Tailhade's is extraordinarily ludicrous. And even Gautier is not spared. We all can remember "Les Arthurs qui vont au bois" in the poem about the obelisk. "Si tu veux, prenons un fiacre" – I suppose this would be called a "quartier" song; at any rate, it has most of the impudence and gaiety which are considered the exclusive possession of the "students."

You have seen M. Tailhade satirizing the *gens urf* by imitating them; in "Vendredi-Saint" we have an ironic picture of the stupid, and the hypocritical religious:

Trop de merluche et des lentilles copieuses –
Seule réfection tolérée aux croyants –
Enjolivent de certains rots édifiants
La constipation des personnes pleuses.[3] [*sic*]

And so on – the hooded nuns getting into the omnibuses, the mournful air of the shops, the fat curates and the nasty little boys going to Sunday School, and – last irony of all – before these people who do not detect its irony a man is putting up an enormous poster:

Concert spirituel à Tivoli Vaux-Hall.[4]

Thousands of pleasant people in Paris have endured the horrors of "Vendredi-Saint," and probably thousands have rebelled, but M.

---

[1] 'Si tu veux, prenons un fiacre...', *Ibid.*, p. 11.

[2] Victor Hugo, 'un peu de Musique', *La Légende des siècles*, in *Oeuvres poétiques complètes* (Paris, 1961), p. 563.

[3] 'Vendredi-Saint', *Ibid.*, p. 12. The misprinted word is *pieuses*. Pound also quotes these lines in his essay on Tailhade in the series 'The Approach to Paris, v', *The New Age*, n.s. XIII, 23 (2 October 1913) 662.   [4] *Ibid.*

Laurent Tailhade was needed to fix the mood for ever in fourteen contemptuous lines.

A superficial glance at these poems may send a reader away faintly annoyed with their writer, but the closer one studies them the more apparent are M. Tailhade's satiric ability and Latin concentration of disdain, his fine injustice. "Pécuchet tient la mappemonde," says he somewhere, and privately determines that even if Pécuchet does keep the map of the world he shall be shown up as the ridiculous, canting, pretentious person that he is. This bourgeois age – how some of us writhe beneath its vulgarity, daily afflicted with its nauseous pretences, its "popular preachers," its "books for the billion," its degrading morale. We live in a time – perhaps not so much worse than other times, but with everything on so much larger a scale – when nothing is desired except the stupid sensualities which masquerade as "improvements" or "comfort." And more than the age of Tiberius, more than that of François I, the age needs to be told unpolitely and unpleasantly of its loathsome qualities. M. Tailhade has begun this task, which others must finish; he has mocked in fierce or obscene phrases the character of the omnipotent bourgeois; he has told him emphatically just how small an animal he is. And who will wonder that the omnipotent bourgeois does not praise the works of M. Tailhade, will not, probably, open to him the door above which is written, "Aux grands hommes la Patrie réconnaisante," and tosses him aside with a "what-a-wicked-man" sort of expression.

M. Tailhade is not sectarian in his denunciations. In "Vendredi-Saint" he derides the cant of the church; in "Sur Champ d'Or" he is just as wroth – not wroth, infinitely amused – with the ridiculous atheism of the small shopkeeper and his class.

> Certes, Monsieur Benoist approuve les gens qui
> Ont lu Voltaire et sont aux Jésuites adverses.
> Il pense. Il est idoine (apt) aux longues controverses.
> Il déprise le moine et le thériaki.
> Même il fut orateur d'une Loge Ecossaise.[1]

Il Pense; there is a long journey among books to travel before finding another example of such swift irony. And the erudite Monsieur Benoist, who "thinks" so originally, actually permits – he is so broad-minded – his daughter to communicate! But then "sa legitime croit en Dieu," and there is wine at eighty centimes the litre to be drunk in commemoration of this august event.

> Or Benoist, qui s'émèche et tourne au calotin,
> Montre quelque plaisir d'avoir vu, ce matin,
> L'hymen du Fils Unique et de sa "demoiselle."[2]

[1] 'Sur Champ d'or', *Ibid.*, p. 22. Punctuation varies slightly.   [2] *Ibid.*

This poem is quoted in "Le Livre des Masques," with the remark that it deserves to be learnt by heart; it has a deadly raillery for the uneducated "atheist" who has not the courage of his doubt when it comes to the test of traversing conventions.

In every one of the poems in "Au Pays de Mufle" some *sottise*, some "cant" is pilloried, or some ignorant pretension exposed. Though the characters are essentially particular and metropolitan, the types to which they belong are as universal as the bourgeois "civilization" which touches every part of the world.

M. Tailhade's political and literary satire is somewhat more special. The poems on L'Affaire Dreyfus are a little confusing to anyone but a Frenchman, but the section of the poems called "A travers les Groins," contains some verses which are amusing enough, whether the literary allusions are taken or not. In "Candidats à l'Immortalité" he sneers at the whole crowd of false poets:

> Les symbolistes, les simplistes, les romans,
> Ceux qui riments [*sic*] à soixante ans leurs pucelages
> Et ceux dont les neurasthéniques mucilages
> Pour Monsieur de Vogüé sont emplies [*sic*] d'agrément;
>
> Frémine plus hideux que les têtes de l'Hydre,
> Et Vicaire pochard comme une pomme à cidre.
> Et ceux qui font des vers pour les cafés de nuit:
>
> Tous veulent sur leur front le diadème esthète,
> Ces palmes dont la fleur améthyste leur duit
> Et l'orgueil des festins à douze francs par tête.[1]

M. Tailhade has a high ideal of literature; he does not seek the *diadème esthète* himself, and knows well how to appreciate at their worth those who cultivate the arts with no higher ambition than to act as hero in "banquets at twelve francs a head." In his writings he has no other motive than to present what he believes to be the truth; however harsh his satire is, it is always deserved. During the time that he was writing his skits on the literary men of his period, M. Tailhade fought a great many duels with people who were aggrieved by his poems. On April 4, 1894, he was badly injured by the explosion of a bomb in a restaurant where he was dining. Since then M. Tailhade has given up his personal satire and has taken to prose. "They are works of an admirable style, of a turned and mannered eloquence, unique products of eloquence. M. Tailhade there shows himself as in his first verses, an indefatigable orator."

[1] 'Candidats à l'immoralité', *Ibid.*, pp. 55–6. The misprinted words are *riment* and *emplis*. There are also slight variations in punctuation.

IMAGISM AND FRENCH POETRY

'The History of Imagism', the essay F. S. Flint contributed to *The Egoist*'s special issue on imagism in May 1915, has long been used as one of the basic documents in any account of the history of the modern movement in English poetry.[1] It has given later readers information – usually lost to history – about the conversations in 1909 in which some of the ideas basic to imagism gained considerable currency, and it has suggested what each of the participants contributed to the discussion. Thus we have Flint's assertion that imagism had roots in the Poets' Club of 1909, that the 1909 group included writers interested in French symbolist poetry and haiku, that nearly everyone in the club was experimenting with free verse and stressing use of the image, that Hulme was one of the leaders, and that Pound was a follower only, with little knowledge of current French work. Later history has supported each of his assertions.

Recent critics have become aware, however, that not all the facts in the history are accurate and that the account itself may have been subject to systematic distortion. Hulme, for example, was not the founder of the Poets' Club, for he was still abroad when a notice of one of its early meetings appeared in the British press in June 1907.[2] What is more, the history occasioned a bitter exchange of letters in 1915 between Pound and Flint.[3] Pound attacked Flint vigorously and charged five errors in the essay. Flint, he said, had distorted the account by failing to acknowledge that the 'drive toward simple current speech' originated with Ford Madox Ford, not with the 1909 club. Further, Pound said, there were such essential differences between the goals of the poets in 1909 and 1913 that Flint was simply wrong to say that the only differences between the imagism of 1915 and the imagist poems of Edward Storer and T. E. Hulme in 1909 were merely those of temperament and talent. H.D. owed nothing to Storer, Pound continued; Flint had tried to imply that Pound wished to minimize the contributions of Hulme; and Flint had ignored Pound's responsibility for 'the whole formation of imagism'. Flint rebutted the charges in a letter on 3 July 1915. Although Ford had made important contributions, Flint said, Pound was over-estimating their significance to the movement as a whole; he was, furthermore, crediting Storer with too little and overestimating both the differences between the poetry of 1909 and 1913 and his own importance, although Flint declared himself ready to give Pound full credit for his energy and organization. Then Flint made the assertion which explains much of what lay behind the controversy: 'You might have been generalissimo in a compact onslaught: and you spoiled everything by some native incapacity for walking square with your comrades,...voilà!'[4] Pound and the other imagists had gone separate ways in 1914, in large part because Pound refused to remain part of a movement which he could not direct.[5] The dissension over this,

---

1 See, for example, Stanley K. Coffman, Jr., *Imagism: A Chapter for the History of Modern Poetry* (Norman, Okla., 1951), p. 34 and Glenn Hughes, *Imagism and the Imagists* (New York, 1960), pp. 11–12. For further discussion of the topics discussed in Flint's 'history' see the General Introduction, pages 30–1.

2 Wallace Martin, 'The Origins of Imagism', in *'The New Age' under Orage, op. cit.*, p. 149. Henry Simpson, the first president of the club, has confirmed in an interview with Martin that Hulme was not the founder.

3 Christopher Middleton, 'Documents on Imagism from the Papers of F. S. Flint', *The Review*, 15 (April 1965) 40–4. Middleton summarizes the two Pound letters (2 July and 7 July 1915) and publishes the Flint letter (3 July 1915) in full. The manuscripts, which came to light after Flint's death in 1960, are held in the Academic Center Library of the University of Texas.

4 *Ibid.*, p. 42.

5 I have discussed the nuances of this conflict in some detail in 'Hulme's "A Lecture on

and over the credit Pound had claimed for making modern French poetry known in England, actively rankled in 1915, and Flint's essay appears to be an attempt to restore proper credit for imagism to participants other than Pound. The essay, thus, is largely accurate so far as it goes, but it must be understood as a selective account that originated in polemical battle.

THE HISTORY OF IMAGISM*

F. S. FLINT

Somewhere in the gloom of the year 1908, Mr. T. E. Hulme, now in the trenches of Ypres, but excited then by the propinquity, at a half-a-crown dance, of the other sex (if, as Remy de Gourmont avers, the passage from the aesthetic to the sexual emotion, *n'est qu'un pas*, the reverse is surely also true), proposed to a companion that they should found a Poets' Club. The thing was done, there and then. The Club began to dine; and its members to read their verses. At the end of the year they published a small plaquette of them, called "For Christmas MDCCCCVIII." In this plaquette was printed one of the first "Imagist" poems, by T. E. Hulme:

Autumn

A touch of cold in the autumn night
I walked abroad,
And saw the ruddy moon lean over a hedge,
Like a red-faced farmer.
I did not stop to talk, but nodded;
And round about were the wistful stars
With white faces like town children.[1]

In November of the same year, Edward Storer, author already of "Inclinations," much of which is in the "Imagist" manner, published his "Mirrors of Illusion," the first book of "Imagist" poems, with an essay at the end attacking poetic conventions. The first poem in the book was called "Image," here it is:

Forsaken lovers,
Burning to a chaste white moon,
Upon strange pyres of loneliness and drought.[2]

Mr. Storer, who has recanted much since, was in favour then of a poetry which I described, in reference to his book, as "a form of expression, like the Japanese, in which an image is the resonant heart of an

Modern Poetry" and The Birth of Imagism', *Papers on Language and Literature*, v, 4 (Fall 1969) 465–70.
* *The Egoist*, II, 5 (1 May 1915) 70–1.
[1] T. E. Hulme, 'Autumn', in *The Life and Opinions of T. E. Hulme* by Alun Jones (London, 1960), p. 156.
[2] Edward Storer, 'Image', *Mirrors of Illusion* (London, 1909), p. 2 (unnumbered).

exquisite moment."[1] A fair example of his practice is this from "Clarice-Henley":

> "Clarice! Clarice! the oasis of lunch,
> We laid Arabian-Night-wise in the green
> And pleasant desert of the field
> For our most welcome selves,
> And that rememberable canopy of white
> And holy linen, that denied your face
> Unto a hundred daisies' peeping glance,
> We placed to bear the bread, the wine – the flowers
> Of you dear hand."[2]

I have always wished that Storer, in his after work, had brought more art to the exploitation of the temperament he displayed in the "Mirrors," which, for me, is a book of poetry. But he changed his manner completely.

At that time, I had been advocating in the course of a series of articles on recent books of verse a poetry in *vers libre*, akin in spirit to the Japanese. An attack on the Poets' Club brought me into correspondence and acquaintance with T. E. Hulme; and, later on, after Hulme had violently disagreed with the Poets' Club and had left it, he proposed that he should get together a few congenial spirits, and that we should have weekly meetings in a Soho restaurant. The first of these meetings, which were really the successors of certain Wednesday evening meetings, took place on Thursday, March 25, 1909. There were present, so far as I recall, T. E. Hulme, Edward Storer, F. W. Tancred, Joseph Campbell, Miss Florence Farr, one or two other men, mere vaguements in my memory, and myself. I think that what brought the real nucleus of this group together was a dissatisfaction with English poetry as it was then (and is still, alas!) being written. We proposed at various times to replace it by pure *vers libre*; by the Japanese *tanka* and *haikai*; we all wrote dozens of the latter as an amusement; by poems in a sacred Hebrew form, of which "This is the House that Jack Built" is a perfect model; Joseph Campbell produced two good specimens of this, one of which, "The Dark," is printed in "The Mountainy Singer"; by rhymeless poems like Hulme's "Autumn," and so on. In all this Hulme was ringleader. He insisted too on absolutely accurate presentation and no verbiage; and he and F. W. Tancred, a poet too little known, perhaps because his production is precious and small, used to spend hours each day in the search for the right phrase. Tancred does it still; while Hulme reads German philosophy in the trenches, waiting for the general advance. There was also a lot of talk and practice among us, Storer

[1] F. S. Flint, 'Verse', *The New Age*, n.s. VI (9 December 1909) 137.
[2] Storer, 'Clarice-Henley', *Mirrors of Illusion, op. cit.*, p. 9.

leading it chiefly, of what we called the Image. We were very much influenced by modern French symbolist poetry.

On April 22, 1909, Ezra Pound, whose book, "Personae," had been published on the previous Friday, jointed the group, introduced, I believe, by Miss Farr and my friend T. D. FitzGerald. Ezra Pound used to boast in those days that he was

Nil praeter "Villon" et doctus cantare Catullum,

and he could not be made to believe that there was any French poetry after Ronsard. He was very full of his *troubadours*; but I do not remember that he did more than attempt to illustrate (or refute) our theories occasionally with their example. The group died a lingering death at the end of its second winter. But its discussions had a sequel. In 1912 Mr. Pound published, at the end of his book "Ripostes," the complete poetical works of T. E. Hulme, five poems, thirty-three lines, with a preface in which these words occur: "As for the future, *Les Imagistes*, the descendants of the forgotten school of 1909 (previously referred to as the 'School of Images') have that in their keeping." In that year, Pound had become interested in modern French poetry; he had broken away from his old manner; and he invented the term "Imagisme" to designate the aesthetic of "Les Imagistes." In March 1913, an "interview," over my signature, of an "imagiste" appeared in the American review *Poetry*, followed by "A Few Dont's by an Imagiste" by Ezra Pound. The four cardinal principles of "Imagisme" were set forth as:

(1) Direct treatment of the "thing," whether subjective or objective.
(2) To use absolutely no word that did not contribute to the presentation.
(3) As regarding rhythm: to compose in sequence of the musical phrase, not in sequence of a metronome.
(4) The "doctrine of the Image" – not for publication.

Towards the end of the year Pound collected together a number of poems [by] different writers, Richard Aldington, H.D., F. S. Flint, Skipwith Cannell, Amy Lowell, William Carlos Williams, James Joyce, John Cournos, Ezra Pound, Ford Madox Heuffer and Allan Upward, and in February–March 1914 they were published in America and England as "Des Imagistes: an Anthology," which, though it did not set the Thames, seems to have set America, on fire. Since then Mr. Ezra Pound has become a "Vorticist," with a contradiction, for, when addressing the readers of *The New Age* he has made Imagism to mean pictures as Wyndham Lewis understands them; writing later for *T.P.'s Weekly*, he made it pictures as William Morris understood them. There is no difference, except that which springs from difference of temperament and talent, between an imagist poem of to-day and those written by Edward Storer and T. E. Hulme.

EARLY RECOGNITION OF A NEW SYMBOLIST

John Middleton Murry's essay on Valéry in 1917 was one signal of the British return to a critical and informed interest in the tradition of symbolism, including both its nineteenth-century masters and its skilled modern followers. The review was but the first recognition in those years of Valéry's achievement. In 1920, for example, Charles du Bos wrote in a series entitled 'On the Symbolist Movement in French Poetry': 'When one reads the last [sic] poems of M. Paul Valéry – "La Pythie", "Le Cantique des Colonnes", "Palme", or, the latest of all, "Le Cimetière Marin" (in the *Nouvelle Revue Française* for June), in all of which the intellectual and the verbal music combine, and are fused, to a degree that one could hardly have imagined within the possibilities of French verse – one feels indeed that none of the Mallarméan efforts, not even the most extreme ones, were in vain.'[1] Du Bos went on to praise Murry's critical perceptiveness in the *TLS* review: 'The day is approaching when M. Valéry will collect his poems. On that day English criticism may proudly remember that the one article in which a discriminating and full justice was done to "La Jeune Parque", the first fruit of M. Valéry's return to poetry, was an English article...'

English appreciation for Valéry was accompanied by a faith that current judgements of French work were critically superior to those made during the 1890s or in the pre-war years. Murry spoke in his essay on 'La Jeune Parque' of 'the heady coryphants of *l'art pour l'art*' in the 1890s who 'tried to palm off upon a guileless British public a sham Baudelaire, a sham Verlaine, a sham symbolism'. Elsewhere in *The Athenaeum* an anonymous reviewer attacked F. S. Flint's 'Some French Poets of To-day' with the declaration that England had seen 'far too much puerile acceptance of French work at its own estimation' and that it was 'the duty of the knowledgeable critic to take every opportunity of restoring the sense of proportion'.[2] A controversy was provoked by this attack, and the result was yet another, though qualified, affirmation of Valéry's importance, this time from the pen of Flint. 'I agree with... [your reviewer] that, of recent French poetry, M. Romains's "Europe", some of M. Caudel's work, and possibly, M. Valéry's "La Jeune Parque" are most worthy of attention'.[3] The attention which Valéry attracted, however, led to fuller understanding of the possibilities of the symbolist method, not to superficial borrowing. English poets, on the whole, entered Valéry's 'enchanted house' to 'explore its darkest rooms with gratitude' and go on their way, in Murry's words, 'comforted that someone should have honourably laboured on the mansion of his dream'.

PAUL VALÉRY'S *LA JEUNE PARQUE**

JOHN MIDDLETON MURRY

The pursuit of beauty for its own dear sake has never been acclimatized among us. We may say with a calm and candid pride that we have been greater. We have followed with all the courage of a blind and tenacious

---

1 Charles du Bos, 'Letters from Paris, v – On The Symbolist Movement in French Poetry', *The Athenaeum* (30 July 1920), 159.

2 Anonymous, 'Poetry', *The Athenaeum* (31 October 1919), 1137.

3 F. S. Flint, 'To the Editor of *The Athenaeum*', *The Athenaeum* (14 November 1919) 1200. The anonymous reviewer with whom Flint was arguing was almost surely either Aldous Huxley or John Middleton Murry, and the reviewer's critical preferences strongly suggest the latter.

* *Times Literary Supplement*, 23 August 1917, p. 402.

instinct art for its own sake; and above all art through poetry. Our poetry has been too prodigal to achieve, save by an accident in the sweep of its own gesture, beauty as an end. We are not clever enough, say the advocates of small perfections, to make the intellectual effort necessary to the full conception of beauty as an end, and to the adequate mastery of the essential means. But in truth, in the realm of literature, ours has been the proud privilege of not needing to be clever. There has been an impulse among us rich and strong enough to break through intellectual limitations on every side. In the years when we were clever we had to yield to the imperious necessity of trampling our discipline underfoot in a riot of unbridled fantasy. Among no other nation in the world could metaphysical poetry be synonymous with quixotic. What it was our poets sought we do not know; if we did know it would be certain that they sought something other, for they sought and found something which no knowing could have given them.

So it was that when the heady coryphants of *l'art pour l'art* came among us not so very many years ago their message fell upon politely sceptical ears. They thought that they had said too much, whereas in truth they had said too little. And there were some wise heads who suspected that they had got even the message which they professed to bring us wrong. In a little while we knew beyond any doubt that they had tried to palm off upon a guileless British public a sham Baudelaire, a sham Verlaine, a sham Symbolism. If they had really learned the French lesson and brought it to us we would not indeed have repeated it, but we might have listened to it with attention and respect. We would have understood perhaps more clearly than we do even now how possible and noble is the activity which devotes a consummate intellectual gift to the achievement of beauty as an end. We might have learned more thoroughly than we have yet how glorious is the mere probity of art that is never free from the torment of divine dissatisfaction, and will not leave even the most unlikely stone unturned or the most forbidding road untrod so its end may be more wholly gained.

All these half-learned lessons, truths wrought into the very texture of French poetry, are suggested to us again with a sudden vehemence by the reading of M. Paul Valéry's poem, "La Jeune Parque." What we know of M. Valéry is extremely little. He belongs, we know, to what is now almost a past generation, and was an intimate of Stephane Mallarmé. A few exquisite poems in a French review, a deeply interesting essay on the method of Leonardo da Vinci, and that is all. He has published no book before this one. "Depuis bien des années," he writes in his dedication to M. André Gide, "j'avais laissé l'art des vers; essayant de m'y astreindre encore, j'ai fait cette exercice." Can it be true? we ask. Is it only an exercise after years of desuetude? Is it not rather true that the intervening years were spent in the slow and subtle elaboration of this certain beauty? Is not M. Valéry the authentic and the sole disciple of Mallarmé himself? Here at least is a poem which has the strange quality of "Hérodiade," and has it not by any groping of painful fingers – that were indeed a paradox – but as surely as the master himself.

> Qui pleure là, sinon le vent simple, à cette heure
> Seule avec diamants extrêmes?...Mais qui pleure[,]
> Si proche de moi-même au moment de pleurer?[1]

That is unmistakable as a string cleanly plucked. This is not an apprentice but a master of beauty, who gives us this unhesitating sense that we are, as they say, in for it. We are in not for a brutal orgy but for a feast so subtle that we need wholly to keep our heads. Without a cool brain we are no less lost than without a delicate ear. For the poem has an argument consonant with its craftsmanship, a fine and bewildering thread of gold which by its own brilliance will evade the eye.

It is night and by the sea. The young goddess is alone listening to her soul, waiting for some inevitable message of her being:

> J'ai de mes bras épais environné mes tempes[,]
> Et longtemps de mon âme attendu les éclairs.[2]

In the deep forest of her soul she saw a snake that had bitten her. The poison runs through her. She is jealous, but of what is she jealous? It is not the snake of a visible longing that has stung her:

> Reptile, au [*sic*] vifs détours tout courus de caresses,
> Si proche impatience et si lourde langueur,
> Qu'es-tu, près de ma nuit d'éternelle longueur?...
> Moi, je veille. Je sors pâle et prodigieuse,
> Toute humide des pleurs que je n'ai point versés,
> D'une absence aux contours de mortelle bercés
> Par soi seule...[3]

So she bids adieu to the mortal sister that lives within her, and she speaks with her harmonious self, "Femme flexible et ferme aux silences suivis d'actes purs." She tells how this self, untroubled by strange longings and stranger insight, was the happy bride of the day, at one with the visible world and with her own desire. But even as she tells of it it is gone. Her self that lives and endures is a stranger to the light of day. With the night it grows up within her and takes possession of her

---

[1] Paul Valéry, *La Jeune Parque, commentée par Alain* (Paris, 1953), p. 61. The annotated edition shows many minor changes in punctuation, not noted in this text.

[2] *Ibid.*, p. 63.

[3] *Ibid.*, pp. 71, 73. The *au* is *ô* in the annotated edition of 1953.

wholly. She tastes the bitter-sweet longing to be no more, while the old riddles and the eternal dreams vex her, and reverie that follows in a mirror a bird changing wing:

> Car l'oeil spirituel sur les plages de soie
> Avait déjà vu luire et pâlir trop de jours
> Dont je m'étais prédit les couleurs et le cours.
> L'ennui, le clair ennui de mirer leur nuance,
> Me donnait sur la [*sic*] vie une funeste avance:
> L'aube me dévoilait tout le jour ennemi.
> J'étais à demi morte, et peut-être à demi
> Immortelle, rêvant que le futur lui-même
> Ne fut qu'un diamant fermant le diadème
> Ou s'échange le froid des malheurs qui naîtront
> Parmi tant d'autres feux absolus de mon front.[1]

Let her die, she cries. The earth is to her only a band of changing colour now, the universe trembles. Death longs to smell this rose beyond price. Let death call her then, and let her soul fill her with despair, so weary of herself is she. She can wait no more. The rebirth of the year foretells to her blood secret motions that she cannot restrain. Regretfully the last diamond of frost will yield in her heart, but yield it must. What mortal can resist the coming of the astonishing spring, and she is only half a goddess:

> Lumière!...Ou toi, la mort. Mais le plus prompt me
>   prenne!
> Mon coeur bat. Mon coeur bat...Mon sein brûle et
>   m'entraîne...
> Ah! qu'il s'enfle, se gonfle et se tende, ce dur
> Très doux témoin captif de mes réseaux d'azur...
> Dur en moi...mais si doux à la bouche infinie...[2]

Is she not made for the delights and the fruits of love? She will put away from her the phantoms that haunt her; they shall not have life from her. She is too full of pity for them and herself together. She will seek an answer only from the tears that have risen to her eyes, she does not know whence, drawn mysteriously from the depths of her being as mortal and mother. But there is no answer. Why should she weep who shrinks from hope? Let the sea-salt earth bear her away. She is faint with the vain endeavour to fathom her own mystery:

> Mystérieuse moi, pourtant, tu vis encore...
> Tu vas te reconnaître au lever de l'aurore
> Amèrement la même.[3]

---

[1] Paul Valéry, *La Jeune Parque, commentée par Alain* (Paris, 1953), p. 87. The 1953 edition gives the reading *ma* for *la* vie.

[2] *Ibid.*, p. 99.   [3] *Ibid.*, p. 109.

Slowly the dawn comes, and she salutes the daylight shining upon the islands in the sea in lines of solemn beauty that to an English memory bear with them an echo of Keats.

> Tout va donc accomplir son acte solennel
> De toujours reparaître incomparable et chaste...
> Salut! Divinités par la rose et le sel,
> Et les premiers jouets de la jeune lumière.
> Iles! Ruches bientôt, quand la flamme première
> Fera que votre roche, îles que je prédis,
> Ressente en rougissant de puissants paradis;
> Cimes qu'un feu féconde à peine intimidées,
> Bois qui bourdonnerez de bêtes et d'idées,
> D'hymnes d'hommes comblés des dons de [*sic*] juste éther,
> Iles...[1]

The night is past. The limpid lines flow into the day. But the goddess is touched by regret for the consummation that has been denied her. She has been betrayed by her body which refused the gift of death, yet she cannot withhold herself from full acceptance:

> Doucement,
> Me voici: mon front touche à ce consentement...
> Ce corps, je lui pardonne, et je goûte à la cendre.
> Je me remets entière au bonheur de descendre,
> Ouverte aux noirs témoins, les bras suppliciés,
> Entre des mots sans fin, sans moi balbutiés.[2]

The abiding impression produced by this poem as it floats out to its calmly shining close is one of musical perfection. The melody, indeed, never falters, but there is more than melody. The theme has been sounded to its depths. The intellectual control has never weakened nor ceased to direct the melody in its mission of discovery. The intention of the poet speaks with the voice of the goddess when she says:

> Cherche, du moins, dis-toi par quelle sourde suite
> La nuit d'entre les morts au jour t'a reconduite?
> Souviens-toi de toi-même, et retire à l'instinct
> Ce fil (ton doigt doré le dispute au matin),
> Ce fil, dont la finesse aveuglément suivie,
> Jusque sur cette rive a ramené ta vie...
> Sois subtile...cruelle...ou plus subtile...Mens
> Mais sache...[3]

If "La Jeune Parque" is obscure (and even a third reading has not made all the shadowy places clear) it is not because the just criticism

---

[1] Valéry, *La Jeune Parque*, *op. cit.*, pp. 111, 113. The *de* of the next-to-last line is *du* in the 1953 edition.
[2] *Ibid.*, p. 127.
[3] *Ibid.*, p. 123.

of sham Symbolism, that it subordinates sense to sound, holds good against it, but because the poet has been guided by the ruthless impulse to full and explicit knowledge. It is obscure because the reality on which it is moulded, the vicissitudes of a woman's soul in the night season, is obscure. The poet has striven to give at once an intellectual explication of a subtle truth and by his music to saturate the discovery with the unique quality which no examination alone could reveal. That neither of these things can exist without the other is fundamental to the tradition of Mallarmé. He would have poetry approximate to the condition of music, but he remembered that music can only be truly built upon a foundation of thought. By this alone the pursuit of beauty as an end is made worthy of a lifetime's devotion. The genius of English poetry demands a broader sweep, a larger argument. It cannot live in such confined perfection. But neither does it do well to pass this by on the other side. French poetry and French symbolism have a message which we should understand – that the achievement of poetry, in whatever kind, is due to the exact probity with which it is pursued. Because of this "La Jeune Parque" is beautiful like an enchanted house set in a haunted garden. We could not live in it; but we enter, explore its darkest rooms with gratitude, peer through its windows as though they were our own, and go on our way comforted that someone should have so honourably laboured on the mansion of his dream.

A CONTINUING TREND TOWARD CLASSICISM

Aldous Huxley's eloquent demand for a 'return to genuine and living classical tradition' has seemed to many critics to have been already nearly fulfilled in England by 1919. René Taupin said of T. S. Eliot's activity in those years, 'Il a l'avantage d'arriver à un moment où de nombreuses expériences viennent d'être faites, où détermination des valeurs a été accomplie. C'est dire qu'un classicisme pouvait s'établir solidement en Angleterre comme il s'en établissait un en France.'[1] Thus Taupin suggested, in concurrence with many of the imagists, that H.D., Aldington, Hulme, and Pound had set a new classicism in motion during the second decade. Huxley, however, pointed out a tendency toward an almost solely formalistic concern (which at one time was strongly supported by Pound and Hulme), and he cautioned that this tendency was really anti-classical. Although his comments were primarily directed towards style in the visual arts, it is significant (and characteristic of the period) that Huxley expanded the range of his observations by noting that 'in literature, in painting, in music, the same phenomenon is observable'. To counteract the tendency, he stressed the importance of subject matter and urged a return to the 'aesthetic arrangement of objects in themselves beautiful and significant'. Clearly there remained in 1919 variations in the application of the term *classicism* much like those prevalent at the time of Murry's and Flint's comments, when interest in the concept first rose in 1913.[2]

Huxley's attitudes had important parallels among his contemporaries. Whether the earlier imagist and vorticist goals had been classical in Huxley's sense or not, T. S. Eliot, for one, showed a viewpoint at about this time that was not greatly different. And from the perspective of current French developments, the essay takes on still broader implications. Dada painters and poets of the day were seeking to destroy subject and aesthetically controlled arrangement alike. Huxley's essay is at once an affirmation of one meaning of a continuing classical revival in England and an explanation of some sources of British reservation about current poetic experiment in France.

ART AND THE TRADITION*

ALDOUS HUXLEY

M. Mauclair is an independent who has lived to find himself a believer in tradition. Ever a hater of official art, he has been outstripped by none in his ardour to overthrow existing academies and institutes. He has been the admirer and, in many cases, the friend of most of the great independent artists in literature, painting and music who have lived and worked in the days of the Third Republic. Now, in his later years, he has come to the conclusion that a tradition and a discipline are profitable and necessary to the existence of the arts. He fears anarchy as much as he hates officialdom. It is not that he has ceased to admire his old friends and fellow-rebels; but he has come to believe that their

[1] René Taupin, *L'Influence du symbolisme français, op. cit.*, p. 212.
[2] See pages 168–71, 201–2, 204–5.
* Review of *L'Art Indépendant Français sous la Troisième République* by Camille Mauclair. *The Athenaeum* (6 June 1919), p. 440.

example is pernicious to those who have inherited from them only the rebelliousness without the compensating genius. There will be many to agree with M. Mauclair in desiring to see the revival of a living classical tradition, which shall check and discipline the unlimited individualism that flourishes in the arts to-day.

Perhaps the most characteristic difference between the modern independents and their classical predecessors lies in their attitude towards the great set-pieces in which the older artists scored their most splendid triumphs. In literature, in painting, in music, the same phenomenon is observable. There are no modern epics, no great over-whelming pictures; the symphony is giving place to the musical lyric. In this contraction of theme, commercial conditions are certainly a contributing cause: nearly a century ago we find poor Haydon groaning over the unwillingness of the aristocracy and the rich burgess to buy his grand historical paintings – an unwillingness due, not as one might have hoped, to the good taste of potential buyers, but to their parsimony and cautiousness. But commercial conditions are not the only cause; the whole theory of the independents themselves has run counter to the idea of large monumental works. Occupied in interpreting their own individual sensations and thoughts, they have abandoned the large classical themes to devote themselves to minuter studies. They have concentrated intensely on the problems of style. Style, of course, is of the highest importance. It is the essentially artistic element in art, the outward expression of the human mind moulding the matter in which it works. But in their preoccupation with style, the independents have largely neglected matter. The "subject," on which the classical authors brought their powers of style to bear, has almost disappeared from modern art; style hangs, self-supported, in the void. Style may be, as we have said, the essentially human, aesthetic element in art; but, divorced from matter, from the beauties of external reality, it tends to become singularly dry and lifeless. Artists brought up in the independent school, preoccupied with the purely aesthetic side of art, are apt to be afraid of beauty, afraid of the great emotions, afraid of universal truths. They are terrified lest they should become "pompier" if they traffick in these things. Some have stylized life out of existence, sacrificing the beautiful to the aesthetic. Some, fearing to be betrayed into senti-mentality, have eschewed emotions for mere sensations. The classical masters had style, but they had also matter. Their painters were not afraid of becoming chocolate-boxy if they represented more or less faithfully some of the inexhaustible beauties of external reality. They had as much sense of the aesthetic as the independents of to-day; unlike their successors, they could stylize the uninformed, indefinite beauty of nature without destroying it in the process. Their pictures are the aesthetic arrangement of objects in themselves beautiful and significant. In literature, too, men were not afraid of the fundamental emotions or of general truths. They could be individual without talking of themselves; they could stamp the impress of their style on large impersonal themes.

Is there to-day any classical tradition to oppose to this disintegrating individualism? Official and academic art is the ludicrous travesty of a classical, traditional art. It illustrates all the faults of sentimentality, over-emphasis and dullness into which the independents are so afraid, too much afraid, perhaps, of falling. The independents have done good work in breaking and discrediting this fossilized classicism. But intransigent individualism is sterile and unproductive. What is needed now is a return to a genuine and living classical tradition.

.   .   .   .

MODERN POETRY AND MODERN PAINTING

The tendency toward the creation of abstract structural forms in poetry, on the analogy of painting and music, was supported by the informed reporting on the visual arts that was available to the poets of London. André Lhote, who contributed articles to *The Athenaeum* with some regularity, was one of the followers of Braque and Picasso during the period of analytical cubism in 1910 and 1911. Thus Lhote's essay on the origins of cubism is the account of one actually a participant in the movement, and such an essay is no isolated phenomenon in British literary journals. His description of the cubist painters' concern with constructive design, 'imbrication of forms' and 'the penetration of objects whose radiations cross each other' recalls the aesthetics of vorticism and the theories advocated by futurist painters and poets in London just before the war. In British literary circles, where Pound had urged the direct application to poetry of Kandinsky's aesthetic theories, and the art and literary criticism of T. E. Hulme had so recently held sway, an essay on the visual arts required no special introduction to be read for its implications for literary as well as artistic form. Any thorough evaluation of the contributions of Paris to the poetry of London, consequently, must keep in mind the potential significance of essays – like this one – that deal with form in the visual arts.

CUBISM AND THE MODERN ARTISTIC SENSIBILITY*

André Lhote

The Paris art season, whose new manifestations we propose to study next month, came to an end with an exhibition of works by Picasso at the Léonce Rosenberg Gallery. There you could meet all kinds of people – vehement adversaries; meticulous amateurs preferring this one of the young master's formulas to this other which they condemned without appeal; the rarer eclectic admirers, and terrible disciples, of old or recent standing, who, as usual "more royalist than the king," exalted beyond measure the most hermetic and mysterious works, and deplored, as sheer betrayals, all the speculations of a more immediate realism towards which the prince of Cubism seems, more and more, to tend.

Anyone who had relied on the remarks he overheard to form a definite opinion would have had great difficulty in finding a solution that would have set his mind at rest. So, too, for us to present an exact image of Picasso, to delimit this fugitive figure, is no easy task. It is certainly a piece of work which passes the limits of a short article. To-day we propose to point out summarily a few peculiarities of this strange art; and the better to elucidate the problems which it poses, we shall reserve our analysis of the works of the "Cubists" for the exhibitions in which they appear – works which are either servile and clumsy

* *The Athenaeum* (19 September 1919) 919–20.

312

copies, or attempts, of a still rudimentary nature, to make a unity out of the hybrid and tangled work of the initiator.

The study of Cubism may be divided into three parts: 1st, the Origins; 2nd, the Realizations; 3rd, the Promise for the Future.

ORIGINS OF CUBISM

When an artistic convention comes to its plenitude there always arises a hero charged with the ungrateful task of sowing doubt in men's minds, of giving form to the vague miasmas floating in the spiritual atmosphere, of aggravating the latent malady and of hastening the decay of a formula that has been drained of all its sap. The phenomenon of gravitation which made its appearance among French painters from the time of Delacroix onwards – that ever more and more rapid attraction of men's minds towards the earth ended in impressionism. Painters plunged, animal-wise, into a wholly material world, accepting without choice a daily bread of the most terrestrial quality. In the midst of the anarchy to which a century of moral disorder had led, Cézanne came. All that this great master represented, from a spiritual point of view, has not yet been said. He embodies, through the Romanticism with which he was impregnated, the avenging voice of Greece and Raphael. He constitutes the first recall to classical order. But the voice in which he put up his claim was so grave and measured among the vehement vociferations of his time that it was necessary, in order that the lesson he gave us might be understood, that an *interpreter* should appear. This was Picasso.

With remarkable intuition the young Spanish painter deciphered the multiple enigma, translated the mysterious language, spelt out, word by word, the stiff, substantial phrases – Picasso illuminates in the sunshine of his imagination the thousand facets of Cézanne's rich and restrained personality.

The first Cubist paintings were the fruit of a process of dissection, or rather of vivisection. Like an anatomist poring over his living victim, he scrutinized with an inquisitor's minuteness the least details of the Cézannian organism. He worked its joints till he dislocated them. But this demonstration was necessary for an epoch in which pictorial analysis, in spite of the obscure example of the Master of Aix, went no further than the superficies of the object.

The "Portrait of Monsieur Sagot" at this exhibition offered a typical example of the earliest Cubist researches. It marks the opening of the period in which Picasso made a study of the imbrication of forms, the penetration of objects whose radiations cross one another. This soldering of separate objects into a single block, which has become the Cubist conglomeration, was too subtly realized in Cézanne's canvases to have any immediate educational value. Picasso discerned the rhythm uniting, by extensions, parallels or convergences, the constructive lines. Knot by knot, he patiently undid the tangled skein of Cézanne's riddle. To lose no detail of the multiple discipline, he decomposed it to its final elements, teaching himself the great lesson by successive fragments as he made his discoveries.

Cézanne's depth, which is obtained by the spirit *and for the spirit alone*, is not a metrical depth. It is impossible to say exactly how far any given object is from the foreground. In the final canvases, indeed, there is no foreground and no background. There is a continuous oscillation of all the different planes, going from the surface of the canvas to the depths of the picture, to come back again towards the eye of the observer. It is this vibration which constitutes the new pictorial volume. This kind of space, less real than *suggested*, has called forth the term "Fourth Dimension," employed in a figurative sense by impatient theorists who have borrowed from the mathematician's vocabulary words whose mysterious meaning is applicable to the mysterious operation which they had to define. Cézanne arrived at this supplementary extra-geometrical dimension, which is a metaphysical dimension attached to the domain of the spirit, by applying, over the whole surface of his canvas, a series of planes like the steps of an irregular staircase. While Renoir, obeying a similar necessity, though less vigorously, constructed his picture from a series of spheres, Cézanne proceeds for the most part by flat planes. It was inevitable that Picasso, intoxicated by his discovery and, in his desire to teach himself, exaggerating every revealing detail of his Model, should have come progressively to reduce modelling till he arrived at flat colours.

It was in this way that the typical method of pure Cubism came into existence, and that little by little, by logical speculation, was evolved that simplified technique which is the parent of that employed by decorative painters. It is, so to speak, the result of a blackboard demonstration of the essential methods of the great painter of Aix. Cubism may thus be defined as the systematic exaltation of the most important and least elucidated peculiarities of the Cézannian formula.

It now remains for us, having defined its origins, to point out the realizations of Cubism, its enrichments and the infinite repercussions which it may make in the art of the future, provided that it be employed sanely, and in a spirit which we will take the liberty of calling "Totalist," by the inheritors of so new and so precious an artistic conception.

A SELECTIVE VIEW OF A NEW GENERATION:
1920

Aldous Huxley's comments on Soupault, Morand, and Cendrars show that his affirmation of classicism did not preclude his critical approval of experimental verse that met his requirements for significant subject matter.[1] His approbation of Cendrars is an accurate appraisal of a French poet only then receiving meaningful recognition in France, although the poems in the two collections Huxley cites were with only one exception written before World War I. Huxley's reflections on Soupault and Morand show considerably less sympathy. His interest in satire – already emerging in his poetry as well – predominated, and he showed no interest in the experimentation with form the Soupault poem represents. His selective view of *poèsie actuelle* was more in keeping with the prevailing English attitudes toward France than was F. S. Flint's extended and well-informed survey of the dada poets in the same year. His review does show, however, that even in literary circles in which the leading poets sought their models from the nineteenth century, the experiments of the contemporary French *avant garde* did not go unremarked.

YOUNG FRENCH VERSE*

Aldous Huxley

M. Soupault is on his guard against saying anything too significant. He does not want to be taken for one of those absurdly earnest folk who strike philosophic attitudes in the face of life or who take human emotions seriously. He presents us in his volume with his sensations and impressions in their native purity, uncontaminated, as far as it is possible, with the faintest tinge of thought. His technique may be a little unfamiliar at first:

> le train passe
>   c'est un nuage
> DÉMÉNAGEMENTS POUR TOUS PAYS
> à l'entresol
> cinq heures
>   le vent part
>   En voiture:[2]

but it is not difficult to see the connection of these phrases with the title of the poem from which they are quoted, "La Grande Mélancolie d'une Avenue." We recognize here a more "advanced" and incoherent form of what our novelists call psychology ("There was a hole in the curtain. She noticed it for the first time. It was shaped like an iguana's head.

---

[1] The essay 'Art and the Tradition' (pages 309–11) provides the background for several of the judgments Huxley renders here.

* Review of *Rose des vents* by Philippe Soupault, *Lampes à arc* by Paul Morand, and *Dix-neuf poèmes élastiques* and *Du Monde entier* by Blaise Cendrars. *The Athenaeum* (21 May 1920) 684.

[2] Philippe Soupault, 'La grande Mélancholie d'une avenue', *Rose des vents* (Paris, 1920), unnumbered.

It became an obsession..." and so on). The novelists go on in this vein for three hundred pages. We are grateful to M. Soupault for his self-restraint in writing no poem more than a hundred words long.

"Lampes à Arc" is the 1920 version of "Poèmes Aristophanesques." Laurent Tailhade celebrated his "ancien bandagiste," his "ioutres au nez circonflexe" in exquisite quatorzains. It is in *vers libre* that M. Morand sings of his motor-load of Spaniards:

> Sur les strapontins trois filles mauves,
> poids lourds,
> avec un duvet sous lequel trop de bouche,
> avec un sourcil sous lequel trop d'yeux
> baignant dans une eau bleue.
> Au fond il y a le fils de famille sans menton,
> avec, en place de nez,
> un petit carré de drap noir.[1]

M. Morand has a good share of that verbal wit which makes the "Poèmes Aristophanesques" such good reading. Phrases like "les cactus ortho-pédiques" remain, a constant source of amusement, in the memory. On the whole, however, we prefer M Tailhade's quatorzains to the "Lampes à Arc." You can get more epigrammatic point into a sonnet than into a loose-knit piece of free verse. Furthermore, by using the sonnet M. Tailhade could produce comic overtones, suggestions of parody and literary criticism, which cannot be got out of a form that has not been hallowed by a long and noble tradition.

The two volumes of M. Blaise Cendrars contain some of the best work that is being done by the younger French poets. His prose poem "J'ai tué," which was noticed in *The Athenaeum* last year, was an only partially successful *tour de force*. "Du Monde Entier" and "Dix-neuf Poèmes Elastiques" show him at his best. Unlike M. Soupault and his collabora-ators in the various little journals in which he is interested, Blaise Cendrars has something to write about. He has travelled from China to Peru, and the whole world, as it passes in a perpetually changing pan-orama before his eyes, is the theme of his poetry. He is a Romantic in his liking for the picturesque, for contrast, for the lavish beauty of the earth: a Romantic, too, in his willingness to talk about his own emo-tions.

> Passion
> Feu
> Roman-feuilleton
> Journal
> On a beau ne pas vouloir parler de soi-même
> Il faut parfois crier.[2]

[1] Paul Morand, 'Au Parc de l'ouest', *Lampes à arc* (Paris, 1920), p. 11.
[2] Blaise Cendrars, 'Journal', *Dix-neuf Poèmes élastiques* in *Poésies complètes* (Paris, 1944), p. 104.

It is just because he is prepared to cry out, without caring if he makes a fool of himself, it is just because he is not afflicted with that over-refinement and that morbid self-consciousness which prevent so many of his younger contemporaries from writing about anything serious at all, that M. Cendrars is a poet whom it is possible to read with pleasure and interest.

APPENDIX

The following quotation is the complete text of the portion of Jules Romains'
'Réflexions' which Pound translated in his essay 'The Approach to Paris, III', in *The
New Age*, n.s. XIII, 21 (18 September 1913) 607–9. For copyright reasons, the excerpts
of Pound's essay which appear on pages 178–82 omit some sections of his translation. In
the original that follows, I have incorporated, in brackets, the sections quoted and
translated by Pound which could not be included in this volume. Wherever ellipses
appear, the omitted material was excluded by Pound from the translation in his 1913
essay.

'Beaucoup d'hommes aujourd'hui sont prêts à reconnaître que l'homme n'est pas
ce qu'il y a de plus réel au monde. On admet la vie d'ensembles plus vastes que notre
corps. La sociéte n'est pas qu'un total arithmétique, ou qu'une désignation collective.
[On croit même aux groupes intermédiares entre l'individu et l'État. Mais ces opinions apparaissent par déduction abstraite ou par expérience rationnelle.] ... Pour
avoir la notion de son corps l'homme n'a pas attendu la physiologie; ... [Car la
raison conçoit l'homme; mais le coeur perçoit la chair de l'homme.]
  'De même il faut que nous connaissions les groupes qui nous englobent non par une
observation extérieure, mais par une conscience organique. Hélas! il n'est pas sûr que
les rhythmes veuillent bien se nouer en nous qui ne sommes pas le centre des groupes.
Nous n'avons qu'à le devenir. Creusons notre âme assez bas, en la vidant des songes
individuels, menons jusqu'à elle assez de rigoles pour que l'âme des groupes y afflue
nécessairement.
  ['Je n'ai pas essayé autre chose dans ce livre. Plusieurs groupes y parviennent à la
conscience. Ils sont très rudimentaires encore, et leur esprit n'est qu'une odeur dans le
vent. Des êtres aussi inconsistants que la rue du Havre et la place de la Bastille, aussi
éphémères que le public d'un omnibus ou l'assistance de l'Opéra-Comique ne
doivent pas avoir un organisme et une pensée bien complexes. Et l'on trouvera
superflu d'avoir tant peiné pour dégager ces brindilles, au lieu de carder une nouvelle
fois l'énorme tas de l'âme individuelle.]
  'Je crois que les groupes en sont à la période la plus émouvante de leur évolution.
[Les groupes futurs mériteront peut-être moins d'amour et nous cacheront mieux le
fond des choses.] ... Un champignon mieux qu'un chêne laisse deviner sous ses
formes l'essentiel de la vie.
  ['Ainsi les groupes préparent plus d'avenir qu'il n'en faut.] Nous avons le grand
bonheur d'assister au début d'un règne, ... Ce n'est pas un progrès, c'est une création
... [Les groupes ne continueront pas l'oeuvre des animaux et de l'homme; ils recom-
menceront tout pour leur besoin, ...]
  'Déjà nos idées sur l'être vont se corriger. [Mous hésiterons davantage à trouver une
distinction de nature entre ce qui existe réellement et ce qui n'existe pas. En pensant
tour à tour à la place de l'Europe, à la place des Vosges, à l'équipe de terrassiers, on voit
qu'il y a bien des nuances de rien à quelque chose. Avant de fréquenter les groupes,
on est sur de discerner un etre d'une simple idée. On sait qu'un chien existe, qu'il a une
unité intérieure et indépendante : on sait qu'une table ou qu'une montagne n'existe
pas; seul notre langage les sépare du néant universel. Mais les rues marquent toutes
les nuances de l'expression verbale à l'être autonome.]
  'On cesse de croire aussi que la limite soit indispensable aux êtres. Où commence la
place de la Trinité? Les rues mêlent leurs chairs. Les squares s'isolent mal. [La foule
du théâtre ne prend de contours qu'après avoir longuement et fortement vécu.] Un
être a un centre, ou des centres en harmonie; un être n'est pas forcé d'avoir des

limites. Il existe beaucoup à un endroit,...; un deuxième être commence sans que le premier soit fini. [Chaque être a un maximum quelque part dans l'espace.] Seuls les individus à ancêtres ont des contours affirmatifs, une peau qui les fait rompre avec l'infini.

'L'espace n'est à personne. Et nul être n'a réussi à s'approprier un morceau d'espace pour le saturer de son existence unique. Tout s'entre-croise, coïncide, cohabite. [Chaque point sert de perchoir à mille oiseaux. Il y a Paris, il y a la rue Montmartre, il y a un rassemblement, il y a un homme, il y a une cellule sur le même pavé.] Mille êtres sont concentriques, On voit un peu de quelques-uns.

'Comment penser encore qu'un individu est une chose qui naît, grandit, se re-produit et meurt? C'est là une manière supérieure et invétérée d'être un individu. Mais les groupes! Ils ne naissent pas véritablement. Leur vie se fait et se défait, comme un état instable de la matière, une condensation qui ne dure pas. Ils nous montrent que la vie, à l'origine, est une attitude provisoire, un moment d'exception, une intens-ité entre deux relâchements, rien de continu, rien de décisif. [Les premiers ensembles prennent vie par une espèce de lente réussite; puis ils s'éteignent sans catastrophe, sans que chaque élément périsse par la rupture de l'ensemble. La foule devant la baraque foraine se met à vivre peu à peu, comme de l'eau chante dans la casserole et s'évapore. Les galeries de l'Odéon ne vivent pas la nuit; chaque jour elles sont réelles quelques heures. Au début, la vie semble momentanée; puis la vie est intermittente.] Pour qu'elle se fasse durable, pour qu'elle devienne un développement et une destinée, pour qu'elle soit nette et ferrée aux deux bouts par la naissance et par la mort, il faut beaucoup d'habitude.

['Toutes ces formes primitives ne se valent pas. Il y a une hiérarchie naturelle des groupes. Les rues n'ont pas de centre fixe, pas de limites vraies; elles se contentent d'une longue vie vacillante que la nuit aplatit jusqu'au ras du néant. Les places et les squares prennent déjà des contours, serrent davantage le noeud des rythmes. D'autres groupes ont un corps façonné; ils durent peu, mais ils savent presque mourir; certains ressuscitent même pas saccades; l'habitude d'exister commence, ils s'y acharnent, et c'est ce qui les essouffle.]

.   .   .   .

['Les groupes ont beau n'avoir qu'une conscience confuse, et n'apercevoir le monde qu'à travers une gelée tremblante, ils sentiront, peut-être, le signe que je leur fais, et il y en aura un, peut-être, qui, pour l'avoir senti, saura devenir un dieu'.]

INDEX